The Insight Discipline

Crafting Marketplace Understanding that Makes a Difference

Liam Fahey

AMERICAN MARKETING
ASSOCIATION

American Marketing Association
Leadership Series
Chicago

Handwritten inscription: Best '18 S&W: Thanks for your contributions to the book. Always a joy to engage with you. Happy living in the west — Happy Reading. Liam

The Insight Discipline
Soft | 978-0-87757-371-5
Hard | 978-0-87757-373-9
Digital | 978-0-87757-372-2

Cover Design by Berge Design

Contents

Preface

For more than thirty years, literally around the world, I've participated in and observed corporate teams conduct many forms of marketplace or environmental analysis. The analysis typically focuses on change in and around one or more of the classic business domains: customers, competitors, suppliers, technologies, industries, government and regulatory agencies, social values, and politics. And, frequently, the analysis involves many individuals, consumes significant resources, and extends over a considerable time.

Increasingly I've been plagued by one question: why do so many analysis teams extract so little of value from the reams of data, spreadsheets, and findings they generate? If you've worked in corporate settings for a few years, few of these observations will be a surprise to you:

- A massive amount of time is spent conducting market analysis, customer analysis, technology analysis, competitor analysis, industry analysis (the list goes on), but little insight is created that rises above the incessant array of tables, figures, and spreadsheets.

- Analysis frameworks are continuously augmented, enabling a greater array of descriptive outputs and findings, yet genuine insight seems as far out of reach as ever.

- The "big data" juggernaut results in many analysis projects becoming scavenger hunts for data patterns; the report card regarding decision value is mixed at best.

- A stunning onslaught of software makes it possible to visualize analysis outputs and findings in ways that were simply unimaginable a few years ago, yet in the view of many business executives I encounter the provision of new marketplace understanding lags considerably behind.

- All too often, where the analysis outputs are rich in new understanding of the external world, for example, why competitors are shifting their strategies, they're not integrated into a set of key insights that can spur fresh thinking or new ways of addressing decisions or challenging action streams.

- Bright and capable "analysts" and analysis teams generate what they consider key findings, but they're unable to discriminate between what's important for the business and what isn't.
- Executives and leaders are at a loss as to how to upgrade the quality and value of the outcomes of all the analysis work being conducted around them and for them.
- Everyone feels at liberty to use the word *insight*; no wonder the word no longer has any distinctive meaning in most organizations.
- A stunning amount of time (our most valuable asset) is simply wasted in what passes for analysis.

Purpose

The purpose of this book is to address the frustrations at the heart of these observations, by helping you to:

- Gain a deep conceptual and practical understanding of insight.
- Adopt analysis and organization methods that support the development and use of insight.
- Build an insight-driven culture.

Some specific goals aim to:

- Depict what marketplace insight is and what it isn't.
- Describe the four high-level phases of insight work.
- Illustrate the types and levels of insight and show how they're connected.
- Provide analysis frameworks to execute specific tasks in crafting insights.
- Demonstrate the four key stages of insight analysis.
- Explain how the six insight factors (6IFs) influence all facets of insight work and how to use them to enhance the quality of your insights.
- Identify common analytical errors that inhibit insight work and learn how to avoid them.

- Provide you with game plans to motivate, oversee, and leverage insight work.

Audience

This book is for anyone who wants to extract maximum value from analysis work, including:

- Analysis leaders
- Analysis teams
- Functional professionals, such as those in competitor intelligence, market research, industry analysis, and technology assessment
- Project and other work groups
- Executives and managers
- Management consultants and professional researchers
- Professional, educational, and training organizations
- Academics

Structure

Chapters 1 and 2 introduce the notion of the insight discipline and the four phases of insight work: preparing for insight work, crafting change insight, developing implication insights, and determining business implications. They explain why insight work requires a deliberate and methodical approach.

Chapters 3 through 6 cover the first two phases of insight work. They detail the 4S cycle: structuring (preparing for insight work), sniffing (drawing preliminary inferences), shaping (crafting suggested change insights), and stipulating (accepting change insights as an input to decision making). These chapters illustrate the deliberations that contribute to effective execution of the 4S cycle and what it takes to build an organizational capability in each S.

Chapters 7 and 8 focus on the final two phases of insight work. They detail the methods involved in transitioning from change insight to implication insight and how the insight discipline enhances the analysis typically deployed in determining business implications—ultimately what the organization should do.

Chapters 9 and 10 address how and why emotions influence insight work, particularly the 4S cycle, and what you can do to establish and sustain an insight culture.

AMA Introduction to Book Series

Welcome to marketing in the twenty-first century—the age of data, social, mobile, automation, and globalization. The field is changing so quickly, it's difficult to keep up. There is increasing uncertainty about the profession's mission and responsibilities. Meantime, the demands marketers face are ever more complex and critical.

This is why the American Marketing Association (AMA) has engaged some of the world's most innovative professionals, academics, and thought leaders to create *The Seven Problems of Marketing*—a seven-book series that introduces and explores a new set of organizing and actionable principles for the twenty-first-century marketer.

Each book in the series takes a deep dive into one problem, offering expertise, direction, and case studies while striking a balance between theory and application. The goal is to provide a contemporary framework for marketers as they navigate the unique challenges and vast opportunities of today's dynamic global marketplace.

Here are the seven problems addressed in the series:

Problem 1: Effectively targeting high-value sources of growth
Problem 2: Defining the role of marketing in the firm and C-suite
Problem 3: Managing the digital transformation of the modern corporation
Problem 4: Generating and using insight to shape marketing practice
Problem 5: Dealing with an omni-channel world
Problem 6: Competing in dynamic, global markets
Problem 7: Balancing incremental and radical innovation

Importantly, the books in this series are written by and for marketers and marketing scholars. All of the conceptual and analytical frameworks offered are born from practice. The authors have applied their tools and methods in client settings, allowing them to test and refine their ideas in the face of real-world challenges. You'll read true stories about how marketers have used innovative thinking and practices to overcome seemingly impossible dilemmas and bring about game-changing success. Theories are explored in a way that busy marketers can understand viscerally. Client stories have been incorporated to illustrate how to apply the analysis frames as well as deal with application and practice-based issues.

Our fundamental aim with this series is to hone the practice of marketing for the twenty-first century. The AMA has asserted that there is a critical tension within every enterprise between "best" and "next" practices. Marketers often choose best practices because they are safe and proven. Next practices, which push boundaries and challenge conventions, can be riskier. Few enterprises, however, transform themselves and achieve breakout performance with best practices alone. The next practices discussed in this series are often responsible for driving outperformance. The books in this series are designed to engage you on two levels: individually, by increasing your knowledge and "bench strength," and organizationally, by improving the application of marketing concepts within your firm. When you finish each book, we are confident you will feel energized and think differently about the field of marketing and its organizing principles. Through the explanation of theory and compelling examples of its application, you will be empowered to help your organization quickly identify and maximize opportunities. After all, the opportunity to innovate and make an impact is what attracted most of us to the field of marketing in the first place.

Russ Klein
CEO, American Marketing Association

Book Series Overview

In 2016, the AMA established its first-ever intellectual agenda. This intellectual agenda focused on complex, challenging, and difficult-to-solve problems that would be of interest to both academics and practitioners. A working team of scholars and practitioners, selected by AMA leadership, identified seven big problems of marketing as the foundation of the agenda. These problems were ranked from a much longer list of challenges. These seven big problems shared three attributes: they were pressing issues that confronted every organization, they were C-suite level in scope, and they could not be solved by one article or book. Indeed, the team felt that each problem could trigger a decade-long research agenda. A key purpose of the AMA intellectual agenda was thus to stimulate research, dialogue, and debate among the entire AMA membership.

The purpose of the AMA book series is to shed a deeper light on each of the seven problems. In particular, the aim of the series is to enable readers to think differently and take action with regard to these big problems. Thus, the book series operates at two levels: individually, increasing your knowledge and bench strength, and at the organization level, improving the application of marketing concepts within your firm.

Given the nature of these problems, no single book or article can fully address the problem. By their very nature these problems are significant, nuanced, and approachable from multiple vantage points. As such, each of the books provides a single perspective on the issue. This single perspective is intended to both advance knowledge and spark debate. While the books may emerge from academic literature and/or managerial application, their fundamental aim is to improve the practice of marketing. Books selected for the series are evaluated on six criteria.

1. Seven Big Problems Focus

Each book is focused on one of the seven big problems of marketing. These problems identify key conceptual issues in the field of marketing that are the focus of emerging academic research and that practitioners are actively confronting today.

2. Audience

The book is written primarily for an audience of thoughtful practitioners. Thoughtful in this context means that the practitioner is an active reader of both professional articles and books, is dedicated to enhancing his/her marketing knowledge and skills, and is committed to upgrading the organization's marketing culture, capabilities, and results. A secondary audience is academics (and students) and consultants.

3. Integrative Framework

The book provides an integrated framework that frames the problem and offers a detailed approach for addressing it.

4. Field-based Approach

The authors have applied their frameworks in client settings. These client settings enable authors to test and refine their frameworks. Conceptual and analysis frameworks are enlivened via practice and case examples that demonstrate application in the field. Named and/or disguised client stories illustrate how to apply the analysis frames, how to deal with application issues, and other practice-based issues.

5. Academic Literature

The integrative frameworks should be new to the marketplace. The conceptual frameworks should extend existing thinking and the analysis frameworks should provide new ways to conduct marketing-related analysis.

6. Readability

The book should be intelligible to the average reader. The concepts should be clearly defined and explained, and cases written so that a reader can understand the content on a first read.

On behalf of the AMA, I am excited to bring these books to market. I am anxious to hear your feedback—both positive and challenging—as we move the field forward.

Bernie Jaworski
AMA Book Series Editor

Chapter 1

The Insight Discipline

Take a look around your organization. I'm willing to bet that every department, team, or function conducts a relentless stream of analysis, generating innumerable outputs. Your colleagues undoubtedly condense masses of data into tables, diagrams, and spreadsheets and, ultimately, PowerPoint presentations. Collectively, these outputs provide rich descriptions of what's happening in the marketplace, from customer behaviors and competitor strategies, to industry change, technology disruptions, and demographic shifts. Yet if my experience in companies around the world is typical of your organization, they provide very little insight that actually can be used to grow your business. Let me illuminate this problem with a story about a small business unit in large conglomerate, which I'll call CommodityCo.[1]

The executive team of one division in the company believed that it fully understood the marketplace in and around its key commodity product. They developed a change dashboard to help "keep on top" of marketplace change. They monitored and analyzed rivals' quarterly product sales and changes in their marketing, sales, and promotion strategies; purchases by key customers; occasional migration of customers from one rival to another; and change in customer buying criteria. Their key findings included differences in rivals' strategies or changes in their sales, change in customer purchase volumes, and the purported rationales for customer migration.

But one executive increasingly felt that if the company's belief that it fully understood the marketplace proved untrue, it might lead to devastating consequences—CommodityCo would be victimized by changes in the behavior of its competitors or its customers. He convinced his colleagues to assemble an analysis team to conduct a comprehensive assessment of all facets of the marketplace.

When the analysis team presented their preliminary outputs, the executive shared his concerns and posed two questions: "You've collected a lot of

1

data, conducted all this analysis, generated all these outputs, and devoted significant time and resources to getting it all done. That said, tell me two things: what are your key insights into this competitive space? And how are they relevant and important to our current and future strategy and operations?"

In short, the analysis team had generated reams of data, but no insight. They provided no new understanding of the CommodityCo's customers, competitors, or marketplace changes. Given a second opportunity to conduct the analysis, as I'll explain later in this chapter, the team generated multiple insights, not the least of which was the realization that their historic commodity product was indistinguishable from its rivals, even after wrapping a genuine customer offer (including technical support, inventory control, and rapid repair service) around it.

The analysis team drew two broad implications that ran counter to the company's prior way of operating: CommodityCo needed to change its product development process to develop products more quickly and it required a new, go-to-market approach tailored to customer segments.

Over a two-year period, the company developed a new marketplace strategy built around new product generation and customized offers to channel and customer segments. As a result, it was able to leapfrog its rivals in product launches, technology reputation, customer satisfaction, and market share gains, causing some competitors to withdraw from the market.

Getting to insight

The executive's questions suggest that crafting and leveraging marketplace[2] insight should be the focus of analysis. They further indicate that insights into the world outside the organization aren't ends in themselves, no matter how brilliantly discerned or elegantly articulated. This focus and the insights derived must enable superior thinking, decisions, and action. Unfortunately, many firms generate masses of data but relatively little insight. Rare is the company that goes beyond the "findings" of any analysis project to craft a small set of crucial insights—the keen new understandings that significantly influence *what* a set of managers think about and *how* they think, the decisions they make and the actions they take.

This book gives you a blueprint for crafting and leveraging marketplace insight. In this chapter, I'll introduce the notion of insight discipline and the four core phases of insight work (Figure 1-1). I'll also provide an overview of different levels of insight. Additionally, I'll illustrate why a deliberate and methodical approach must reside at the heart of insight discipline. I'll conclude by identifying a variety of desired insight attributes.

FIGURE 1-1

A Disciplined Approach to Insight Work

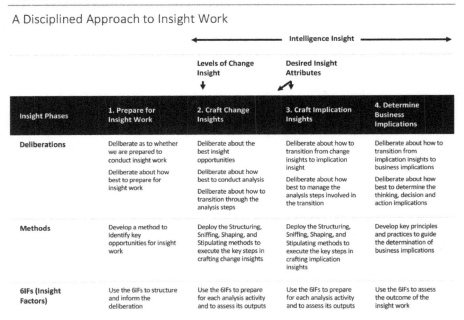

Insight Phases	1. Prepare for Insight Work	2. Craft Change Insights	3. Craft Implication Insights	4. Determine Business Implications
Deliberations	Deliberate as to whether we are prepared to conduct insight work Deliberate about how best to prepare for insight work	Deliberate about the best insight opportunities Deliberate about how best to conduct analysis Deliberate about how to transition through the analysis steps	Deliberate about how to transition from change insights to implication insight Deliberate about how best to manage the analysis steps involved in the transition	Deliberate about how to transition from implication insights to business implications Deliberate about how best to determine the thinking, decision and action implications
Methods	Develop a method to identify key opportunities for insight work	Deploy the Structuring, Sniffing, Shaping, and Stipulating methods to execute the key steps in crafting change insights	Deploy the Structuring, Sniffing, Shaping, and Stipulating methods to execute the key steps in crafting implication insights	Develop key principles and practices to guide the determination of business implications
6IFs (Insight Factors)	Use the 6IFs to structure and inform the deliberation	Use the 6IFs to prepare for each analysis activity and to assess its outputs	Use the 6IFs to prepare for each analysis activity and to assess its outputs	Use the 6IFs to assess the outcome of the insight work

The executive's questions further illuminate that insight is about understanding change[3] in and around a competitive space and its business implications. Change gives rise to inevitable marketplace characteristics: uncertainty, turbulence, discontinuity, and, above all, ambiguity. Analyzing change in your rivals' strategies, products, customer preferences, technologies, and governmental proclivities presents some daunting challenges. The future doesn't yet exist. So any depiction of the transition from the present to the future is a cognitive construction. In other words, the future is a product of your mind.[4]

Consequently, how well your organization develops an understanding of the present and anticipates what the future might be depends entirely on your conceptual abilities. Change ensures that the world as you see it won't hold together at some point in the future—and that day may be closer than you realize! Change therefore demands that you continually adapt your mental models[5] of the world. As you gather new data, develop new information, encounter alternative viewpoints and perspectives, and confront new assumptions, you must ask whether your long-held concepts and mental frames are adequate to describe and explain the world around you now, or the world as it might be at some future time.

You can better address these challenges—and thus the questions posed by the CommodityCo executive—when you have a clear understanding of what insight is and what it isn't; know how to craft and test an insight; and embed insight discipline throughout your organization.

What is insight?

Asking and answering the executive's questions presumes that both the executive and the analysis team understand the concept of insight. But all too often that's not the case. Ask any manager and their support staff to define insight or describe the focus of insight work or list the desired attributes of value-generating insight. Their answers will be all over the map.[6] Although it's typically presumed that everyone knows what insight is, confusion about the concept reigns supreme. The result is that analysis rarely focuses on *crafting Insight*. Instead, analysis findings are vague and seldom provide the value you need. So let me clearly define what I mean by insight.

At the broadest level, insight is a new understanding of some facet of marketplace change that makes a difference. This new understanding, as I'll discuss later in this chapter, must represent a distinct break from your prior thinking. It must change how you see and think about the marketplace and, eventually, what you do.[7] Following are three examples of insights that required market leaders to make a dramatic shift in their understanding of the current marketplace.

A competitor insight: A currently insignificant player in one product area, could, through a single acquisition and a change in direction in its research and development (R&D) investments, generate within three years a new customer solution that is a generation or two ahead of all current rivals in that product space.

Previously, a company I'll call AbsoCo believed that smaller firms couldn't exert any significant degree of product or solution change in their competitive space, or that a dramatic product breakthrough would occur within the next three years.[8]

AbsoCo's R&D investment stream was considerably riskier than previously believed. The firm partnered with a technology source to revamp the product and immediately launched an action program to reconfigure its marketplace assumptions, prune its existing R&D portfolio, search for potential R&D partners, and identify opportunities in related product lines.

A customer insight: The customer didn't understand the extent to which product operations could be improved due to inexperience in plant management and the absence of more sophisticated processes. Achieving significantly higher operating efficiency would be cost effective and some enhancement to product quality (plant output) would also be possible.

Previously, based on customer statements, the firm believed the customer had a sophisticated approach to plant management and that little could be done to enhance its operations.

To take advantage of this opportunity to create a solution for the customer, the firm initiated an action program to develop alternative solutions and test them with a small set of customers.

A technology insight: A set of emerging technologies showed that if the company progressed in specific directions, converging these separate paths over the next three years could open up a whole new market space that would render obsolete many of today's dominant products.

Previously, the firm accepted as fact that technology change, although it was pervasive, wouldn't lead to new "white spaces" that would render its current dominant product line obsolete.

Realizing that the firm's dominant product line might have a shelf life of just two years, the CFO initiated an action program to examine the financial consequences. Not surprisingly, the results were potentially devastating. The executive team then asked how the firm might quickly pull out as much cash as possible from the current products. They also launched a major initiative to leverage the firm's competencies in related product areas.

What is insight content?

Content is what the actual insight is: what it says about what. Consider the content of AbsoCo's competitor insight above. The insight's content tells us that current small market share rival has the potential to leapfrog existing rivals in one product area within three years, through the combination of a single acquisition and a change in its R&D program.

The content of AbsoCo's competitor insight—that is, the new understanding of the competitor's potential actions—enabled the analysis team to determine what difference the insight makes to its understanding of the competitor and what difference the insight makes in potential business implications—hence, the importance of assessing an insight's attributes, which I'll discuss later in this chapter.

Insight into what?

To gain the insight needed to make a decision, you need to understand the different types of insight. This work requires thoughtful responses to the following questions:

- What should be the insight focus of the analysis work? In other words, what are you gaining insights into?
- What different levels of insight are applicable? And how do they relate to one another?
- How do you get from insight to marketplace change to business implications (a combination I call intelligence insight)?[9]

Failure to answer to these questions can severely limit the robust analysis needed to generate insight. How often have you heard these questions posed? If you've been fortunate enough to hear one or more of them, did they give rise to serious deliberation?

In answering these questions, the first tendency is to focus on just one or two domains: customers, competitors, technology, governmental policies, or some combination of these.[10] But other domains may have significant potential to affect your business's emerging or potential strategies and operations. Whatever domain has been top-of-mind for whatever reason dominates the collective attention.

The second tendency is to adopt a narrow view of the emphasized domains, which further restricts the attention focus. Perhaps only large market share rivals are subjected to extensive data collection and analysis.[11] In the case of customers, former customers and rivals' customers hardly make it on to the radar screen. If the concern is technology, only those technologies that have long been at the heart of the business warrant significant attention.

The third tendency is to dig deeper and deeper into the narrowly defined domains, solidifying the narrow field of vision. The intent would seem to be to learn everything possible about the large market share rivals, current customers, or the key technologies. But learning "more and more about less and less" only ensures that early detection of change outside the analysis focus is certain to be missed.[12]

The insight funnel

The insight funnel (Figure 1-2) provides a framework to address these tendencies. It identifies different but interrelated levels of change insights (domain, competitive space, generic marketplace) and implication insights (implications and business implications). It also guides you through key questions that test the business relevance of change at each level. I'll describe each of these in detail in upcoming chapters, but here's a brief introduction, using the CommodityCo case for illustration purposes (Figure 1-3).

FIGURE 1-2

The Insight Funnel: Insight Levels and Relationships

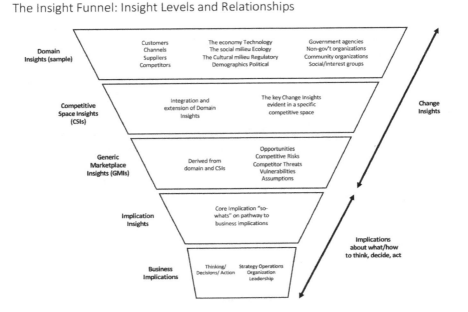

FIGURE 1-3

Intelligence Insight: The CommodityCo Case

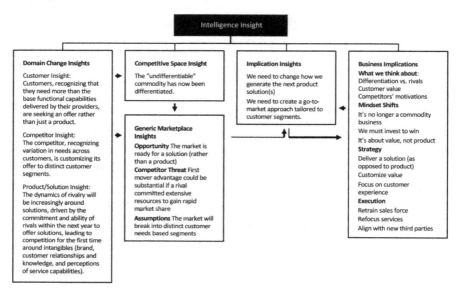

Change insights

Change insights—those related to your domain, the competitive space, and the generic marketplace—can make a powerful difference in your thinking, decisions, and actions.

Domain insights

Domain insights are the basic unit of analysis in insight work. They can take many forms, as shown in Figure 1-2. Three key domain insights—customer, competitor, and product/solution, emerged in the CommodityCo case (Figure 1-3). You can subject each domain insight to scrutiny and quality test results that I'll share in later chapters.

Competitive space insights

How often have you observed the following in your organization's efforts to make sense of marketplace change?

- Inability to synthesize change across two or more domains

- Lengthy, inconclusive deliberations about which domain change is more important
- Belief that change in one domain is more important than the others
- Disagreement about how dominant change factors interrelate
- Unwillingness to accept integration of change across multiple domains

These tendencies reflect the fact that a company doesn't "live in" only one domain. If your organization obsesses on the world of customers, you may get sideswiped by disruptive change spawned by technology breakthroughs or an imaginative strategy launched by a rival or a sudden shift in rules by a government agency. Although each domain influences facets of your business, it lives in a space broader than any single domain—what I refer to as the competitive space. Understanding change at the level of your competitive space provides distinctive insight compared to your domain insights—what I refer to as competitive space insights (CSIs).

In the CommodityCo case, the analysis team converged around a central CSI, the "undifferentiable" commodity that has now been differentiated. This CSI summarizing change in a competitive space was a shock to many individuals within the firm. They had long seen the market as consisting of rivalry among undifferentiated products. They didn't see rivalry as involving solutions, that is, products surrounded by service and other support.

Generic marketplace insights

How often have you observed the following in strategy development or execution in your organization?

- Conflicting assertions about whether and to what extent an opportunity is real
- Debate about the nature and extent of marketplace risks, such as technology change or regulatory shifts
- Divergent projections of whether and how rivals might amend their current strategy in view of changing market conditions
- Differing opinions about the vulnerabilities of the current strategy
- Assumptions accepted as givens despite refuting data and reasoning

This type of dialogue reflects, in part, a gap in the analysis inputs to strategy making or decision making more broadly—what I call generic marketplace insights (GMIs). GMIs beg the question of how domain insights and CSIs can help with strategy making, strategy execution, and organizational change. For strategy purposes, five GMIs are relevant:[13]

- Marketplace opportunities
- Competitive risks
- Competitive threats
- Strategy vulnerabilities
- Assumptions

Only when this change in focus occurs can you tie marketplace change directly to the major issues and challenges at the heart of strategy decision making.

CSIs such as understanding how technology could cause a rapid dislocation in product composition (and, thus, customer functionality), how regulatory change could allow the entry of a new type of product substitute rival, or how customer migration toward foreign rivals could lead to significantly more intense rivalry, must be subjected to the following questions:

- What are the marketplace opportunities?
- What specific competitive risks exist?
- Are there competitor threats that may face many rivals?
- How might any rival's current (or potential) strategy be vulnerable?
- What assumptions about the future might be emerging?

Subjecting the dominant CSI in the CommodityCo case to these questions led to three GMIs (Figure 1-3):

Marketplace opportunity insight: The market is now ready for a solution rather than a product. This realization repudiated the long-held view of most firms that the competitive battle in the marketplace would revolve around the tangible product, especially its technical features.

Competitor threat insight: First-mover advantage could be substantial if a rival committed extensive resources to gain rapid market share. This possibility gave rise to extensive dialogue that speed in strategy change and execution was likely to become a new dynamic in this product market space.

Assumption insight: The notion that the market will break into distinct customer needs-based segments was likely a challenge to how every firm in the business had traditionally viewed the market.

Given these three GMIs, it's little wonder that assumptions with respect to the competitive space for all firms would eventually have to be updated.

Implication insights

Implication insights, which I'll address in more detail in Chapter 7, are the high-level, key business takeaways that emanate from one or more change insights. In the example of the AbsoCo competitor insight noted above, two significant implication insights emerged:

- Continuation of the firm's current R&D investment path was considerably riskier than previously understood.
- The firm needed to partner with a leading technology source to quickly revamp its product line.

These two implication insights provided significant guidance for what the business should do next. They suggested a series of questions:

- What new marketplace and organization assumptions is the firm willing to accept as an input to strategy development?
- How should the firm amend its current R&D investment path?
- What type of technology partner(s) would be ideal?
- Should the firm move to quickly pull cash from its current product lines?

In the CommodityCo case, the CSI, the undifferentiated commodity was now differentiated, in conjunction with the three GMIs just noted gave rise to two implication insights (Figure 1-3): the company needed to change how it generated the next product solution(s), and it needed to create a go-to-market approach tailored to its customer segments.

You'll see shortly how these two implication insights contributed to specific thinking, decisions, and action implications—what are broadly referred to as business implications.

Business implications

If specific implication insights are accepted for decision-making purposes, determining their business implications becomes the obvious next task. They are addressed at three interrelated levels:

- Thinking
- Decisions
- Actions

In the CommodityCo case, the firm had to think about, for the first time, how to achieve differentiation versus rivals, how to deliver customer value beyond the physical product, and what was motivating rivals to commit to differentiation. It had to decide what solution it would provide customers, how to customize it to specific customers—in short, what customer experience it should strive to create. Some specific actions quickly became a focus of sustained attention:

- Retraining the sales force
- Developing specific services
- Aligning with third parties

Intelligence insights

Intelligence insight—the combination of change insights and implications—provides answers to the two questions asked by the CommodityCo executive. It constitutes the ultimate prize in insight work: it offers the best judgments to the analysis team as to what the organization should think about, decide, and do. I'll focus on intelligence insight in Chapter 8.

Change insights, no matter how unique, interesting, revealing, or counterintuitive, don't indicate by themselves what their business implications might be. Indeed, a change insight manifesting these characteristics may not have any significant business implications; it's just not relevant to the business. So the business value of a change insight isn't the insight content itself. It also resides in the implications that enable the business to outperform its rivals—competitively and financially—in the marketplace.

Insight: A shift in understanding

The most fundamental characteristic of any quality[14] change or implication insight is that it manifests a substantial difference between the old and new understanding specific to the topic, issue, problem, or challenge at hand. The technology insight in the AbsoCo case offers a preliminary illustration of how extensive and significant the pre- and post-change insight difference can be, and how that can lead to significant difference in the implication insights and business implications compared to what was previously identified.

The pre- and post-change insight worldviews are radically different. AbsoCo's understanding of competitors, customers, technology, rivalry, and its own strategy and investments shifted in unexpected ways. The management team no longer believes that small rivals are unimportant to the future of its business. It no longer assumes that its current market strategy will continue to win and generate the performance and results of the recent two years.

Further, it recognizes that its investment commitments may not be sufficient, as previously presumed, to outperform rivals. In short, the difference between pre- and post-change insight leads you to modify, and in many instances, reframe how you "see" and think about specific parts of the external world.

Insight: Data and analytics are necessary but insufficient

Asking what the insights are and what they mean for your strategy presents the analysis team with a challenge: get beyond data and analysis frameworks to generate the small set of critical insights that inform decision making.

As the examples in this book attest, getting to change insight and then to intelligence insight requires you to draw inferences and make judgments that go far beyond data, no matter how abundant, and far beyond analysis or analytics, no matter how sophisticated the tools and techniques.

Availability of data, for the most part, is often not the constraining factor in generating valuable decision-making inputs—insights.[15] Analysis tools, techniques, and frameworks abound in relation to every business function and every business decision context. Big data[16] or, more broadly, business intelligence,[17] is the latest type of "analytics" involving massive databases and software that enable configuring and analysis of data in ways that were simply unimaginable even five years ago. Indeed, analysis frameworks gain so much popularity they become known by their authors' names,[18] some catchy acronym,[19] or memorable phrase.[20] These frameworks capture many indicators of change—such as product change, sales shifts, and competitive dynamics—that enable the depiction of innumerable trends, patterns, and discontinuities.[21]

Fundamental to the quest for insight, however, is that data, no matter how meticulously arrayed and thoroughly analyzed via your favorite analysis tools or techniques, doesn't automatically give rise to quality insights. Insight, as the understanding of change, doesn't jump off exquisitely detailed, computer generated, output "visualizations," nor does it leap from the carefully configured spreadsheets or appear on the page as a self-evident a-ha.

Insight emerges only through the intervention of the human mind to determine implications.[22] Further, it's your mind that assimilates and integrates the nuances and details embedded in any simple or elaborate data array or set of analysis outputs. An understanding of the relevant context enables your mind to (eventually) extract something—an inference or an insight—that is most often not readily observable in the data and analysis outputs. Doing so often requires deep immersion in the (relevant) data, organization, and business contexts.[23] For example, spending a day in the life of a customer provides an intimacy in understanding the customer's needs and aspirations that simply can't be obtained in any other way.[24]

A logical outgrowth of acceptance of the human mind's critical role is that the derivation or crafting of insight in organizational settings requires a disciplined process—getting to insight can't be left to chance. The pathway from data to change insight to intelligence insight, even though it can't be predetermined, must be managed.

Insight discipline: Deliberations and methods

Insight is typically portrayed as occurring at a specific instance in one individual.[25] You hear phrases like "then the insight hit me," or "the breakthrough [insight] came to me out of nowhere," or the "aha moment occurred when," or "I'm still looking for that big aha." These observations are reminders that insight starts with one person mentally processing data and information.[26] Thus, an organization doesn't have an insight; rather, one or more individuals within it do.

But insight can't be left to chance. The analysis team needs to learn how to craft change and implication insights, while the executive team needs to learn how to enable the team to do so. And it's important that insight work be deliberate and methodical, with insight discipline brought to bear at each phase (Figure 1-1):

- Preparing for insight work
- Crafts change insight
- Crafting implication insights
- Determining business implications

As you'll see in later chapters, insight discipline's emphasis on method has profound implications for analysis. When your intent is to "get more out of analysis than we do today" as some managers have phrased it, how you think about and approach analysis must change from what is common practice in most firms. Far too much time is spent on data and perfecting analysis outputs and far too little on searching for, shaping, and leveraging insights.

Six insight factors (6IFs)

Insight—whether it's about domain, competitive space, generic marketplace, or implications—involves a shift in understanding, one that significantly enhances your organization's marketplace and financial performance. To generate insight, it's critical to ask two questions:

- What influences whether and how the team craft change insight?
- What must change insight influence to give rise to superior performance?

I've come to believe that six insight factors (6IFs) influence and reflect both the input and output sides of the deliberations and methods involved in this work in organizational settings. Each of them revolves around a verb: see, think, intend, decide, act, and feel. This emphasis on verbs is no accident. Verbs imply that individuals will do something to advance insight work. Others have also noted the relevance and influence of individual IFs.[27]

The 6IFs challenge you to consider whether you're ready to engage in the deliberations at the heart of each insight phase. Each IF poses a challenge: are you willing to act differently to facilitate the likelihood of insight?[28] On the input side to insight work, each IF addresses a different facet of the inhibitors and impediments to insight work. If you're not willing to "see" differently, you'll miss a lot of what's around you or available to you.

If you resist thinking in different ways, you'll find it difficult to challenge how you make sense of the world. If you adhere to your aspirations and goals, you circumscribe the world you pay attention to. If you limit how you decide and what you make decisions about, you miss other possibilities. If you act largely in the same way over time, you shut yourself off from engaging with the world in new ways. If you don't pay attention to how you feel, it's highly likely you won't understand your own motivations, attitudes, and behaviors. In short, the ability to be different along the 6IFs greatly influences the content of deliberations within each insight stage.

The 6IFs strongly influence whether you aspire to be methodical in your analysis work. They also directly influence your choice and execution of methods—the organized and systematic approaches to the many data and analysis tasks necessary to translate disparate data into carefully articulated change insights, and ultimately implications. Each IF plays a role:

See: You need to see and understand how different analysis methods give rise to distinct data sets and indicators,[29] and thus why structuring the analysis context is fundamental to generating insight that makes a difference.

Think: What you think about and how you think requires carefully crafted methods to draw preliminary inferences from assembled indicators and then shape suggested change insights and accept change insights.

Intend: You need to be clear about the organization's intent to adopt appropriate methods. A business purpose provides the rationale for why you're embarking on insight work. In the CommodityCo case, a clear intent drove the analysis: what is changing in the marketplace that might affect the strategy choice? It's equally important to have clear insight intent: it is to generate a small set of change insights to enable decision makers to see and think better and to decide and act in ways that enhance business results.

Decide: Decide which analysis methods to adopt and how to deploy them. In the CommodityCo case, the analysis team decided to proceed through the change insight levels—domain, CSI, and GMI—slowly and comprehensively, allowing time to oscillate back and forth between the levels.

Act: The act and feel IFs bring insight methods to life. For example, you need to understand and manage the analysis back-and-forth that character-izes your team's efforts to get to a change insight. You'll translate the indi-vidual methods described in the next five chapters into questions that focus deliberations.

Feel: Emotions are always present and influence every facet of analysis. So it's important to monitor and manage how emotions affect involvement in and contribution to each insight phase.

Case: AbsoCo

The AbsoCo competitor insight is a classic example of how a single domain insight can lead to a profound difference in each IF that results in dramatic business implications. Once AbsoCo could see the competi-tive context differently, a new competitive space would likely unfold. It could no longer simply think about how to gain market share; it would have to think about what it needed to do to stay in the market. Its intent had to shift; it could no longer aim to win with its current products, but rather it had to create new customer offers.

It had to make new decisions: maximize existing products and/or acquire or develop new products. It had no choice but to act to achieve its new goals. The executive team developed a new action plan to develop and introduce its own new product. Emotions ranging from excitement to exuberance characterized the feelings of some executives once the key decisions were made but others had dominant feelings of dread, hesi-tancy, and discomfort that the projected action plan would be difficult to execute.

Case: CommodityCo

The 6IFs provided a focus for deliberations that addressed the fundamen-tal implication questions: what difference do these change insights make to what you should be thinking about, what decisions you need to make and what you should do? Each IF resulted in new understanding for the analysis team and others involved in the deliberations (Box 1-1). They saw that the old way of doing business was a guaranteed loser; it was no longer a commodity-like business. They had to think about new issues and challenges: how to craft new customer value, how to shape different customer experiences, how to capture a competitor's motivations. The firm's intent clearly had to change: it needed a new strategy aimed at winning new customers and retain existing ones because the long-established strategy would result in customer migration to rivals.

New decisions could not be avoided: should CommodityCo commit to the next product generation or wait for further marketplace data to establish how fast the new marketplace conditions are unfolding? Both internal and external actions were mandatory: for example, organizing discussions to refine what the new assumptions implied for current and potential decisions, initiating relations with potential external technology partners, and undertaking preliminary market segmentation analysis. Finally, emotions always had to be considered. The analysis team recognized that during the deliberations around implications, many individuals became enthused and excited that CommodityCo could successfully move to the new strategy and the significant shift in operations that it required.

Box 1-1

Case: CommodityCo—The Business Implications of Change Insights

The focus here is the output side of insight work. The intent is to illustrate how the 6IFs detect and assess the business implications of a set of change insights (Figure 1-3).

See: The analysis team (and, later, the executive team and others) began to "see" the competitive context in a new light: the old way of competing would no longer win in the rapidly emerging new marketplace. It had to imagine new notions of customer value. As noted by one executive, "We see what could be a very different world coming at us."

Think: The organization had to think about different issues, challenges, and possibilities. It had to think through what a new go-to-market strategy might be, how it might generate the next generation product/solution, how it might create modest solution customization. In short, the firm had to reframe its thinking, not just make an incremental change to its point of view about the future: it had to reconfigure its base business assumptions.

Intend: The change in what you see and think, if significant, almost inevitably leads to a change in what our goals are likely to be. The firm, spurred by the outputs of the analysis team, had to address new goals: can you develop a strategy that will allow you to stay in and win in this market? The organization's purpose or intent with respect to this market could not remain what it had been.

Decide: Insight, as genuinely new understanding, often eventually gives rise to new decisions and/or significant shift in the configuration of existing decisions. The firm was immediately faced with new decisions: do you maximize your current products in this market sector? Do you alter and/or extend your R&D project portfolio? Do you need to hire personnel with experience in market segmentation and related technologies?

Act: Insight can only lead to enhanced marketplace performance and financial results when it directly affects action. And, sometimes the actions may take an organization on a new pathway and in a new direction. The firm's actions, of course, depended upon its decisions: it decided to "go for it," that is, take a sequence of actions to develop and introduce the next product generation.

Feel: Any insight that causes new "seeing," thinking, intentions, decisions, and action can't do so without affecting the feelings (emotions) of those involved. Some members of the organization felt engaged, exhilarated, and adventurous at the prospect of taking on new analysis and thinking challenges; some others felt anxious, dismayed, and hesitant that they had to embark on a new learning journey.

In summary, the 6IFs help you assess the marketplace and organization implications of any change insight. In particular, they focus attention on how change insight shifts your understanding of the world and to methodically determining what that new understanding means for thinking, decisions, and actions. In short, these potential shifts in understanding and decision implications reinforce the importance of addressing the three insight-related needs noted earlier in this chapter: to understand what insight is, to know how to generate and leverage insight, and to lead and mobilize the organization in the pursuit of insight.

The importance of insight: Entrepreneurship and strategy

The executive understands the value of insight and how it can enable winning strategy. The analysis team enables winning strategy when it helps to answer the executive's two questions.

Executives and others often don't appreciate the capacity of insight to result in the consequences just discussed: to shape and drive how you see, think, intend, decide, act, and feel. Thus, they grossly underestimate how change and implication insights influence shifts in mental models, the development and choice of strategy and decision alternatives, and, more generally, the content and direction of everyday deliberations. I find that those skeptical of a deliberative and methodical approach to insight (for whatever reasons) tend to ask two related questions: Does insight really make a difference to our understanding of the world around us? Is it worth the effort to craft and test insight?[30] Take two areas critical to the organizational success, entrepreneurship, and strategy, to illustrate the power and value of insight.

Entrepreneurship: The big Idea

A start-up business stems from a business idea. And, what's come to be called "the big business idea" necessarily involves some understanding of current and/or prospective change—a possible insight—that hopefully evolves into a business that opens a new market space. Table 1-1 summarizes customer insights that gave rise to the top twelve entrepreneurial growth businesses identified in a *Fortune* magazine article.[31]

None of the customer insights in the table tell us whether a real market opportunity exists: whether the customer need is real; how many customers might possess this need; or, how the need might evolve over time. Thus, as described in Chapter 2, each domain insight, such as a customer or competitor insight, if they're contributing to strategy, must eventually be transformed into a CSI or GMI that begins to answer these questions.

Table 1-1   Insights That Gave Rise to Large Enterprises

Company	Founder(s)	Initiating Customer[44] Insights
Apple	Steve Jobs and Steve Wozniak	Customers want a computer interface that's easy to understand and easy to use.
Microsoft	Bill Gates	Customers realize more value from the applications (created by hidden software) than in what the physical machine looks like.
FedEx	Fred Smith	Small business customers need an integrated air-ground shipping system, similar to what large corporations already had.
Amazon	Jeff Bezos	Customers would like to buy almost anything they want from their home/office, from an unlimited offer range, at lower cost, with extremely high service.
Google	Larry Page and Sergey Brin	Customers could do many things if we downloaded the entire web on to computers.
Starbucks	Larry Schultz	Customers want more than just coffee; it's the context in which it's consumed.
Facebook	Mark Zuckerberg	Customers want to be connected for social purposes.
Whole Foods	John Mackey	Customers want to eat better, mostly for health reasons, and will pay for the quality food experience.
Southwest Airlines	Herb Kelleher	Customers will fly with us if we reconfigure the airline cost structure while enhancing customer service using secondary airports
Walmart	Sam Walton	Customers will respond if we buy low, stack it high, and sell it cheap.

The relevance of the 6IFs is evident. From Steve Jobs and Herb Kelleher to Mark Zuckerberg, each insight "sees" the potential for market or technology or customer change that others hadn't yet detected. Each insight spawned thinking that focused on how to get the business off the ground and rapidly evolved into an intent specific to each business but with a common theme: to create a new market space. Each insight provided the basis for a business model that enabled the creation of a novel customer solution—these entrepreneurs could act in ways that others could not even dream about. Additionally, each insight unquestionably resulted in feelings that motivated these individuals to "go for it": they were propelled by the belief that their insight could be the stepping-stone to creating or transforming a whole business sector.

Strategy: Competing for insight

Strategy, as rivalry, is about outwitting, outmaneuvering, and outperforming the competition.[32] Outperforming is typically measured in standard marketplace and financial metrics. Outmaneuvering entails acting faster, better, smarter, and with more agility than rivals. However, both outperforming and outmaneuvering aren't likely to generate superior results unless the current and potential competition has been outwitted. Developing a better understanding of current, emerging, and potential future change constitutes the core of outwitting or outthinking rivals. Thus, rivalry at its most fundamental is about insight: who creates the change and implication insights (intelligence insight) that encapsulates a superior depiction of emerging and potential marketplace change.

Many others have emphasized the centrality of insight to strategy. For example, a former CEO asserts, "The battle for superior insight is increasingly becoming the real starting point of business competition."[33] Two leading strategy theorists note, "Senior management teams compete in the acquisition of industry foresight," by which they mean a "point of view about the future."[34] One of the most respected strategy academics, Richard Rumelt, perhaps puts it most incisively: "An insightful reframing of a competitive situation can create whole new patterns of advantage and weakness. The most powerful strategies arise from such game-changing insights."[35]

The challenge therefore for the strategist and others within any organization isn't only to understand the role and importance of insight in shaping and executing strategy but also to know and understand how to craft and leverage insight.

Desired attributes of a change or implication insight

The executive needs high quality insights. The analysis team needs criteria to guide the development of superior quality insights. As used in everyday organizational parlance, most alleged (change) insights aren't real or quality insights. The word (insight) is used so indiscriminately that it loses its meaning. However, it begs the question, what *is* a "quality" insight?

Change insights

The more an alleged insight manifests the following attributes, the more likely it is a quality or genuine insight and thus serve as the basis for potential intelligence insight.

New understanding: At the most basic level, as discussed above, a change insight affords a depth of new understanding of some entity, issue, topic, or phenomenon that you didn't previously possess. Stated differently, it's not a surface-level familiarity. As noted above in the AbsoCo and CommodityCo cases, the shift in understanding from pre- to post-insight can reflect a dramatic difference.

Novelty: New understanding should be new not just to your organization, but to the world—or at least, not already be discerned by your current and prospective rivals. Thus, a genuine insight can't be common knowledge. Say, for example, you develop what you think is a change insight around water availability,[36] namely that a water supply and demand imbalance will cause production costs for a particular product in one geographic area to increase by a factor of two or three over a period of a decade or less. But what if your rivals have also created this understanding? Then your presumed insight is essentially common knowledge and unlikely to give rise to decisions and actions that will significantly enhance marketplace performance compared with rivals.

Obviousness: If the insight is counterintuitive or not obvious, it's less likely to be discerned by others. Competitor and customer insights sometimes meet this test. If a competitor insight indicates that the competitor is moving down a pathway that is opposite to its prior behaviors and statements, observers may miss the strategy direction change because it runs counter to prior expectations.[37] In one study of a utility's consumers, the crucial unexpected, indeed counterintuitive, consumer insight was that one segment of consumers felt embarrassed to be associated with the brand. They felt badly about themselves because they were associated with the brand.

Congruence: Alleged insights must also be scrutinized for congruency: does the articulated understanding reflect the current world and/or the world you're heading into? Congruency can only be validated over time.[38] The more congruent the change insight, the better informed those charged with crafting intelligence insights. Congruence is always a judgment call; it can't be otherwise, because you can't know the future with certainty.[39] It's why you need to scrupulously and ferociously vet and vouch for every suggested insight, as described in Chapters 5 and 6.

Explanatory: A quality insight typically goes beyond description; it entails a degree of explanatory power that sometimes may be more implicit than explicit. A customer insight that captures why customers behave in a particular way should explain rather than simply describe their behaviors. A technology insight that paints a picture of how specific technologies could interconnect over the next few years or how a technology could disrupt rivalry in a specific product sector should explain why a particular product solution might be in the marketplace in a few years or why the dynamics of rivalry might be very different in a specific product sector in the near future.

Enduring: If an insight satisfies the above attributes but only lasts a few months before it's overwhelmed by marketplace change, it's not likely to generate significant decision value. The CommodityCo CSI (Figure 1-3) proved enduring. Evidence for the insight mounted over time and the firm could take it as a critical input to its strategy development and execution.

Implication insights

Change insights must always be value tested: do they lead to outcomes along the 6IFs that contribute to superior organizational performance? So you can ask of every change insight that meets the six tests: does it lead to one or more implication insights that reflect and lead to superior thinking, decisions, and actions—the ingredients for enhanced business performance? As detailed in Chapter 7, you can also subject Implication insights to the six tests of new understanding, novelty, obviousness, congruence, explanation, and endurance.

Business implications

The ultimate test of change and implication insights is whether they lead to thinking, decisions, and actions[40] that contribute to superior marketplace and financial performance. Thus, executives and analysis teams must ask the question: what are the business implications?

Business domains

As discussed in detail in Chapter 8, implication insights eventually must be connected to thinking, decisions, and action in business domains, including strategy, operations, organization, and leadership. The quality of the thinking, decisions, and actions in these business domains determines whether and how intelligence insight contributes to winning in the external marketplace.

Performance results

The ultimate test of thinking, decisions, and action is whether they lead to a meaningful difference in performance outcomes and results. Outcomes include marketplace performance—preempting rivals, market share, share of customer, and enhanced brand position—and financial performance—margins, profitability, and cash flows. Results involve a comparison that enables an assessment of better or worse along some criteria: for example, compared to our own goals, expectations of others, a competitor's position and goals, or industry standards or performance.

Is your company insight-oriented? A preliminary assessment

You may have just begun reading this book, but it's not too early to ask whether your organization is insight-oriented. Although your organization no doubt conducts analysis across all functional areas and hierarchy levels related to many facets of marketplace and organization change, the answer to the question may be unclear. Your answers to the key questions posed in Table 1-2 will help you determine whether and to what extent your organization (or your segment of it) focuses on insight and not just analysis. Each question emphasizes an element of the deliberations and methods that determine how far down the road your organization has traveled (or must travel) in its quest to move beyond analysis to the land of insight. I'll address each of the questions in detail in later chapters.[41]

Table 1-2   Is Your Company Insight-Oriented?[45]

Key questions	Follow-up questions
Is there a shared understanding of insight among key individuals, teams, and functions? (Chapter 1)	Do key professionals and decision makers know the attributes of a "quality" insight (as opposed to an unvetted insight)? Are they aware of the different levels of insight (domain, competitive space, generic marketplace, and implication insights)?
Is a specific individual or group charged with integrating insights across (insight) domains and levels? (Chapter 2)	Is a specific individual or team responsible for crafting and testing insights in key functional areas/units? Is a team designated to synthesize insights crafted across functional teams/units?
Are insights integrated into decision making? (Chapters 2, 8, 10)	Are insights used to frame (and reframe) decisions? Are decisions tested against insights? Are potential decisions used to determine relevant insight projects?
Is insight a focus of managers'/executives' attention? (Chapter 10)	Do they ask that insights be an output of key analysis projects? Do they initiate dialogue about a change insight's implications? Do they typically raise insight questions in key meetings?
Is insight a required output in most types of analysis? (Chapters 6 and 7)	Is insight a standard output in "analytics" work? Is insight a routine output in analysis conducted by key groups (for example, marketing, operations)?
Is insight a focus of deliberations in meetings? (Chapters 7 and 8)	Do meetings distinguish between findings and insight? Is insight a required part of analysis presentations? Is there discussion around the validity of insights?

Are efforts made to "structure" an analysis context (to enhance the likelihood of insight)? (Chapters 3 and 9)	Are different types of data and data sources sought? Are multiple analysis frames used to generate alternative outputs? Is the perspective of different stakeholders brought to bear? Are the participants encouraged to use their imagination to "see" differently?
Is there an established method (set of analysis protocols) to get from data to some form of insight? (Chapters 4 and 5)	Has the organization developed a broad set of analysis protocols to identify relevant data and indicators, to transform indicators into inferences, and inferences into insights? Has the team been trained in how to use the protocols?
Are suggested insights subjected to stringent vetting and validating? (Chapters 5 and 6)	Are formal analysis steps used to critique proposed insights before they're accepted for decision-making purposes? Are "accepted" insights assessed for their potential decision value?
Are implication insights developed as a routine analysis output? (Chapter 7)	Do analysis teams develop implication insights (high-level business consequences) before determining specific business implications? Are implication insights then used as a critical input to determining strategy, operations and organization implications?
Are specific processes in place to monitor and validate insights over time? (Chapter 6)	Are indicators specific to each change insight identified for purposes of monitoring whether the insight remains valid over time? Is someone charged with monitoring the indicators and assessing whether individual insights need to be amended or discarded?

Do professionals focus on enhancing their insight-related knowledge and skills? (all chapters)	Has the team been charged with conducting analysis of change (for example, analysts and researchers in varied disciplines) work to hone their knowledge of different types of insight, skills in insight analysis methods, ability to lead insight deliberations, and, capacity to inspire and lead insight projects.

Notes

1. CommodityCo is a pseudonym for an actual company.

2. The focus in this book is marketplace insight, that is, insight about the broad context external to the organization. We especially focus on customer insight and competitor insights.

3. The thesis advanced in this book is that understanding marketplace change is the source of marketplace insight. We view the current marketplace as in a process of change, that is, evolving from the past into the future.

4. Both philosophers of science and cognitive scientists leave us in no doubt that our conception of the future can't but be a creation of our own minds. See, for example: C. West Churchman, *The Design of Inquiring Systems* (New York: Basic Books, 1971), and Steven Pinker, *How the Mind Works* (New York: W.W. Norton, 1997).

5. For a detailed discussion of the role, importance and implications of mental models, see, Peter Senge, *The Fifth Discipline: The Art and Practice of the Learning Organization* (New York: Doubleday-Currency, 1990.)

6. Let me invite you to ask any number of your colleagues these questions. Document the responses. You'll discover how little agreement exists as to what they mean by insight, where the focus should be in insight work, and what might be desirable insight attributes.

7. The linkages between insight and the verbs *see, think, decide,* and *act* will be fully explored later in the chapter on the six insight factors (6IFs).

8. AbsoCo is a pseudonym for an actual company.

9. As defined later in this chapter, intelligence insight is the combination of change insight and its business implications.

10. The tendency to narrowly focus insight work and how to deal with it are treated in Chapter 3.

11. This is a common tendency in how "competitor intelligence" is applied in many corporate organizations. See, Liam Fahey, "The Future Direction of Competitive Intelligence, Some Reflections," *Competitive Intelligence Magazine* 12, no. 1 (January/February 2009): 17–22.

12. This is a major rationale for the emphasis on structuring as the initial stage in the 4S cycle detailed in Chapters 3–6.

13. These five items cover a spectrum of strategy relevant issues that typically need to be addressed as the outputs of any marketplace analysis: they focus on the upside (opportunities) and downside (competitive risks and competitor threats); they identify vulnerabilities of possible strategies; they address what assumptions need to be accepted about the broad marketplace.

14. A quality insight is one that exhibits the insight attributes noted in the concluding section of this chapter.

15. Experience has taught me that how individuals or a team deals with the data they already possess, in short, how they think and analyze, is far more influential in generating insight than data per se. This doesn't deny the need for more data or for better data. It does reinforce the assertion that how the mind works is the most influential factor in generating change insight. The influence of the mind in insight work is explicitly addressed in Chapters 3–6.

16. For a general introduction to the big data evolution, see Bill Franks, *The Analytics Revolution: How to Improve Your Business by Making Analytics Operational in the Big Data Era* (New York: John Wiley & Sons, 2014).

17. For a good discussion of the emergence and approaches to analysis under the rubric of Business Intelligence, see Thomas H. Davenport and Jeanne G. Harris, *Competing on Analytics* (Boston: Harvard Business School Press, 2007).

18. For example, Porter's Five Forces. Michael E. Porter, *Competitive Strategy: Techniques for Analyzing Industries and Competitors* (New York: Free Press, 1980).

19. For example, the political, economic, social and technological (PEST) approach to analysis of the macro-environment. See Liam Fahey and V. K. Narayanan, *Macroenvironmental Analysis for Strategic Management* (Saint Paul: West Publishing Company, 1986).

20. For example, the real options approach to analysis strategy and investments alternatives. Marion A. Brach, *Real Options in Practice* (Hoboken, NJ: John Wiley & Sons, 2003).

21. These three modes of depicting change are addressed in Chapters 2–6.

22. The role and importance of the mind in insight work require that we prepare the mind for insight work. In Chapters 3–8, we describe what is required to prepare the mind to conduct specific analysis tasks in crafting and leveraging insight.

23. The point of view has been advanced by many others. See Thomas H. Davenport and Lawrence Prusak, *Working Knowledge: How Organizations Manage What They Know* (Boston: Harvard Business School Press, 1998).

24. The power of the "day in the life of a customer" approach to understanding the customer context is detailed in the customer migration case in Chapters 3–6.

25. I'll address this observation in more detail in Chapter 2 and in Chapter 4 when I consider the role of the mind in drawing inferences and crafting insights.

26. The mind as an information processing machine has been developed by a wide range of authors across many disciplines. See especially Steven Pinker, *How the Mind Works* (New York: W.W. Norton & Company, 1997).

27. Klein, for example, notes that insights change how we understand, act, see, feel, and desire. Gary Klein, *Seeing What Others Don't: The Remarkable Ways We Gain Insights,* (New York: *Public Affairs*, 2013), 23. More fundamentally, Pinker notes the special thing the brain does, information processing or computation, "makes us see, think, feel, choose, and act." Steven Pinker, *How the Mind Works* (New York: W. W. Norton, 1997), 24.

28. If we all see and think and act in the same way, it's impossible to possess distinct understanding of the world around us or gain an advantage over

others. Thus, is it impossible to possess insight that exhibits the desired attributes discussed at the end of this chapter.

29. The role and importance of indicators in capturing marketplace change and enabling inferences are described in detail in the next two chapters.

30. It's interesting to note that the executive who asked the two questions at the beginning of this chapter had already answered both questions in the positive.

31. John A. Byrne, "Great Ideas Are Hard to Come By," *Fortune,* April 9, 2012, 68–86.

32. For a detailed discussion of these three modes of rivalry, see Liam Fahey, *Competitors: Outwitting, Outmaneuvering and Outperforming* (New York: John Wiley & Sons, 2000).

33. Willie Pietersen, *Reinventing Strategy: Using Strategic Learning to Create and Sustain Breakthrough Performance* (New York: John Wiley & Sons, 2002), 70.

34. Gary Hamel and C. K. Prahalad, *Competing for the Future: Breakthrough Strategies for Seizing Control of your Industry and Creating the Markets of Tomorrow* (Boston: Harvard Business School Press, 1994), 77.

35. Richard P. Rumelt, *Good Strategy, Bad Strategy: The Difference and Why It Matters* (New York: Crown Business, 2011), 10.

36. In other words, the water change insight embodies significant new understanding for our firm.

37. In effect, this is what happened in the CommodityCo case discussed in this chapter.

38. The process of validating a suggested or tentative insight is fully detailed in Chapters 5 and 6.

39. As noted earlier in this chapter, the future is a cognitive construction—you construct what you think the future will be. Hence, you can never be certain that your construction gets it right. What you can do is be clear on the judgments you make and the data and rationales you use in making those judgments.

40. Again, it's worth remembering that thinking, deciding, and acting constitute three core insight factors.

41. The numbers in the left-hand column of Table 1-2 indicate the chapters in which the key question is principally addressed.

42. The notion of peripheral vision as a means to looking where you don't normally look is one example. See George S. Day and Paul Schoemaker, *Peripheral Vision, Detecting the Weak Signals that Will Make or Break Your Company* (Boston: Harvard Business School Press, 2006).

43. The influence of emotions in insight work is the subject of Chapter 9.

45. The chapter(s) in which each question is most directly addressed is noted at the end of each question.

Chapter 2

The 4I Diamond Framework

Rideshare companies like Uber have transformed the taxi marketplace in the last five years. Whether or not you're a fan, the company's value proposition—cheaper, convenient, and, often faster from point A to point B—comes from a core customer insight: people are more than willing to use a web-based app to connect to and pay their transportation carrier. Such value-generating insight doesn't simply fall like manna from heaven. It's the culmination of four stages of analysis: indicators, inferences, insights, and implications—what I refer to as the Four-Insight (4I) Diamond Framework (Figure 2-1).[46]

FIGURE 2-1

The Four I (4I) Diamond Stages

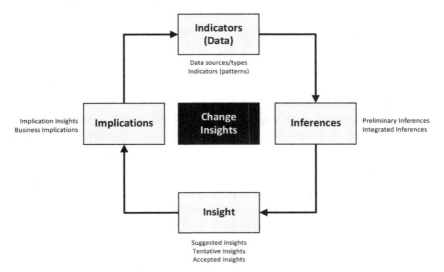

For illustration purposes, I'll use a firm called VP as a case throughout the book. [47] The firm conducted both customer and competitor analysis to provide an initial overview of each stage of analysis (Box 2-1). I'll focus on indicators and inferences here; I'll address insights and implications in detail in later chapters.

Box 2-1

Case: VP

VP, an industrial product firm, sells products to corporate customers in multiple geographic regions. It has always considered one, large rival as its most direct and serious competitor. The two rivals are among the large market share rivals in the competitive space. The competitor begins to make changes to its historical customer-value proposition.

The changes initially appear modest, but VP starts to lose customers to this competitor. It decides to observe and monitor how customers are responding to the competitor's emerging value proposition.

After a few months, VP begins to analyze the data it has collected on the shift in the rival's value proposition and customer responses to it.

Indicators

Insights may, and often eventually do, arise spontaneously. But they never come out of nowhere. Something sparks an inference. Something causes you to see differently.[48] Something gets connected to something else that allows you to craft an insight. That something is what I call *data,* or more precisely, *indicators.* In short, indicators about change—past, present, and future— enable inferences and insights. However, you need to be clear on the distinction between indicators and inferences (Box 2-2).

The disciplined approach to insight requires deliberation about indicators: how they manifest change, how they relate to one another, how they give rise to inferences, and how they enhance learning about a competitive space. This approach also requires methodical management of indicators: how to search for them, how to move from data to indicators, and how to categorize them.

Box 2-2

Data and Indicators: Confuse Them at Your Peril

Confusion among data sources, data forms, and indicators constitutes a prevalent and dominant inhibitor of insight. When data sources and indicators are confounded, indicators, as the focal point of detecting and projecting change, tend to be overshadowed by an emphasis on data sources and the search for new sources of data. Also, without a clear sense of what constitutes indicators, data more quickly recedes into a mass of disconnected bits and pieces.

This confusion and its consequence are exemplified in the case of statements. In many contexts, statements about any topic may be either a source or an indicator. Clearly, for example, statements by a competitor or customers or government agency leaders, frequently give rise to many *indicators of change*: what the competitor plans to do; how and why customers are migrating to a new entrant; policy or regulatory change that the government agency may introduce some months hence. In some instances, however, a statement may constitute a critical indicator.

For example, a technology development entity that historically doesn't make public comments about the state or direction of its work may find it necessary to issue a statement denying or supporting a contention by another party about the imminence of a technology breakthrough. The statement itself serves as (but one) indicator of the current state of the technology and its potential evolution.

Data about change in specific domains or broad competitive contexts, of course, comes in many forms:[91] from incidental comments to dense analysis;[92] from simple forecasts to complex projections; from anecdotal observations to deep, detailed ethnographic observations. And, of course, data may be quantitative or non-quantitative. It should be remembered, however, that a strong preference for either quantitative or non-quantitative data always comes with costs: numbers only have meaning when placed in context; and, numbers clearly help shape our understanding of any context.

The sources of data are almost innumerable. Any organization that develops a data base of data sources finds that categorizing and prioritizing sources is the challenge, not searching for sources! Every successful intelligence-driven organization shapes a network of critical external sources that can be tapped selectively when specific types of data are required. It must also be emphasized here that sources internal to the organization (for example, personnel in marketing, sales, engineering, manufacturing, R&D, finance, human resources, and line management among others) possess extensive (and sometimes) amazing amounts of data and have access to external bountiful primary and secondary sources.

So, accessing data on and about change isn't the issue. What's central to crafting insight, however, is capturing key indicators of current and potential change. Compared to the volume of data that could potentially be generated with respect to any topic or issue or domain, indicators will be relatively small in number, specific and revealing.

Table 2-1 gives some examples of the role of indicators as the source of suggested[49] insights in the macroenvironment.[50] Sometimes, a single indicator leads to a powerful change insight. More frequently, patterns across indicators give rise to insights, leading to significant business implications. The following section illustrates and reinforces how and why indicators play a crucial but often overlooked role in crafting change insight in organizational settings.

Indicators and inferences: Preliminary observations

Indicators assume a position of importance because they enable inferences. In other words, if you miss an indicator, you miss an opportunity to draw what might be a crucial inference. For example, if you don't capture a statement[51] by a customer who is deeply disappointed in the performance of a rival's product, you may not infer that you have an opportunity to compete for the customer's business until you discover another rival has already won it.

Indicators as the source of inferences, or more broadly, the process of *inferencing*, are common and crucial in everyday life.[52] Consider these simple examples:

- **You're driving close to the waterfront and see deep, dense clouds coming in (indicator).** You infer that heavy rain could be on the way and you'd be well advised to quickly leave the area.

Table 2-1   Indicators as a Source of Suggested Insights: Macro Environmental Domains

Topic area	Sample indicators	Potential insights
Potential government policy shift.	Political party statements Electoral candidates' verbal commitments Legislative initiatives Interest group activities Media visibility.	The historic governmental position could be reversed within 18 months with strong political party and public support (thus suggesting it wouldn't likely be reversed for the foreseeable future).
Water as a source of major conflict between two countries.	Supply trends Demand trends Projected economic activity and consequences of insufficient supply Major potential supply interruption factors Public interest groups' statements and activities Government departments' considerations of possible actions.	A further decline in water availability for both countries would most likely lead to intense political battles between the countries in many arenas (media, regional organizations, UN), resulting in one country potentially losing a significant portion of its water supply, which would increase the likelihood of military skirmishes at the border.
Technology developments (next generation technologies).	Statements by scientists, technology developers, science reporters, public policy experts, professors, government agencies, consultants, among others Actions and comments by government agencies, specialist agencies (for example, patents office), corporate entities, research institutes, investor entities, science journals, investment banks, consulting firms, among others.	The intersection of three technology developments (previously viewed as relatively independent) could lead to a breakthrough that would solve a specific surgical problem, resulting in a range of current surgical procedures becoming obsolete.

Economic (shift in overall economic activity)	GNP, GDP; income levels and inequality, savings and expenditures; corporate margins, profits, and investments; prices, wages, and productivity; employment rates; housing starts; stock market indices; currency exchange rates; monetary policy decisions; imports and exports; among many others.	Despite a shift in government policies and continued near zero interest rates, inflation will remain low (as opposed to many assertions by political actors and some economists).
Regulatory (shift in emphasis in implementation of a rule or regulation)	Statements by executive branch departments, political representatives, regulatory agency leaders, experts at regulatory hearings, interested and affected social interest groups, industry and trade representatives, among others Actions by all of these parties and other interested and affected groups	The new regulation would have extensive enforcement discretion that could lead to delayed application in many circumstances.

- **You're driving in a city for the first time and observe cars frequently "beating the yellow light" (indicator).** You infer that taking off fast when the light turns green is likely to be dangerous to your physical well being.

- **You come up behind a car with a large "learner driver" sign (indicator) prominently displayed in the back window.** You infer that the driver may do some unexpected and even dangerous things, so you decide to keep a healthy distance back from the car.

Shifting back to capturing and understanding marketplace change, the interplay between indicators and inferences can be even more complex, sometimes not self-evident, and, often, not well understood (Box 2-3). I'll address some of this complexity in the next section, and will detail the process of extracting inferences from indicators in Chapter 4, Sniffing.

Box 2-3

The Interplay between Indicators and Inferences

The relationship between indicators and inferences is complex, not self-evident, and often not well understood. Here are some key items to help you understand the interplay between indicators and inferences.[93]

Timing of change: Indicators may give rise to inferences about past, current or prospective change. Thus, change insights may give rise to a new understanding of the past, present or the future.

Alerting indicators/inferences: A sequence or pattern of indicators is typically associated with a significant marketplace change. Therefore, indicators are typically captured and assessed over time. So it's important to note the role of "alerting" indicators: the initial one or two indicators that enable us to draw the first inferences about some specific or potential change. For example, a new, unique comment at a trade show or a statement in a governmental report may provide our first indication of a change in competitor's strategy or the potential emergence of a new customer need or the possibility of a change in the implementation of a specific governmental regulation.

Confirming and refuting inferences: Later indicators can then be used to confirm or refute the alerting inferences. Change evidenced in the later indicators can be assessed as to whether it lends further credence (or not) to the alerting inference. This analysis resides at the heart of vetting—a primary focus of Chapter 5.

Indirect inferences: The human mind knows no bounds in its capacity to draw inferences from one or more indicators. This is evidenced by the ability to draw indirect inferences: those that focus on change in one thing or domain even though the indicator is about something different. For example, indicators addressing change in social values lead to inferences about change in future election results or change in judicial decisions or governmental policies. Without the capacity for indirect inferences, the ability to craft insights would be extremely limited. Indirect inferences also validate the need for vetting and vouching, addressed in Chapters 5 and 6, respectively.

Faster inferencing: The sooner indicators are detected and inferences drawn, the faster inferencing occurs. Thus, organizations need to pay attention to shortening the "detection lag," that is, the length of time between when an indicator becomes available and its detection and capture. For example, if customer statements about their challenges, problems, and pain points aren't detected until months after they're uttered, it's likely that rivals will already be well on their way to addressing the underlying customer needs.

But they also need to pay attention to the "inference lag"—the time between detecting an indicator reflecting change and drawing an inference. If the customer statements are captured, but inferences about possible underlying customer needs aren't drawn for another six months, then even more time has elapsed before the customer-change indicators become of value to the business. Reducing both the detection and inference lags contribute to greater efficiency and effectiveness in insight work: the shorter both lags, the more time the organization has to craft a response to the relevant change.

Strong versus weak inferences: Whether inferences are direct or indirect, you can ask whether they're strong or weak. In other words, how credible are the inferences? Credibility depends upon both the indicators and the interpretation at the heart of the inference. A number of reinforcing and supporting indicators lends credibility to the inferences. A competitor's behaviors, words, and investments that support each other add to inference strength. A compelling story or narrative also adds to inference strength. A narrative around a competitor's current and planned moves with evident intent and motivation will add to inference strength. Yes, weak inferences—those with limited data and not yet supported logic or argument, or even conflicting logic—may be powerful alerting inferences. A comment passed by a third party may produce a weak inference that alerts you to the possibility of a significant and unexpected move by a competitor or a possible shift in the implementation of regulatory rule or regulation.

Indicators: Trends, patterns, and discontinuities

Indicators provide the means to detect, track, and project trends, patterns, and discontinuities. They offer the basic staples of capturing, anticipating, and assessing marketplace change.[53] Any trend line represents change along an indicator. For example, a customer's purchases each year constitute one trend line that might show the ups and downs in that customer's purchases over a number of years. Any chart or figure presenting a set of trends reflects change over time along a set of indicators. Change patterns (for example, assertions that a region is becoming more conservative, the population is becoming less migratory, technologies are diffusing faster than a decade ago) involve connecting change along multiple indicators.

To demonstrate that a region is becoming increasingly conservative, you need to track change along the following indicators:

- Voting patterns in local, state, and federal elections
- Decisions by different governmental agencies
- Judicial decisions
- Speeches, statements, and actions by politicians, religious, and other public leaders
- Newspaper stories and editorials, among others

Current or projected change in one indicator (a trend) or more indicators (a pattern) representing a significant disjuncture from a prior trajectory indicates discontinuity. Some examples of discontinuity could be:[54]

- A switch in control of a political assembly, such as Congress or a state legislature, from one political party to another
- A large and rapid downturn or upturn in the economy, as occurred with the slump in the 2008 financial markets
- Apple's unrelenting rise in market share in the mobile phone market interrupted by Samsung's market surge; established product positions overturned by so-called disruptive technologies[55]

The role of indicators

Indicators play a critical role in the overall insight process beyond sparking you to draw an inference. Identifying potential *indicator categories* often helps you develop a deeper understanding of the issue, topic, or domain.

VP case: The analysis team spent some time developing the list of indicator categories pertaining to the competitor's value proposition and customers' responses.[56] As the team began to examine the competitor's value proposition, it realized that a winning value proposition is never dependent on only one component such as service, functionality, image, or relationships. Rather, it's a combination of several components. And, each component then has a number of dimensions to it with associated indicators. For example, functionality involved several indicators: application uses, performance levels, and breakdowns.

Indicators also focus attention on specific aspects of change that might not have been previously identified or captured, or if they had, hadn't been noticed.[57] For example, one company recently discovered a consultant's comments (the source) about the changing landscape of an industry. It generated multiple indicators pertaining to shifts in strategies of existing competitors, the likely entry of a specific type of rival, small but significant change requirements in winning value propositions, and the rapid evolution of distinct customer niches. Here, each indicator led analysts and managers to address specific aspects of emerging and potential industry change.

VP case: Negotiations between the competitor and some customers had previously not been considered relevant to capturing and understanding how and why customers responded to the competitor's offer. As a consequence, key aspects of the competitor's value proposition around relationships with customers were missed.

Indicators also allow an analysis team to detect, develop, and test patterns that go way beyond the raw data. Patterns that aren't obvious[58] are more likely to give rise to fresh and valuable new understanding.[59] This is the hope that lies behind the current enthusiasm for big data analysis.[60]

VP case: As you'll see later, patterns across indicators within indicator categories, such as functionality and service, and across indicator categories will help your team draw higher-level inferences that aren't immediately evident (Figure 2-2).

In addition, indicators help you derive, test, and refine different, and often, conflicting inferences. As you'll see throughout this chapter and others,

FIGURE 2-2

Insights: The Role of Inference: The VP Case

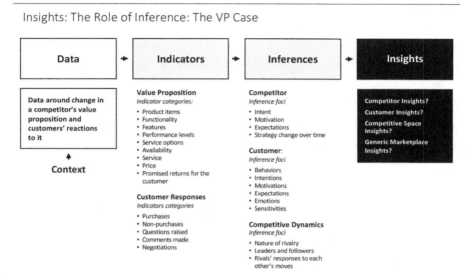

change along indicators furnishes the data and evidence to develop and vet these conflicting inferences.[61]

Moving from data to indicators

The transition from data to indicators lies at the heart of both efficient method and effective deliberations in insight work. Efficiency here refers to timely extraction of indicators. The sooner the right indicators are noted, the faster inferences can be derived.[62] Effectiveness refers to deriving quality insights. The higher the quality of the insights, the greater the likelihood that you can develop significant business implications.

The method and deliberations inherent in the data-to-indicators transition require you to "read" the data with an eye toward identifying and categorizing potential indicators. It involves addressing three interrelated questions:

What change indicators are evident in the data?

This open-ended question invites you to sift through the data in search of indicators that (may) indicate a change.[63] Focusing your mind in this way is central to any effort to move from data to indicators.[64] The value derived from reading a document submitted to a regulatory agency, an industry study, a technology assessment, a governmental report, or even an article in your local newspaper or favorite business magazine is greatly enhanced if you concentrate on identifying indicators of change. Noting the indicators and the type and extent of the change they embody or potentially suggest makes you more attentive to change and its potential implications. You're mind-set shifts from reading to detecting and thinking about change.[65]

VP case: As the team recognized the importance of understanding the shift in the competitor's value proposition, they began to note possible indicators as they reviewed the data from internal and external sources: sales force reports, written comments from the marketing group, feedback summaries from executives who had visited customers, public statements from the competitor, the competitor's own website, and reports from third-party consultants and technology specialists.

What indicators might be specific to previously determined categories?

If you don't ask this question early in the process of data collection and review, you'll be confronted with a crucial analytical challenge: how to organize the indicators into meaningful groups. This closed-ended question compels you to read the data for indicators that will shed light on critical issues and questions with respect to specific domains, topics, or issues. For example, in reading an industry-level market research report or a series of sales force call cards, you might seek indicators pertaining to current or latent customer needs, potential migration to rivals, customer assessment of your firm's and rivals' value propositions, or customer points of view about emerging technologies.

VP case: The analysis team captured and inserted indicators into a number of predetermined categories (Figures 2-3, 2-4, and 2-5). The iterative nature of insight work was evidenced in the addition of indicators as the team progressed through the steps in data collection.

What topic categories emanate from the data?

This question reflects the iterative nature of the movement from data to indicators. It's unlikely that your team will identify and separate all relevant indicator categories *before* serious reading and reflection on the available data. So,

FIGURE 2-3

Change in a Competitor's Value Proposition: The VP case

Indicator Category	Sample Indicators	Sample Inferences	Integrated Inferences	Insights
Product	Product lines; Product line items	Competitor wants to create a unique solution space	Competitor understands that it must focus on a specific product space (it can't be all things to all customers)	The Competitor Insight: The competitor wants to establish a new solution space; it is driven by the desire to transform the customer experience; it is willing to transform its value proposition in order to outperform all its rivals
Features	Design Style	Competitor not interested in design uniqueness	Competitor recognizes that to "win big" it must win both in terms of functionality and brand (image, reputation and service)	
Functionality	Performance levels	Competitor aims for massive superiority		
Availability	Wholesale channels Retail channels	Competitor will eventually consolidate its channels	Competitor will invest significantly to build the desired distinctive brand and customer relationships	
Service	Service options	Competitor sees service as a critical customer value point		
Image	Message content; Brand elements	Competitor building image around rapid service		
Reputation	Actions and words of others	Competitor wants to be seen as service leader		
Selling	Behaviors of sales force; messages used	Competitor willing to spend to build a consultative sales force for most segments		
Relationships	Words and actions	Competitor now values relationship with customers		
Price	List prices Discounted prices	Competitor aims for prices above direct rivals		

as you review data for change indicators, new indicator categories are likely to emerge and/or predetermined categories will be redefined. This is consistent with the observation that consideration of relevant indicators compels further thinking about the phenomenon of interest.

VP case: As the VP analysis team identified and categorized indicators, they refined individual indicator categories and introduced some additional categories. In the case of the competitor's value proposition, they hadn't anticipated the role and importance of reputation or of non-purchases in understanding customers' responses.

Open-ended search for change indicators

Unfortunately, you don't know what you don't know. You're reminded of this fact when you come across an indicator that alerts you to something that you

FIGURE 2-4

Customers' Responses to the Shift in the Competitor's Value Proposition: The VP case

Indicator Category	Sample Indicators	Sample Inferences	Integrated Inferences	Insights
Inquiries about the offer	Questions asked	Customers eager to learn about the offer	Customer are responding in very different ways	THE CUSTOMER INSIGHT:
Negotiations with provider	Content of conversations	Some customers proving to be a hard sell	The competitor's new value proposition (offer) is delivering real functional benefits	Customers are falling into distinct needs-based segments requiring customized solutions and some segments WILL walk away fast from their long-time providers
Product trials	Who doing so; when, where.	Some customers will to learn about the product	Customer needs-based segments appear to be emerging	
Purchases	Which customers; Volume; types;	Customers buying who value the seller relationship		
Non-purchases	Who not purchasing; Statements	Customers not buying who are highly price sensitive		
Experience in use	Problems; Benefits; Results	Customers seeing real benefits		
Statements about the product/ experience	Expectations met (or not); Areas for product improvement	Some customers eager to point out next product generation attributes		

FIGURE 2-5

Potential Competitive Dynamics: The VP case

Indicator Category	Sample Indicators	Sample Inferences	Integrated Inferences	Insights
Emerging/ potential product change	Product dimensions/ attributes Solutions propagated (rather than products)	Product change will speed up; Solutions will be the focus of rivalry (not products); Will be a rapid evolution of solutions	The move toward solutions willcause some current rivals to fade from this market; Without a service capability, it will be almost impossible to survive in this marketplace	THE COMPETITIVE SPACE INSIGHT Strategy will need to be based on multiple dimensions of value; it will transform which rivals win and which lose; some will not be able to make the transition.
Competition around service	Service types Service levels Service options	Service will no longer be optional — will key to evolution of solutions		
Competition around intangibles	Brand investments Brand positioning Emphasis upon relationships Sales force pushing "value"	Heavy investment will be required to reposition most brands; Collaboration will be the focus of relationship development	Marketing increasingly will be critical to creating and enhancing the "intangibles" required to win Strictly price rivals will find it difficult to gain market share	
Competition around price	Price changes Price/value relationships Price discounts Competitors' pricing moves	Value will need to be identified and delivered to allow and sustain price premiums; Dropping price will be less likely to attract customers;	Customer segments seeking different forms of value are likely to emerge (in the next two years)	

didn't know you didn't know.[66] Many times these indicators of change aren't anticipated. And they typically arise in places and ways that hadn't been the object of search or attention.[67] Indeed, stories of insight capture passed down in the folklore of organizations often reveal how chance encounters or reflection upon issues or topics or data not typically encountered led to intriguing inferences and insights (Table 2-2). If an indicated change has potential implications for the organization, then the possibility for an intelligence insight is real.

Table 2-2 Unexpected Occurrences as the Source of Inferences

Unexpected comments from customers

- If you guys are so smart, why can't you fix this problem?
- Let me tell you what our real operating challenge is!
- If we could connect these two technologies, think of what we could do!

Chance encounters

- My friend sat beside a lady on a plane who told him how emotionally upset she was with the service his company had provided her business. He inferred that two key elements of service were grossly underemphasized and probably ignored entirely.
- An engineer at a trade show sat beside a purchasing department leader from one of his firm's customers and learned that the purchasing group was about to change key purchasing norms and criteria for key suppliers and their product. He quickly inferred that the product attributes his firm had worked long and hard to develop would make its products less attractive to this customer organization.

In the interest of generating insight, don't leave coming across such indicators to chance. Instead, conduct an open-ended search for change indicators.[68] By open-ended, I mean seek (change) indicators in places and in ways that aren't constrained by your organization's current strategies, operations, issues, or interests. For example, scientists might scan R&D work in related industries, or even in unrelated industries, to identify science developments that might one day affect the scope and focus of your organization's science and technology work. Marketers might scan consumer behaviors, interests, and commitments in unrelated product areas for indicators suggesting consumer contexts that they might one day face or may already be confronting without knowing it.

Inferences: The bridge from indicators to insights

The pathway from indicators to insights leads through inferences (see Figure 1-1). So it's important to understand the nature of inferences, what's involved in extracting them, the value of context in deriving them, and the role of the human mind in interpreting them.

Indicators provide the means to detect, monitor, and project market-place change. The change detected may be current and well established; for example, a set of technology indicators might indicate how the technology is penetrating specific market segments. Or the indicator may be a portent of change that has yet to unfold; for example, presentations at an industry conference might collectively suggest an imminent technological breakthrough that could lead to a radically new customer solution. The verbs "indicate" and "suggest" clearly imply that new understanding of change doesn't emerge directly from indicators. Stated differently, indicators don't speak. The human mind needs to intervene.[69] In simple terms, you infer something from one or more indicators; that's something I call an inference. The automobile driving examples earlier in this chapter provide some everyday instances of how you might infer something that was not evident in the indicators, per se. Here are some common business examples:

- **The EPA announces a policy change establishing new coal industry emission guidelines (indicator).** The head of R&D in one firm infers that all rivals now have a large incentive to invest R&D dollars in replacement technologies.

- **A customer complains that an established manufacturing technology continues to malfunction (indicator).** The firm infers a major market opportunity may exist for anyone who develops a solution that wouldn't involve the long-established technology.

- **A firm successfully adapts its product to enter a specific geographic region (indicator).** Key rivals then infer that the firm will further adapt the product to enter adjacent geographic markets.

I can't repeat often enough that no indicator about a facet of change constitutes an inference by itself, much less an insight. Dense, data-filled trends detailing the change in and around the economy don't throw off insights in the form of understanding emerging or potential economic change. Nor do they neatly encapsulate the forces shaping the direction of emerging or future economic change. Worse still, if the economic trend lines are all positive (for example, GDP is increasing, housing starts are growing, interest rates are declining, the Federal Reserve isn't constraining money supply, and corporate profits are improving), a mind untutored in the vicissitudes of the economy could quickly draw what might turn out to be a decidedly false inference: the economy will continue to grow, and it won't go into decline in the next year. Getting to this false conclusion alerts you to the role, importance, and influence of inferences in any effort, conscious or subconscious, to craft insight.

Consider the following as a preliminary set of observations on the process of inferencing (that is, drawing inferences from indicator change):

- Shifting from the description about the past or present to consideration of the future necessarily requires you to draw an inference; that is, to infer something about the future based on the available indicators. Thus, you infer that the economy will continue to grow based on the performance purveyed along the key indicators noted above.

- Any inference necessarily entails a judgment. You make an assessment—a judgment—that the economy will continue to grow.

- You may make the judgment(s) at the heart of inference consciously or subconsciously.[70] So the inference that the economy will continue to grow may take place in ways you can't explain. And, in some instances, it may take place almost instantaneously.[71]

- Any inference entailing one or more judgments results from the intertwining of data and reasoning.[72] And, the reasoning may be implicit (the unconscious at work) or explicit. In most instances, reasoning overpowers data. The logic imposed upon the economic indicators (all the change trends represented along the indicators "clearly" argue for a continued upsurge in general economic conditions) typically overwhelms any desire to seek counter data along a different set of indicators.

These general observations suggest the need to examine in more detail the phenomenon of inferences and the process of inferencing.

Inferences: An overview

Insight is impossible without inferences. So it's critical to understand the nature of inferences. An inference always manifests a number of characteristics. Each contributes to your understanding of what an inference is, and perhaps even more importantly, what you refer to as the inferencing process.

An inference occurs when you infer one thing from another—when you infer something from an indicator. An inference is always drawn by *someone* in a specific *context* from one or more *indicators* pertaining to *something* (for example, a person, organization, trend, or event) that addresses *change* (for example, an action, behavior, future state, or motivation).[73]

Because any inference is drawn by a human, another set of characteristics emerge. An inference is always an *interpretation* that involves *judgments* and, thus, must be buttressed by *data and logic* (hopefully, the intersection of solid data and compelling logic) that is necessarily subject to all the machinations, foibles, biases, and tendencies of the human mind.

I'll discuss the role and importance of these characteristics of inferences and the inferencing process, continuing with the VP case for illustration purposes.

Drawn by the human mind, not software

An inference can only be a product of your mind. Computer-driven analytics don't generate inferences. Irrespective of the complexity of the factors it can incorporate and manipulate, the best that software can do is show you patterns not evident in the raw data, identify potential causal relationships, and surface linkages you hadn't previously detected. These software outputs serve as inputs to your brain's crafting of inferences.

VP case: Members of the analysis team individually and collectively work to understand the change in the rival's value proposition and customer responses to it over time.

In a context

An inference is *always* drawn in a context. It can't be otherwise.[74] Familiarity with the context of the relevant indicators enables you to draw the inferences.

This is especially important in any business situation because the relevant context is likely to be in a state of flux. What may be a reasonable inference today might not be so tomorrow.

VP case: Analysis team members have extensive knowledge of the key rivals' histories, strategies, and behaviors; the dynamics of competition among these rivals; and how customers have previously responded to value proposition shifts. Thus, they have a basis in competitor, customer, and competitive knowledge to develop possible interpretations and explanations of the change in the competitor's value proposition.

From one or more indicators

An indicator gives rise to an inference and, thus, the possibility of insight. It reflects the change (past, present, emergent, or potential). You may draw an inference from one, a few, multiple, or many indicators.

It's important to note that the source indicators may not be evident in the expressed inference (or insight). In fact, this is often the case, and it's true at all levels along the insight funnel. Thus, a generic marketplace insight (GMI)—for example, a competitor threat, that *a competitor is likely to move quickly to enter an emerging product market to preempt certain later entrants by locking in a set of key accounts,* doesn't refer to the indicators from which it was drawn.

VP case: A string of pertinent indicators was evident. Indicators were associated with each key dimension of the competitor's value proposition (Figure 2-3), each dimension of customers' responses (Figure 2-4), and the potential competitive dynamics that might be unleashed because of change in the competitor's value proposition (Figure 2-5).

Pertaining to an object

Although it may be obvious, an inference always pertains to an object. For example, you might draw an inference about what some entity—a competitor, customer, channel, supplier, or government agency—might do at some point in the future. Or, you might infer when an event will take place, or when a trend might change, or what type of significant disruption or discontinuity might occur.

What's less obvious is the role and importance of *indirect inferences.* Sometimes the object of an inference emerges only as you reflect on the change embedded in the indicators. For example, a competitor's projected move, such as the launch of a new product or the announcement of its withdrawal from a product line, could give rise to an inference about what might happen in an adjacent market, what the response of a government agency might be, or what executives in the competitor's related business units might do.

VP case: As illustrated in Figure 2-3, the inferences are drawn by team members from the indicators associated with the competitor's value proposition shift addressed three domains (or macro objects): the competitor's strategic intent and motivation, the customer's behaviors and motivations, and the potential competitive dynamics. As illustrated in Figures 2-3, 2-4 and 2-5, inferences were drawn about individual aspects of these three domains (or micro-objects).

About change

By now it should be self-evident that inferences (and thus insights) always address change. Every example of inference and insight in this book involves change: inferences about change that might occur in the future, and inferences about current and emerging change.[75] Change legitimizes the need for inferences and insights.

VP case: The inferences explicitly address change in each of the three domains just noted: the competitor's strategy direction, intent, and motivation; the customers' behaviors, motivations, and concerns; and the potential direction and evolution of competitive dynamics. As you'll see, change in these three domains is intimately interrelated. Change in one sheds light on the others.

An interpretation

Because inferences, and thus insights, connect one form of change with another, are often about the future, and are rarely axiomatic or purely deductive, an element of judgment is always involved. Drawing the inference requires you to make a judgment that the data represented by one or more indicators in some specific context will lead to some future state—something about the object. To infer that customers will move quickly from one rival to another if a particular regulatory restraint is eliminated requires you to make a number of judgments—why customers will switch, how fast they'll do so, the level of switching costs, and the inability of the current dominant rival to protect its product position. If the team judges poorly, that is, gets it wrong or is substantially "off," the inference is likely to prove incorrect.

VP case: A moment's reflection will convince you that members of the VP analysis team were making an interpretation when each inference was drawn, no matter how tentative it might be. To cite one example, to connect a change in the competitor's service content and levels to some customers' motivation to work more closely with the competitor requires you to make an interpretation, that is, to make a judgment based on some data and some type of reasoning.

Data and logic (reasoning)

Inference, by definition, requires data (indicators) and reasoning. For instance, an inference that total sales growth in a specific product-market segment will decline this year for the first time in ten years requires indicators (for example, growth in the economy, penetration of customer segments, marketing investments of rivals, customer order patterns) and judgments about the change represented along the indicators (for example, how a stagnating economy affects customers purchasing habits, and whether rivals' marketing investments will attract new customers to the product-market segment). As I'll discuss later, you need to assess both the data and the reasoning—what I refer to as inference (or insight) vetting, vouching, value testing, and validating (Table 2-3).

Subject to your mind's tendencies

Inference occurs only because your mind imposes itself on the situation. Your mind creates the linkage (makes the judgment) that enables an inference. Often the inference isn't evident in the indicators or even in the context, per se. But your mind works in ways you may not fully understand, and many of its biases and proclivities are well established.[76] You need to be aware of the brain's capacities, as discussed in the next chapter, and its biases to manage the inferencing process and derive the highest possible quality inferences (and, thus, insights).

VP case: In tracking customer responses to the change in the competitor's value proposition, the analysis team discovered that some customers were already suggesting attributes for the next generation of the product. Some team members immediately judged that these product attributes didn't make sense and therefore were implausible. They made this judgment almost instantly (a distinctive capacity of the brain). But upon further reflection caused by other team members asking whether and how the product attributes could add value for customers, the team drew the inference that these

Table 2-3   A Summary of 4V Activities

Activity	Description
Vetting	The analysis team must assess every suggested change insight against the desired attributes: new understanding, novelty, congruence, obviousness, explanatory power, and endurance.. Vetting provides the opportunity to critically test and reframe suggested change insights.
Vouching	After vetting, the team should take one last opportunity to review and test each insight. The insight moves from suggested to accepted for decision-making purposes when the team vouches for the insight—they have taken the analysis as far as they can.
Value testing	Next, the team value tests each accepted change insight. The intent is to identify implication insights and business implications. Value testing determines how each change insight might enhance your organization' s thinking, decisions, and actions as inputs to superior marketplace performance and financial results.
Validating	Change and implication insights, by definition, have a shelf life. They don't last forever. The team needs to monitor each insight over time to assess whether or not it still holds up.

attributes (and extensions of them) could be present in products in the market within three years.

Sequences of inferences

Inferences always lead to further inferences. Sometimes, a single inference kicks off a sequence of inferences. You might infer from recent statements by the company and by industry experts that Apple's next iPhone will contain a set of specific features. Presuming that this feature set will be present, you might then infer that Apple will have a distinct product functionality advantage over rivals' current products. This, in turn, might allow you to infer that a certain volume of customers will trade in their current phones for the new iPhone.

VP case: An inference that some customers who are highly price sensitive aren't buying the product could lead to the inference that highly price-sensitive customers may represent a needs-based segment (that is, "we want a basic functionality at a relatively low price") which might, in turn, lead to an inference that some competitors might see this segment as large enough to warrant a dedicated value proposition. Each inference in the chain, of course, needs to be vetted and vouched for, as discussed in Chapters 5 and 6, using available data and solid reasoning.

A hierarchy of inferences

Much of the complexity of creating insights stems from the fact that inferences can be integrated into higher levels and eventually to a point where you're willing to declare an insight. Thus, you might draw many inferences from a set of indicators about the impending emergence of new technology, what I refer to as preliminary or preliminary inferences. You might then integrate a number of these "preliminary" inferences into one or more integrated inferences about specific aspects of the technology (for example, potential value dimensions for customers), when the technology might be launched, or which customers might be most likely to adopt the new technology. Integrating inferences constitutes an unavoidable and critical component of any pathway to crafting insights.

VP case: Figures 2-3, 2-4, and 2-5 illustrate how a set of preliminary inferences was aggregated or integrated into higher-order inferences. In the case of customer responses, the team drew inferences for each indicator category (Figure 2-4). They then analyzed those inferences to determine how they might be aggregated or integrated. The process begins by asking what inferences are related to each other. For example, which inferences relate to value delivered to customers or to potential distinct needs-based segments? This questioning process led to the three integrated inferences shown in Figure 2-4.[77]

Again, judgment is always involved in moving up the inference hierarchy. Sometimes, higher-order inferences won't be self-evident in the preliminary inferences. This is especially so when the inferences are more indirect than direct. Thus, the process of moving to integrated inferences must always entail vetting and vouch for the higher-order inferences. I will briefly discuss this in the next section, Insight.

Connecting to the insight funnel

The insight funnel, described in Chapter 1, embodies both a sequence and levels of inferences and insights. The levels of insights begin with domain insights (the lowest level) and lead to competitive space insight (CSIs) and GMIs, and eventually to intelligence insights. The road to insight in any domain (see Figure 1-1) such as suppliers, technology, regulatory, social values, or ecology, is marked by the inference steps described in the VP case. Each eventual *domain* insight emerges from a sequence of inferences that create the bridge from preliminary inferences through integrated inferences to a suggested and finally an accepted insight.[78] A similar sequence of inferences typifies getting to a CSI or GMI.[79]

The 6IFs and drawing inferences

Here are some preliminary indications of how the 6IFs influence the deliberations and method involved in identifying indicators and drawing inferences.[80] Attention to the 6IFs should propel you and any analysis team to generate higher-quality inferences and superior insights.

See: Immerse yourself in the relevant indicator content and its context so you can escape long-established points of view. In the VP case, for example, the team had to imagine how and why customers were responding in ways that weren't evident in the preliminary inferences. If they had remained in the data, they wouldn't have seen how or why customer needs-based segments might evolve.

Think: Without focusing on different and new connections among preliminary inferences, asking questions you wouldn't have previously asked, and challenging others' suggested preliminary and integrated inferences, you won't think about new things or think in new ways. In the VP case, the deliberations pushed the team to ask why specific indicators would lead to the suggested inferences and what might be the basis for suggested integrated inferences.

Intend: Embarking on a systematic approach to drawing inferences and managing the analysis back and forth and interpersonal ebb and flow, as discussed in the next section, doesn't come easily to most people. So they need to be animated by an overarching purpose: the intention to craft the highest-quality inferences and insights.

Decide: If you don't commit to digging deep in the deliberations around any data set for new understanding, and even new explanations of what might otherwise be taken for granted, you won't search for elusive indicators, look for less obvious inferences, and push to generate quality (integrated) inferences. In the words of one manager, you need to decide to draw on your mental energies to do things that may be entirely new to you.

Act: Living the intent and decisions requires specific behaviors, many of which entail trial and error: learning how to draw preliminary inferences, how to wordsmith them, how to articulate the reasoning succinctly underpinning them. In short, you learn new behaviors and adapt old behaviors—how you previously identified relevant indicators and drew inferences.

Feel: Emotions may severely inhibit or strongly facilitate deriving and articulating preliminary inferences. In the VP case, a few team members expressed negative emotions about executing the steps involved in moving from indicators to preliminary inferences; hence, their reluctance initially to fully commit to the method.

Insights: Transitioning from preliminary inferences to change insights

The generation of preliminary inferences gives rise to a challenge: how to get to one or more change insights (Figure 2-1). The third stage in the 4I Diamond Framework addresses how to transform preliminary inferences into the levels of change insight introduced in Figure 1-2. It typically involves extensive back and forth and interpersonal ebb and flow.

The insight perspective comes into full flower in the transition from preliminary inferences to change insights. Because insight involves a new understanding of change that represents a significant departure from your old understanding, which may have been largely implicit or not on your mental radar at all, intensive deliberations typically mark the transition to the new understanding. This is especially true because the focus and content of insights vary greatly depending on whether you're crafting domain insights, CSIs, or GMIs. The deliberations address a number of questions:

What preliminary inferences relate to each other? How do you connect preliminary inferences to craft higher-order inferences? What do you need to do to get to domain insights? The methodical approach, the second lynchpin in executing the insight discipline, involves a set of individual *analysis* steps that are summarized in this chapter and detailed in Chapter 5.

An insight always presumes an act of inferencing. Thus, all of the attributes and characteristics associated with inferences discussed above also pertain to insights. Insight is crafted by someone; it's always with respect to change in some context; judgment is necessarily involved; it addresses the future, either directly or indirectly. Before you stipulate an insight, as with significant inferences, you need to test and vindicate the data and reasoning that gives rise to it. Because an insight is stipulated at one point in time, that is, you accept it for purposes of decision making, you need to subject it to continual assessment and refinement, that is, insight validating, which I'll address in detail in Chapter 6. Insights, by definition, have a shelf life.

VP case: The VP case illustrates the crucial analysis steps involved in moving from indicators to inferences to insights. The sample of preliminary inferences shown in Figures 2-3, 2-4, and 2-5, constitute the input to the collective deliberation required to begin the analysis journey to change insights. Integrated inferences provide the crucial stepping-stone from preliminary inferences to domain insights. But it's a long way from the preliminary inferences to carefully crafted insights. The VP analysis team members immersed themselves in this task. In Chapter 5, I'll detail the steps undertaken by the VP analysis team in shaping insights from the preliminary inferences.

My purpose here is to briefly delineate the transitions from preliminary inference to domain insights and then to CSIs and GMIs.

Analysis back and forth

My emphasis on a deliberative and methodical approach to crafting change insight stems in large part from key characteristics of the analysis process inherent in getting to insights. Each of the transitions—from preliminary inferences to integrated inferences to domain insights to CSIs and, finally to GMIs—takes time. It's never a linear process. Each transition involves extensive analysis back and forth. For example, every integrated inference subsumes two or more preliminary inferences. A substantial number of preliminary inferences, of course, are likely to give rise to more than one integrated inference (though the number will certainly be significantly smaller than the number of preliminary inferences). Typically, an analysis team develops many potential integrated inferences as trial balloons to test whether they make sense; that is, do they offer a higher level of understanding? The deliberations around the analysis go back and forth as you advance an integrated inference and provoke responses from other members of the team.

VP case: The analysis back and forth was evident in the team's deliberations. For example, in the case of the competitor's value proposition, a team member might connect preliminary inferences pertaining to image, reputation, relationships, and price to generate a potentially integrated inference regarding the brand or the experience the competitor desires to create for customers. Others then reword the integrated inference based on the connections they see among the preliminary inferences.

Interpersonal ebb and flow

You make judgments that help you connect two or more preliminary inferences or to develop a suggested integrated inference, or even to advance a suggested domain or higher-level insight. In the same vein, you make judgments about others' suggested inferences and insights. As differences become evident in the suggested inferences and insights, an interpersonal ebb and flow emerge: you may contest each other's suggestions. Frequently, the ebb and flow are driven less by differences in judgment and interpretation—the reasoning supporting individual points of view—than by reactions to who is advancing specific inferences and the relationships and alliances among individuals that evolve over the course of an analysis project.

VP case: Some individuals insisted that they had the "correct" interpretation (inference) given specific indicator change. The insistence sometimes provoked a reaction: "You might want to think about the following inference about customer behaviors given the change we observe along these indicators." But when properly managed, the interpersonal ebb and flow often led to a different inference; this was especially so in the case of integrated inferences.

Integrated inferences

Preliminary inferences are a long way from insights. Integrated inferences facilitate the *analysis* journey to insights. However, the pathway from preliminary to integrated inferences can be contorted, circular, and full of *tentatively* suggested integrated inferences that are initially (often vehemently) rejected. No wonder analysis reflects the back and forth noted above. And, the pathway can be tension-filled as you advance and defend your initial and refined statements of integrated inferences—thus, giving rise to the interpersonal ebb and flow just noted.

Both the analysis back and forth and the interpersonal ebb and flow stem in part from the fact that the transition to even an initial statement or draft of an integrated inference requires you to combine at least two, and often more, preliminary inferences into one suggested integrated inference. As in the case of preliminary inferences, personal judgments and knowledge of the relevant context underpin the transition. Consequently, it's not surprising that a given set of preliminary inferences often gives rise to a surprising number of *suggested* integrated inferences.[81]

VP case: The team quickly suggested a number of integrated inferences. Combinations of the preliminary inferences gave rise to different ways to articulate a more integrated inference. For example, combining three preliminary inferences (Figure 2-3)—*the competitor will eventually consolidate its channels, competitor wants to be seen as the service leader, competitor now values relationships with customers*—led to a series of deliberations that, when combined with other preliminary inferences, eventually led to the integrated inference: *the competitor understands that it must focus on a specific product space (it can't be all things to all customers).*

The power and value of integrated inferences are that they manifest a level of understanding of change that simply can't be detected in preliminary inferences. The move toward integrated inferences enables greater scope and explanation than is possible in any single, and even sometimes, a small set of preliminary inferences. Hence, the important role they play in the pathway to insights.

VP case: In the case of the competitor's value proposition (Figure 2-3), the integrated inference, *competitor recognizes that to "win big" it must win both in terms of functionality and brand (image, reputation, and service)*, emerges from and extends beyond several preliminary inferences. None of the preliminary inferences alone suggest or enable this integrated inference.

The transition pathway to integrated inferences may prove straightforward or complex. In either case, judgment and reasoning enable the transition. A simple pathway might involve a small number of preliminary inferences that quickly give rise to an integrated inference. For example, in considering the competitor's value proposition, a number of preliminary inferences including *competitor wants to create a unique solution space, competitor aims for massive performance functionality,* and *competitor building image around rapid service,* led to the integrated inference, *competitor will invest significantly to build the desired distinctive brand and customer relationships.* The transition is especially straightforward when individuals largely concur with the initially suggested integrated inference. The analysis back and forth leads to a modest change to the suggested integrated inference and the team moves on to considering the next integrated inference.

A complex path involves extensive analysis back and forth, fueled in part by interpersonal ebb and flow. The back and forth stems from the fact that the preliminary inferences can be grouped in different ways to generate different initial integrated inferences. As you immerse yourself in preliminary inferences and ways to integrate them, you develop a richer understanding of the changing context.

VP case: As the deliberations revolved around a number of suggested integrated inferences, the team members began to realize that the competitor was committed to a dramatic shift in how it wanted to compete and that its eventual customer value proposition would likely create a new experience for customers—one that might be very difficult for rivals to emulate or exceed.

Domain insights

Domain insights represent the preliminary unit and level of analysis in insight work (see Figure 1-2). But it's important to remember that a given domain can always be refined. For example, the competitor domain might be broken down into current, emerging, potential, substitute, and invented competitors. Each of these subdomains then serves as the focus of analysis and will likely lead to subdomain-specific insights. As described in Chapter 5, you can synthesize the subdomain insights into one or more competitor domain insights, and possibly into other domain insights (and then contribute to the development of CSIs and GMIs).

Integrated inferences provide the raw material from which domain insights are crafted. It's here that the new understanding shaped by the deliberations involved in getting to the integrated inferences becomes instrumental in crafting each domain insight. In analyzing complex change situations such as a deep dive into multiple competitors or into changing behaviors and motivations across multiple customer segments, integrated inferences provide the pivotal stepping-stone toward domain insights. The intent is to create an understanding that isn't contained or represented in any single integrated inference, but that isn't yet at the level of insight. Typically, as indicated in Figures 2-3, 2-4 and 2-5, analysis gives rise to a small set of integrated inferences.

As with the transition from preliminary to integrated inferences, the transition from integrated inferences to insights typically involves analysis back and forth and interpersonal ebb and flow, which will be addressed in detail in Chapter 5.

VP case: The analysis team eventually settled on one competitor insight (Figure 2-3) and one customer insight (Figure 2-4). Each insight reflected a significant shift in understanding. The customer insight, *customers are falling into distinct needs-based segments requiring customized solutions and some customers will walk away from their long-term providers,* refuted the firm's long-held beliefs that all customers' needs were basically the same and that incremental changes to the value provided to customers *would keep them in the fold.* The competitor insight, *the competitor wants to establish a new solution space, it's driven by the desire to transform the customer experience, it's willing to transform its value proposition to outperform its rivals,* refuted the firm's stated beliefs that the competitor was content with its strategic position and that the marketplace wouldn't undergo turbulence initiated by any existing rivals.

Vetting integrated inferences and domain insights

Suggested insights remain untested until they're vetted. Vetting is one of the 4V activities (Table 2-3) critical to moving through the insight *analysis* stages from preliminary inferences to accepted or stipulated insights noted in Figures 2-3, 2-4, and 2-5. Vetting aims to determine if the suggested insight brings new understanding to the business, is relatively distinct compared to rivals, is not obvious, is reasonably congruent in its depiction of the present and projection of the future, helps explain the change being investigated, and is likely to be enduring.

Vetting, described in detail in Chapter 5, should be conducted in two related ways. Vet the insight to determine whether it is of high quality or merely a mistaken output of deliberative analysis or instantaneous thinking. A quality insight withstands scrutiny, whether data and reasoning support it. Then test whether the insight is novel; if it's common knowledge or has already been discerned by one or more rivals, it's less likely to be the basis of distinctive decision value. The quality and novelty tests are intimately related: it doesn't make sense to spend considerable time conducting the quality tests without a sense that the insight possesses some degree of novelty. By the same token, investing extensive time testing insight novelty may prove worthless if the quality of the alleged insight crumbles under scrutiny.

VP case: The competitor and customer insights and CSI indicated in Figures 2-3, 2-4, and 2-5, respectively, were outcomes of extensive vetting, detailed in Chapter 5.

Competitive space insights

In moving to CSIs, the focus shifts from individual change domains to the broader competitive space, which may be an industry as commonly defined or a substantial segment of it. The intent is to generate an understanding of change that isn't specific to any single domain. Domain insights and general knowledge of the competitive space furnish the inputs to CSI generation.

CSIs are likely to be a novel element in insight deliberations in most firms. In my experience, teams applying industry or competitive space analysis, for example, Porter's Five Forces[82] or Blue Ocean analytics,[83] are too easily satisfied with generating domain analysis outputs, often in excruciating detail. They dive deep into competitor, customer, or supplier analysis or shifts in product dynamics, but shirk or avoid the challenge that then confronts them: how to integrate the analysis into a smaller set of key change drivers and their consequences. They inevitably end up with an excessive amount of detail in the analysis "findings," culminating in a PowerPoint deck that is overwhelming in its level of minutiae yet misses the core and necessary insights.

New understandings

CSIs frequently give rise to new understandings that aren't evident in any single domain integrated inference. Each CSI noted in Table 2-4 signals a profound shift between old and new understandings; the new understandings shatter traditional and long-held viewpoints and perspectives pertaining to which players will shape competitive dynamics, the stability of product configurations, the unlikelihood of technology generating dramatic product disruption, the stability of consumer buying behaviors, and the inability of substitute products to emerge as a direct rival.

Table 2-4   Sample Competitive Space Insights

New understanding	Old understanding
Small rivals, driven by the need to isolate themselves from the value propositions at the heart of the three major rivals' strategies, are developing and introducing winning value propositions in select customer segments that will dramatically alter competitive dynamics across these customer segments.	Competitive dynamics will be shaped by the marketplace interactions among the large rivals; smaller share rivals will have minimal, if any, impact on competitive dynamics in any product sector or customer segment.
The competitive space is rapidly moving to a new generation of products spurred by R&D breakthroughs that will allow a new generation of market leaders to emerge.	Product change is reasonably stable in the competitive space due to little new R&D trajectories, especially on the part of the smaller market share rivals.
A rapidly- evolving technology, driven by a well-funded small firm, could be a viable substitute for one of the industry's current leading product lines and would solve a major customer need.	Various rivals are working on new technologies, but the evidence suggests that no major product disruption is expected in the next three years.
Consumer purchasing habits, especially among lower-income groups, are shifting toward smaller packets and less frequent purchases, and therefore are likely to be a persistent attribute of consumer behavior.	Consumer buying behaviors in the food industry, broadly defined, are well-established and unlikely to change significantly.
An impending regulatory shift driven by new legislation will expedite the arrival of a new substitute product that could transform customer functionality.	Our products are unlikely to face competition for substitute products over the course of our five-year strategic plan.

CSIs generate distinctively different deliberations than a focus on one domain or a few domains. Any of the CSIs noted in Table 2-4 provoke deliberations at the competitive space level rather than at the level of an individual domain. Thus, the dialogue addresses how competitive dynamics might unfold in the competitive space, where opportunities and risks might reside, what strategies are likely to win and lose and why, and what assumptions might be appropriate heading into the future.[84]

The 6IFs

The power and importance of CSIs are exemplified in their capacity to sometimes fundamentally shift a number of the 6IFs.[85] It's easy to imagine how each CSI noted in Table 2-4 might impact each IF: how the organization *sees* the relevant market space, what it *thinks* about (for example, the need to reconfigure its assumptions), how its *intent* might shift (for example, consider market opportunity outside its historical product portfolio), what it might *decide* (for example, shift resources from one or more current products to the exploration of emerging market segments), how it *acts* (for example, asking key managers to visit potential customers in the emerging market segments), and how organization leaders and others *feel* (for example, recognizing the need to shift resources to emergent customer opportunities might lead to feelings of excitement, joy, and self-worth for some and feelings of hesitancy, discomfort, and insecurity for others).

Shifts along one or more of the 6IFs heavily influence the transition to GMIs and on to implications. If an analysis team sees a real possibility that change in the competitive space will result in new marketplace opportunity, it commits to identifying the scope and scale of that opportunity (leading to a GMI) and what it might mean for the organization's mind-set about what it takes to succeed in the emerging market space (a possible implication insight).

VP case: The analysis team eventually settled on the CSI noted in Figure 2-5, that strategy will need to be based on multiple dimensions of value; it will transform which rivals win and which lose; some won't be able to make the transition. This CSI had significant implications for the GMIs that were eventually generated.

Generic marketplace insights

No matter how richly and accurately a CSI captures and projects change in and around a marketplace, it must be transformed into a specific business implication. This requires a two-step process. Generic marketplace insights (GMIs) constitute the intermediate step (see Figure 1-1). When this step is executed, competitive change becomes immeasurably more meaningful and relevant to decision-makers: a shift occurs from focusing on change in the competitive space to identifying the critical inputs for strategy making and execution.

In my experience, almost without exception, organizations move too quickly from analyzing the competitive space to identifying business implications. The following question propels the transition from CSIs to GMIs: What are the *generic consequences* of the CSIs (and the domain insights) for the competitive space, *broadly defined*. Generic here refers to consequences, for example, for the auto or computer or pharmaceutical or shoe or medical instrument space without regard to any individual entity within the space. Consequences refer to factors that could influence how any single entity might view the competitive space or specific segments of it. And "broadly defined" isn't a throwaway comment here. The scope of relevant competitive space, as discussed in the next chapter, may include current or potential substitutes; it's often not sufficient to consider merely largely lookalike products or solutions.

Generic consequences can be grouped into five GMI foci: marketplace opportunities, competitor threats, competitive risks, strategy vulnerabilities, and broad assumptions. CSIs such as understanding how technology is causing a rapid dislocation in product composition (and, thus, customer functionality) or how regulatory change will allow the entry of a new type of product substitute rival or how customer migration toward foreign rivals could lead to significantly more intense rivalry must be subjected to the following questions:

- What marketplace opportunities may be here?
- Are there competitor threats that may face many rivals?
- What specific competitive risks may lurk here?
- How might any rival's current (or potential) strategy be vulnerable?
- What assumptions about the future might be emerging here?

VP case: Team members had to work hard to keep their focus on GMIs and not allow themselves to slip into considering business implications. Four key GMIs emerged:

Marketplace opportunity: an opportunity is rapidly emerging for a new customer offer

Competitive risk: potential rivalry dynamics would necessitate heavy marketing investments

Strategy vulnerability: some rivals will find it impossible to make the transition

Assumptions: almost all historic assumptions about the marketplace won't hold going forward

Each GMI served as a summation of extensive deliberations intended to develop answers to the five questions just noted.

Implications: Value testing change insights

The final stage in the 4I Diamond Framework (Figure 2-1) addresses implications: what do the change insights mean for the organization's thinking, decisions, and actions. No matter how extensively and intensively it's vetted and vouched,[86] a genuine change insight doesn't necessarily generate organizational value; it may not enhance thinking, decision-making, or action. Insight work succeeds not when it leads to vetted and vouched for domain insights or CSIs or GMIs but when it results in performance-enhancing business implications. Hence, you continue to emphasize intelligence insight. Testing the business value of domains insights, CSIs, and GMIs, takes us to business implications, the focus of Chapters 7 and 8. Here I briefly complete the discussion of the VP case and highlight the role and importance of the 6IFs in focusing analysis that aims to determine implication insights and key business implications.

Implications insights

Managing the deliberations in the transition from change insights to implication insights represents a central element in the disciplined approach to insight work.[87] Though rarely addressed, implication insights serve as a pivotal step on the way to determining key business decisions, choices, and action plans. An implication insight constitutes a fundamental implication so-what *about consequences for the business* that is derived from consideration of change insights. In large measure, because they're specific to the marketplace and not to any individual firm, GMIs often heavily influence implication insights.[88] As with every other type of insight, an implication insight involves a old and new understanding. Here are some examples:

- Our major marketplace opportunities increasingly will be in emerging Asian markets (not, as previously believed, in the more developed countries).
- Alliances with distribution channels will be critical to a rapid launch of our new product line (previously we viewed key channels as antagonists).
- Our core capability may be deteriorating faster compared with rivals that any of us believed (previously most of us thought it was at least on a par with rivals).

Implication insights, as the pivotal so-whats emanating from a collection of change insights (and especially CSIs and GMIs), enable an analysis team to better understand their organizational consequences *before* they burrow down into the details of the thinking, decisions, and actions that constitute business implications.

VP case: The deliberations around the pivotal "so-what's" led to two implication insights: how to think about winning and retaining customers needs to shift; and the need to massively reconfigure how the organization is managed.

The insight discipline ensures that sufficient time is invested to ferret out what is often profound and critical change in what *should be* the focus of the organization's thinking including its underlying point of view about the future, assumptions, and beliefs.

Business implications

An implication insight, by itself, doesn't indicate the specific "what, where, how and when" of business implications. Once the implication insights have been tentatively accepted, full attention can then turn toward determining the key thinking, decision, and action implications—the three core factors in the 6IFs. I'll use the VP case and the 6IFs to frame the analysis scope that typifies determination of business implications.[89]

Seeing and thinking

Although analysis teams, and indeed, entire organizations, tend not to separate out, describe and document specific seeing and thinking implications, as the crucial first stage in determining business implications, the VP case illustrates why it's critical to do so.

VP case: The implication insights clearly illustrate how the organization underwent a significant shift in its point-of-view about the future—one that would have dramatic implications for its decisions and actions. In short, the management team began to *see* the future of the competitive space and their strategy within it very differently. The future wouldn't belong to those entities selling just a product, technology alone could not be the source of sustainable customer-based advantage, and customers would continue to seek value along multiple dimensions beyond the core tangible product.

The point-of-view was reflected in and contributed to the development of three *new* core assumptions:

- Competitive dynamics will increasingly be less about price, and more about intangibles.
- Customers will leave us if we don't adjust our value proposition (and do so quickly).
- Our obsessive internal focus (on costs and processes) will become an even greater impediment to customer success if you don't act aggressively to change it.
- A mind-set built on these assumptions can't accept the firm's historic strategy as the basis for future marketplace success; thus, it leads to deliberations that address decisions and actions that will also be new to the organization.

Intent and decisions

Intelligence insight ultimately connects to intent and decisions specific to the four core implication domains—strategy, operations, organization, and leaders. The deliberations are driven in part by the *seeing and thinking* outcomes. The GMIs also can be suggestive of changes to the intent and consequent decisions.[90] For example, a GMI may indicate the need to change the current strategy: to go after a specific new opportunity, or to preempt or respond to a competitive threat, or to anticipate and modify the strategy to avoid or mollify a competitive risk or to shift the strategic direction to counter a clear vulnerability.

VP case: The management team identified four decisions: whether and how fast to move toward creating and testing customer-focused solutions; whether to commit fully to developing distinct customer value propositions; whether to extend the firm's marketing and sales capabilities; how fast and how much to invest in these activities. It was agreed to move quickly on all fronts—thus a new intent evolved: develop a solution-driven strategy aimed at preempting current rivals.

Actions and feelings

Actions, of course, are required to execute decisions. And, decisions and actions unavoidably provoke both positive and negative emotions. And the action timeline always involves immediate, shorter term and longer-term actions.

VP case: Once the commitment was made to move quickly on all fronts, sets of actions were almost inevitable: designate a cross-functional team to develop possible customer solutions; promote a manager to be the new head of marketing with the charge to retool the whole marketing and sales functions; establish a task group consisting of senior managers across a number of functions to assess the amount of investment required and how it should be allocated. Over time, individuals' positive emotions reinforced the desire and commitment to execute the chosen action plan: feelings of excitement and expectation at the prospect of succeeding in a new approach to the marketplace replaced prior feelings of hesitancy and discomfort at the prospect of what needed to be accomplished to win in the new marketplace.

Does your analysis reflect the insight discipline?

The story of the VP analysis team moving through the four core analysis stages—indicators, inferences, insight, and implications—suggests a series of questions you can pose to identify and test whether and to what extent the insight discipline informs your organization's approach to analysis (Table 2-5). Any individual or analysis team needs to deliberate about how best to identify relevant indicators, capture data along indicators, draw inferences from change represented along the indicator change, transform inferences into one or more insights, and then leverage the insights in thinking, decisions, and actions. The questions posed in the left-hand column will help you make a preliminary assessment of such deliberations. The questions in the right-hand column will help you quickly determine whether insight-related method elements characterize analysis projects. Each cell is addressed in detail in later chapters.

In summary, the VP case illustrates why higher-quality insight occurs when individuals and analysis teams adopt the insight discipline—the deliberate and methodical approach to insight work. The VP case also shows why the insight discipline's deliberations and methods must be managed. The generation of change and implication insights should not be left to chance. The next four chapters detail what needs to be managed in the generation of change insights.

Table 2-5   Does Your Analysis Reflect the Insight Discipline?

Analysis Stage	Deliberations	Methods
Indicators	Do you/your analysis team deliberate about: The role of indicators in capturing change? Types of indicators and their importance? The distinction between data and Indicators? How to transition from data to indicators? Indicators as the source of inferences?	Do you/your analysis team possess a method to: Capture data from a wide variety of sources? Conduct open-ended search for data? Detect change indicators across domains? Connect indicators to a priori categories? Develop indicator categories from the indicators?

Inferences	Do you/your analysis team deliberate about: What you mean by inference? What you draw inferences about? The role of judgment in any inference? The influence of context on inferences? How and why a sequence of inferences arises? How and why levels of inferences are critical to generating insight?	Do you/your analysis team possess a method to: Show individuals what is involved in drawing a preliminary inference? Draw sets of preliminary inferences? Encourage individuals to draw more than one inference from one or more indicators? Highlight the reasoning supporting an inference?
Insights	Do you/your analysis team deliberate about: What you mean by an insight? Why levels of insight are critical to building understanding of the marketplace? How analysis back and forth influences the generation of insight? How interpersonal ebb and flow influences the generation of insight? How domain insights give rise to competitive space insights (CSIs)? Why it is important to generate generic marketplace insights (GMIs)?	Do you/your analysis team possess a method to: Transform preliminary inferences into one or more integrated inferences? Transform integrated inferences into suggested insights? Highlight the reasoning underpinning integrated inferences and suggested insights? Vet each key integrated inference and suggested insight? Execute the steps involved in vouching for each accepted insight?

Implications	Do you/your analysis team deliberate about: What you mean by implication insight? The distinctions between implication insight and change insight? How implication insight contributes to determining key business implications: thinking, decisions, and actions?	Do you/your analysis team possess a method to: Transition from change insights to one or more implication insights? Vet and vouch for implication insights? Transition from implication insights to specific and comprehensive business implications?

Notes

46. Analysis stages are distinct from insight phases discussed in Chapter 1. For example, the first three analysis stages, indicators, inferences and insights are executed in the middle two insights phases, crafting change insight and crafting implication insight (Figure 1-3)

47. VP is a pseudonym for an actual company.

48. This is a classic example of the IF (insight factor) "see."

49. By "suggested" insights I mean insights proposed by one or more individuals that have not yet been vetted.

50. The broad working definition of the macro environment is the environment external to the industry: the political, regulatory, economic, social, technological and economic milieu. Also, see Figure 1-2.

51. A statement may be a data source or an indicator. A statement may include many indicators. A statement itself may also constitute an indicator. For example, a customer's statement about its purchase behaviors that refutes statements of others might serve as an indicator of its purchase intentions.

52. Inferencing is intended as a shorthand way to refer to all the steps involved in moving from one or more indicators to one or more change insights—the steps involved in the inferences and insights stages noted in Figure 2-1. It also emphasizes that inferences often result from a

process—a set of steps—as distinct from a single one-time event. The inferencing process is detailed in Chapters 4 and 5.

53. For a description of types of indicators and their uses in many domains in the macro environment (political, social, economic, technological, regulatory and ecological milieu) see, Liam Fahey and V.K. Narayanan, *Macro environmental Analysis for Strategic Management* (St. Paul: West Publishing Company, 1986).

54. For an early powerful and cogent argument on the role of discontinuity across many societal areas as a source of indicators of emerging and potential marketplace changes, see, Peter F. Drucker, *The Age of Discontinuity* (New York: Harper & Row, 1968).

55. For a vivid discussion of many forms of disruptions as a means to anticipating marketplace change, see, Clayton M. Christensen, Scott D. Anthony, and Erik A. Roth, *Seeing What's Next: Using the Theories of Innovation to Predict Industry Change* (Boston: Harvard Business School Press, 2004).

56. The importance of identifying indicator categories *before* gathering data can't be over emphasized. Among other things, it prepares people to "see" indicators that might well otherwise be missed.

57. In other words, an opportunity to draw some inferences isn't perceived—a topic that is addressed in detail in the next chapter.

58. This comment reinforces the observation in Chapter 1 that a desired attribute of a quality insight is that it should be non-obvious or possibly counterintuitive.

59. A shift in understanding was noted in Chapter 1 as fundamental to insight.

60. We have seen a veritable explosion of books on the topic of big data and, more generally, analytics in the last five years. See, for example, Foster Provost and Tom Fawcett, *Data Science for Business: What you Need to Know about Data Mining and Data Analytics* (New York: O'Reilly Media, 2013).

61. The process of vetting inferences and insights is introduced in this chapter and fully detailed in Chapter 5.

62. Experienced researchers, analysts, and intelligence professionals develop the capacity to "see" change indicators where others may see only a stack

of data. Thus, an experienced person reading an industry report or a statement by a rival's CEO or viewing a video released by an NGO will quickly identify the relevant change indicators and, as a consequence, will begin to draw inferences about current and potential change far sooner than those who don't recognize the indicators. Hence, we speak about efficiency in doing the early steps in insight work.

63. As noted earlier, this capacity invokes the IF seeing: to ability to see change indicators where others may only observe data.

64. The transition from data to indicators will be addressed in detail as part of sniffing in Chapter 4

65. Here the IF thinking is invoked: change indicators cause you to think about new things and perhaps even to think in new ways.

66. The importance of addressing what we don't know we don't know has long been emphasized in the knowledge management literature. See, for example, Eric Lasser and Laurence Prusak, eds., *Creating Value with Knowledge: Insights from the IBM Institute for Business Value* (Oxford: Oxford University Press, 2004).

67. The IF, intend, clearly comes into play here: we need to be conscious of the goal to capture indicators.

68. This recommendation is common in the work that addresses analysis of the external analysis. It's explicitly treated in Liam Fahey and V. K. Narayanan, *Macroenvironmental Analysis for Strategic Management* (Saint Paul: West Publishing, 1986).

69. The role of the human mind in drawing inferences will be fully addressed in the next three chapters.

70. Neuroscience has now developed convincing evidence that we are only conscious of about 5 percent of the "thinking" that goes on in our mind.

71. Several key characteristics of how the mind works are addressed in detail in the next chapter.

72. The interplay of data and reasoning is addressed in detail in Chapters 4 and 5.

73. Dictionary definitions of inference are similar to the description given in this book: "to infer, to derive by reasoning, conclude or judge from premises or evidence." *Webster's College Dictionary* (New York: Random House, 1991).

74. For example, if I know extremely little about a foreign country, say Latvia or Ukraine, it's impossible for me to draw any reasoned inferences about what the details of what life is like there for the "average" family.

75. Remember from Chapter 1 that marketplace change is the object of all the analysis frameworks presented in this book.

76. A number of *cognitive* biases and their insight practice implications are discussed in Chapter 5.

77. The steps described here are elaborated in Chapter 5 (the analysis steps involved in moving from preliminary inferences to change insights).

78. The distinction between a tentative and an accepted insight is fully developed in Chapters 5 and 6.

79. The transitions through the levels of inferences in the case of CSIs and GMIs are discussed briefly later in this chapter and detailed in Chapter 5.

80. Each IF's influence on various facets of *inferencing* will be addressed in detail in later chapters.

81. Suggested integrated inferences refer to the integrated inferences that are first articulated. Once they're vetted, then a smaller number of tentative integrated inferences emerge. The tentative integrated inferences are then further vetted and those that survive are deemed to be accepted integrated inferences. This process is detailed in Chapters 5 and 6.

82. Michael E. Porter, *Competitive Strategy: Techniques for Analyzing Industries and Competitors* (New York: The Free Press, 1980).

83. W. Chan Kim and Renée A. Mauborgne, *Blue Ocean Strategy: How to Crete Uncontested Market Space and Make the Competition Irrelevant* (Boston: Harvard Business School Press, 2005).

84. These questions serve as the focus of GMIs, the topic of the next section.

85. This is an example of the use of the 6IFs as output assessment: does it make a difference and to what?

86. What it means to vouch for an insight is addressed in detail in Chapter 6.

87. This is Phase 3 in the insight stages introduced in Chapter 1 (see Figure 1-3).

88. The connection between GMIs and implication insights is fully developed in Chapter 6.

89. Chapter 8 details the application of the insight perspective to the determination of business implications.

90. This is an example of how the IF *intend* addresses the possibility of new intent or objectives. An analysis team must ask itself what new goal possibilities may result from the change and implication insights.

91. We intentionally take a very broad view of what we mean by "data." It's in effect all inputs into the inferencing process, described in this and later chapters.

92. As noted earlier in this chapter, analysis outputs such as the projections of a competitor's strategy or the determination of customers' needs or the elaboration of alternative industry scenarios may serve as the source of inferences. Data in this sense doesn't just refer to disparate, inchoate, standalone bits of raw data.

93. For a more detailed discussion of the linkages between indicators and inferences, see, Liam Fahey, *Outwitting, Outmaneuvering and Outperforming* (New York: John Wiley & Sons, 2000).

Chapter 3

Structuring: Preparing for Insight Work

The 4I Diamond Framework—indicators, inferences, insights, and implications—discussed in the last chapter are the focus of insight analysis. Intelligence insight, that is, change insights and their business implications, requires mastery of each stage. However, the discussion left untouched many critical aspects of how to manage each stage. The VP case surfaced the need to generate a breadth of relevant indicators, capture preliminary inferences as a matter of course, transform them into higher-level integrated inferences, and vet and vouch for the change and implication insights that ultimately emerge. The 4Ss detailed in this chapter and the next three chapters are intended to meet these needs. Each S connects directly to one or more stages of the 4I Diamond Framework (Figure 3-1). Understanding what each activity entails enhances

FIGURE 3-1

Connecting the 4I Diamond and the 4S Cycle

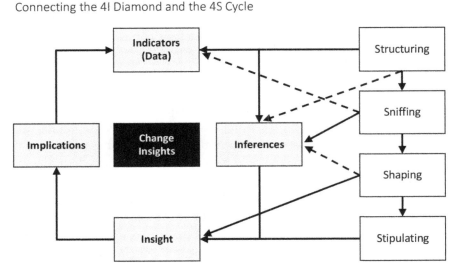

79

the likelihood that higher-quality insights emerge and, as a consequence, that the 4I Diamond Framework leads to superior decision value and organizational performance.

Structuring: Managing the early deliberation and method

The possibility for insight is far too frequently foregone before any form of analysis or reflection has begun. Deliberation and method are both poorly focused as insight work is getting off the ground. This occurs in at least three ways. First, the team devotes too little time to finding opportunities to create change insight that will make a significant difference in decision making. This is common in organizations that are unfamiliar with the role and importance of insight work. Second, the team spends too little time addressing how to manage the context of an insight project: for example, how to determine what data sources to use, how to identify different types of indicators, how to bring different perspectives to bear on extracting inferences from indicators—to name just a few of the challenges.[94] This isn't surprising if data and analysis routines are strongly embedded in how the organization deals with understanding the external world. Third, the team gives only minimal consideration to who should be involved in the various facets of insight work, such as scoping an insight project, arraying data in different ways, or drawing preliminary inferences.

What I call *structuring* addresses these three tasks: deciding where to focus insight attention, orchestrating the analysis context, and determining who should be involved. Structuring exemplifies the deliberative approach to insight: managers and others deliberate where to spend insight time and attention, which insight projects should be initiated, and which ongoing analysis projects might most benefit from the insight discipline. The methodical approach manifests itself in the steps and questions involved in ensuring that insight attention is focused on appropriate opportunities, managing the analysis context, and getting the right people involved.

Structuring helps ensure that change and intelligence insight aren't left to chance. At the organization level, it ensures that the insight discipline is brought to bear on the opportunities that will make the greatest contribution to the organization's thinking, decisions, and actions. At the level of any insight project, it ensures that the pathway is set to craft high-quality change insights.

It's important to note that structuring challenges aren't new to any organization. Given limited time and resources (talent, capital, knowledge, expertise), leaders are always confronted with the issue of where resources will generate the greatest knowledge and insight returns—that is, which analysis opportunities should be the focus of attention. Leaders of any analysis project are concerned with whether the analysis approach could be enhanced so that it will lead to outputs that genuinely inform decision makers and impact decision making.

Preparing your mind for structuring

The insight discipline's deliberations and methods don't just happen. If insight isn't to be left to chance, your mind needs to be stimulated and nourished so you can see and think[95] in ways that increase the odds of deriving interesting and substantive inferences that lead to value adding insight.

Although there are no simple solutions for how to prepare your mind for insight work, several mind[96] principles and data perspective[97] principles offer specific guidance. The mind principles (Table 3-1) suggest you can fertilize your mind by questioning the arguments in others' thinking and viewpoints, sustaining your curiosity, and recognizing that inferences and insights don't last forever. Your answers in understanding marketplace change always give rise to more questions. Commit yourself to "continually learning how to see current reality more clearly."[98] Developing new understanding—the heart of insight— requires that you put your presuppositions, beliefs, and assumptions on the table: commit to subjecting them to critique from all quarters and be willing to reject them when the evidence and reasoning suggest that you should.

Your brain requires something to process in order to generate outputs— that something, in this case, is inferences and insights. I'll broadly refer to this as data. As treated here, data subsumes all the inputs to the insight process, irrespective of their form or source.[99] Although from the vantage point of both neuroscience and day-to-day practice, it's difficult to fully separate "data" from how the mind works,[100] the data principles noted in Table 3-2 indicate several practice prerequisites to successful execution of the 4Ss. Never take data at face value. Consider it tentative and presumptive, and contaminated by biases.[101] Be careful not to privilege any one form of data or data source. And remember that the context of data always profoundly matters. In short, data only partially represents the change being investigated and data is never final; as change takes place, new data emerges.

Table 3-1   Preparing the Mind for Structuring: Mind Principles

Principle	Rationale	Structuring principles and practices
Start with an open mind.	Your own beliefs, presuppositions, and assumptions (your "mental models") can blind you to what is happening or may happen in the world.	Assume that nothing is self-evident, axiomatic, or exempt from firm and penetrating questioning.
Seek disciplined diversity in perspectives.	Unless you enable others to challenge your mental models, you're likely to hold to them. Tension between ideas and viewpoints opens the possibility for change in your point of view.	Ensure that analysis isn't closed within one definition of the problem, issue, or opportunity. Use different modes of thinking, types of analysis, conflicting assumptions.
Encourage tolerance for ambiguity.	Nothing is ever as it seems. Multiple interpretations of any change situation are always possible.	Develop different depictions of key change situations. Look for alternative explanations of change.
Remember that an inference or insight is always provisional.	There's no guarantee that despite your best intellectual and analytical efforts that any inference or insight represents the true state of the world.	Articulate your best judgments (at the core of any inference or insight) so they can be assessed by others.
Evoke enduring curiosity.	Given the persistence of change in the world around us, you can never cease our inquiries into the direction, speed and intensity of change.	Recognize that our "answers" in understanding change always give rise to more questions; our inquiries should never cease.
The non-referential mind.	You can't know how your own mind's understanding of the world is inadequate; you need the perspective of others.	Subject your judgments to the critique and challenge of others.

Table 3-2   Preparing the Mind for Structuring: Data Principles

Data principles	Rationales	Structuring principles and practices
Data is always in question.	There's no guarantee that data represent or reflect the real (current) state of the actual world.	Consider all data as tentative and presumptive—in describing change the data may be "off" Data can never be the final arbiter in our judgments.
Data is always contaminated.	Data are a function of who created them and how they did so.	Treat all data as biased.
Data is never privileged.	If you privilege one type of data or one data source, you forfeit learning from other data types/sources.	Use many different sources to generate data; insist on different data types.
Data context profoundly matters.	The meaning of data resides in its context (not in the data, per se).	Always elaborate the context of data; interpret data within the context; vary the context to challenge what the data mean.
Data is always time dependent.	Data always refers to a specific time period (though it's often implicit).	Make explicit the relevant time period; ask whether the data would hold over an extended time period (why/why not).
Data is often not the impetus to analysis work.	You can have multiple starting points: purpose of the analysis; a question raised by someone; an issue that emerges.	Clarify purpose (of analysis) before embarking on data search; treat data as but one starting point; look for multiple data starting points.

The value of data volume is some-times misguided.	Data volume is only as good as the quality of the inferences you can extract from it.	Deploy large data analysis tools where appropriate but insist on developing inferences buttressed by the analysis outcomes.
Small data dif-ferences can be significant.	A modest data incre-ment can sometimes dramatically shift the inferences that can be drawn.	Look for data differences; ask how a minor data change might lead to dif-ferent, even conflicting, inferences.

The combination of your mind and data principles will help you prepare for insight work. Your mind will be more open to new observations and experience; it's fully committed to questioning how and why change is occurring; it treats data in all its forms with great care; it's willing to be self-critical; it recognizes that data is always evolving. In the words of one manager, "we need to get our minds right for this kind of work." Your mind and data principles contribute to a mind-set that is pivotal to the 4Ss—structuring, sniffing, shaping, and stipulating—detailed in this and the next three chapters (Box 3-1).

Box 3-1

The 4S Cycle

Structuring sets the stage for insight work. It addresses three issues: identifying key opportunities to execute the insight discipline; developing principles to extend the range of data and indicators; and determining who should be involved in the early stages of insight work. Data literally involves playing with the data using procedures ranging from highly orchestrated and regimented to largely informal and ad hoc. The intent is to capture and arrange data in different ways to prompt inferences that might otherwise be missed.

Sniffing is the handmaiden of data structuring. You ask what inferences you might draw from individual indicators, data structures, or arrangements. It's a perceptual act: you sense the possibility of an inference and pursue it until you can articulate it. Sniffing lies at the heart of the sample inferences noted in Tables 2-3, 2-4 and 2-5 and discussed in the previous chapter.

Shaping constitutes the core, and usually the most difficult and involved, stage in crafting insight. Typically, it requires amalgamating and integrating multiple preliminary inferences into a smaller inference set which is then synthesized into one or more "refined" or integrated inferences that are a key in crafting insights, as briefly described in Chapter 4. This activity necessitates significant judgments: the human mind is imposing itself upon the inference set.[133]

Stipulating represents the final throes of the 4S cycle in which those involved finalize the insight that will be accepted for the moment as an input to decision making. As you'll see, this isn't a trivial or inconsequential aspect of crafting insights; small changes in wording can make a substantial difference to the stipulated insight.

Reference to the 4S cycle conveys the iterative and interactive nature of any pathway through the four activities. Rarely will it be a one-time linear flow through the activities. Sniffing may cause a need for further structuring; for example, developing some preliminary inferences about a competitor may suggest the need to adopt the vantage point of customers or channels as a frame from which to draw further competitor inferences. Shaping suggested insights frequently give rise to the need to revisit the data and reasoning supporting individual or sets of preliminary inferences. Stipulating an insight always causes an analysis team to review the prior vetting of the suggested insight: it's the last opportunity to critique the data and reasoning supporting each insight.

Structuring insight work: Where to focus attention

The insight discipline begins in large measure by stepping back from the cut and thrust of day-to-day analysis activity to consider where the opportunities exist for insight work that will make the greatest contribution to decision making. Two questions need to be posed: what new analysis initiatives is the organization likely to undertake, and what major analysis projects are currently underway?

New opportunities

An organization is always contemplating several analysis initiatives that address many forms of marketplace change. Change across the marketplace domains noted in Chapter 1 (see Figure 1-1) underpin what executives and others deem to be marketplace opportunities, issues and challenges. The range of possible analysis contexts is large and varied: potential acquisitions, new R&D initiatives, global supply chain realignment, the potential entry of new substitute rivals, shifts in customers' purchasing behaviors, the emergence of new technologies, regulatory shifts, to name but a few.

Once a listing of likely analysis contexts is determined, you need to pose three questions:

- Which analysis contexts are most important to the business? In other words, what opportunities, issues, and challenges would have the greatest influence on the future of the business?
- How could the insight discipline aid the analysis?
- How might the analysis outcomes add distinctive value to the organization's thinking, decisions, and actions?

Consider a recent example I encountered where the insight discipline could have made a real difference to decision making and organization performance. A member of the strategic planning team in a global manufacturer identified the impact of digital capabilities on its integrated supply chain as a potential major threat to its current business model. It conducted a preliminary analysis that concluded the threat was overstated. A set of interviews quickly revealed that many of the mind and data principles noted in Tables 3-1 and 3-2 were violated: The organization's collective mind was not open to a detailed critique of the forces driving digital change; it rejected the suggestion that alternative hypothesis be developed and assessed; senior executives apparently were no longer curious as to why the "digital sphere" was likely to continue to change; some internal and external data sources were exceedingly privileged to the point that assumptions underlying their "data," especially projections, were never questioned. In short, the deliberations that should have taken place never got off the ground.

Existing opportunities

Many different types of analysis are ongoing in any organization at any one time. Each analysis probably constitutes a structuring opportunity. Ideally, the insight discipline is brought to bear on each analysis initiative. However, in the early stages of moving toward adoption of the insight discipline, it's necessary to screen ongoing analysis initiatives to identify the most productive structuring opportunities. Three questions need to be addressed:

- Is the analysis addressing an opportunity, issue, or challenge of significant importance to the organization?

- Is there evidence that those involved in the analysis typically violate the mind and data principles and/or don't apply the structuring components (addressed in the next section)?

- Can you develop an argument that structuring if properly applied would likely lead to an enhanced outcome—superior insight that would make a real difference in decision making?

Consider the following case where the insight discipline dramatically shifted the analysis outcome. A market share leader in an industrial component market was in the midst of identifying and analyzing rivals' value propositions across a few distinct customer segments. The intent was to determine how its own value proposition might be enhanced across the market segments. Even modest value proposition change could lead to winning new customers and would be especially critical to retaining existing customers, given that rivals were committed to experimenting with changes to their value propositions.

However, it quickly became apparent that almost every mind and data principle was being violated. For example, what the team considered to be a value proposition was not open to review—a closed mind dominated the discussion of what constituted rivals' value propositions. Hence, some of the real value being experienced by customers was missed. Prior work conducted by a marketing consulting firm overrode some inputs received by members of customer organizations: one data set and source was given undue privilege due to the relationship between some managers and the consulting organization. A thirst for data volume seriously diminished the possibilities of new understanding emerging from small(er) data sets. Interviews with customers that identified potential emerging needs were dismissed because the data "represented small numbers of individuals." Only when the mind and data principles were brought to bear upon the project, mostly through the execution of the analysis components discussed in the next section, did the conception of a value proposition shift from its historical narrow focus, new data sources receive attention, and critical assessment of the firm's own value proposition from the perspective of customers become the norm.

Structuring the analysis context: Some guiding principles

The insight discipline drives structuring in the early stages of any analysis context. It requires everyone involved to deliberate about the scope of the analysis and the perspective from which it should be addressed. The deliberations unavoidably challenge the routines inherent in how most organizations traditionally conduct analysis. They also require the people involved to methodically develop and apply a set of practice principles to guide data collection and indicator detection. As you'll see, the practice principles are heavily influenced by the mind and data principles noted in Tables 3-1 and 3-2.

But what does structuring an analysis context entail? Think of it as managing a number of analysis components. Each component affords an ability to break through some of the inhibitors of insight work that may be lurking in the organization's long-established ways of conducting analysis. Each raises several issues and involves specific choices. How these issues and choices are addressed and resolved affects what inferences are derived (as you'll see in the next chapter) and the insights that accrue in the later stages of insight crafting. Each component gives rise to a specific question

- Scope: What should be the scope of the insight work?
- Frame: What analysis frame(s) should be adopted?
- Focus: How might the focus be shifted?
- Perspective: What or whose perspective should be deployed?
- Context: Do we understand the analysis context?
- Imagination: What role should imagination play?
- Data: What are the appropriate data and data sources?
- Indicators: What indicators should be emphasized?

A distinct mind-set stemming from the mind and data principles lies at the heart of structuring's deliberations and methods dealing with these questions. It strives to sustain an open mind about key method issues: how to scope, frame, and focus; how to incorporate multiple perspectives; how best to engage imagination. It strives to question data, to remember that data no matter how detailed and comprehensive doesn't fully reflect current (not to mention future) reality. Its spirit is captured by the following phrases: "We're missing key data but we don't know what that data might be," "We need to live in the context," "We need to walk in the shoes of another person or entity," and "Only by playing with the data can we discern what's there." It implies an open-ended view of dealing with data: indeed, how we engage with data may be limited only by our imagination, ingenuity and willingness to invest some time in capturing, arraying, and analyzing data in multiple ways. The mind-set is consistent with theorists and practitioners[102] who pioneered the study of systems, equilibrium, and chaos in the context of organizations and change. They emphasize the importance of adaptive learning: they see data as the creative energy of both the universe and organizations, the fuel that drives learning—and, thus, the understanding of any change context. The critical point is that by adopting methods that adhere to the mind and data principles we may "see" connections that aren't obvious or may be surprising or even counterintuitive; thus, enabling our ability to think differently.[103]

Scope of insight work

All too often I've seen the potential for significant change insight severely limited before any data is collected or analysis has begun. An open and curious mind isn't present: the scope or purview of the change context to be examined gets defined too narrowly. As a consequence, potentially relevant data are never considered. Here as three simple but pervasive examples:

- Analysis of competitors, in many instances, focuses primarily on current, dominant market share rivals.[104] Small rivals, emergent rivals, substitute product rivals and potential rivals such as alliances, don't get considered. Yet, as so many companies have discovered, future winning customer value propositions are frequently first evidenced in the successful efforts of these types of rivals to gain initial spurts of market share.

- The commonly deployed political, economic, social, and technology (PEST) analysis in most instances doesn't include ecological (physical environment) analysis unless it's strikingly obvious as in the case of a food firm that executes deep dive analysis of weather patterns, water abundance/ scarcity, soil conditions, and farm acreage available for specific crops.

- Many firms focus their technology analysis predominantly, if not exclusively, on their core or base technologies thus missing current or emerging change in disruptive technologies with the potential to replace their major products.[105]

Adjusting the scope of an analysis project sometimes gives rise to intense deliberations: those wishing to adhere to the organization's long-established ways of analyzing competitors, customers, technology or marketplace dynamics don't readily accept the suggestions of those who advocate significant change to scope. It's typically better to scope widely rather than narrowly in the initial phases.

Analysis frame

Irrespective of a wide or narrow scope, data needs to be collected, organized and synthesized as input to and part of the inference derivation process. The choice of analysis frames or methods strongly influences each of the three data tasks just noted. Framing thus constitutes a non-trivial choice in structuring. Here are two examples of how shifting the analysis framework alters the issues addressed and the questions raised, and thus the possibility of distinctly different inferences emerging:

- One firm decided to adopt a business eco-system frame[106] rather than a Porter's Five Forces[107] frame to depict the structure of and relationships in and around an industry segment. It immediately became evident that relationships with entities in adjacent product areas and non-market players (for example, technology houses, NGOs, government agencies) would become increasingly critical to competitive success. The initial Five Forces analysis paid little attention to the "non-market" players.

- Many firms have discovered how assumptions analysis offers a distinct but related frame for strategy analysis. Shifting analysis away from assessment of strategy alternatives to identification and analysis of the relevant marketplace and organization assumptions reframes how the alternatives are viewed. In one instance, accepting the assumption that two competitors would retaliate rapidly and strongly to a significant price reduction caused that alternative to be rejected.

- A "wicked problems" approach[108] to identifying the business challenges in marketplace environments that are undergoing unpredictable change and in which it's obvious that traditional strategies won't succeed offers a frame in which it's not apparent what data to collect, how to organize the data, or how to synthesize (for example, how to define the core problem or opportunity). The breadth of stakeholders considered widens, new data extends the range of questions asked, and tentative answers provide a new set of questions.

Focus shift

Related to but distinct from scoping and framing is the notion of focus shift. Focus shift entails changing the key questions asked. The mind principles encourage an open mind: we can't accept the world as we think it is. The data principles encourage questions, especially questions that have not previously been asked. Here are some examples that illustrate how shifting the focus can lead to the possibility of inferences that otherwise wouldn't be generated:

- Shifting the focus in customer analysis from understanding customers' functional needs to their emotional needs always challenges the conventional wisdom about customer behaviors. In one case, the insight that consumers felt deeply insecure and uncomfortable by being associated with the firm's brand provided a more powerful and action-relevant explanation of customers' reluctance to purchase the product than anything that was revealed by in-depth functionality analysis.[109]

- Shifting the focus in competitor analysis to what the competitor will do in the future as opposed to what it's doing currently leads to distinctly different analysis issues and questions. In a recent analysis, a shift from the rival's current value proposition to what it might be in a few years gave rise to new questions about the possible future competitive context: for example, how would customers' needs be driven by emerging technology shifts?

- The simple notion of working from the future back to today instead of from the present to the future enables fundamentally different questions. Even simple scenarios detailing how driving forces might combine to shape alternative competitive futures, allows an analysis team to ask: what marketplace opportunities exist in each competitive future, a question unlikely to be asked in the absence of distinct competitive futures?[110]

Perspective

Scope, framing, and focus shift raise the following issue: from what or whose perspective(s) should the analysis be addressed? The mind principles support the notion of adopting the stance or point of view of others to challenge your mind-set. The data principles support the notion that no data provided by an external source should be privileged to the point of ignoring or downplaying other data sources. Adopting more than one perspective helps deal with the biases—personal, functional, organizational—inherent in taking only one perspective on any issue, challenge, or problem.[111] Here are two examples of the power of different perspectives as a means to broadening the swath of potential inferences about customers and competitors:

- Simply asking people to take the customer perspective has on occasion radically shifted their point of view. In one case, the individuals playing the role of customers immediately recognized that the product's features and functionality compared with rivals was not the dominant point of differentiation they had previously assumed. What was the truly distinguishing advantage had to do with the customer's ability to work with the firm to customize the "solution" to address some specific technical requirements.

- Competitive gaming exercises compel teams to adopt the position, point of view, and commitment of different competitors and then attack the "host" firm's strategy. This typically unearths inferences and insight into the host firm's ability to win against rivals that were not previously detected or surfaced. Sometimes the insights that emerge (for example, you can't win with your proposed strategy because one or more rivals will overwhelm you through their resource superiority and their commitment to win) cause a major shift in strategy choice and/or how the strategy will be executed.

Context

As noted throughout this book, indicators and the change they reveal only make sense within a (broader) change context. The mind principle that all inferences and insights are provisional is a reminder that unrelenting marketplace change eventually makes every inference or insight obsolete. The data principles assert that data is always time dependent and that the meaning of data resides in its context, not in the data per se. Thus, identifying and clarifying the relevant context constitutes a crucial element in structuring any analysis.[112] This is especially so in the case of a single data point or indicator: understanding its context is often the precursor to extracting more powerful inferences. Consider this classic example:

A competitor announces a price increase. Understanding the relevant context requires assessment of the current and recent competitive conditions including the dynamics of rivalry among the current players, the competitor's current marketplace strategy as well as the stated and unstated reasons for the price increase and the expected consequences of it. If rivals are close to full plant utilization and margins are low, one inference might be that the competitor wants to lead in moving prices upwardly and it doesn't expect price retaliation (reduction) by any rival. If the rival has significantly enhanced its customer value proposition and customers have reacted positively, then an inference might be drawn that the rival can do so because of the established customer response to its new value proposition.

Understanding context is also crucial in making sense of patterns across trends. And, it may be especially important in drawing inferences in the case of discontinuity, such as a major and abrupt change in a trend or a pattern. A change or a reversal in a regulation or administrative rule by a federal or state agency can't be understood in the absence of its context. Some regulations affecting technology transfer across country borders would be difficult to interpret and explain unless one knew that some firms had illegally sold technology to foreign unfriendly governments or other entities within these countries.

Imagination

Nothing constricts structuring as much as lack of imagination. Einstein's comment that imagination is more important than knowledge is strikingly apt. Imagination embodies the open mind principle. Imagination literally creates data as the three examples below illustrate. It helps to overcome the privileged position of specific data types or data sources. Without question, imagination plays a role in all the structuring components discussed in this section. Sometimes it's the driving force. Consider these three examples:

Inventing competitors, an established process to conduct analysis of rivals, revolves around inventing (imagining) a competitor[113] that could enter the market in the foreseeable future (frequently defined as five years or less) with a strategy that would demolish existing rivals. An analysis team invents (that is, imagines) how the competitor could come to be, what its strategy and winning value proposition might be, how the competitor might execute the strategy, and how it might enhance the strategy over time. The invented competitor's strategy affords opportunities to infer potential new customer needs, how rivalry might unfold over time and key competitive vulnerabilities for rivals' current strategies (competitive space opportunity inferences).

Imagining the ideal customer experience is just one of many examples where imagination is pivotal to structuring a data context that enables people to break out of a present-dominated purview. Specifying what that ideal customer experience might be, how it would be different to today's experience and why customers would consider it ideal also offers many opportunities to draw inferences about customers' needs, motivations and aspirations, what rivalry might entail (a competitive space insight) and potential customer needs (a generic marketplace insight).[114]

Imagination also plays a role in another simple technique to structure data, especially with a future focus and emphasis: ask the question, what would happen if? It leads to data arrays distinct from any structuring around the present (or the past). What would happen if a competitor significantly shifted its strategy or if technology breakthrough occurred or if a regulatory change happened two years earlier than projected? Among other things, each question helps to identify the critical indicators that must be monitored to assess whether and how that future might unfold.

Data

The mind and data principles establish what I call the "data mind-set" that is essential to successful structuring. The mind-set speaks directly to many data issues and challenges in structuring any analysis situation, especially in the early phases of the work. The mind principles remind you never to accept descriptions of change no matter how "good" the data. If you take customers "for what they are" and "how they behave" as essentially givens, then you're hardly likely to question their behaviors, motivations, commitments, and intentions. Avoid data becoming your intellectual and action prison. The data principles forewarn about many of the hazards of unthinkingly treating data as congruent with the realities they address: they're contaminated in many ways, subject to biases of those who created them, specific to time and place, and assume meaning only in context.

Scope, framing, focus shifting, and perspective affect what data is collected and how it's organized and synthesized (and thus, influence the indicators generated and the inferences and insights derived). The purpose here isn't to delve into data types, data sources, programs to collect data, ways to store and retrieve data, and all the other classic elements inherent in managing data. Rather, it's to emphasize that structuring frequently leads to deliberations about what data is required, what data is currently missing, what data sources we currently ignore or neglect, what data and data sources we might not be aware of, and whether and how you might need to engage differently with specific data sources.

The combination of scope, framing, focus shift and perspective often suggests that it's necessary to get closer to customers, suppliers, channels, NGOs, government agencies, and other entities. For example, you may need to extend the customer scope to include customers who have left us and broaden the analysis frame to include customers' motivations: you need to understand the rationales for their supplier choices and how they see the strengths and limitations of our offers and our organization. If you want the perspective of individual customers, then you need to get customers' viewpoints in their own words. To achieve these goals, you need to spend considerable time with these customers to understand their business model, organization practices, decision choice criteria in choosing suppliers, their organization culture and the biases and perspectives of key decision makers. The depth of the data generated, and more importantly, the context of the data, requires ethnographic research;[115] they can't be obtained through "quick" data collection processes such as surveys or even telephone interviews.

Indicators

Structuring ultimately results in identifying key indicators and current, past and future change along them. The VP case in the previous chapter illustrated the role and importance of identifying indicators and their contribution to drawing inferences and crafting insights. The mind principles remind us that the search for change indicators ought not to be constrained by your beliefs, assumptions, and presuppositions (our mental models) or by our adherence to one problem or situation definition. The data principles remind us that indicators and change along them often require us to tap many kinds of data sources, to insist on different forms of data (to generate different sets of indicators), and, to seek differences in change patterns across indicators (to eventually extracting different, even conflicting, inferences).

Some other structuring observations

The eight analysis context components apply to every analysis situation. The principles associated with each component influence how any analysis methodology is deployed, irrespective of how formal or informal it may be: they raise issues and questions that otherwise are likely to be missed or all too easily glossed over.

Formal extensive methods

The insight generating potential of formal analysis methodologies such as scenario learning,[116] simulations[117], competitive gaming,[118] alternative hypothesis testing,[119] and big data methods[120] can be enhanced when attention is paid to the eight analysis context components. Each of these methodologies is amenable to structuring: they take place over an extended period, create and use extensive amounts of data, involve many people (some of whom may be outside the organization) adopting different perspectives, and utilize data from many sources internal and external to the organization.

Scope considerations inevitably raise questions about whether an analysis methodology is addressing the "right" context. For example, a scenario exercise may be designed to explore what-if questions about future direction of technologies when it might generate more valuable industry insights if the what-if questions were shifted to the relevant competitive space. Analysis frame considerations might suggest that a competitive gaming exercise is more relevant than other methodologies if the intent is to anticipate rivals' potential responses to the firm's planned new product launch in new geographies.

Scenarios enable people to live in one or more specific futures, thus allowing a radically different perspective to frame their thinking. Competitive gaming exercises shift the analysis frame away from classic industry analysis approaches to adopting an analysis frame that places competitor rivalry (actions and reactions) at its core. Each of the methods noted should generate critical indicators to be monitored to detect and project the emergence of possible futures before they occur.

Big customer and other data sets can be more systematically "interrogated" through application of the analysis context components. Scope compels assessment of a wide swath of topics; for example, not just looking at buying behaviors but what aspects of the buying experience consumers find rewarding or off-putting. Focus inspires questions that might not historically be asked in trying to make sense of the data patterns generated from the data. Perspective exhorts teams to involve not only "data scientists," but also those from varied functional backgrounds who may possess deeper understanding of the business in exploring inferences that might be extracted from the data outputs. Imagination grants people permission to develop novel interpretations of the data patterns to stimulate deliberations that might not otherwise occur.[121]

Informal, simple methods

Sometimes, structuring benefits rather simple and straightforward arraying of data. It compels people to deliberate about whether they're asking the right questions and to review how they might enhance their data configuring and analysis methods. One key outcome is the detection of indicators that may not be obvious in the raw data. Thus, the range of potential inferences may be greatly expanded. Consider the following two brief customer examples:

- A marketing team reframed all the negative comments passed by customers in a survey about the firm's flagship brand by categorizing them into "buckets" of related comments with respect to customer complaints about service, delivery, price, and broken promises. They then shifted the focus to asking how customers appeared to feel about the company, the brand, and themselves. A set of indicators emerged that addressed directly and indirectly how segments of customers felt about doing business with the firm. The marketing team eventually drew a strong integrated inference[122] that many customers appeared to be saying negative things about themselves because they bought the brand.

- People manning a booth at a trade show conducted informal interviews with attendees who visited the booth. Rather than simply writing "interview reports," they went through their interview notes and categorized the interviewees' statements into key issues and topics, including customers' possible needs, technology change, and various rivals' strategy shifts. These data buckets enabled the team to shift the scope and focus of the questions they asked. For example, they had never previously used trade show data to ask and test questions about rivals' technology shifts. Eventually, they drew the inference that customers saw one technology's capabilities as grossly overstated; thus, an opportunity potentially existed for its replacement.

Linkages to the insight funnel

The insight discipline challenges how analysis is often conducted within and along the marketplace change levels in the insight funnel (see Figure 1-2). As many of the examples in this book attest, analysis rarely can be constricted to any single change domain. Change along indicators in one or more domains serves as a precursor to change in other domains. For example, competitor change such as projected shifts in one or more rivals' marketplace strategy enable inferences about customers' potential choices and purchase behaviors. Precursors of change in the regulatory domain reside in the political, legislative, judicial, and social values domains.

In short, scope often needs to be extended to include additional domains; analysis frames may need to be extended to include indicators from other domains that typically might not be addressed; perspective may need to shift to that of change in the domains serving as change precursors; focus clearly shifts to asking questions that might previously be disregarded or suppressed or simply not asked. In short, the likelihood of generating lead indicators is greatly enhanced.

The eight analysis components also contribute to movement from domain insights to CSIs to GMIs. In the transition to CSIs, scope, frame, focus, perspective and context challenge prevailing analysis methods and deliberations. For example, when scope and focus was extended in one industry analysis using the Five Forces framework to include political strategy considerations, a CSI addressing the role and importance of political strategy as a precursor to winning in the product-market domain emerged. Adopting the perspective of other players in the marketplace including government agencies, community groups, labor unions, and NGOs led to raising issues and questions that previously had received minimal attention. One outcome; the analysis team identified sets of political indicators that required monitoring to aid in anticipating the actions of individual external entities.

In the transition to GMIs, scope, frame, focus, perspective, and context greatly influence how an analysis team may view each GMI element (marketplace opportunity, competitive risk, competitor threat, strategy vulnerability and marketplace assumptions). Simply applying scope, focus and imagination considerations to marketplace opportunity in one analysis led to a redefinition of opportunity: it moved from opportunity associated with existing products and technology to opportunities that would result in new customer solutions that would reconfigure a large segment of the industry. In the same vein, the analysis components almost always extend the range of strategy vulnerabilities. In the political strategy case noted above, the lack of a coherent and well-executed political strategy was deemed a major vulnerability that many firms were poorly positioned to rectify.

Connecting trend lines

Structuring at its simplest addresses relationships among and between trends. Productive structuring sometimes involves asking: what might be the connection between these two trend lines? The result may be a shift in scope, frame, and focus. Consider the intersection of these two trends: number of people who view automobile use as an on-demand mobility and car ownership among millennials. If the trends indicate more on-demand mobility and less car ownership, scope and focus suggest questions about the broader lifestyles of millennials that, among other things, may help explain the trend lines. The context of their lives including discretionary income, expenditure patterns, work and leisure preferences, provides the background to make sense of the trends.

Sometimes, change in one trend portends future change in another trend line: growing sales in the first year of a substitute product may indicate a potential downturn in sales of the rival product at some point in time. Sometimes, the trend lines are correlated: recently, a downturn in unemployment assistance was reflected in a downturn in sales in Walmart. The great caveat here, of course, is that the human mind can see connections where none exist;[123] thus, alleged interconnections among trends always warrant the vetting and vouching processes discussed in the next three chapters.[124]

Assimilating data (patterns)

As many others have noted,[125] identifying patterns or connections among trends lies at the heart of enhancing understanding of change irrespective of the context, type of analysis, or purpose of the reflection. Patterns across indicators are evident in the VP case addressed in Chapter 2 (see Figures 2-3, 2-4, 2-5). To cite a simple example, a pattern in a competitor's behaviors (for example, investments, market behaviors, advertisements, executive or other personnel changes) and words (for example, announcements, presentations at trade shows and conferences, and responses in newspaper interviews) may provide a distinctly stronger (and maybe different) inference as to the competitor's imminent strategy move than might be derived from change along any two of these indicators. Each analysis context component affects the search for and interpretation of patterns across indicator change—and thus the inferences and insights that ensue.

Scope encourages analysis teams to move beyond established routines in searching for change patterns. Some years ago, a pharmaceutical firm reluctantly extended its monitoring of R&D indicators to include biotech and related industry indicators. It quickly drew a strong inference: pharmaceutical firms could no longer depend upon traditional R&D approaches to create winning product pipelines. A high-tech firm moved beyond technology to include competitor and customer indicators to refine an inference that a new competitive space was likely to emerge and far sooner than the technology indicators alone suggested.

Analysis frame suggests using different analysis methodologies, for example, eco-system analysis and scenarios to detect indicators that might lead to different, and perhaps conflicting, patterns: for example, one pattern leads to an inference of increasingly intense rivalry around price and another pattern allows an inference that service and relationships will be the focus of rivalry.

Focus compels asking questions about patterns that simply wouldn't otherwise be asked: Which indicators might generate a pattern reflecting current, emerging or potential change that would surprise us? Which trends might be combined to suggest an emerging competitive space that no one in our organization has previously considered?

A perspective shift from the present to the future generates potential patterns that may be the source of distinctly new inferences. Projecting a series (a likely pattern) of a competitor's marketplace moves enables inferences about competitive dynamics at some point in the future that simply could not be drawn from the pattern noted in the competitor's current behaviors and words—no matter how extensive and detailed the current pattern.

Small data

The structuring principles and practices noted in Tables 3-1 and 3-2 help unleash the insight potential hidden in small data.[126] Many "methods" exist to structure small amounts of data (Box 3-2). Each method initiates deliberations resulting in inferences that could give rise to value generating insight. Awareness of these simple structuring approaches often allows early inferences to be drawn that then guide the search for supporting or refuting inferences. Consider the following summary case of many industry data conflicts I've observed.

Box 3-2

Using Small Data to Augment Structuring

Connecting small sets of data should not be overlooked as a means to sniffing significant inferences. Here are some examples of where a few data points, and even a single date point, can serve as the input for new and different inferences, and perhaps powerful inferences.

Data source contradictions: A contradiction in the observations or assertions of two or more data sources may suggest interesting inferences. One technology guru predicts the decline of a technology solution while another forecasts significant growth for it.

Data conflicts: A search for conflicts in data can lead to inferences that would otherwise be missed. Differences in customer purchasing behaviors in the case of the same product can lead to inferences about latent customer needs.

Anomalies: Data points about entities or processes that lie outside the "normal range" or what was expected. For example, the one customer that complains bitterly about a product's application or the one competitor that doesn't use a particular component or technology.

Outliers: An unusual or strange condition or circumstance that is way outside the norm or what might be expected, for example, the suggestion that a driverless car is a real possibility.

Dilemmas: Exploring how others deal with a choice situation is often the pathway to inferences. For example, a customer that is finding it difficult to choose between two specific offers: once a choice is made, you can draw inferences as to why.

Causal differences: Two obvious explanations in the form of distinct causal relationships. For example: two experts provide alternative or directly opposing "explanations" as to how a technology will evolve or why two organizations have adopted distinctly different approaches to developing a technology can lead to distinctly different cause-effect linkages.

Bottlenecks: Where a flow of activities doesn't move as it should or as has been forecast. A unit in a regulatory process sometimes becomes the bottleneck that slows up the development of multiple rules or the response to the interpretations of others.

Constraints: Limitations and constraints often alert analysts to possibilities. For example, a rival's production process may encounter a constraint due to a production capacity issue (the manufacturing technology can only produce so many units).

The intentional pursuit of data conflicts pushes people to consider many of the analysis context components. Conflicting statements from industry gurus about whether or not a significant sales downturn is imminent lead to an active search for indicators that support or refute either statement. The scope of the data search extends to capture indicators relevant to the changing industry context. Nontraditional industry prognosticators might be sought for their perspectives about alternative industry futures. A shift in focus compels the team to ask questions it has not previously posed. When the question, what if the industry were to undergo a major sales discontinuity (for example, a massive sales downturn) is asked, imagination is required to posit possible industry trajectories—and, in the process, identifying indicators that need to be monitored to project industry change before it happens.

Structuring insight work: People procedures

Because human minds generate insight, structuring must address who should be involved in all phases of insight work, or more specifically, the attributes they should possess. The intent is to find or educate people who will drive the necessary deliberations involved in identifying insight opportunities and applying the analysis context components discussed above.

The 6IFs suggest one overarching desired attribute: people willing to do what in necessary to see, think, intend, decide, act and feel differently. The 6IF challenges and questions noted in Chapter 1 can be used to assess people's ability and willingness to be different.

The mind principles (Table 3-1) suggest some facets of the practice orientation at least some individuals should possess to move toward the desired 6IF differences (Table 3-3): a willingness to assume that nothing is self-evident, to challenge prevailing mental models, to articulate their best judgments and engage in challenges to them, and to avoid accepting the first answers offered to any question. The data principles suggest further facets of the desired practice orientation (Table 3-2): a willingness and ability to seek diverse forms of data from many different data sources, to address the biases inherent in data and sources, to deploy various methodologies to differentially array data and analysis outcomes.

Table 3-3   The 6IFs and Structuring: Deliberations and Methods

6IFs	Readiness for structuring (inputs to structuring)	Influence of structuring on each insight factor (outputs of structuring)
See	Envision how deliberations might be managed to motivate involvement in structuring; see how structuring's elements might be managed differently.	See questions that now should be asked; see issues that should be explored; see connections that might otherwise have been missed; see what could be, as opposed to what is.
Think	Be willing to challenge historic modes of thinking (reasoning); use different analysis frames to spur new questions; accept different modes of reasoning; identify and address influence of biases on thinking modes.	Think about new topics, issues, challenges; apply thinking (reasoning) in new ways (for example, future backward); understand the context of analysis, not just data in isolation; look for conflict and differences and explanations that resolve them.

Intend	Advocate for the need to engage in structuring and to try individual analysis components; collaborate with others to learn how to deploy each structuring element.	Plan to systematically identify structuring opportunities; commit to deploying the analysis context components in key analysis projects; educate analysis teams in the fine art of structuring.
Decide	Assess structuring readiness; assess whether and how structuring is now conducted; determine when and how to introduce structuring into ongoing deliberations.	Determine which structuring opportunities to pursue; decide how to sequence the opportunities; decide who should be involved in structuring; determine how to educate analysis teams in the details and nuances of structuring.
Act	Learn how to identify structuring opportunities and how apply the analysis context components; learn how to seek new data and indicators; learn how to elaborate the context of any analysis project.	Develop a team to identify structuring opportunities; use each analysis context component to push the needed mindset to execute structuring; ask questions that may challenge how analysis has been historically executed.
Feel	Explore how emotions influence all facets of applying the analysis context components; reflect on your own emotions about embarking on structuring and the work it entails.	Identify how others' emotions support or inhibit execution of each of structuring's three elements; bring consideration of emotions into structuring's deliberations.

The desired mind and practice orientations must then be infused into structuring's deliberations and method. One or more individuals schooled in the mind and data practices should be involved in any application of the eight analysis context components. The purpose is straightforward: ensure that each analysis component is fully applied.

Some other steps may enable and reinforce the desired mind and practice orientations: involve people from different organization disciplines and functions; sometimes new employees who have not yet been acculturated to the organization may more willingly adopt the desired practices; it may also be possible in some instances to involve people from external organizations such as channels, suppliers, technology or regulatory experts.

Case: DipCo

While conducting intensive B2B customer domain analysis, a customer analysis research team in an industrial product firm I'll call DipCo[127] discovered through an alert from a member of the sales force that a mid-sized corporate customer had gone public with its decision to migrate to DipCo's staunchest competitor. A combined marketing and sales team took it upon themselves to analyze why it occurred and to address how to prevent other customers from following suit. As the team began its work, it made many structuring choices.

Scope: Don't restrict the analysis project to an economic analysis of the migration decision. The initial intent was to understand the customer; consider all issues and decisions relevant to the customer. Doing so immediately broadened the analysis context. Scoping the project initially to examine the whole customer, and not just the economic rationale for the decision to switch to the firm's number one rival, led to a series of new questions about the customer's strategy, investment plans, motivations of senior executives, and, especially the customer's relationship with the competitor. The option to extend the analysis to other customers was left open.

Analysis frame: Go beyond the firm's traditional customer needs-based analysis. The intent was to identify the firm's value proposition and that of its rival and then compare and contrast them. They committed to analyze all facets of the customer's experience with DipCo and relevant rivals rather than simply conducting the long-established product and price comparison.

Focus: Ask questions suggested by the data as it's collected. The intent was to avail of opportunities as they arose to invoke new series of questions. The team especially wanted to avoid falling into the trap of raising only a set of a priori designated questions, a characteristic of the organization's culture. As the inquiry progressed, the team found itself asking questions about the competitive context that it hadn't anticipated including which non-high market rivals might be the source of new breakthrough products.

Perspective: Ask individuals to adopt the customer's perspective. The intent was to surface and challenge the firm's predominantly latent presumptions and point of view about customers, rivals and marketplace rivalry. Two members of the team were designated to "walk in the shoes of the customer." One result: few statements about the customer's strategy, behaviors and actions went unchallenged; some statements didn't hold up in the face of critical questioning. For example, the customer's loyalty to any provider could no longer be taken as a given; it had to be earned.

Context: Identify how changes in the competitive context might influence the customer's behaviors. The intent was to ensure that the deliberations would aim to learn as much about the competitive context as about the customer. One result: the analysis required individuals who could bring competitive knowledge to the deliberations.

Imagination: Make asking what-if questions a core element of moving from data to indictors (and on to preliminary inferences). The intent was to encourage team members to "dig beyond the obvious:" to ask if there were other explanations of the customer's migration decision, if a refocusing of the customer's strategy was causing it to behave in ways that were a departure from its previous behaviors, if the migration decision was a harbinger of decisions for which there was yet limited if any indications.

Data: Place no preference on any one type of data or any source of data. The intent was to encourage team members to seek multiple forms of "data" including the opinions and judgments of a diverse range of external sources and not to simply accept data "as true" from historically trusted external sources including industry experts, recognized technology leaders and individuals within suppliers, channels and end-users.

Indicators: Insist on Identifying change indicators as a focal point of the data collection and analysis. The intent was specific: remind all team members of the purposes and uses of indicators.[128] Each structuring component orients data collection to the detection and assessment of indicators; the emphasis is upon capturing and understanding change, not the aggregation of data.

Structuring led the analysis team to set forth a distinctly new approach for DipCo to understanding a customer. It provided a set of preliminary principles to guide the initial approach to collecting and analyzing customer data.

Case: VP

The analysis team in the VP case also made several structuring choices.

Scope: Address the competitor, customer, and competitive context; don't limit your focus to the competitor. Change across these domains is interconnected; understanding the shift in the competitor's value proposition requires understanding customers' responses.

Analysis frame: Develop a comprehensive competitor value proposition analysis. Understand all facets of the value delivered to customers; don't detail only the product and price.

Focus: Ask questions which it historically neglected. Every question should be asked; use data to spawn questions about the competitor's value proposition, customer motivations, and the dynamics of change in the competitive context.

Perspective: Ask individuals to play the role of the competitor and the dominant customer. Insist that one or more individuals "assume the mantel of the competitor" as it adapts the value proposition over time.

Context: Address how change in the competitive context might influence both the competitor and customers. It was not enough to consider the current competitive context. For example, it would be helpful to capture what product attributes might be in the market in one or two years.

Imagination: Ask individuals to draw multiple inferences from each indicator. The aspiration: individuals would "see" what was not immediately evident in the indicators and their context. Also, be willing to derive a sequence of inferences to detail connections across indicators that also might not be immediately obvious.

Data: Move beyond traditional data types and sources. Developing a full understanding of the competitor's emerging value proposition and customers' responses required access to data and data sources the firm previously ignored or neglected.

Indicators: Be obsessive in identifying indicators and tracking change along them. The competitor's value proposition and customers' responses could only be fully detailed if the analysis team noted all relevant indicators.

The VP analysis team developed these structuring principles in the early stages of their efforts to document the competitor change and customers' reactions. It broadened the scope and focus of their approach and led to a broader and deeper understanding of the competitor's value proposition, the how and why of customers' behaviors, and change expected in the competitive context.

Structuring and the 6IFs (Insight Factors)

The 6IFs influence whether and how an analysis team adopts structuring to augment the value extracted from analysis (Table 3-3). The mind and data principles (Tables 3-1 and Table 3-2) enable change along the 6IFs—what people see, think, intend, decide, do and feel—as they engage in structuring.[129]

These 6IF consequences, as you'll see in the next three chapters, strongly influence how insight work is conducted and the quality of the insights that ensues. In this section, I'll emphasize structuring's impact on the 6IFs—how structuring makes a difference along the 6IFs—and how in many instances it motivates greater commitment to insight work. Some typical comments heard from individuals as they participate in structuring illustrate the role and importance of structuring's impact on the 6IFs.

See

The eight analysis context components aim to enable individuals to see differently. Scoping, framing, focus, and perspective place you on a "perch" from which you should see differently—for example, who the relevant competitors are, what shifts might be emerging in customers' behaviors, or how regulatory agendas might unfold. Provoking imagination lies at the heart of seeing what could be as opposed to what is. Imagining an invented competitor has caused analysis teams to see the limitations of the strategies of all current rivals. Without seeing differently, new preliminary inferences won't be drawn. Here are two comments that illustrate how structuring influences what individuals see:

"It was only when I immersed myself in a day in the life of a historic customer that I came to see its inability to be a long-term customer for us"

"Once we included emerging substitute product providers as potential rivals, we quickly saw that what we had designated as new marketplace opportunities would most likely be obliterated by this new product"

Think

Structuring also challenges where you focus your thinking on and how you think. Scoping and framing, for example, prompt thinking about a customer instead of focusing only on its needs or thinking about a competitor and not just its current marketplace strategy or its value chain or its cost structure. If you assume the position of a customer or a rival or a regulatory agency, you think about issues, challenges and problems from their vantage point, some of which may be new to us, some of which may cast a different light on how you have previously thought about them.

The influence on how you think may be even more critical. A shift in analysis focus from a conventional industry structure analysis to an ecosystem analysis causes systems thinking to come to the fore. The actions of internal and external players in the industry are now assessed for their impact on the entire system of relationships in the broadened definition of the industry. Using scenarios to frame thinking about competitor or customer or competitive change requires an analysis team to think future-backwards: take a position in the future and work backwards to its implications for competitors or customers or the competitive context.[130]

Adhering to the mind principles noted in Table 3-2 implies you're willing to challenge what you think about and how you think. If you're not, you can hardly say you're prepared for structuring: identifying structuring opportunities, applying the eight analysis context components, or managing structuring's participants. Here are some typical customer-focused comments that evidence the influence of structuring on thinking:

"Because we applied a variety of frames to analyze our key corporate customer including finance, marketing, supply chain, cost structure, profiles of key executives and linkages to its customers, we eventually realized that our focus needed to shift to the customer's business strategy—otherwise we simply could not explain many of its recent behaviors and decisions."

"Once we widened the scope of our analysis of consumers to address the social networks in which they were embedded, the questions we now had to ask led us to think about consumers as networks and not as individuals."

Intend

The absence of the intent to advocate and deploy structuring guarantees it dies on the vine. Because the value of structuring is often not self-evident, the need to embark on structuring sometimes isn't an easy sell. Moreover, analysis teams, especially if they're under pressure from managers to generate findings and outputs, have built-in motivations to spend less time on structuring. The implied motto: what we're doing is good enough.

In these instances, structuring preparedness is at the low end: individuals need to experience structuring, as noted in the see and think comments above, to appreciate its potential value. The good news is that as structuring proceeds, individuals' intent to engage in the active pursuit of new inferences (and therefore the possibility of insight) typically intensifies; they recognize the value of scoping, framing, focus shifting and adopting other perspectives. Here are some comments that illustrate the importance of a shift in intent:

"We had firmly believed we knew how to craft marketplace insight, it was part of our annual environmental analysis; it was only when we were asked to address competitor and customer and channel insights that we understood we had to change how we conducted marketplace analysis."

"A senior manager asked us to identify key opportunities for structuring. We found several critically important missed opportunities. Consequently, we established an intent to conduct an opportunity review on a regular basis."

Decide

Intent needs to transform into decisions. Most likely, the decisions involve new choices and commitments. Individuals decide (for example) to assess their readiness to follow the mind and data principles noted in Tables 3-2 and 3-3 and, more generally, to review how well they understand what structuring is. If an individual commits to structuring to enhance analysis quality, he or she must then decide how best to do so: which analysis projects to address, how to introduce structuring to the deliberations, which structuring components to emphasize, how to apply each component (for example, how broadly to apply scope or perspective), how to sequence the components, who should be involved, how fast to move the structuring deliberations. Another key decision involves determining how best to incorporate the structuring approach into existing analysis methodologies such as scenarios, simulations, competitive gaming, and many forms of business analytics. At a more micro level, structuring comes alive when individuals decide to seek out connections between trends and search for patterns in disparate indicators. Here are some comments that exemplify the importance of the "decide" IF to the advancement of structuring:

"I was completely locked into my way of doing analysis; it was only when I was compelled to be involved in adopting different frames and perspectives that I decided to structure differently how I approach every analysis project."

"My analysis team grudgingly agreed to identify new and existing opportunities to apply the structuring components. Once we saw the benefits of bringing imagination to how we might apply each component, we decided to ask how we might quickly bring structuring to all our key analysis projects."

Act

The mind and data principles beget action; otherwise, they remain as merely words on paper. Implicit in executing the three structuring elements are behaviors that require individuals to act differently. They critically assess what current or future analysis projects offer the highest potential insight returns. They conduct analysis differently: they insist on applying a number of the analysis context components, they ensure that no single frame or perspective dominates, they seek supporting and refuting indicators. They always ask whether the analysis scope, frame, and perspective, are appropriately applied; they ask questions they might not otherwise when the focus shifts from the present to the future in a competitor or industry or political or regulatory analysis; they ask how more imagination might be brought to bear. Here are some comments that illustrate how involvement in structuring shapes behaviors:

"We always did analysis as the projects emerged. Once we did our first review of existing projects to identify the most critical structuring opportunities, we've made it an ongoing analysis routine."

"Traditionally, we asked a predetermined set of questions as the core of our customer, competitor and industry analysis—indeed every type of analysis we did. Once we applied the structuring components, we quickly shifted to developing sets of questions specific to each analysis project."

Feel

Emotions may stifle if not prevent or support and maybe even accelerate key aspects of each of the three structuring elements. If involvement in structuring leads to individuals feeling more positive—more energized, engaged and hopeful—as they recognize the possibility of a pathway to valuable insight, they encourage all around them to engage in seeing and thinking differently. And, the range of preliminary inferences derived is likely greatly extended. If on the other hand, it leads to more negative emotions—individuals feeling more fretful, hesitant and insecure—as they recognize the personal and team commitment required to fully engage in structuring, it's likely they'll only grudgingly enter the tasks required. And the range of preliminary inferences derived will be severely limited. Here are some comments to illustrate the power of emotions:

"The apparently simple task of determining the major opportunities for applying the analysis context components left us feeling aggravated, belittled and diminished because the management team didn't approve our choices. We didn't wish to have anything to do with it again."

"Watching the reactions of the team to the new questions being addressed when we shifted the focus and adopted the perspective of different external stakeholders, I suddenly felt jubilant and relieved that we could accept new analysis routines."

Structuring errors

Experience has taught me that an organization inexperienced in structuring is prone to commit four errors[131] that critically limit structuring's deliberations and method. First, haphazardly identifying key structuring opportunities: insufficient time is devoted to identifying non-obvious analysis projects that could benefit from structuring's method. The result: analysis deliberations are hamstrung by a lack of understanding of the power of structuring and its method most likely is applied only to lower-value insight projects. Second, adopting only one or two of the eight analysis context components. The result: deliberations don't avail of the possible inputs that might be generated by the other analysis components and the structuring method is severely shortchanged. Third, not infusing fresh DNA in analysis teams or projects. The result: the deliberations are dominated by individuals' historic mind-sets and the analysis method hews to what has previously worked. In short, many of the structuring principles and practices noted in Tables 3-1 and 3-2 are never considered. Fourth, each structuring application isn't viewed as a learning opportunity. The result: structuring isn't seen as something that can be enhanced over time.

Enabling and enhancing structuring

Structuring is rarely a finely honed capability. Here's a sequence of steps that help you embed and enhance structuring in your unit or broader organization:

Deliberate on the mind and data principles

The mind and data principles (Tables 3-1 and 3-2) provide a focus for deliberation before any effort is made to execute any of structuring's three elements—identifying insight opportunities, executing the analysis context components, determining appropriate structuring participants. A discussion of the structuring principles and practices noted in the right-hand column in Tables 3-1 and 3-2 enables an analysis team to bring the right frame of mind to the tasks inherent in structuring. For example, something as apparently simple as assuming that nothing is self-evident or that any data source should not be privileged suggests to individuals that they should not take any data as a given—they need to be hyper-inquisitive.

Assess the state of structuring in your organization

Unfortunately, structuring is too often overstated: people typically fail to recognize the full scope of structuring's deliberations and method. So it's imperative to pose a set of questions designed to describe and assess the actual state of structuring in your unit or organization (Table 3-4). The less that structuring's method is evident, the more important it is to ensure that serious deliberation occurs around the mind and data principles and that the 6IFs are used to assess readiness for structuring.

Use the 6IFs to assess structuring readiness

Each IF gives rise to sets of questions that allow you to assess the readiness of the analysis team to execute structuring. You'll need to document the

Table 3-4   Assessing the State of Structuring in Your Organization

Key questions	Sub-questions
In your function, unit, or the entire organization, does one person hold recognized responsibility for structuring?	Is there a person with recognized expertise in structuring? How has that person developed his/her expertise? Do others call upon that person to share his/her expertise in analysis projects?
Is there a formal assessment of structuring opportunities associated with new analysis projects?	Does the organization or your unit create a listing of new analysis projects? Has a set of criteria been developed to assess which projects could benefit from structuring? Is there a formal effort to apply the criteria?
Do you identify the key structuring opportunities across existing analysis projects?	Does your unit or organization develop a list of ongoing analysis projects? Do you create a set of criteria to prioritize the projects for structuring? Do you carefully choose the individuals who are involved in the assessment?
In a recent analysis project, what was the evidence that structuring was seriously applied?	Who was involved in leading the structuring? Which structuring elements received the most attention? How did each analysis context component lead to new generation of new data? How did each component give rise to specific indicators?
Can you identify any meeting in which structuring issues and questions were raised?	What was the purpose of the meeting? What specific structuring issues and questions were raised? Who raised them and for what purpose? What were the follow-up actions?
Has your unit or organization engaged in any structuring education efforts?	Has any "training" in how to execute structuring been afforded to one or more analysis teams? How has the training proved helpful? Was the training connected to specific insight projects?

evidence that the team has the capacity to see, think, intend, decide, act, and feel in ways that accept the need for structuring and a willingness to put it into practice. Many of the relevant issues and questions are noted in Table 3-4.

Appoint a structuring leader

Especially if structuring receives minimal attention or is haphazardly executed, appointing someone to initiate and oversee the application of the three structuring elements becomes mandatory. In most instances, accountability for structuring can be added to the responsibilities of an existing analysis leader or senior player in a specific analysis project. The leader's role in part is to ensure the decisions noted above in the discussion of structuring and the 6IFs become part of the deliberations so that all involved recognize the choices they confront and the rationales for each decision.

Identify structuring opportunities

Structuring opportunities abound in the everyday analysis life of any organization. Choose an initial one or two analysis projects where structuring might be critical to their success. Use the following three questions to identify the initial project(s):

- Is the current or anticipated analysis associated with an issue, opportunity, or risk of significant importance to the organization?
- Is there evidence that those involved in the analysis typically fail to apply the structuring elements?
- Can you develop an argument that structuring if properly applied would likely lead to an enhanced outcome—superior insight?

If the answer to each of these questions is yes, you've probably identified one or more significant structuring opportunities.

Apply the analysis context components

Make the eight analysis context components a core building block in one of the identified structuring opportunities. The structuring leader raises each component and asks how it might be applicable to the analysis project. This deliberative approach allows everyone the opportunity to consider how each analysis context component could influence the inputs to the analysis and therefore its outputs.

Evolve some structuring ground rules

As illustrated earlier in the DipCo case, deliberation around some key ground rules proves a highly effective means to kick-start a structuring initiative. In part, the ground rules serve to operationalize the choices that stem from deliberations around the mind and data principles. For example, choosing to project and assess a competitor's potential future strategy alternative[132] and not just to analyze its current strategy significantly influences all facets of the competitor insight project.

Learn from each structuring engagement

Each structuring assignment begets learning: how to apply the three structuring elements individually and collectively; what issues and questions to raise with respect to each analysis context component; how to move the analysis along at an appropriate speed; how to sense that further time invested in structuring may not pay commensurate dividends.

For purposes of educating others about the nuances and merits of structuring, composing a brief report on the structuring experience creates a compelling story—one that enables others to experience what structuring is all about.

Extend structuring's reach

The final step is to extend the three structuring elements to each analysis domain considered critical to the organization's decision making and performance. In marketing, for example, the structuring elements might be applied to determining the key analysis opportunities, then applying the analysis context components and ensuring a DNA mix.

A final comment

Structuring represents the early intervention into insight work. The three structuring elements—deciding where to focus insight attention, orchestrating the analysis context, and determining who should be involved in insight work—prepare the organization to conduct the analysis activities involved in the early stages of insight work. The intent is to ensure that insight work generates value-generating inferences, the crucial step on the pathway to change insights—the focus of the next chapter.

Notes

94. In short, few of the questions noted under Methods in Table 2-5 receive little if any attention.

95. Indeed, we need to orient the mind so that we not only "see" and "think" better but that we perform better along each of the other IFs (insight factors): intend, decide, act and feel.

96. The principles have been culled from a variety of literatures including philosophy of science, organizational decision making and organizational learning including: Nicholas Rescher, *Philosophical Reasoning: A Study in the Methodology of Philosphizing* (Malden, MA: Blackwell, 2001); Philip, E. Tetlock, *Expert Political Judgment: How Good Is It? How Can We Know?* (Princeton: Princeton University Press, 2005); James G. March, *The Pursuit of Organizational Intelligence* (Malden, MA: Blackwell, 1999).

97. The data perspective principles draw heavily from the philosophy of science and some knowledge management literature. C. West Churchman, *The Design of Inquiring Systems* (New York: Basic Books, 1971); Ikujiro Nonaka and Hiro Takeuchi, *The Knowledge Creating Company: How Japanese Companies Foster Creativity and Innovation for Competitive Advantage* (New York: Oxford University Press, 1995).

98. This pursuit is one element of the personal "mastery" advocated by Peter Senge to understand the world around us. Peter Senge, *The Fifth Discipline: The Art and Practice of the Learning Organization* (New York: Doubleday-Currency, 1990).

99. This conception of data reinforces the broad view of data advanced in Chapter 2.

100. This is a core theme in Steven Pinker, *How the Mind Works* (New York: W.W. Norton & Company, 1997).

101. Many cognitive biases and their implications for insight work are noted in Chapter 4.

102. See, for example, Margaret J. Wheatley, *Leadership and the New Science: Learning about Organization from an Orderly Universe* (San Francisco: Berrett-Koehler Publishers, 1992), and Ralph D. Stacey, *Managing the*

Unknowable: Strategic Boundaries Between Order and Chaos (San Francisco: Jossey-Bass Publishers, 1992).

103. Seeing and thinking differently connect directly to the 6IFs (insight factors) introduced in Chapter 1 and discussed later in this section.

104. Most firms focus their competitor analysis on their large market share rivals. The learning costs of doing so are extensive. See, Liam Fahey, *Competitors: Outwitting, Outmaneuvering and Outperforming the Competition* (New York: John Wiley & Sons, 1999).

105. See, Clayton M. Christensen, *The Innovator's Dilemma: When New Technologies Cause Great Firms to Fail*, 2d ed. (New York: Harper Business, 2000).

106. Eamonn Kelly, "Business Ecosystems Come of Age," Deloitte Consulting, last modified April 15, 2015, https://dupress.deloitte.com/dup-us-en/focus/business-trends/2015/business-ecosystems-come-of-age-business-trends.html.

107. For a full discussion of the Five Forces Framework, see Michael E. Porter, *Competitive Strategy: Techniques for Analyzing Industries and Competitors* (New York: MacMillan, 1980).

108. John C. Camillus, *Wicked Strategies: How Companies Conquer Complexity and Confound Competitors* (Toronto: University of Toronto Press, 2016).

109. The role and importance of framing in customer analysis work will be illustrated in the Customer Migration case example used in this chapter.

110. Scenarios generate distinctly different competitive futures. Each one enables descriptions of what the opportunities and risks might be, what strategies might be required, and how they might be different than the firm's current strategy.

111. The influence of biases will be addressed in Chapter 5.

112. The importance of context will be evident in the Customer Migration case used later in this chapter.

113. See, Liam Fahey, "Invented Competitors: A New Competitor Analysis Framework," *Strategy and Leadership* 30, no. 6 (2002): 5–12.

114. Yet the role and importance of imagining and detailing *potential* customer experience is often missed or understated in conceptual and empirical

work addressing customer experience. See, Katherine N. Lemon and Peter C. Verhoef, "Understanding the Customer Experience Throughout the Customer Journey," *Journal of Marketing* 80, no. 6 (2016): 69-96.

115. Ethnographic research entails living with customers. For a vivid description of what it entails, see, Abbie Griffin, "Qualitative Research Methods for Investigating Business-to-Business Marketing Questions," in *Handbook of Business-to-Business Marketing*, eds. Gary L. Lilien and Rajdeep Grewal (Cheltenham, U.K.: Edward Elgar, 2012).

116. For those interested in broad treatment of scenario learning, see Liam Fahey and Robert M. Randall, *Learning from the Future: Competitive Foresight Scenarios* (New York: John Wiley & Sons, 1998).

117. William Hall, *Shift: Using Business Simulations and Serious Games* (San Francisco, Create Space, Independent Publishing Platform, 2014).

118. For a good discussion of Competitive Gaming, see, Benjamin Gilad, *Business War Games: How Large, Small and New Companies Can Vastly Improve their Strategies and Outmaneuver the Competition* (Franklin Lakes, NJ: Career Press, 2009).

119. Alternative hypothesis testing is an established method in business research to test alternative possibilities or ways of thinking about the future.

120. For a useful discussion of big data analytics, see, Thomas H. Davenport and Jeanne G. Harris, *Competing on Analytics: The New Science of Winning* (Boston: Harvard Business School Press, 2007).

121. The value of the analysis context components is implicit in many recent reports on the use of big data analysis. See, for example, Peter Horst and Robert Duboff, "Don't Let Big Data Bury Your Brand," *Harvard Business Review*, November 2015, 79-86.

122. The notion of an integrated inference was developed in Chapter 2.

123. The capacity of the mind to draw instantaneous inferences is explicitly addressed in Chapter 4, especially Table 4-2.

124. Remember that all inferences need to be vetted and vouched for, as discussed Chapter 5.

125. The ability to see and consider patterns among change variables is central to the ability to develop alternative views of how the future might

unfold. See, for example, Peter Schwartz, *The Art of the Long View* (New York: Doubleday-Currency, 1996).

126. For a powerful discussion of the importance of small data as a source of marketplace insight, see, Martin Lindstrom, *Small Data: The Tiny Clues that Uncover Hugh Trends* (New York: St. Martin's Press, 2016).

127. DipCo is a pseudonym for an actual company.

128. The purposes and uses of indicators were detailed in the previous chapter.

129. The discussion of the analysis context component earlier in this chapter emphasized how specific mind and data principles provided the impetus for deployment of scoping, framing, focusing and the other analysis context components.

130. Scenarios essentially enable backward thinking—from the future back to now. Many examples of how to frame such thinking can be found in Liam Fahey and Robert M. Randall, eds., *Learning from the Future: Competitive Foresight Scenarios* (New York: John Wiley & Sons, 1998).

131. The first three errors refer to the three structuring elements.

132. This is an example of the analysis context component, scope. It broadens the domains to be considered: the multiple different competitor futures constitute "domains."

133. As noted earlier, the role of the mind as an influence on the execution of each of the 4S activities is addressed in this and the next three chapters.

Chapter 4

Sniffing: Deriving Preliminary Inferences

Structuring generates marketplace data, especially indicators of change that otherwise would be missed. Indicators constitute the raw material out of which the mind creates inferences and insights. Yet, all too often, you recognize in retrospect that you should have drawn an inference about something or other from data (indicators) that were readily available and known to us. Indeed, sometimes you're so buried in the data, or more precisely in the context of the data, that you may miss the "obvious" inference (insight). One competitor analyst at a trade show was so focused on understanding the major rival's recent marketing shifts that she entirely missed the likely strategy shift that might stem from its announcement that it would consummate an acquisition within six months. Have you been close to a family member or colleague or friend and not recognized that something was deeply "wrong" even though you noted some unusual behaviors or words or tendencies?

In this chapter, I'll detail the method involved in moving from indicators to preliminary inferences, what I call *sniffing*. I'll begin by describing what sniffing entails, the three core acts that constitute sniffing, and the questions typically posed in sniffing. Then I'll illustrate the connections between structuring and sniffing and use the DipCo and VP cases to illustrate the steps involved in the sniffing method. I'll conclude with a set of prescriptions to enhance your personal or organization's sniffing capability.

What is sniffing?

Sniffing is the act of drawing base or preliminary inferences. The inference is preliminary because it's typically drawn within a short time of the indicators being noted and, sometimes very quickly, if not instantaneously, and it has not yet been vetted. Sniffing occurs as data unfolds, as indicators are detected in the process of structuring. Sniffing, as the generation of yet-to-be assessed inferences, constitutes the second step in the pathway from data to quality inferences that enable value-generating insights.

The ubiquity of sniffing

Here are some further examples that illustrate the ubiquity of sniffing opportunities:

- An executive watching the evening TV news saw a report that an inter-governmental department study group is about to publish strong evidence of the growth of large infrastructure projects (roads, bridges, rail, and subways) in the next ten years. She immediately asked what it might mean for the industry. She jumped to a GMI inference: demand for the outputs of her industry could be substantial.

- A major customer noted in passing in a casual phone conversation with a marketing executive that she didn't think that her firm's performance results in a particular product area would be anywhere near the prior year's. The marketing executive inferred that sales of his components that were used in related products might well have reached a plateau (the firm's lavish sales forecasts notwithstanding).

- A footnote in a global industry analysis produced by an international bank noted a potential major water shortage in two adjoining countries if an agreement was not reached with neighboring countries not to redirect water flows. The analyst immediately inferred that if a water conflict were to arise, production capacity and output could be severely restricted for several rivals in that region.

In short, sniffing can occur in almost any context at any time. A variety of change situations giving rise to sniffing opportunities are noted in Table 4-1. In each situation, once one or more indicators emerge or are determined, analysts, and managers set about identifying what, if any, inferences might be drawn.

Although it has received minimal attention in a variety of relevant literatures[134] and it's rarely noted in practice, sniffing occurs in almost all incidences of insight work that take place over some time. As data are structured, sniffing should be an inherent element of the process.

Table 4-1 Examples of Sniffing Inferences

Data/indicators	Sniffing (preliminary inferences that might be drawn)
Competitor: Small rival has won a number of mid-sized customers in its local region.	Infer: The competitor may have found a winning value proposition that might be relevant beyond its local region; customers are seeking solutions (radically) different than those previously available.
Customer: Longtime customer migrates to a rival.	Infer: A superior value proposition has been developed by the rival; we let slip our attention to delivering value to this customer.
Most competitors experience an unexpected upturn in sales in one industrial product area.	Infer: Customers have found a new application for the product; the products have been marketed and positioned differently (compared to the historical approach); demand has increased because customers' sales have increased.
An industry technology guru asserts in an interview in an industry trade publication that technology developments, mostly in related industries will obsolete the industry's core products within five years.	Infer: Assumptions about the mid- and long-term future could be substantially overstated; key players in the industry have had a major blind-spot in their environmental scanning; many rivals' current R&D investments may well be wasted; if customers became aware of the potential or immanence of these technologies, they could pull back on purchases of the industry's current products.
A supplier is negotiating with one of its suppliers to obtain access to its patented advanced technology component.	Infer: Our supplier plans to introduce a significantly upgraded version of its current product line with a year or so; the potential is high for rivalry to become far more intense between the supplier and its rivals.
A leading channel member has announced new, more demanding, terms to carry a product, irrespective of the supplier.	Infer: The channel management team believes the product will be on a growth trajectory; the management team sees little future in the product and wants to get it off its selves; the management team knows that its role is critical to all providers.

Sniffing: Three core acts

If sniffing is to become central to the deliberative and methodical approach to insight work, individuals need to recognize that it involves three distinct acts. Each contributes to transforming data (indicators) into insight.[135]

An act of perception

People perceive that the opportunity exists to sniff—to draw preliminary inferences. The intent of structuring, of course, is to generate sniffing opportunities. The senior executive meeting with customers or the manager listening to a rival's quarterly security analysts' conference call, needs to be aware of the opportunity for sniffing. Yet, all too often, sniffing doesn't occur. Great effort might be expended on adopting the perspective of different customer segments or competitors or reframing an analysis framework (for example, detailing the firm's eco-system) while postponing sniffing until the structuring is complete or almost so. Or, new indicators become available and it's treated as just another occasion for data collection, so sniffing doesn't occur. Analysts often read studies or reports obtained from many different types of sources where their exclusive focus is to summarize the key findings, sometimes with great specificity. What they don't do is make any attempt to generate preliminary inferences.

An act of derivation

Once the sniffing opportunity is recognized, one or more inferences need to be derived from the relevant data or indicators. It's one thing for an individual role-playing a customer or reading a consultant's report on technology change to sense that the data might tell you something interesting about emerging competitive dynamics in a specific product-market. It's another thing to expend the mental energy to derive some specific inferences about what the competitive dynamics might be and why.

An act of articulation

Extracting inferences is a mental process. Thus, the immediately derived (sniffed) inference must be articulated, that is, expressed in a form that allows it to be captured and documented in written form. It requires the exercise of thought to express what the inference is; in fact, it may be many inferences at roughly the same time! Thus, the sniffed inference might be: current products may be obsoleted faster than previously expected or in a year or two there may be considerably more product differentiation than projected. Table 4-1 illustrates a variety of articulated inferences.

Guiding questions: Entities

I'm frequently asked, "What do we draw preliminary inferences about?" The answer depends on whether you're talking about "actors" in the external environment, including both organizations and individuals, or inanimate trends, patterns, and discontinuities. Where the focus in on an organization specific indicator (for example, a statement by a senior executive or a decision the organization has just made or change in marketing strategy) or indicators specific to one or more individuals (for example, what they said or did), here as some general questions that typify the thrust of early stage preliminary inferences with respect to any entity or actor in the external environment.

- What does it (possibly) suggest about the entity's current or potential intentions or goals? What might the corporate customer's queries and questions indicate about its immediate procurement goals? What might the consumer's question about next generation products indicate about her intent to buy products currently on the market?

- What does it tell us about that entity's future behavior? How do its recent statements suggest a government agency might shift the execution of a specific set of regulations? How might the shift in consumers' statements about their life priorities affect their purchasing patterns?

- What explanation might it suggest about that entity's current or future behaviors? How might the rumored alliance with a component provider enable the supplier to exert more power over its customers? How might shifts in consumers' disposable income affect their brand preferences and thus the products they buy or don't buy?

- What does it indicate about a specific action the entity might take in a related context? How might the competitor's recently announced action in one geographic market suggest what it might do in other geographic markets? How might consumers' commitment to allocating disposable income to one purpose (for example, education) affect their expenditures in other areas?

- What might be the motivations behind the entity's potential strategy moves, actions, apparent intentions or goals, or recent announcements? Are the competitor's sudden actions to prune its product portfolio a reflection of its new CEO's desire to significantly reduce the firm's cost structure? Is the consumer's commitment to specific product types caused by new ecological awareness?

These questions remind us that change along even a single indicator can provide the genesis for many types of preliminary inferences. Each inference opens a new avenue of inquiry that may spur distinctly new understanding of the entity: for example, knowing a consumer's potential behavior causes a desire to understand the motivations that might explain the behavior.

Guiding questions: Trends, patterns, discontinuities

It's remarkable to observe how much time managers and analysis teams invest in detecting and corroborating trends, patterns (a combination of trends) and discontinuities and then how little time is committed to drawing inferences from them about current, emerging, and potential change. It's a powerful indication that the sniffing mind-set isn't present. It also means that the potential insight value of the confirmed trends, patterns, and discontinuities is likely to remain unrealized. Here are some general change questions that enable individuals to expand the scope, frame, and focus of their quest for preliminary inferences:

- Degree of change: What is the extent of the change in the trend, pattern, or discontinuity? Is the change in sales in a region greater or less than what you had projected? Is the sudden downturn in the rival's sales after many years of growth (a discontinuity) a new phenomenon in this product sector?

- Emerging/future change: what might change in the trend or pattern portent about the future direction of the trend or pattern?

- Causal influences: Who may be involved in driving this change in one direction or another?

- Causal factors: what factors other than "entities" might be driving the trend or pattern or discontinuity?

- Domain connections: How is this change related to change reflected in other trends, patterns, and discontinuities within its domain (see Figure 1-2)?

- Cross-domain connections: How is this change related to change in other domains?
- CSIs and GMIs: What might be the consequences of this change within and across domains for competitive space insights (CSIs) and generic marketplace insights (GMIs)?

Preparing the mind for sniffing

Sniffing constitutes the first activity involved in making sense of the change captured in data and along indicators. The mind and data principles (Tables 3-1 and 3-2) detailed in the previous chapter imply that making sense requires a human mind. Without the intervention of our mind, the sequence described in the VP case in Chapter 2: data transform into indicators, indicators give rise to inferences, and integrated inferences eventually cumulating in insight—doesn't takes place, irrespective of whether the overall flow or process occurs instantaneously or emerges due to deliberation over a protracted period. In the words of an eminent neuroscientist "the mind is what the brain does, specifically the brain processes information and thinking is a kind of computation."[136]

While the workings of the mind aren't fully understood, neuroscience has identified many of the brain's innate capabilities (Table 4-2). Without these fundamental brain capabilities, the human inferencing abilities necessary for sniffing (and the entire 4S cycle) would be impossible. The mind can generate inferences instantaneously, craft multiple inferences from a single indicator, develop a sequence of inferences at lightning speed, and sometimes even draw conflicting inferences. Of critical importance for sniffing, the mind can draw inferences that invoke views of the future that aren't evident today.

The brain capabilities give rise to sniffing principles and practices (Table 4-2). Be prepared to let the preliminary inferences flow, willing to draw multiple and even conflicting inferences form a single indicator or a set of indicators, and, where possible, use different perspectives to derive inferences. Individuals should be especially encouraged to draw inferences that at first glance may well conflict with the organization's prevailing mental models or a team's assumptions and beliefs.

Ideally, sniffing becomes a team or even an organizational mind-set. Each member persistently looks for sniffing opportunities (perception). They might ask what inferences can be drawn from the data or indicators

Table 4-2   The Human Mind as an Amazing Inference Generator

Capacity of the mind	Sniffing principles and practices
Generative mind: The mind can generate many inferences from any given data set (or set of indicators).	Sniffing should be driven by a purpose: unleash relevant brains to derive preliminary inferences. Engage different "types of brains" to generate potentially different change inferences.
Generative mind: Even a single data point can spark one or several inferences.	Sniffing should not frown on drawing inferences from single data points or indicators. A single indicator may give rise to inferences about many different things.
Instantaneous mind: The mind works at stunning speeds! In many instances, the inference is generated (almost) instantaneously.	Let the inferences flow should be the sniffing motto! Don't resist the temptation to spew forth preliminary inferences.
Complex mind: The mind can shape inferences that often-times are a string of related inferences.	Sniffing has the capacity to describe a series of interconnected inferences that may not be evident in one or more indicators.
Dexterous mind: The mind can also draw inferences that may well be in conflict, and some-times, diametrically opposed.	Don't constrain conflicting inferences: they may the source of different perspectives leading to fresh understanding sniffing must treat all preliminary inferences are extremely tentative.
Mind involving: The mind uses existing data and extant theories to draw inferences (especially with respect to the future).	Sniffing is facilitated and constrained by the mind's built-in mental models, shaped in part through experience. Sniffing needs to be driven by different perspectives.

Mind invoking: The mind is able to invoke views of the future that aren't evident today.	Sniffing can generate preliminary inferences that invoke "pictures" of the future that go beyond relevant current indicators and their context.
Non-referential mind: You can't know how your own understanding of the world is inadequate; you need the perspective of others.	You can't presume you have accurately depicted or projected change. Even preliminary inferences need some degree of fast assessment or vetting.

as they become available to us (derivation). They immediately script, orally or in writing, what the inference is or might be (articulation). The ultimate in a sniffing mind-set is that an individual practiced in the art of sniffing executes these steps, especially perception and derivation subconsciously: perceiving, deriving, and articulating preliminary inferences essentially go on automatic pilot.

However, people grapple with understanding change in individual marketplace domains. In the broader competitive space (see Figure 1-2), you must recognize the most fundamental fact of epistemology: the mind has no direct access to "truth" about the external world.[137] The mind is thus confined to "estimating" how the world outside it is and it has no way of ever confirming that its estimate (judgment) exactly corresponds or even comes close to depicting the "external reality."[138] Judgments about the future state of parts of the world are, of course, even more problematic. Integrated inferences, as described in the VP case in Chapter 2, and stipulated insights, that is, insights you're willing to accept as inputs to decision making must be viewed as your best estimates or judgments for the moment about the underlying phenomena or issues or topics.

The notion of "for the moment" is critical in insight work. The pervasiveness and constancy of the marketplace turbulence noted in Chapter 1 implies that at any one point in time the mind's understanding ("estimating") of change and what is actually happening (and, of course, what may happen) in the external world may be incongruent.[139] Some elements of our understanding, often described as our mental models, may have to be abandoned. Some other elements may have to be reconfigured; yet, some other elements may have to be constructed de novo. In simple terms, therefore, you can depict the mind, and collectively an organization, as being in a never-ending battle to understand change.

Sniffing: Key steps

The challenge, therefore, isn't with the capacity of the human mind to draw inferences but with the need to guide and nourish it to do so—prudently, efficiently, and effectively. Thankfully, the brain doesn't need much to stimulate it. The insight discipline's emphasis on deliberation and method guides the approach to sniffing. The three core acts in sniffing—perception, derivation, and articulation—suggest a sniffing method, a set of analysis steps (Table 4-3). The steps provide a set of protocols to ignite the drawing of preliminary inferences and to help ensure that the inferencing capabilities noted in Table 4-2 are fully deployed. The intent is to ensure that sniffing provides the best possible inputs to shaping, the next 4S activity.

Table 4-3   Sniffing: Key Steps

Perception: Perceive and clarify the initiating indicators

> Step 1: Recognize the sniffing opportunity.

> Step 2: Clarify and refine the relevant indicators.

Derivation: Draw immediate and preliminary inferences

> Step 3: Draw immediate inferences.

> Step 4: Ask questions pertaining to the indicators and their context.

> Step 5: Draw preliminary inferences.

> Step 6: Consider if other inferences can be drawn.

Articulation: Test and state the preliminary inferences

> Step 7: Conduct an initial "mental test" of the inferences.

> Step 8: Articulate the preliminary inferences.

Sniffing, as a method, isn't a one-time activity, that is, you draw an inference and that is all there is to sniffing. There's probably no limit to the questions you might ask in the form of "what does or might this data or indicators possibly tell us about…? *Possibly* is a critical word here because, as discussed later in this chapter, any given indicator about A could give rise to multiple direct inferences about A and many indirect inferences about B to Z. *Possibly* also reminds us that our first or immediate efforts to extract some meaning from the change and context reflected in and around the specific indicators are our preliminary inferences: they need to be further developed and vetted. Thus, you refer to them as preliminary or base inferences.

Sniffing: The link to structuring

Sniffing is inextricably intertwined with structuring; in many respects, they're nearly impossible to separate. Structuring explicitly aims to provide the mind with occasions or opportunities for sniffing. It's why you structure data, search for indicators, and seek to understand their context. Each structuring analysis component outlined in Chapter 3 enables application of the sniffing steps summarized in Table 4-3.

Scope

Scope broadens the purview of the insight context to be explored. It generates new opportunities for sniffing. Researchers, analysts, and others need to be aware that new data and indicators generated by extending the analysis scope offer immediate opportunities for sniffing (step 1 in Table 4-3). Here's a common example:

Customer win-loss analysis[140] and other methodologies often generate significant data from past customers. Clarifying indicators (step 2) that caused them to leave such as the provider's behaviors (for example, actions of the sales force, price increases, treatment by its senior executives) opens the possibility for inferences (step 3) that might never arise from innumerable conversations with current customers. As the customer details its experience with the provider in response to follow-up questions (step 4), the analyst draws inferences (step 5) regarding the aspects of the offer from its current supplier or behaviors of its former provider's employees that its current customers may not be aware of or may be disinclined to bring to its attention. Preliminary inferences, for example, about the rival's product functionality in turn cause that analyst to search for indicators about the provider's product performance and how it compares to that of other rivals (step 6). Any individual participating in this inferencing process can do a quick "mental test" (step

7) to assess if each key preliminary inference withstands some initial scrutiny. For example, one could ask what data and reasoning supported the inference that service functionality, that is, providing the requisite quality service in a timely fashion, was becoming a major point of differentiation compared to product performance functionality. Finally, the analyst or research team lists the preliminary inferences they have derived (step 8).

Analysis frame

Shifting the analysis frame always gives rise to new data and indicators. The value of any new analysis frame is largely missed if members of the analysis team fail to perceive the opportunity to sniff preliminary inferences. The potential insight value of extending the analysis frame is powerfully illustrated in this example:

As a study team in a health care firm began to develop an eco-system analysis of the increasingly pervasive and complex interconnections among entities in the firm's competitive space, they noted the need to explore the role of nongovernmental organizations (NGOs). As they gathered data and identified indicators (step 2 in Table 4-3) around the number of NGOs including their geographic presence, the demands they were placing on specific players in the industry, and how some were apparently partnering with individual rivals, team members quickly sniffed a number of preliminary inferences (step 5): *NGOs are increasing in prominence; NGOs are aligning around a point of view that could strongly support our firm's position in an upcoming court proceeding; NGOs will become a stronger influence on acceptable marketing practices.* Consideration of these inferences quickly suggested a changing competitive space. The NGO example confirms that derivation is a multitask process (Table 4-3).

Focus

Shifting the focus of the key questions asked opens a sniffing opportunity: it typically results in new data and indicators. The more the object of the new focus is outside the traditional purview of the organization or analysis team, the greater the need to clarify and refine the indicators as they emerge (step 2 in Table 4-3). Here's one example:

Several industrial product firms have generated new data and indicators and drawn fundamentally different inferences when they focus on the end-user or the consumer as well as their transactional or immediate customer.

In one case, a manufacturer of the ingredient for protective materials and clothing decided to focus intensively on the users or wearers of the materials and not just their immediate or focal customers, those who manufactured the products to be worn by the users. The team developed a set of indicators based on the statements and behaviors of the users or wearers (step 2 in Table 4-3). Among the immediate inferences (step 3): *users want best possible protection; users want to stay alive; users don't care who makes the product; users never look at the label or brand; users listen to the judgments of others.* They asked a variety of questions pertaining to the indicators and their context (step 4). For example, in what circumstances might they be concerned with an ingredient brand?

Respondents argued persuasively that it just didn't matter; what did matter was safety. The analysis team derived two key preliminary inferences (step 5): users were indifferent to the "ingredient brands," and what they cared about was the promise that the clothing would protect them in specific conditions. It didn't seem that the opposing inferences could be derived (step 6). The absence the ability to support opposing inference served as the initial "mental test" of the two dominant preliminary inferences (step 7). The analysis team refined and articulated the two inferences noted in step 5 and a small set of other inferences. The team also noted that these two inferences clashed with long-held presumptions about end-users' preferences.[141]

Perspective

Adopting the perspective of others creates a unique opportunity for sniffing; it fundamentally shifts the vantage point from which you experience the world. Asking people to adopt or assume a different perspective in effect asks them to immediately sniff from that perspective. Here's one common example that illustrates the power of shifting perspective:

In competitive gaming, teams play the role of a competitor: they're asked to think and act like that competitor.[142] As soon as they embrace the mantle and persona of the competitor, teams begin to think like the competitor. They confront new indicators (step 2): for example, investments being made by the competitor, actions being considered by the competitor, expressions of intent that hadn't previously been recognized. They begin to sniff, that is, draw preliminary inferences (step 3), about the competitor they're role playing (for example, this competitor possesses an asset base that is poorly leveraged in its current strategy), other competitors in the game (for example, one competitor's current strategy is based on stronger premises than you had previously believed), and the competitive context (for example, this specific product custom segment could easily be dominated by a specific rival were it to adopt a particular strategy). As they delve further into the competitor's strategy, intent, assets, and behaviors (step 4), they draw further preliminary inferences (steps 5 and 6). They do a quick test of viability of individual inferences (step 7) and generate a list of preliminary inferences (step 8). Unquestionably, walking in the shoes of a competitor results in preliminary inferences that otherwise wouldn't be generated.

Context

Elaborating the context around an indicator not only enhances understanding of the indicator, but also creates sniffing opportunities:

Legislation: As the amendments to a legislative initiative are proposed by powerful legislators, sniffing generates inferences about possible final forms of the legislation, when the legislation might be passed, how and when it might be transformed into regulations, who would benefit and who would lose.

Technology: Many analysis teams have discovered how learning about the emergence of potential technologies enables drawing inferences about the potential growth rates of existing product-customer segments or the focus of rivalry that quickly challenges traditional views of the marketplace.

Imagination

The ability to imagine what isn't now evident enables preliminary inferences that simply can't be crafted by individuals or teams locked into the organization's culture, belief systems, and mind-sets. Imagination powers what-if questions, builds images of what different futures might be, and challenges acceptance of preliminary inferences. Here are some examples:

Invented competitors: Developing an invented competitor's strategy offers many occasions for sniffing domain inferences (such as potential customer needs, possible products or solutions, competitors' resource limitations), competitive space inferences (such as how the rules of the competitive game could change over time), and generic market inferences (such as the profile of marketplace opportunities, lurking vulnerabilities facing rivals' current strategies).

Big data analytics: Data patterns around consumer behaviors and buying propensities provide an opportunity to draw preliminary inferences about the ideal buying experience—an experience that may not be represented in the current data sets.

Data

Each of the six structuring analysis components discussed above is a reminder that new data offers a natural opportunity for sniffing. Ask what the data implies or suggests about possible change around some topic, issue, entity, trend or pattern, or phenomenon of interest. Here's an example I recently encountered:

A conversation with a recognized technology expert in a medical supply business about the emergence of substitute products as part of a study of new product developments afforded the ability to draw immediate inferences (step 3 in Table 4-3) about new product possibilities, impediments to their development, who may be likely to first come to market, and possible consequences for the competitive space. Further questioning (step 4) of the expert about his assessment of the likely time path around the emergence and market penetration of the substitute product spurred two more preliminary inferences: recognition of the emergence of the substitute product would cause some current rivals to begin withdrawing from the market and some current customer segments for technology reasons might have a difficult time adopting the product (steps 5 and 6). A quick assessment of these and other preliminary inferences (step 7) led to a series of articulated inferences. A review of the set of inferences drew attention to the need to review several of the firm's implicit views about the marketplace.

Indicators

Indicators are the means to both identify and monitor change. Thus, they constitute the focal point of sniffing. Yet, frequently, the focus remains on data, not indicators. The faster structuring leads to the identification, categorization, and assessment of indicators, the faster sniffing can take place. Indeed, in the presence of a sniffing mind-set, perceiving a sniffing opportunity and deriving preliminary inferences should automatically kick in. However, in the absence of a sniffing mind-set, indicators often aren't detected, and even when they are, people don't take the time to derive preliminary inferences. Here are two examples of missed sniffing opportunities:

Big data analytics: What's now referred to as analytics or big data generates reams of carefully identified trends and patterns, often with respect to customers' behaviors and their possible causes. What I've noticed is that the data analysts and others don't stop to identify what preliminary inferences might be derived from key indicators. They tend to jump to some of form of finding or conclusion. And, sometimes, they spend little time identifying and deliberating about the relevant change indicators.

Customers: In a recent case, the analysis team identified a customer trend: customers were taking longer to make a purchase decision. In effect, the trend becomes the indicator enabling sniffing (step 1 in Table 4-3). It should lead immediately to sniffing (step 4). But it didn't. The team lost the opportunity to draw preliminary inferences about whether the trend will continue, what direction it might take, whether it will intensify, who might influence it, and what its consequences might be for one or more domains or for the competitive space.

Case: DipCo

Chapter 3 described how DipCo[143] used a set of structuring principles to guide the early stages of the analysis of why a presumed loyal customer had migrated to DipCo's rival. The case illustrates the steps of each sniffing stage: perception, derivation, and articulation. The team's structuring choices were a critical influence on how it approached sniffing and its outputs.

Perception

In this case, the act of perceiving a sniffing opportunity was thrust upon the analysis team: the customer's announcement about leaving DipCo for another supplier quickly became an indicator of change that attracted the attention of many people within the organization. The company obviously had to ask why the customer was leaving. However, the act of perception is never as simple as it seems, as steps 1 and 2 in Table 4-3 illustrate.

Step 1: Recognize the sniffing opportunity

Capturing an indicator, in this case, the termination announcement doesn't automatically mean that a sniffing opportunity is recognized, in particular, the opportunity to sniff multiple inferences, some of which may well be contradictory. All too often, data and/or indicators are noted and described and then communicated to others, but the people involved don't ask what preliminary inferences might be drawn. In this case, because the team documented key structuring principles, they didn't fall into the trap of quickly drawing a few inferences—in effect, their judgments answering the "why" question—and then, implications—what you can do about it. The scope principle—don't restrict the analysis to the migration decision—immediately led the team to recognize that the opportunity to sniff went considerably beyond the customer's announcement to migrate to the rival. The team needed to better understand the customer, the competitor, and the competitive context.

Step 2: Clarify and refine the relevant indicators

The customer, who had always been identified as satisfied and loyal, announced rather suddenly the decision to migrate to the competitor. The rival, to the extent that DipCo knew, hadn't significantly shifted its basic value proposition. In short, the move to the rival came as a shock. The surprise element in part spurred the acceptance of many of the structuring principles described in the prior chapter. For example, the analysis frame principle—go beyond the firm's traditional customer needs-based analysis—indicated that the team understood that the alerting indicator was insufficient to generate a full understanding of the customer's migration decision. Many other indicators of change in and around the customer would have to be identified.

Derivation

The structuring principles and the pursuit of indicators are meaningless unless the team draws inferences, that is, makes judgments about how (change along) the indicators suggest possible change about something or other.

Step 3: Draw immediate inferences

Almost as soon as the announcement was reported, the team began to draw immediate inferences. This shouldn't be a surprise; it's a normal human tendency.[144] The basic question was straightforward: What should they infer from the customer's switch to DipCo's rival? Even before any further data was collected pertaining to the alerting indictor and its context, based on some observations provided by the sales force and some understanding of the customer, two inferences were immediately drawn: the customer perceived some previously unrecognized value in the competitor's offer, and perhaps as a result of miscommunication on the part of the DipCo's senior executives, who had recently visited the customer, a serious misinterpretation of DipCo's commitment to the customer had occurred on the part of some individuals within the customer's organization.[145]

Derivation of preliminary inferences presumes availability of indicators. Thus, the search for additional inferences is always present. The DipCo team, as discussed throughout this case, sought further customer specific indicators including its past behaviors, current performance results, and changes in the management team as well as competitor specific indicators and indicators pertaining to the competitive context.

Step 4: Ask questions pertaining to the indicators and their context

The mind's inclination and capacity to draw inferences, even though the data may be extremely flimsy and the indicators ill-described, means it's no surprise that the analysis team quickly drew the two preliminary inferences just noted. However, that doesn't excuse an individual or team from elaborating and refining key indicators and their context. Remember that understanding change along any indicator depends on understanding the indicator's context.

Two structuring principles adopted by the DipCo team influenced the commitment to understand the context of the alerting indicator and related indicators. The perspective principle—appoint two people to walk in the shoes of the customer (as distinct from DipCo's shoes)—forced consideration of key questions from the customer's vantage point, in effect an intended antidote to the firm's historic way of thinking about customers. The data principle—place no preference on any type of data or any source of data—spurred the team to seek as many types of indicators and as many depictions of the alerting indicator's context as possible. The intent was to avoid falling prey to one or a few data types or data sources and thus bringing the sniffing phase to a premature close and limiting the likelihood of genuine insight.

As soon as deliberation occurred around the alerting indicator, the announcement of the move to the rival, the analysis team asked a set of questions to better understand the indicator: What did the announcement say specifically? Who made the announcement? What was the occasion when the announcement was made? Where was it made?

Answers to these questions could be extremely misleading in the absence of an understanding of the relevant context. Another set of questions addressed the context: What do you know about the customer's business? Was there any prior relationship between the customer and the rival? Did you miss any indicators that might have suggested the customer was dissatisfied with our offer? What was happening in the competitive context that might have influenced the customer's move?

Step 5: Draw preliminary inferences

As data was collected in response to these questions, the structuring focus principle, asking questions suggested by the data as it was collected influenced the flow and volume of preliminary inferences. The deliberation, even at this early stage, was propelled by the rapid fire of inferences stemming from attempts to furnish answers—and at the early stage, preliminary inferences—to the these and many related questions including: Why did the move occur? What had the competitor done to entice the move? How and why was the customer dissatisfied with our firm?

Several inferences were quickly sniffed:[146]

- The competitor has altered its value proposition to meet a specific need articulated by the customer.
- The competitor may be entering a new phase in its strategy—moving to customize its offer across market segments.
- The customer has redefined what it requires in an offer or solution (from any rival).
- The customer may have had a prior relationship with the rival and had been moving toward the rival for some time.

Step 6: Consider if other inferences can be drawn

The temptation to prematurely close off inference derivation is high. Team members conclude they've exhausted the inference possibilities or new indicators aren't readily apparent. Thus, it's always appropriate to ask what other inferences are possible. Two structuring principles fight against premature closure. The imagination principle, make asking what-if questions a core element of moving from data to indicators to suggested inferences, encourages questions that might not otherwise be asked. For example, an individual might ask: what if the customer had a few relationships with the competitor that you didn't know about? The structuring indicator principle, insist on identifying change indicators as a focal point of data collection and reflection, encourages the team to search for change indicators and not just to collect and organize data. Thus, a search of comments from the sales force switches from collating comments into groups to asking what change indicators are embedded in the comments.

The analysis team reflected on the relevance of the competitive context and drew two further inferences:

- The customer may be concerned that some suppliers may pull out of the market entirely and thus it's seeking a contractual relationship with its new supplier;
- The intensity of rivalry among suppliers may have caused the customer to become concerned with the functional quality of the components it might receive from some suppliers in the coming years.

Articulation

The structuring principles push any analysis team to extend the range of preliminary inferences derived. They may also suggest when it's time to stop: the time spent capturing more data and indicators reaches a point of diminishing returns. Articulation, however, involves not only describing and developing a list of preliminary inferences, but also conducting an initial "mental test" or fast and largely informal vetting of individual preliminary inferences.

Step 7: Conduct an initial mental test of the inferences

Each of the generated preliminary inferences at face value may seem plausible. Obviously, all need to be quickly vetted. This isn't the formal vetting that occurs in shaping as discussed in the next chapter.[147] Informal vetting here involves any member of the analysis team subjecting each inference to a rapid mental test: What data and reasoning might support or refute one or more of the preliminary inferences? As they quickly review each preliminary inference, it may be necessary to quickly reword the inference—but not to spend much time on getting the preliminary inference absolutely right.

Step 8: Articulate the preliminary inferences

Finally, as an input to shaping, it's essential to develop a written list of the preliminary inferences and sometimes to develop categories of the inferences—the output of sniffing. The list may seem overwhelming at first glance, but any concerns with the length of the list or with possible redundancies can easily be address in shaping—the focus of the next chapter.

Case: VP

The VP case extends several points in the DipCo case above. Remember that sniffing is an activity that takes place over time.

Perception

Perceiving the opportunity to conduct sniffing often isn't a one-time event. In the VP case, some marketing and other functional professionals quickly noted the business challenge posed by the competitor's shift to a new value proposition and the apparent positive customer responses, but they didn't immediately engage in sniffing. They detected and clarified some specific indicators; yet they didn't derive and articulate preliminary inferences until others became involved in assessing the competitor's intent and actions. Unlike the DipCo case, the benefits of sniffing early preliminary inferences were missed.

Derivation

As noted in the DipCo case, deriving preliminary inferences is propelled as new indicators are captured. The structuring principles detailed in Chapter 3 in the VP case compensated for the absence of a sniffing mind-set: they guided members of the analysis team to extend their purview in both the capture of change indicators and the derivation of preliminary inferences. The elements of a sniffing mind-set evolved as the analysis proceeded: individuals learned the importance of drawing preliminary inferences; they did so as soon as indicators were added to each relevant indicator list (see Figures 2-3, 2-4, 2-5); they saw the merit in mentally testing each preliminary inference (see step 7 in Table 4-3). In short, the practice of formal sniffing sets the stage for the evolution of a sniffing mind-set.

Articulation

Preliminary inferences drawn over time add to the importance of articulating each inference. The analysis team in the VP case, as they saw a sequence of specific preliminary inferences emerge realized how important it was to extend the range of inferences with respect to each key analysis domain— the competitors value proposition, customers' responses, and the competitive context. Team members sensed, even before shaping and stipulating occurred, that they had to reframe their understanding of any competitor's value proposition as well as the interconnections between value propositions and customers' responses.

Sniffing inferences: Beyond single inferences

Viewed as a powerhouse for processing information, involving forms and speeds of computation that you don't yet fully understand, you can appreciate how the brain instantaneously derives indirect inferences, sometimes deriving a range of both direct and indirect inferences at lightning speed, and, most spectacularly, extracts a sequence of inferences. Each of the brain capacities noted in Table 4-2 enables derivation of preliminary inferences that goes way beyond capturing inferences one at a time.

Inferences: Direct and indirect

The power and value of early[148] inferences are enhanced when you recognize that change along an indicator about A often leads to indirect inferences about B and maybe C and D as well. The mind makes these indirect connections, often in ways that surprise, if not shock us. You need to be aware of and nourish this brain capacity. Exposure to the details of indicators and their context serves to enable indirect inferences. In short, the brain establishes connections when it's appropriately fertilized.

Indirect inferences present a particularly difficult analysis conundrum. The unique characteristic of the human mind is its ability to ask what-if questions, to ponder future possibilities that are a distinct break with the past, to imagine what might be both about the present[149] and the future. Thus, the mind is admirably able to draw indirect inferences: to connect change in one context with change in another. The upside for sniffing is the possibility that indirect inferences that may seem particularly weak or speculative, that is, without an evident rationale, prove highly productive: they initiate a line of inquiry that leads to new understanding. Consider this case that I encountered a few years ago:

A business analyst sitting in a trade show auditorium hears the VP of a major rival make the following statement (the indicator): "My company might be compelled to do an acquisition in the next eighteen months, something we have never previously done." She immediately drew an indirect inference: "Within three years, the dynamics of rivalry in our largest product-customer space could be altered greatly (with possible dire consequences for our current strategy)." She took the indirect inference to her VP of strategy. Between them they developed the business case for what the competitor might be able to do if it did an acquisition of one or other of two specific rivals. They took their analysis to the executive committee. It heavily influenced the firm's decision to do an acquisition of its own.

The downside for sniffing as an influence on later stages of analysis and insight work is that individuals derive indirect inferences that data and reasoning could never support; they're flights of imaginative, and perhaps even, naïve minds. The good news is that the sniffing steps noted in Table 4-3 are designed to detect and eliminate such indirect inferences. The "mental test" or very early, largely informal, assessment of individual inferences provides an opportunity to weed out, at a minimum, the most egregious culprits.

The importance of context

The indirect inference conundrum reinforces the importance of understanding an indicator's details and its context. For example, it's not possible to draw plausible indirect inferences about customers' potential responses to the launch of a substitute product without an understanding of the "fit" of the product in customers' operations, the customer pain point or challenge the product would resolve, and customers' ability to purchase the product. In short, the more an individual or team knows about the relevant context, the faster they can derive indirect (and direct) preliminary inferences and the more plausible they're likely to be.

The ubiquity and importance of indirect inferences

The opportunity to derive indirect inferences occurs far more frequently than you might realize.

Trends

Indirect inferences occur at the level of individual trends—the most basic unit of analysis. Change in a trend, that is, change along an indicator, frequently leads to an inference about the future direction of the trend—a classic example of a direct inference. For example, a downturn in overall sales in a specific customer segment might lead to a quick preliminary inference that sales will remain relatively stagnant or increase or decline depending upon the individual's expectations about change in the competitive context of the customer segment. However, in terms of understanding change, the value of capturing deviation in a trend is more likely to reside in indirect inferences: it potentially informs us of change in areas other than the domain of the trend. Thus, the sales downturn in a customer segment might lead to inferences about change in current and potential competitive dynamics (for example, some rivals will resort to reducing prices; others will augment product features), explanations of customers' behaviors (for example, some customers are awaiting a new product entry) or the potential emergence of a superior product (for example, a specific new entrant is bringing a product with superior performance to the market).

Within domains

Preliminary indirect inferences dominate analysis within individual domains (see Figure 1-1). For example, change reflected in a competitor's imminent

R&D announcement (for example, it's confirming an R&D breakthrough) leads to indirect inferences about the competitor's new product launch time, shifts in its marketing and sales strategy, where and how it might do manufacturing, and the talent that might be required.

Across domains

It's perhaps even more important on many occasions for an individual to ask what an indicator change might mean for other domains. Impending regulatory change may allow the analyst to draw immediate preliminary inferences about the actions of specific competitors, likely development in the political arena, or the evolution of technology change. Change in a competitor's value proposition frequently affords the ability to draw inferences about customers' needs.

Patterns

Strong indirect inferences often emanate from patterns across indicator trends both within and across domains. Multiple trends around the consumer behaviors of millennials domiciled in cities might allow indirect inferences to be drawn about their automobile purchasing and use behaviors. Trends across domains suggesting a pattern in voting behaviors might allow indirect inferences about cases that might be brought before the courts or investments in different types of physical infrastructure.

Discontinuities

Inferences that might be the source of eventual insights frequently stem from discontinuities. A Supreme Court reversal of a lower court decision almost always enables indirect inferences about potential change in one or many other domains—political, social, regulatory, technological, economic, ecological—depending upon the issue and decision. A sudden and rapid downturn in a competitor's sales in a specific product line often leads to indirect inference about customers' purchasing behaviors, technology developments in a related product domain, or imminent change in specific regulatory rules.

Indirect inferences need to be vetted: the reasoning that underpins the linkage from the indicator change to the inference must be carefully explicated and tested. So it's important to clearly articulate indirect inferences.

A range of inferences

Sniffing loses some of its potential value when individuals or a team suspend it too quickly; they're comfortable having derived one or a few preliminary inferences. As many of the examples above illustrate, sniffing, by its very nature, often leads to multiple indirect and direct inferences. Indeed, in many instances, it leads to a surprising range of quickly derived inferences. Again, indirect inferences need to be especially encouraged. Consider the following:

In structuring data around an impending vote in any governmental (federal, state, or local) assembly or administrative or regulatory agency, you could draw direct inferences with respect to the governmental domain (for example, who may influence the outcome, whether the vote will follow party lines, how individuals might vote, and why they might vote one way rather than another), indirect inferences with respect to the governmental domain (for example, how the vote outcome might affect other impending votes, how it might bring new issues on the agenda), and indirect inferences pertaining to other domains (for example, judicial decisions the vote might ultimately give rise to, consequences for business affected by the vote).

Given a sniffing mind-set, your mind goes on automatic pilot in the derivation of these inferences as data accumulates, as events unfold, as conditions change. You aim to gain a sense of what may happen and why, that is, how the vote may turn out, rather than wait for it to happen.[150]

A sequence of inferences

The marvel and ingenuity of the human brain is best exemplified in its capacity to craft a sequence of interdependent inferences in the form of: if A then B, if B then C, if C then D, etc.[151] The competitor domain frequently serves as the source of an extensive preliminary inference sequence.

Returning to the impending competitor R&D announcement noted above, the sniffed inference that the competitor is about to announce a technology breakthrough could immediately lead to a string of interdependent preliminary inferences: the technology breakthrough will lead to new manufacturing plant requirements which in turn will lead to new supplier commitments and in turn to some new talent acquisition. The combination of these and related preliminary inferences could give rise to inferences focused on other domains: inferences about potential new customers coming into the market that might in turf influence the long-term actions of current rivals that might affect how they manage their near-term strategy in the existing marketplace. The analysis team night then draws further preliminary inferences suggesting the potential to reshape the competitive space (a potential CSI in the language of Chapters 1 and 2); the CSI in turn might be quickly judged to possibly translate into a major risk for most existing rivals (a GMI as discussed in Chapters 1 and 2) that would then give rise to the inference that some current leading rivals might have little option to craft a significant shift in their historic strategy.

A sequence of interdependent direct and indirect inferences illustrates the importance of articulating the interconnections—the third act in sniffing discussed earlier—so that they can be informally and formally vetted.[152]

Connecting to the insight funnel

Sniffing is relevant to each transition in the insight funnel (see Figure 1-2). As noted in the discussion of a sequence of inferences above, the human mind can quickly sniff inferences that result in CSIs (competitive space inferences) and GMIs (generic marketplace inferences) and even all the way to implication insights and ultimately to business implications. Indeed, it's the capacity to draw indirect inferences that enables the rapid identification of possible CSIs or GMIs. Following are some examples:[153]

Domain to CSIs

A pattern in a set of preliminary customer inferences often leads individuals to jump to a CSI, for example, an inference about a potential discontinuity in the growth rate of a specific product market or market segment. An announcement of a new manufacturing technology or of one competitor's intention to pull out of a specific region may give rise to rapidly derived indirect inferences about likely shifts in competitive rivalry and intensity.

Domain to GMIs

Early preliminary inferences about potential change in a competitor's strategy may quickly give rise to an indirect GMI, for example, an inference about the likely diminution of a projected marketplace opportunity.

CSIs to GMIs

In the VP case in Chapter 2, early deliberations in the development of the eventual CSI, strategy will need to be based on multiple dimensions of value; it will transform which rivals win and which lose; some won't be able to make the transition, led to preliminary inferences suggesting that key long-held assumptions about the marketplace and what was required to win in the marketplace would need to change significantly.

GMIs to implication insights

The team can jump, almost instantaneously, in deliberations about GMIs to preliminary inferences about implication insights. Early efforts to describe emerging marketplace opportunities or strategy vulnerabilities lead to rapid preliminary inferences about whether specific opportunities might be relevant to the firm or whether the firm's current strategy might be subject to the newly detected vulnerabilities.

Again, it's important to note that these are preliminary inferences. They may not stand the scrutiny that will be detailed in the next section. Thus, they can't be the basis for decisions and action—they're but the preliminary inferences drawn as data is collected or accessed and somehow quickly structured.

Sniffing and the 6IFs

The 6IFs can be used as a diagnostic to assess the presence or absence of a sniffing mind-set. If individuals or a team don't see that sniffing enables new points of view, don't intend to encourage others to engage in sniffing, and don't act to derive and articulate multiple inferences, it's hard to argue that a sniffing mind-set prevails. If a team doesn't see the value of extracting multiple inferences from one or more indicators or doesn't want to think about the connections generated by indirect inferences or shows little intent to seek sniffing opportunities, it's unlikely to act to execute the sniffing method.

Even in the absence of a sniffing mind-set, the 6IFs can be used to test the readiness of an individual or group to engage in sniffing. Questions can be asked about different facets of sniffing along each IF to assess whether individuals or a team are likely to engage in sniffing as one component in crafting insight (Table 4-4). For example, in one case, some individuals proved highly resistant to drawing and considering indirect inferences; they wanted only to draw inferences where the connecting logic was foolproof. In another case, I found that some individuals didn't believe it was fruitful to map out a sequence of inferences or to seek indicators that might lead to non-obvious inferences or inferences that might raise questions about the firm's major resource commitments. These individuals were only prepared to conduct limited sniffing.

Table 4-4   Linking Sniffing to the 6IFs

6IFs	Input to sniffing	Output of sniffing
See	Sense a sniffing opportunity. Recognize the potential value of how sniffing may enable seeing things very differently. Recognize the importance of patterns as a source of inferences.	See the need to extend the range of indicators. Understand how current change can be a precursor of emerging and future change. Realize the need to reassess long-held elements of the prevailing mental model.
Think	Extract indirect inferences. Tease out sequences of direct and indirect inferences. Think differently given new data or change along an indicator.	Address new linkages among indicators. Focus on new change elements. Ask new questions about change. Push for non-obvious inferences.
Intend	Commit to sniffing as a mind-set. Encourage others to engage in sniffing. Be serious about testing your own sniffing capabilities.	Invest time and attention to going beyond preliminary inferences. Develop sniffing skills and capabilities.

Decide	Determine that sniffing is important and make time to do it. Extract inferences where possible. Articulate inferences so that others can test the underlying reasoning.	Commit resources to leveraging sniffing's outputs. Create formal settings to generate and integrate preliminary inferences.
Act	Actively seek sniffing opportunities. Extract more than one inference. Search for indirect inferences. Map out sequences of inferences. Ask others to assess inferences.	Learn about sniffing errors and how to avoid them. Engage with others to discuss and test preliminary inferences.
Feel	Manage emotions so that you feel positive about drawing and testing preliminary inferences.	Feel positive about inferencing process. Reflect on how emotions influence each step in sniffing.

The diagnostic results provide guidance for what is required to inspire a sniffing mind-set and motivate a commitment to adopting the sniffing method (which will be addressed in the next section).

As in structuring, once a team develops some experience with the sniffing method, the 6IFs provide a means to assess the output side of sniffing. From the vantage point of institutionalizing insight work, three assessment criteria merit special attention. First, skills and knowledge: do individuals intend to invest some time in honing their sniffing abilities and decide how to do so? Second, deliberations: does the team use the outputs of sniffing—preliminary inferences, sequences among inferences—as an explicit means to drive dialogue so that they think and act in new ways? Third ongoing learning: do individuals, and maybe teams, commit to reviewing how they act: learning from each sniffing activity and from applying the sniffing method in an insight project? For example, do they create formal settings to review how sniffing might be enhanced—in particular, identifying and eliminating errors that have crept into executing the method?

Sniffing: Role and importance

Sniffing's role and importance in insight work can hardly be overstated. If you fail to advocate and support sniffing as a mind-set, as a recognized and persistent practice, the pathway to insight is greatly inhibited. Consider the common example of executives who visit customers, engage in deep and wide-ranging conversations that cover many critical aspects of the supplier-customer relationship but who don't actively sniff for inferences about latent or emerging customer needs or likely reactions to products about to reach the market. Without question, the potential implications of many statements and observations of the customer's personnel will be missed. Even those that are noted won't be assessed for their importance and consequences. The value of the customer visit is significantly short-changed.

Sniffing reminds us that structuring isn't the end; structuring facilitates and affords an opportunity for sniffing. Sniffing (and structuring) helps set up the subsequent 4S activities; the intent isn't to obtain the perfect data configuration.

Sniffing emphasizes the importance of not waiting until the data have been fully structured before embarking on inference derivation. Doing so delays inference extraction. Perhaps, even more importantly, it may lead to data structuring assuming attention and importance beyond any reasonable expectation of a commensurate return in insight value. This is a common error in organizations that have become fixated on getting the highest possible "quality" data, data from the widest array of sources, and especially, data with the highest degree of accuracy.

Once you initiate sniffing, early preliminary inferences, no matter how tentative, often suggest the need to refine or extend structuring. Thus, structuring the analysis context components takes on a different direction than would otherwise be the case. In the DipCo case discussed above, the first preliminary inferences led the analysis team to scope and focus the analysis differently: understanding of the competitor became just as important, if not more so, than understanding the customer—the team recognized that the context of the customer's decision had to include the competitor and the broader competitive context.

Sniffing: Avoiding some key errors

Sniffing as a mind-set and practice doesn't come easily to individuals work-ing in organizational cultures dominated by complete-the-template fixations or reporting to superiors who demand fast answers. Thus, the sniffing errors noted in Table 4-5 should not be surprising. Recognizing and preempting these errors contributes greatly to more efficient and effective sniffing. I emphasize here some errors that reflect the vital importance of sniffing to insight work.

Table 4-5   Fundamental Sniffing Errors

Perception

- Denying the need for sniffing as a mind-set: "I'll recognize the oppor-tunity for sniffing when it presents itself."
- Devoting little time to structuring the data and the context: "It's pretty obvious what this situation is; there's no need to look at the data from multiple vantage points."
- Ignoring other available indicators: "The other data/indicators won't tell us anything new."

Derivation

- Delaying sniffing until all or most data are collected, organized, and synthesized: "I'll be in a better position to draw the 'right' inference once I have all the data."
- Remaining within one conceptual frame or perspective: "There's no need to draw inferences about anything other than marketing."

Articulation

- Not articulating and refining the immediate inference (especially if it's perceived as a potential contributor to a valuable insight): "I've got it; I'll remember it; I know what it is."
- Locking in too quickly on one inference: "This is the key inference that can be drawn from this data or data set."

Perception

Individuals who appreciate the role and importance of sniffing sometimes fail to actively seek sniffing opportunities: in short, they limit the deliberations that sniffing is intended to generate. Even some individuals in the DipCo case initially didn't see the value in focusing on the competitor as a source of valuable learning.

Derivation

Insight as new understanding of change that makes a difference frequently challenges individuals' and the organization's prevailing mind-sets.[154] If these mind-sets prove unshakable, sniffing countervailing inferences—even at a very preliminary level—and engaging in deliberations about them is unlikely to occur. Thus, a grievous sniffing error occurs when individuals perceive that an inference runs counter to the embedded mind-sets and decide not to articulate and circulate it to others for comment.[155] In one case, two individuals didn't state the inference that at least some customers appeared to value service as the most important differentiating factor because the senior management team had declared that service was not a significant factor in customers' purchasing criteria.

Drawing only one inference from a single or set of indicators sometimes stultifies the sniffing activity; often it's the second or third preliminary inference that sparks the pathway to a novel integrated inference or insight. Here's where having more than one individual charged with drawing preliminary inferences from an indicator or range of indicators validates the purpose of structuring: changing the scope or focus or perspective can lead to different inferences.

Another common error is to lock in on and accept a preliminary inference before it's informally vetted either as a single inference or in the context of other inferences. Even though the inference may be accurate, it may not be important in helping explain a specific marketplace change. For example, an individual may lock in on an inference that a set of customers rated very highly a product's functionality but if that product is about to be made obsolete by a new product, the inference is likely to have little value.

Articulation

Deliberations about emerging and potential marketplace change often prove short-lived or may not even happen when preliminary inferences aren't fully articulated. A preliminary inference that a corporate customer is likely to be sold by its corporate parent or that consumers are getting critical product data from an ill-informed social media source if it's not articulated and circulated to members of the analysis team and others, can't give rise to deliberations about its validly and business implications.

Enhancing your sniffing capability

Look around your organizational function or unit and maybe even the broader organization and ask yourself the following three questions: How much attention is paid to extracting full value from indicator change? Who is a good role model of sniffing? How do you rate yourself as a Sniffer? Based on my experience across different types of organizations, I suspect your answers indicate that a dedicated effort is required to enhance the organization's sniffing capability. Here's an overview of the method designed to build sniffing capability:

Assess current state of sniffing

Determine whether and to what extent sniffing is deployed in analysis projects. Ask individuals pointed questions about each step in the sniffing method. For example: Do they clarify the context of indicators? Do they actively search for additional indicators? Do they move quickly to derive preliminary inferences? Do they do a fast mental-test of some preliminary inferences? Do they articulate and catalogue the inferences?

Deploy the 6IFs

Use the 6IFs in the case of individual analysis teams. Again, ask pointed questions about specific aspects of sniffing (Table 4-4). For example, do individuals see the value of sniffing? Do they derive preliminary inferences from so that they can think about questions about customers and competitors? Do they deliberate about the role of sniffing so that they can develop new sniffing intent? If they've been involved in sniffing, how do they feel about the sniffing experience? The IF-inspired questions quickly paint a picture of any team's understanding and practice of sniffing.

Develop a sniffing tutorial

If the team doesn't see the importance of sniffing as a source of the inferences required to stimulate and fuel the insight process and don't know how to act to conduct sniffing, it suggests the need for some form of tutorial on what sniffing is all about. It addresses: the purpose of sniffing; the sequence of steps in the sniffing method (Table 4-3), the types of deliberations it generates, and how to avoid typical sniffing errors. Even a one-hour session, using a set of sniffing examples, educates an analysis team about key do's and don'ts in the execution of the sniffing method.

Diagnosis: Are you a sniffer?

Ultimately, sniffing is something each individual executes. So it's appropriate to engage in self-assessment—how effective are you as a sniffer? Asking and answering the questions listed in Table 4-6 will help you quickly judge where you may be strong or weak in the three sniffing acts.

Table 4-6   Are You a Sniffer?

Perception

- Do you think about what it means to be a sniffer?
- Do you look for sniffing opportunities in your day-to-day work?
- Do you seek out sniffing opportunities that wouldn't typically occur in your daily activity?
- Do you search for a variety of indicators specific to a topic, or issue or challenge?
- Do you engage others in deliberations about the need to identify sniffing opportunities?

Derivation

- Do you immediately draw one or more preliminary inferences?
- Do you pay attention to indirect inferences?
- Do you develop a sequence of inferences?
- Do you look for a pattern in your inferences?
- Do you do a quick "mental-test" of preliminary inferences that seem important?
- Do you involve others in deliberations about the preliminary inferences you derive?

Articulation

- Do you pay attention to articulating the preliminary inference?
- Do you articulate it in different ways?
- Do you ask others to challenge the preliminary inference?

Enhance personal sniffing skills

A sniffing self-assessment typically identifies sniffing deficiencies that need to be remedied. Some suggestions to enhance desired sniffing skills (Table 4-7) involve both critical self-reflection and the judgments of colleagues. One useful approach: take an analysis project, map what you did (or didn't do) along the sniffing method steps, and then assess how well or poorly you performed each step. Then be careful to determine what you need to do to enhance your performance. For example, if you didn't search for indicators beyond those traditionally used by the analysis team or the organization, identify how you could do so. If you typically only derived inferences about specific topics or entities, for example customers or technology, consider how you might extend the scope of your preliminary inferences.

Table 4-7   Ways to Improve Your Sniffing Skills

Perception

Identify a current analysis project you're involved in and answer the following questions:

- Can you determine where are the sniffing opportunities?
- Can you see how sniffing could add value?
- Do you check with others to determine if you missed some sniffing opportunities?
- Learn about key perception errors and how to avoid them (Table 4-5)

Derivation

- Choose an indicator: What types of inferences can you draw from it?
- How quickly could you derive the inferences?
- Can you derive inferences about other topics or entities?
- Can you observe any patterns across the inferences?

- Can you see possible conflicts in the inferences?
- Check with others to see what inferences they might draw from the indicator.
- Did you miss any inferences? Why?
- What would you need to learn about the business and its competitive context to be able to draw new inferences? Better understanding of customers, competitors, and marketplace dynamics?
- Learn about key derivation errors and how to avoid them (Table 4-5).

Articulation

- Can you quickly articulate an inference and put it on paper?
- Do you revisit the written inference as you learn more about the context?
- Ask others if an inference can be better stated?
- Learn about key derivation errors and how to avoid them (Table 4-5).

Avoid sniffing errors

Knowing and avoiding common sniffing errors (Table 4-5) reinforces the actions that stem from self-assessment and the commitment to enhance your sniffing skills. For example, if you know that sniffing should not be postponed until the late stages of data gathering, then you'll likely begin deriving preliminary inferences as soon as data becomes available.

Institutionalizing sniffing in projects

Assuming one or more members of an analysis team have been through the steps just noted, as data is gathered and indicators are noted or crafted,[156] sniffing is executed. Individuals recognize the opportunity for sniffing, derive preliminary inferences, and articulate them as one of the early stages of any analysis project. As individuals gain experience in sniffing, it's executed automatically.

A final comment

Sniffing embodies the movement from indicators to inferences. It challenges the mind to see and think about change that may not be immediately evident in the indicators. The sniffing method provides a set of analysis steps that can be deployed with respect to one or many indicators. The output often entails a laundry list of preliminary inferences that then become the fodder for shaping one or more insights—the topic of the next chapter.

Notes

134. This is in part because insight is viewed as a single act in which an individual goes instantaneously from an indicator to the insight, as discussed in Chapter 2. Viewed from this vantage point, sniffing isn't necessary to generate preliminary inferences.

135. These three acts serve as another illustration of the deliberative and methodical nature of *insighting*: people commit to executing a set of steps (the method) to get from data to insight and the deliberations that take place as the method is executed.

136. Steven Pinker, *How the Mind Works* (New York, W.W. Norton and Company, 1997).

137. Philosophers of science as well as many neuroscientists have emphasized this point. For an early influential discussion of this point, see, Patricia Smith Churchland, *Neurophilosophy: Toward a Unified Science of the Mind-Brain*, (Cambridge, MA: MIT Press, 1986).

138. Nicholas Rescher, *A System of Pragmatic Idealism, Volume 1: Human Knowledge in Idealistic Perspective* (Princeton: Princeton University Press, 1992).

139. In Chapter 1, we noted congruency with the external world as one of the critical desired attributes of any insight.

140. Win-loss analysis is a common process employed by business firms to assess why they won or lost one or more customers against rivals.

141. This observation constitutes a key input to shaping insights (addressed in the next chapter) and most likely to determining business implications (addressed in Chapters 7 and 8).

142. For a good discussion of Competitive Gaming, see, Mark Chussil, "Learning Faster Than the Competition: War Games Give the Advantage," *The Journal of Business Strategy* (January/February 2007).

143. Again, DipCo is a pseudonym.

144. Neuroscience and many streams in philosophy assert that drawing inferences is an automatic function of our brains/minds.

145. These inferences are good examples of the speculative nature of many preliminary inferences and why such inferences need to be vetted against the available data and the reasoning that connects the data and the inference.

146. The differences between these inferences and two preliminary inferences just noted are attributable to the learning that resulted from investigation of the indicator and its context. Thus, the additional data and the discussion among the team members allowed more solid inferences to be drawn, that is, they're better supported by data and reasoning. These inferences could of course be subjected to the vetting that is discussed later in this chapter.

147. The form of fast mental vetting should not be confused with the formal vetting of integrated inferences and suggested insights described in Chapter 5.

148. Early here means not just the first in a sequence of inferences. It also means the inferences that are derived from alerting indicators, as discussed in Chapter 2.

149. It's not outlandish to consider the mind imagining what is going on now. For example, it might be imagining what might be the causes of an entity's current actions or statements.

150. Considering how and why the vote might turn out and what its consequences might be is a classic example of the mind's capacity to invoke possible futures, one of the mind's capacities noted in Table 5-2.

151. Drawing indirect inferences connects directly to the discussion of indirect indicators in Chapter 3.

152. Preliminary inferences are informally vetted as part of sniffing (see Table 4-1). Vetting as a formal process takes place as part of shaping described in Chapter 5.

153. Examples of the power of sniffing along the insight funnel (see Figure 1-2) are also evident in the discussion of shaping in the Chapter 5.

154. If individuals or teams are unwilling to see and think differently (two of the 6IF's described in Chapter 1) then the prevailing mind-sets are less likely to be challenged.

155. The importance of deriving, articulated and circulating such preliminary inferences as a factor in establishing an insight culture is addressed in Chapter 10.

156. Indicators are not just captured or collected. sometimes they're crafted—they're the output of analysis. For example, a competitor's annual cash flow is a powerful indicator from which many types of inferences might be derived. However, the cash flow needs to be calculated.

Chapter 5

Shaping: Crafting Change Insight

The deliberative side of insight work is perhaps best exemplified in the transition from sniffing's outputs to some form of change insight. Because of the analysis back and forth as well as the interpersonal ebb and flow, many pathways from preliminary inferences to insight are possible. Allowing a contentious and protracted pathway flies in the face of timely decision making. However, allowing a pathway that moves too quickly likely results in lower quality insight. Hence, a deliberative and methodical approach becomes mandatory. The method entailed in moving from preliminary inferences to integrated inferences to suggested insights briefly discussed in the VP case in Chapter 2 requires active management, what I call "shaping the insight."

This chapter details the steps at the heart of the shaping method, illustrates how they're interrelated, indicates the role of deliberations, and specifies what an organization needs to do to enhance its shaping capability. I'll illustrate the steps using the DipCo case addressed in the previous chapter, the VP case, as well as what I'll call the Gorilla Competitor case.

Shaping change insights: Deliberations and methods

The two pillars of the insight discipline, deliberations and methods, intertwine and fuel shaping and its outputs, tentative insights. The analysis method, summarized in Table 5-1, guides you through the analysis back and forth required to get from preliminary inferences to suggested insights. Each of these steps was touched on in the VP case. The method's intent is to greatly enhance the likelihood that quality insights emerge that can't be observed in the raw data or the preliminary inferences. Following these steps helps ensure that the analysis effort isn't short-circuited in the interests of meeting an arbitrary deadline or sabotaged by individual team members' intent on having their point of view prevail.

Table 5-1 Shaping: Key Steps

Because of the analysis back and forth and the interpersonal ebb and flow, many pathways from preliminary inferences to insight are possible. Yet several steps are likely to be evident in any insight pathway that requires some time to complete:

Refine understanding of indicators and context

> Step 1: Refine understanding of the context.

> Step 2: Identify critical new data points and indicators, leading to new inferences.

Work toward integrated inferences

> Step 3: Categorize preliminary inferences.

> Step 4: Look for connections within and across the categories.

> Step 5: Develop initial integrated inferences.

> Step 6: Vet initial integrated inferences.

> Step 7: Condense and refine initial integrated inferences into suggested integrated inferences.

Work toward suggested insights

> Step 8: Vet suggested integrated inferences.

> Step 9: Integrate suggested integrated inferences into suggested insights.

> Step 10: Vet and transform into suggested insights.

Analysis back and forth

The VP case illustrates that getting from preliminary inferences to a tentative insight involves many twists and turns. Analysis back and forth is thus not incidental; it's a natural outcome of the steps involved in getting from a set of preliminary inferences to a suggested insight: as individuals learn more about the insight context, their judgments shift and the points of view they advocate change. So it's worth noting why analysis back and forth along the steps noted in Table 5-1 characterizes the pathway to tentative and accepted[157] insights.

Interpersonal ebb and flow

The analysis back and forth causes and is, in part, driven by a related dynamic: the interpersonal "ebb and flow" that characterizes the interactions among those involved in the transitions toward an insight. Given the differences in interpretation and judgment that typically arise among individuals along the analysis steps, it should not be a surprise that significant interpersonal ebb and flow becomes evident in the deliberations. The analysis method summarized in Table 5-1 by itself doesn't reveal or explain the dynamics of the deliberations.

Individual members of an analysis team react to each other's suggested and refined preliminary inferences, inference categories, integrated inferences, and initial assertions of potential insights. Differences of opinion are likely to arise as individuals advance and advocate for their interpretations and judgments that lie at the heart of any suggested inference.[158] And, it's important to recognize that some degree of tension among different viewpoints is desirable and hopefully creates a degree of creative turbulence;[159] it forces individuals to challenge each other's interpretations and to seek higher level inferences—the transition from preliminary to integrated inferences or insights.

The interpersonal ebb and flow also arises for several reasons, many of which can be directly connected to execution of the shaping steps outlined in Table 5-1:

- Team members may have a different shaping intent: some may wish to complete the analysis process quickly, while others are willing to spend as much time as required to fully understand the context (step 1).
- Some "dig their heels in" in support of their preferred preliminary inferences, indicators (step 2), or suggested integrated inferences (step 7), and thus are reluctant to hear countervailing arguments.
- Often people don't respect or trust the judgments of others, so they directly or inadvertently cause clashes that often have little to do with specific inference categories (step 3) or with shaping as a whole (all the steps in Table 5-1).
- Something as apparently straightforward as categorizing preliminary inferences (step 3) or offering connections within and across categories (step 4) provokes intense responses from others who see it differently.

- As individuals advance initial integrated inferences (step 8), suggested insights (step 9), and tentative insights (step 10) disagreements burst into the open;[160] resolving the differences often takes significant time.

Multiple potential pathways in shaping

Because of the analysis back and forth and the interpersonal ebb and flow, many pathways are possible through the shaping method (the steps noted in Table 5-1). It's always difficult to anticipate what the pathway will be. Moving along the pathway is hard work: it requires extensive reflection and judgment; it demands doggedness in pursuing the analysis to get to what seems to be an insight that builds upon the inference set. It requires immersion in the data and inferences.[161] Rarely will a suggested integrated inference or suggested insight be self-evident; rarely will it be stated first time in a way that doesn't require later change. In short, as with structuring and sniffing, you need to prepare the mind for shaping.

Preparing the mind for shaping: Reasoning

The deliberations along each shaping step involve data and reasoning. These two facets of the brain's computations are extremely difficult to unravel and separate.[162] Yet the mind must somehow work on its inputs, irrespective of the form they take, to compute or create some outputs, including inferences and insights. Some form of reasoning lies at the heart of the judgments involved in each shaping step. It enables the inferences that go beyond what is evident in the data. Most reasoning resides at the tacit level:[163] people are unaware of how they reason or why they reason in specific ways. Although, we don't know precisely how the brain reasons, we can identify several reasoning principles[164] and their specific implications for how to manage deliberations during the shaping steps noted in Table 5-2.

The reasoning principles noted in Table 5-2 compel you to recognize that there's no one best way to reason, that is, to develop an argument that supports asserting the presence of a specific category of inferences or drawing a tentative integrated inference or one of the small set of suggested insights. No analysis or other rules are available to us to claim that we have used the best mode of reasoning.[165] The shaping implications are clear: don't privilege one mode of analysis over others and, to the extent possible, identify the critical judgments underpinning any proposed inference or insight and the argument

Table 5-2   Reasoning Principles

Reasoning principles	Rationale for principle	Shaping principles and practices
Reasoning often defies (easy) retrospective articulation.	Only five percent of the mind's work is at the conscious level. You're unaware of what the mind is thinking about and how it's thinking.	We don't know when an "integrated inference" or insight will hit us. We need to mull over data (indicator change) and subject any inference to multiple forms of argument (reasoning).
Intuition is often the spark that ignites reasoning.	Intuition is the mind's subconscious at work; the brain on automatic pilot detects linkages (patterns) that generates (instant) inferences.	Encourage intuition as the brain's functioning to generate all forms of inferences. Subject the mind to many "cues" (indicator change) as a mean to spurring inferences of all types. Build "memory" as the understanding of context as an aid to inference generation.
Reasoning is always infiltrated by biases.	The mind isn't a blank slate. How the mind computes (reasons) is influenced by many factors.	Be attentive to your own biases Identify personal and organizational biases. That may be influencing why an individual or a team or a team is advocating specific integrated inferences of suggested insights.
Reasoning involves the need for (immediate) testing and refinement.	The logic or argument at the heart of reasoning may be filled with unidentified flaws.	All inferences (no matter the level) must be regarded as tentative and thus necessitating critique.

Reasoning has no "one best way".	Inviolable rules that lead to one best way of reasoning simply don't exist.	Develop clear explicit arguments (modes of reasoning) to assess the "reasons" underpinning the judgment(s) at the heart of an inference or suggested insight.
Reasoning allows no one individual to be privileged.	In the face of dynamic and complex change, no one individual can claim a privileged status for his/her conception of how the future may unfold.	Ensure that individuals with differing "mental models" are allowed to develop alternative and maybe even competing inferences and insights Ask individuals or teams to provide the reasons (judgments) supporting their judgments.
Reasoning can't be separated from emotions.	Emotions are hardwired into your brain; thus, emotions influence reasoning in many ways (and often in ways we don't realize).	Identify and assess how emotions influence all facets of analysis (the data we emphasize, the data sources we use, the types of reasoning we employ and deprecate, whose judgments we support and oppose, the types of inferences we propose and oppose).
Reasoning often leads to conceptual innovation (new descriptions and explanations).	The mind's models, theories, frameworks, concepts, etc. are open to change; thus, new descriptions and explanations are possible.	Encourage individuals to develop ways of "seeing" and "thinking" that are clearly different than prior ways of doing so. Request individuals to articulate new connections among trends, new patterns, new descriptions of what the future might be, new explanations (as a way to test unstated reasoning and implicit judgments).

Reasoning is never-ending.	Change in and around the marketplace never ceases.	Insist the shaping's outputs are always regarded as subject to change over time.
Reasoning often doesn't generate one best (dominant) inference.	Given the complexity of a competitive and organizational context at any point in time, it's unlikely that reasoning will generate an inference or insight that totally dominates all others.	Encourage all involved in shaping at every step in analysis to generate multiple outputs. Ensure that the inevitable haste to complete the analysis doesn't lead to a premature acceptance of one integrated inference or suggested insight as "obviously" correct. Insist that all suggested insights are fully vetted.
Reasoning and its outcomes change over time.	As the mind absorbs new inputs, it develops new modes of computation.	Over time, it's probably necessary to intentionally develop new modes of analysis—new ways of executing each step in the shaping method.

(line of reasoning) supporting each judgment. In this way, others can see the reasoning and assess it.

The absence of one best way of reasoning adds to the importance of recognizing that only five percent of the mind's reasoning is at the conscious level; we're simply unaware of what the mind is thinking about and how it's thinking (reasoning). Thus, we need to stimulate the mind to "let it go to work." Although an inference (at the heart of an insight) may occur at an instance, getting to that instance may take time.[166] In short, we will cycle back and forth on a convoluted and tortured path through data and reasoning.[167] The shaping implications are clear: we need to organize "data" to draw inferences, mull over the inferences, subject them to multiple forms of reasoning, and in some cases, to directly opposite or at least, conflicting modes of argument (reasoning). We're preparing ourselves to reach that instance—that aha moment—even though you don't know when it will arrive, that is, when it will "hit" you. And, amazingly, at the end of it, when the aha moment occurs, you won't be able to describe how you got there—the mental path that landed you with the aha moment.[168]

The predominantly tacit nature of how the brain works implies that intuition is often the spark that ignites reasoning:[169] the brain on automatic pilot detects linkages (patterns) that generates (instant) inferences. Intuition can be viewed as a process, a distinctive aspect of the brain as a computation machine.[170] Most authors, broadly speaking, see the brain picking up some form of a cue (for example, a data point or indicator) that sparks the mind to see a connection or a pattern.[171]

The link between the cue and connection or pattern is aided by what is stored in memory; it enables us to know without knowing why we know.[172] Thus, you intuit inferences; stated differently, inferences reside at the heart of intuition. In fact, intuiting inferences (inferences as the output of intuition) is a fundamental staple of mental life.[173] The shaping implications are clear: you have to subject your mind to many indicators of change so that it builds a memory of the relevant context and can thereby aid in deriving inferences and insights that otherwise wouldn't occur.[174]

The relevance and importance of intuition as an initiator and driver of reasoning reinforces the need to recognize that the mind isn't a blank slate: reasoning is always infiltrated by cognitive biases[175] and organizational biases.[176] It's now well established in the neuroscience, psychology, and behavioral economics that human reasoning, or more broadly, how we make sense, is subject to many biases.[177] The computations performed by the brain don't follow the stipulations of the philosopher's analytic logic or the rationality theorems of economic or decision science. A number of the more dominant cognitive biases and their implications for reasoning are noted in Table 5-3. The shaping implications are clear: the unavoidability of these cognitive biases reinforces the need to treat preliminary and higher-level inferences and any suggested insights as especially provisional.[178] It also argues for the inclusion of people who bring different mental models[179] in the shaping steps and to enable them to openly challenge the dominant reasoning that may be evident in each phase of vetting, as described later in this chapter.

The collective mind of an analysis team also needs to recognize that reasoning is never-ending and that often it doesn't generate one best or dominant inference or insight. Change in and around the marketplace never ceases. Given neverending external change, interpretations of the change in

Table 5-3   Cognitive Biases: Influencing How the Mind Works

Bias type	Description	Implication for reasoning	Implications for shaping
Confirmation bias	The search for data and information to confirm your preliminary inference or insight.	Counterinferences aren't a focus of attention.	Ensure that counterarguments are used in vetting inferences and insights.
Recency Bias	Recently seen data is given priority.	Reasoning is unduly influenced by data most recently seen.	Ensure the "older" data are brought to bear in drawing inferences and insights.
Hindsight bias	Reframe your opinions to enable you to say, "I knew it all along."	Don't ask the fundamental questions that could give reasoning a very different focus.	Challenge the judgments underpinning suggested inferences and insights.
Framing bias	How you frame an issue or situation colors how you see it.	When one frame eliminates others, one logic overwhelms other possible logics.	Use multiple frames to generate inferences and insights.
Outcome bias	The outcome of the event or decision influences judgments you make about those involved.	You may pay more or less attention to the reasoning of others.	Insist on multiple team members contributing to the development and vetting of inferences and insights.

Belief bias	Judgment about the logic and correctness of an argument is based your belief of the truth or falsity of the conclusion.	You may too easily accept or reject an argument's reasoning without assessing the reasoning.	Don't accept inferences and insights based on respect for the person advancing them.
Anchoring bias	Give excessive weight to an unimportant but salient feature of a situation or issue.	Reasoning may be based on lesser important items.	Don't allow inferencing to be unduly influenced by unimportant data.

a competitive situation by different people influenced by different life experiences, education, training, and modes of reasoning lead to alternative inferences. Often, no single inference dominates. For example, inferences about the likely reactions of a competitor to a regulatory shift or the emergence of a substitute product can lead to a set of inferences suggesting different action paths, with distinct explanations.

Again, the shaping implications are clear: because your understanding at any point in time in any domain such as competitors, customers, government, ecology or technology, not to mention interactions across domains, is likely to be incomplete, and, it can quickly become incongruent with the current reality,[180] all preliminary inferences and suggested insights need to be immediately tested, and most likely refined.[181] When an inference catches your attention or an insight hits you, don't take it as final. Turn to testing it. Indeed, it's in the testing and refinement (vetting) of integrated inferences and suggested insights (steps 8 and 10 in Table 5-1) that you'll develop an appreciation for the insight—can it stand the test of refinement or does it whither in the heat of reflection on its validity?

Fundamental to shaping is the capacity of the mind to innovate conceptually:[182] to reason in ways that enable new descriptions, projections, and explanations of change.[183] The mind's capacity to invoke "pictures" or project views of what the world might look like at some future point in time is due to its ability to resort to assumptions, suppositions, and hypotheses. That the mind can conceive of the hypothetically possible means that it can think in terms not just of "what does happen" but "what would happen if." It's not con-strained to the descriptive "facts of today" or to the "real world" as we know it today. The shaping implications are clear: encourage and enable people to invoke new points of view, to look for new relationships among indicators and inferences, to develop and test new suppositions or lines of argument, especially those that challenge long-held beliefs about customers, competi-tors, the marketplace, and their own organization.[184]

Case: DipCo—Customer migration shaping at work

Chapters 3 and 4 highlighted how the DipCo analysis team deployed structuring's analysis components and sniffed a long list of preliminary inferences. Here, I'll highlight the method (Table 5-1) and deliberations involved in getting from the preliminary inferences to a set of tentative insights.

Refine understanding of indicators and context

The DipCo analysis team quickly recognized that shaping takes time; it doesn't happen in one afternoon meeting. Thus, extensive opportunity existed to expose and test people's tacit understanding[185] of the customer, competitor, and marketplace context.

Step 1: Refine understanding of the context

The sniffed inferences noted in the previous chapter are the outcome of the analysis team's initial reflections on the customer's announcement that it was migrating to the rival. Each inference emanated from and reflected the team's understanding of the relevant context. However, it's important to note that understanding of context evolves as the team continues to gather data about: significant shifts in other rivals' strategies; changes in value propositions aimed at specific customer segments and geographies; how rivals are responding to each other's moves including value proposition adjustments; which customers are switching rivals and why they may be doing so; customers' public statements about decisions and choices, prod-ucts, solutions, state of the industry, and, needs and wants. The enhanced understanding of the context enables rewording preliminary inferences as well as the derivation of new inferences.

Step 2: Identify critical new data points and indicators, leading to new inferences

Several new data points and indicators emerged as one outcome of the team's efforts to develop a better understanding of the context. The structuring analysis components detailed in Chapter 3 contribute to superior understanding of both the context and new indicators. For example, shifting the focus from the customer's current needs to its possible future needs compelled the analysis team to ask questions about the direction of the customer's potential strategy: specifically, what kind of value proposition might it want to offer its customers. Shifting the analysis frame from the customer's infrastructure to the customer's value chain allowed the analysis team to identify and assess whether and how the solution it provided to the customer was enabling the customer to enhance its operating efficiency or to add value for its customers.

As the analysis team noted new data and indicators specific to (for example) the rival's offer and the customer's recent behaviors, it could generate additional new preliminary inferences:

- This customer and others had become increasingly disenchanted with the solutions in the market in this product space.
- The customer had begun an internal project to determine the underlying sources of the its discontent with this product area.
- The competitor was indeed trying hard to customize its solution for this customer.
- The competitor was about to adopt a new technology that would significantly enhance the offer or solution it could provide customers within twelve to eighteen months.

Working toward integrated inferences

As you saw in the VP case, integrated inferences play a crucial role in the pathway to tentative insights. They enable understanding of domains such as customers, competitors, and technology that is simply not evident in the preliminary inferences. Even initial stabs at articulating integrated inferences involve a synthesis of two or more preliminary inferences. They often involve judgments that may be difficult to articulate and not easy for others to accept. The absence of one best way of reasoning necessitates elaborating the strings in the argument (reasoning) underpinning key judgments.

It's no surprise therefore that extensive back and forth, fueled in part by interpersonal ebb and flow, is especially characteristic of generating and agreeing on a set of integrated inferences.

Step 3: Categorize preliminary inferences

The relatively easy part of the analysis in the DipCo case was to segment the inferences into broad groups around the customer who had migrated, other customers, the competitor to whom the customer had migrated as well as technology and competitive change. Each group was then subdivided into categories based on connections across all the preliminary inferences. For example, the customer who had migrated was broken into several categories: the customer's behaviors, the customer's motivations, the customer's intent, and the customer's internal organization.

Step 4: Look for connections within and across the categories

Connections within and especially across categories of preliminary inferences are frequently anything but self-evident. It's here that intuition as the initiator of reasoning needs to be unleashed. Seeking these connections is also one of the ultimate tests of people's capacity to innovate conceptually. It requires living in the inferences: reading each inference, thinking about why the inference might have been drawn from an indicator, how one inference might connect to another, and, how and why inferences relating to different topics, for example how one about the rival and one about the customer might together suggest another inference.

Living in the inferences allows tacit reasoning to occur: connections across inferences strike us even though we were not explicitly focusing on these specific inferences. For example, connecting two of the preliminary inferences just noted, this customer and others had become increasingly disenchanted with the solutions in the market in this "product space" and the competitor was about to adopt a new technology that would significantly enhance the offer or solution it could provide customers within twelve to eighteen months might lead to a CSI inference: new customer solutions could transplant all existing product offers in the next two years.

Step 5: Develop initial integrated inferences

Connections across the preliminary inferences enable the generation of initial integrated inferences. This step can't be overlooked even though analysis teams tend to downplay it, if not avoid it entirely. When asked to do so, people quickly generate possible integrated inferences by connecting two or more preliminary inferences. The DipCo analysis team generated a long list of initial integrated inferences but they recognized that this listing eventually had to be boiled down to a small number, a few at most.

Step 6: Vet initial integrated inferences

In this step, reasoning needs to be made explicit. The DipCo team applied a simple vetting test to each initial integrated inference: is there some support for it or can it be refuted? So people articulate, however briefly, a line of reasoning that others can observe and react as they deem appropriate. The intent of this level of vetting is to challenge each initial integrated inference and, if necessary, to rephrase it. This preliminary vetting gives everyone and the team another opportunity to better understand the context as well as connections across the preliminary inferences. It's no surprise that the analysis back and forth and interpersonal ebb and flow become manifestly evident.

Step 7: Condense and refine initial integrated inferences into suggested integrated inferences

Reasoning as the spearhead of "conceptual innovation" characterizes the transition from a list of initial integrated inferences to a small set of suggested integrated inferences. The innovation in thinking becomes manifest in integrated inferences that cut across the preliminary inference categories and thus could not be derived from any one inference category alone.

The team iterated several times to get to a general agreement around three suggested integrated inferences:

- The customer is seeking a new solution for a need that it was aware of for some time but had never fully articulated partly because of differences of opinion within the organization;

- A set of rapid developments in a number of related technologies were enabling emerging and potential solutions that most customers were only becoming aware of;
- The competitor was in the process of significantly reshaping its customer value proposition with the intent of locking in several new key customer accounts.

Work toward suggested insights

The suggested integrated inferences provide the platform for the development and vetting of suggested and tentative insights. Each step in the progression toward tentative insights (see steps 8, 9 and 10 in Table 5-1) provides a sharper focus on insights that meet the desired insight attributes outlined in Chapter 1.

Step 8: Vet suggested integrated inferences

Vetting the refined integrated inferences brings to the fore two key reasoning principles noted in Table 5-2: don't privilege one individual's judgments and opinions above others or allow any one mode of reasoning to dominate the deliberations. Vetting requires people with differing perspectives and vantage points to express their judgments and the reasons supporting them. The analysis back and forth and the often-intense interpersonal ebb and flow become understandable when we consider the questions that must be posed as people posit and vet the refined list of integrated inferences as they pursue one or a few suggested (and later tentative) insights:

- What other preliminary inferences might be relevant to the refined integrated inference as tentatively stated?
- How might these inferences support or refute the stated integrated inference?
- How might these inferences conflict? Might some of them be diametrically opposed?
- Is there a way to reconcile conflicts among these integrated inferences?
- How might the integrated inference (insight) be further refined?

These judgments and reasoning buttressing them aren't self-evident; they open the possibility of extensive deliberations around the 'logic" and supporting evidence for each articulated integrated inference. The interpersonal ebb and flow becomes evident when team members support and oppose each other's refinements of stated integrated inferences.

Step 9: Integrate suggested integrated inferences into suggested insights

The capacity to conceptually innovate—to invoke pictures of the future and explanations of possibilities that extend beyond prevailing understanding of current marketplace realities—enables the transition from vetted integrated inferences to suggested or tentative insights. The focus on generating an insight that reflects new understanding beyond the integrated inferences drives the deliberations. Hence, the need to be explicit in articulating the "whys" at the heart of each suggested insight.

Step 10: Vet and transform into suggested insights

The DipCo analysis team eventually agreed that there were two key tentative domain insights: one a customer insight and one a competitor insight:

Customer insight: A new customer need (a particular operation's problem) with specific technology specifications was emerging (driven in part by evolving technology and by customers' discontent with existing solutions). The team was confident that the judgments underpinning the declaration of this customer need could be supported by the available data and their reasoning.

Competitor insight: The competitor would be able to launch its new offer within twelve to eighteen months. The competitor was already testing its potential offer concept with some customers and had begun to test specific elements of its potential offer in customers' operations.

From domain to CSIs and GMIs

Once the tentative domain insights were agreed, another reasoning principle suddenly kicked in: reasoning (thinking) is never-ending. It can always be applied in new directions. The DipCo analysis team quickly realized the two tentative domain insights had significant potential consequences for CSIs (competitive space insights) and GMIs, (generic marketplace insights).

As soon as the deliberations shifted to CSIs, the shaping steps noted in Table 5-1 could again be applied. The team could describe the emerging and future competitive context in view of the two domain insights (step 1), look for possible indicators of change (step 2), develop preliminary inferences about competitive space change (step 3), categorize the preliminary inferences (step 4), develop initial integrated inferences (step 5), vet them (step 6), condense into a small set of integrated inferences (step 7) and vet them (step 8), finally working toward a small set of suggested CSIs (step 9) that are then integrated into one or a small number of tentative CSIs. Two CSIs emerged:

- All the old product, price and service rules of competitive space rivalry wouldn't be relevant to rapidly emerging competitive space conditions;
- Some rivals (because of their internal asset, capability and culture configurations) won't be able to make the transition to the new competitive context.

Another reasoning principle strongly influences the need for and development of GMIs: reasoning is always infiltrated by cognitive and organizational biases. GMIs, as noted in Chapter 1, are created without reference to any individual competitor. The analysis focus is on marketplace consequences of domain insights and CSIs. Hence, the intent is to try to get analysis participants to step outside their personal predilections and organizational interests (biases).

The DipCo analysis team generated four specific GMIs:

- Marketplace opportunity: A new marketplace opportunity (driven by an emerging customer need and the ability of at least one firm to serve that need) significantly larger than the current product solution would evolve over the next two years.
- Competitive risks: Customers might move slowly toward trial and acceptance of the projected new product.

- Strategic vulnerability: Key rivals' current strategies would be extremely vulnerable to the rapid emergence of the new competitive conditions
- Assumptions: All key elements of marketplace dynamics including product rivalry, service, relationships and price would be radically different in two years compared to a year ago.

Stipulating insights

Once the domain, CSIs and GMIs, noted above are vouched for, they're accepted as inputs to business implications—thinking, decisions, and actions. The transition to accepted insights serves as the focus of the next chapter.

The surprise element

Insight, as described in earlier chapters, involves a shift from an old (and, often implicit) understanding to a new understanding of marketplace change. And, that shift can be extensive and often surprising, as in the DipCo case. The tentative insights suggested a new customer need that the analysis team didn't expect. The projected competitor launch of a new offer within twelve to eighteen months was not considered in any of the team's prior competitor deliberations. Clearly, the tentative insights, once they were vouched for and finally stipulated would lead to a critical GMI, new assumptions about the competitive context for the purposes of strategy development. The new assumptions would entail a radical "view of the future" compared to what might have been projected a mere two months earlier.

Case: VP—The role and power of vetting

The shaping discussion in the DipCo case illustrates the role and importance of vetting integrated inferences and suggested and tentative insights. The reasoning principles and their associated shaping principles and practices (Table 5-2) heavily influence the method and deliberations that typically characterize shaping. The VP case, initially discussed in Chapter 2, offers more detail about the analysis framework to vet suggested and tentative insights (the framework can also be applied to integrated inferences).

The VP insights noted in Chapter 2 were:

Customer insight: Customers are falling into distinct needs-based segments requiring customized solutions and some segments *will* walk away fast from their longtime providers

Competitor insight: The competitor wants to establish a new solution space; it's driven by the desire to transform the customer experience; it's willing to transform its value proposition in order to outperform all its rivals.

CSI: Strategy will need to be based on multiple dimensions of value; it will transform which rivals win and which lose; some won't be able to make the transition.

Vetting suggested (and tentative) change insights

Vetting's focus stems from the desired insight attributes noted briefly in Chapter 1: new understanding, novelty, non-obvious, congruence, explanatory, and endurance. They dictate two related modes of insight testing as an insight moves from suggested to tentative. Assess the tentative insight to determine if it's a quality insight, that is, whether the new understanding exhibits congruence and some explanatory power, or is merely a mistaken output of deliberative analysis or of instantaneous brain activity. A quality insight withstands scrutiny: whether data and reasoning support it. Second, test whether the insight is novel: if it's common knowledge or has already been discerned by one or more rivals, it's less likely to be the basis of distinctive decision value. The quality and novelty tests are intimately related: it doesn't make sense to spend considerable time conducting the quality tests without a sense that that the suggested or tentative insight possesses some degree of novelty. By the same token, investing extensive time testing insight novelty may prove worthless if the quality of the alleged insight crumbles under scrutiny.

Vetting is predominantly an exercise in reasoning. As you'll see with each VP change insight, the more it involves the future, the more dependent a change insight is on the underlying reasoning. A line of argument must be made that builds the "case" for the suggested or tentative insight. Thus, attention to the implications of the reasoning principles noted in Table 5-2 become imperative: for example, expose the prevailing personal and organization biases that may be afflicting the reasoning; treat each suggested insight as immediately requiring critique; engage multiple people with diverse perspectives, perhaps even some who have not heretofore been involved, so that the implicit reasoning underpinning each case for a specific insight can be exposed and assessed. In short, the conceptual innovation necessary to generate an insight, at any level of the insight funnel (see Figure 1-2), must be elaborated and tested.

Vetting insight quality

Insight quality largely refers to its congruence with the current or potential marketplace change; what philosophers might refer to as its "truth quotient" or what academics might call "reality congruence."

If the VP analysis team discovers that a variety of indicators, for example, executives' statements, security analysts' statements, absence of required investments, major capital and personnel commitments to existing products and supplier relationships, suggest the competitor has little intention of establishing a new solution space, then the competitor insight noted above doesn't meet the basic quality (congruence) test—it's untrue. To cite another common example, an alleged customer insight that asserts customers are responding to a rival's reduced prices when it was in fact the rival's superior product functionality that was winning the day exemplifies poor insight quality (and, of course, the potentially negative decision consequences).

Does the suggested insight stand scrutiny? The scrutiny tests may well alter the substance (content) of the insight but they're not likely to dramatically alter its novelty. The scrutiny test is best executed by asking two related questions:

- What data and reasoning support the thrust of the insight?
- What data and reasoning might refute the thrust of the insight?

These questions drive a reappraisal of the suggested or tentative insight. They force a review of the "logic" connecting base inferences to integrated inferences and on to the insights.

For the VP analysis team, the scrutiny test caused a lengthy review of the data and reasoning underpinning a suggested competitive dynamics insight, strategy will need to be based on multiple dimensions of value; many firms will have difficulty adapting to this need. The deliberations evidenced intensive back and forth as team members offered what they saw as compelling evidence to support and refute reformulations of the suggested insight. As the team moved toward settling on a final statement of the tentative insight, they added some elements to broaden the insight's content:[186] strategy will need to be based on multiple dimensions of value; it will transform which rivals win and which lose; some won't be able to make the transition. They also tested how the tentative customer and competitor insights (see Tables 2-3 and 2-4) supported or refuted the need for strategy to be based on multiple dimensions of value, and whether and how the new strategy requirements would lead to winners and losers and why some rivals might need to exit the market.

An important side benefit of vetting: it always generates significant learning. For many in the analysis team, the deliberations served as an opportunity to learn about what it takes to win customers, how and why winning value propositions change over time, and of course, how their own organization viewed the marketplace and why that too would need to change over time.

Does the insight possess explanatory power? Insights involve more than mere description.[187] Insights that reflect genuinely new understanding frequently help "explain" something or other: we can peer beneath the surface of what is apparent, we see the reasons why something has happened or why events will turn out one way rather than others, we understand what will give rise to success or failure. Two reasoning principles are especially important: reasoning is never-ending and reasoning and its outcomes change over time. As an insight's context unfolds, old explanations may become less appropriate, and in some instances, may prove wrong.

In terms of the VP case, to revert to the competitive dynamics insight just noted, it indicates what will be necessary for strategy to be successful and suggests why some firms will likely fall by the wayside. It helps explain why some rivals stuck in a price competition mentality aren't likely to win if they can't transition to multi-dimensional customer value propositions. The tentative customer insight, customers are falling into distinct needs-based segments requiring customized solutions and some segments *will* walk away fast from their longtime providers, helps explain customers' behaviors (for example, what they're looking for in offers from providers), and why some customers would break from their traditional suppliers (for example, they're looking for an offer or a solution not being delivered by the traditional supplier).

The deliberations here also afford a great learning opportunity for the analysis team's members: the need for constant vigilance to test whether key elements of the firm's mind-set—its point of view, assumptions and beliefs—are congruent with current realities and those that might prevail at some point in the future.[188]

Vetting insight novelty

A suggested insight without novelty in its content is no insight at all. Yet, suggested and even tentative insights are sometimes asserted as if they're new to the world. Novelty has at least two reference points: your own organization and the external world. Thus, at a minimum, it's important to ask two questions:

- Does the insight involve new understanding for the organization?
- Is the new understanding already known to others?

Is the understanding (significantly) new to the organization? Two reasoning principles need to be especially heeded. Assessing an insight's new organizational understanding can easily fall prey to numerous personal and organizational biases. For example, recency bias may impel one or more people to support the suggested insight most recently articulated even though the reasoning supporting earlier suggested insights may be stronger. Hindsight bias may lead team members not to ask penetrating questions; they assert that they were moving in the direction of the asserted insight.

If the proffered insight doesn't provide new understanding for the organization, we can immediately eliminate what is asserted as an insight. The shift from the old to the new understanding should be significant (as discussed in Chapter 2).

Each suggested and tentative insight in the VP case must be subjected to this insight criterion. Consider the tentative competitor insight: the competitor wants to establish a new solution space; it's driven by the desire to transform the customer experience; it's willing to transform its value proposition in order to outperform all its rivals, and it will invest what it takes to win. If the old understanding was the opposite, for example, the firm didn't have any sense that the competitor intended to create a new solution space and believed that it was content with the customer experiences it was creating, then significant new understanding was created.

Is the insight new to the world? If the insight is new to the organization but is in fact part of "common knowledge" in the broader world, then we can safely assert it's not a genuinely new insight in the world at large. It therefore will have limited potential to generate value in thinking, decisions, and actions. Reasoning here may be particularly influenced by the belief bias: people may too easily accept that the insight is new without subjecting to assessment why is it so.

The analysis team can ask, for example, whether the tentative customer insight, customers are falling into distinct needs-based segments (some want a full solution, others want a basic solution) requiring customized solutions and in the full solution segment customers *will* walk away fast from their longtime providers has already been captured by one or more rivals. If it has, then it signals that the organization is merely catching up to its rivals in terms of understanding customers! The team concluded that elements of the insight had probably been crafted by the competitor but whether it was a fully integrated insight was open to question.[189]

A final comment

Vetting generates tentative insights; they serve as input to stipulating, the final inferencing activity (described in the next chapter). Vetting any tentative insight can't go on forever! At some stage, an individual or an analysis team must declare that they've taken the analysis as far as they can: they vouch that the inference or insight has been subjected to their best analysis efforts; they're willing to accept it for purposes of assessing its business implications.

Case: Gorilla Competitor—The influence of interpersonal ebb and flow

Shaping competitor insights typically involve weaving your way through disparate and often conflicting indicators, preliminary inferences, and even integrated inferences. This shouldn't come as a surprise: competitor change may be open to multiple interpretations; competitors can make significant change to their longstanding strategy or marketing or operations; competitors often try to conceal their real marketplace intent. The analysis back and forth is thus likely to be open to extensive interpersonal ebb and flow for all the reasons noted above. This case illustrates how the interpersonal ebb and flow may influence positively and negatively the analysis back and forth.

The "800-Pound Gorilla," as the competitor was affectionately called, had for many years dominated a large and growing global product sector in a technology market. It had recently made noises about the need for a shift in its historic strategy including executives' comments about unfavorable potential market shifts, emerging rival product technologies, and expected slow global market growth.

The core analysis challenge was succinctly summarized by the analysis team: clarify the Gorilla Competitor's current strategy, project its likely future strategy, assess these outputs for insights into the competitor, and then, if possible, assess whether the competitor insights might contribute to CSIs and GMIs.[190]

Refocusing shaping's intent and focus

Before it could formally move to shaping, the interpersonal ebb and flow quickly made its presence felt. Some team members insisted shaping could not be restricted to the inferences derived from a single projection of the competitor's strategy. The strongly admonished the team's other members and some others outside the team that they had to resist the temptation to develop only one projection of the Gorilla Competitor's strategy and then jump immediately to identify and assess its thinking, decision and action implications. They claimed that the insight discipline suggested a different approach: a shaping process driven by attention to concerns, issues, and questions that aren't asked and addressed if only a single strategy projection is made. They asserted, for example, no matter how comprehensive in scope, accuracy and detail a single projected strategy for the Gorilla Competitor, it doesn't address, much less answer, the following two questions:

- What insights into the competitor are missed due to only projecting the competitor's strategy (and not taking the analysis any further)? For example, not assessing why the competitor might take its strategy in this specific direction rather than others?
- What insights might be missed by not developing alternative projections of the competitor's strategy?

When the team agreed to address these two questions, some team members greatly irritated others when they asserted in strong terms that they wouldn't participate in any further discussion of executing the shaping steps until another set of questions were addressed as part of the analysis:

- What's the business model at the heart of the competitor's current strategy? What changes to it might be indicated by the projected strategy (or alternatives to the projected strategy)?
- What assumption change on the part of the competitor is suggested by the projected (competitor) strategy?
- How has the competitor overcome specific strategy inhibitors that had been previously identified?
- What new leverage points might underpin any potential shift in the competitor's strategy?

The deliberations around these questions caused a drastic shift in the intent and scope of shaping: use alternative projections of the Gorilla Competitor's strategy to understand not just the competitor, but many facets of its competitive context. The presumption stated by the advocates of the extended analysis approach was that it would lead to superior CSIs (competitive space insights) and GMIs (generic marketplace insights). The logic of this line of reasoning was not self-evident; the team had to sell its point of view with great care to specific team members.

Moving through the analysis steps

The projected alternative Gorilla Competitor strategies caused another distinct interpersonal ebb and flow: individual team members took different approaches to how fast the analysis could proceed. Some wanted to move immediately to developing integrated inferences. Others asserted they must use the projected strategies to develop another round of raw or base inferences. They argued with some vehemence that doing so would likely extend the team's understanding of the competitor's strategy possibilities and thus the competitor's leverage points and constraints given alternative views of its strategy. After considerable discussion, the team agreed, though not with complete consensus, to generate additional base inferences.

Categorizing the base inferences

As the team progressed through the shaping steps, members moved at different speeds as they organized the inferences into groups suggested by the content of the preliminary inferences. The groups included customers, channels, products, solutions, R&D, technology, customer value, competitors and some other categories. Some inferences were placed in more than one category.

As is always the case, the object of the preliminary inferences isn't constrained; they can be grouped into competitor and non-competitor foci. The non-competitor foci such as marketplace change, potential opportunities and threats, serve as input to developing potential CSIs and GMIs.

Moving toward refined integrated inferences

As the team focused in on individual groups of preliminary inferences or topics to determine if an underlying or integrated inference could be drawn, some team members pushed their colleagues to identify and articulate initial integrated inferences (step 5 in Table 5-1) rather than waiting to articulate a carefully worded integrated inference after considerable and deep personal reflection. This intervention resulted in team members identifying many more possible integrated inferences, thus, providing more varied raw material than would otherwise have occurred for the development of integrated inferences.

When the team began to identify and vet the initial integrated inferences (step 6), another major interpersonal ebb and flow emerged. People were quick to adopt and advocate specific preliminary inferences as the source of potential integrated inferences and even insight. Others often vehemently disagreed. These analysis conflicts, however, generated productive tension: people were asked to make the strongest possible case for their judgments. Consequently, stringent vetting of even the most provisionally proposed integrated inference quickly became the norm (step 6). One result: all involved learned a lot about how to draw inferences and articulate and present them to their colleagues.

Condense and refine into a set of suggested integrated inferences

Reasoning has no one best way and reasoning often doesn't generate one best (dominant) inference, but these two reasoning principles almost inevitably give rise to intense interpersonal ebb and flow in any collective effort to condense the number of initially suggested and vetted integrated inferences into a small set (step 7). As people developed their own rationales for linking two or more initially suggested inferences into one refined integrated inference, it became increasingly evident that different combinations could give rise to a refined integrated inference that no one had yet suggested. The team iterated their way through a deliberation that resulted in general acceptance of several "refined" integrated inferences (step 7) including;

- The Gorilla Competitor will continue to augment its investment in two established R&D projects over the next three or more years in order to hit the market with a solution that will enable it to eliminate most rivals from the market.
- The Gorilla Competitor will be generating increasing free cash from its current product portfolio over the next three to five years due to both economies of scope (compared to rivals) and economies of scale (due to continued operational enhancements).
- The Gorilla Competitor will invest in a small set of alliances and possibly one or two acquisitions to augment its marketing and sales competencies to extend its global market reach.

Vetting the suggested integrated inferences

Perhaps more than in any other shaping step, two reasoning principles—that reasoning is always infiltrated by biases and that reasoning can't be separated from emotions—become manifest in vetting the refined integrated inferences (step 8). Personal biases clearly led people to promote specific integrated inferences. For example, those with experience in R&D (a functional bias) firmly believed that the Gorilla Competitor was committed to extending its investments in R&D as the driving force in its marketplace strategy. They pushed for the R&D integrated inference noted above.

As discussed in Chapter 9, emotional commitments to specific judgments such as those necessarily involved in vetting refined integrated inferences led some people to hold on to their viewpoint longer than the counterevidence might suggest. They resisted accepting the supporting rationales of others' initial statements of refined integrated inferences, thus prolonging the deliberation without necessarily advancing the quality of the ultimately refined integrated inferences.

Generating suggested and tentative insights

It's worth reiterating that a key reasoning principle, reasoning often leads to conceptual innovation (Table 5-2), underpins the generating and vetting of suggested insights. The analysis team leaps to a suggested new understanding that may not be obvious in a set of refined integrated inferences. Thus, it won't come as a surprise that the analysis became protracted when the team endeavored to move from the suggested integrated inferences (step 8) to a small number of suggested insights (step 9) and then on to one or two tentative insights (step 10). Indeed, a few people, reflecting their biases and emotional commitments,[191] wanted to vet the entire analysis outputs to buttress and reinforce their choice of suggested insights—a desire that was strongly opposed and eventually rebuked by a "vote" of the team.

The interpersonal ebb and flow came into full view as the team moved toward specifying a small number of suggested insights including:

- The Gorilla Competitor can leverage its R&D capabilities to achieve global market dominance.

- The Gorilla Competitor can build a network of alliances as a base from which to extend its global reach.
- The Gorilla Competitor is augmenting its marketing capabilities through astute investments and investment in personnel.

When the analysis team looked for connections across the suggested insights, the first drafts of insights became the focus of intense deliberations. One or two people argued for simply accepting the suggested insights as tentative. In their view, no further analysis was required. However, as others generated insights that combined elements of the suggested insights and that seemed to be a more complete and deeper understanding of the competitor, they recognized that the suggested insights could be greatly improved. Eventually the analysis team generated two tentative insights:

- The Gorilla Competitor was intent on reaching a new level of global market dominance through its R&D and marketing commitments that would make it exceptionally difficult for some current rivals to remain in the business;
- The Gorilla Competitor was already well down the path to creating localized marketing and sales competencies across countries and regions through astute alliances and channel relationships that would render it almost impossible for national rivals to win against it.

These two tentative insights represented a new understanding of the Gorilla Competitor; the direction of a strategy that was not evident in its disparate actions and statements suddenly became apparent.

Key shaping errors

Shaping's method and deliberations outlined in the DipCo, VP, and Gorilla Competitor cases necessitate time, commitment, and attention. Several errors specific each analysis step contributes to shortchanging the process (Table 5-4). These errors indicate how execution of the method's steps can go off course and why the deliberations become less rich than they should be. Here I'll emphasize three errors that affect the entire shaping experience.

Table 5-4   Common Errors along the Shaping Steps

Shaping step	Common errors
Refine understanding of the context.	Assume that it was fully crafted in structuring. Assume that no change occurs during the shaping period.
Identify critical new data points and indicators.	Downplay the ongoing need to seek new change indicators. Resist adding to the list of preliminary inferences developed in structuring.
Categorize the preliminary inferences.	Not asking if a category can be usefully subdivided. Not asking individuals to independently suggest possible categorizations.
Look for connections within and across the categories.	Failing to push individuals to ask how specific inferences in one category might connect to one or more inferences in other categories.
Develop initial integrated inferences.	Avoiding identifying non-obvious integrated inferences. Not reviewing how an initial integrated inference might be extended.
Vet the initial integrated inferences.	Not taking seriously the need to specific the underlying reasoning. Paying little attention to rephrasing initial integrated inferences.
Condense and refine the list of integrated inferences.	Moving too quickly to get to the refined list of integrated inferences. Not seriously challenging the rationale for each refined integrated inference.
Vet the refined integrated inferences.	Assuming that the reasoning supporting each refined integrated inference is obvious. Not taking seriously the possible need to combine or further reduce the number.

Integrate into a small set of suggested insights.	Not asking each individual to propose one or more suggested insights. Not considering how each suggested insight provide clear and distinct new understanding.
Vet and transform into one or a few tentative insights.	Moving too quickly to reduce the suggested insights down to one or two. Not vigorously applying the scrutiny and novelty tests.

A rush to complete shaping doesn't allow the deep immersion required to enable the mind to make connections across inferences that are simply not evident in the preliminary inferences or the inference categories. Although there are no firm rules to determine when to cease shaping, taking too little time severely limits insight potential.

Not engaging collaboratively constitutes perhaps the most damaging error. Shaping is as much about sparking productive connections among the people involved as it's detecting and advocating inference and insight possibilities. Thus, managing the interpersonal ebb and flow crucially influences the analysis back and forth.[192]

The principles and practices of structuring are also relevant to shaping and should not be forgotten. Shifting scope, focus and perspective often bring a fresh challenge to identifying and assessing integrated inferences and suggested and tentative insights.

The 6IFs: Enabling and driving shaping

The shaping method detailed above in the DipCo, VP, and Gorilla Competitor cases often doesn't come naturally to people accustomed to quite different analysis routines and interpersonal behaviors. The 6IFs enable you to identify critical inhibitors to the shaping method and some foci for deliberations. In this chapter, I'll focus on the input side of shaping; in the following chapter, I'll address how the 6IFs enable assessment of the outputs of shaping and stipulating. I'll use the three cases discussed above for purposes of illustration.

See: Visualize how and why inferences might connect to each other

Many of the reasoning and data principles (Tables 5-2 and 3-1, respectively) challenge people to "see" what may not be immediately evident in the data and, indeed, in the analysis output along the shaping steps summarized in Table 5-1. For example, what may seem like straightforward analysis tasks such as identifying new indicators (step 2) and developing possible integrated inferences (step 5) required people in each case to look beyond how their own organization traditionally configured indicators in its scanning and monitoring of marketplace change. Seeing was especially critical in moving from initial to suggested integrated inferences. Some people had great difficulty visualizing how a set of initial integrated inferences might be recast as a suggested integrated inference; they just couldn't see how they connected (steps 6 and 7). Deliberation around these inhibitors surfaces personal biases and organizational barriers that prevent people from seeing differently.[193]

Think: Reason about new things and in new ways

Shaping's method compels people to think about new things and to think (reason) in new ways. Some had to work hard to adopt the mode of thinking that allowed them to draw multiple inferences from single indicators (step 2); they often wanted to stop once they had articulated one inference. The transition from preliminary to integrated inferences (steps 3–7) also proved difficult for some to contemplate and master: they wanted proof that they had got it right. This was especially the case in step 5, developing initial integrated inferences: they found it difficult to suggest a possible integrated inference without being highly confident that is would withstand the scrutiny and novelty tests. In short, for many people, thinking about new things such as preliminary and integrated inferences needed to be encouraged and supported.

Intend: Create a shared shaping (and business) purpose

Without a shared and convincing intent people won't take on the shaping method and deliberations evident in the three cases discussed above. That shared intent was present at the initiation of the DipCo work but was not present when the VP work was initiated. The analysis leader had to sell the value of the insight project to the VP team. The Gorilla Competitor case exemplified the need for the insight shaping work to be driven by a business intent: how do we compete against the Gorilla Competitor? In the VP case, as the analysis proceeded, the team recognized the potential strategy benefits of enhanced customer and competitor understanding. As the suggested change insights were articulated and vetted (steps 9 and 10), they sensed a new marketing purpose: creating a winning value proposition to outmaneuver and outperform key rivals.

Decide: Establish the commitment to complete the shaping method

In each case, the team had to make a series of decisions: to be involved in the analysis; to commit to participating fully in the analysis; to push themselves to draw preliminary and integrated inferences; to challenge suggested insights; and, later, to derive implication insights and business implications. Some individuals wavered on some of these decisions. The team leader in the VP and Gorilla Competitor cases had to intervene to ensure that all team members were fully committed to the insight work.

Act: Execute the analysis steps

Shaping's principles and practices dictate that analysis back and forth and interpersonal ebb and flow dominate the pathway from preliminary inferences to tentative insight.[194] Thus, the team had to tread carefully through the analysis steps. Some members had to engage in new behaviors specific to new analysis contexts: collaborating with others to better understand the relevant context (step 1) and to identify relevant indicators (step 2); working with fellow team members to offer up additional preliminary inferences and categorize preliminary inferences (step 3); striving to remain fully involved even though some of the inference contexts were outside their areas of competence and familiarity (steps 4 and 5); challenging others to support their preferred integrated inferences (step 5, 6, and 7); asking questions to better understand the rationales for individual suggested insights (steps 8 and 9). Team leaders frequently invested time to help people understand the purpose of each step and the benefits of maintaining a collaborative spirit.

Feel: Create and leverage positive emotions; ameliorate negative emotions

Feelings frequently rose above the surface in each case—they were vocalized. Initially, feelings of concern, disbelief, and hesitancy were expressed by some team members in the VP and Gorilla Competitor cases, and to a lesser extent in the DipCo case, that this insight work was being initiated and their participation was ordered. As the teams progressed through execution of the analysis steps, positive and negative feelings were expressed about the inherent thinking and analysis challenges. Team leaders and senior members of each team as part of the interventions noted above encouraged people to express these feelings and discussed them in full view of the team.

Enhancing your organization's shaping capability

Building a shaping capability takes time. It requires an understanding of shaping's method and a willingness to manage its deliberations. Some tasks should precede application of the shaping method in an analysis project (Table 5-5).

Table 5-5   Enhancing Your Organization's Shaping Capability

Develop shared understanding of key shaping concepts

- Discuss rationale and purpose of shaping.
- Develop familiarity with shaping's method (Table 5-1).

Assess current analysis approaches to shaping change insights.

- Identify key current analysis projects.
- Delineate dominant modes of analysis.
- Assess against shaping's method.
- Determine key gaps in shaping.

Conduct some self-assessment

- Assess against the 6IFs.
- Determine the significant issues.

Reflect on the shaping errors

- Anticipate likely errors (Table 5-4).
- Monitor each method step for indicators of presence or emergence of key errors.

Apply the shaping steps in a specific analysis project

- Choose one or two analysis projects.
- Execute the shaping method (the sequence in Table 5-1).

Manage the deliberations

- Monitor execution of each method step.
- Observe and manage the analysis back and forth.
- Observe and manage interpersonal ebb and flow.
- Identify need for interventions.

Identify key learning

- Note key learnings about execution along each step in shaping's method.
- Note key learnings about managing deliberations.

Embed shaping across projects

- Identify key shaping learnings.
- Apply learnings in next shaping projects.

Develop a shared understanding of the key shaping concepts

The team needs to understand why a shaping method is necessary, what the shaping method entails, and what might be the focus of deliberations as shaping proceeds. It's always helpful to walk a team through shaping's method before embarking on a shaping project.

Assess current analysis approaches to shaping change insights

Analysis teams aim to develop new understanding of the relevant competitive context or customers or competitors or some specific change domain. The modes of analysis deployed can be assessed against the shaping steps identified in Table 5-1 to determine how well or poorly any analysis team or the organization crafts change insights. For example, a competitor analysis team can document if they execute each of the shaping steps, how systematically they follow the routines within each step, how long it takes to complete the steps.

Conduct some self-assessment

Team members can assess themselves against the 6IFs to determine their level of preparedness for shaping. The findings may require specific interventions. For example, if some don't see how shaping might lead to new marketplace understanding or don't believe that new modes of thinking are necessary, then the suggestion above to develop a shared understanding of key shaping concepts is indeed mandatory.

Even before they undertake a shaping project, team members can evaluate their shaping skills. For example, they can rate themselves on whether and how they execute each of the shaping steps noted in Table 5-1. They should pay particular attention to whether they short-circuit the analysis steps; for example, moving quickly from some preliminary inferences to a suggested integrated inference that then becomes an accepted insight because it's never vetted or exposed to the critique of others.

Reflect on the shaping errors

Another focused way to prepare for shaping involves acknowledging and reflecting on the errors associated with each step in the shaping method (Table 5-4). It helps avoid common pitfalls and speeds the process.

Apply the shaping steps in a specific analysis project

Executing the shaping steps in a specific analysis project serves as the ultimate way for any team or organization to learn and augment its ability to enhance any team's or organization's shaping capability. The following sequence of actions is helpful:

Choose a domain and topic area: Ask how urgent it is to develop some change insight(s) in the domain area. For example, it might be critical to embark on crafting some customer or competitor insights because of current or anticipated change in these domains.

Identify the decision purpose of the analysis work: The customer or competitor insights might provide crucial input to strategy change or a decision to enter or exit from a specific product market.

Establish a team to execute the shaping steps: Typically, shaping involves a set of individuals who commit to delivering a possible set of insights. It's always helpful, to the extent possible, to invite individuals from multiple functions or pockets of expertise.

Choose a shaping knowledgeable leader: where possible, this should be someone with shaping expertise can guide the team along the shaping steps and help avoid committing the errors noted in Table 5-4.

Organize a review of the preliminary inferences: This task gives people the opportunity to become familiar with the basic analysis challenges in transforming indicators and data into inferences. Doing so explicitly is often a new experience for many. So, also, may be the need to articulate and script inferences that connect two or more preliminary inferences.

Develop suggested integrated inferences: Allow the team sufficient time to develop highly provisional suggested integrated inferences and then synthesize them into a much smaller set, probably no more than four or five.

Vet the suggested integrated inferences: In this task, it's especially important to support and encourage people to follow the vetting sequence of questions detailed in the DipCo and VP cases. The intent is to ensure that the team won't short-circuit the process or adopt the first one or two integrated inferences that are addressed.

Articulate the refined integrated inferences: Avoid the temptation to skip this step in the analysis. Give people the opportunity to challenge and refine integrated inferences as they are proposed. The team learns about the context of the inferences.

Vet and articulate the tentative insights: Ensure that sufficient time is devoted to identifying suggested insights and then vetting them to get to one or a few tentative insights. Sometimes, asking one or more individuals to provide the reasoning supporting each suggested insight helps others to see connections that might not be apparent.

Manage the deliberations

Shaping rarely flows smoothly. The task sequence just described necessarily involves extensive back and forth. It thus requires one or more people who dedicate themselves to observing, assessing, and guiding the pathway through the tasks. The individual observes breakdowns and blockages in the pathway, where and when more time may be required, and whether the analysis is being stretched sufficiently to extend the range of suggested integrated inferences or suggested insights.

Participants and leaders in any shaping project need to be attentive to the influence of the interpersonal ebb and flow on the back and forth along the task sequence. It's not enough to monitor the negative influences noted earlier in this chapter. It's often imperative to intervene to, for example, build tension in various tasks—to get people to openly and constructively challenge the thinking or logic underpinning individual integrated inferences.

Identify key learnings

It's imperative to be obsessive in noting key learnings about the execution of each analysis step and managing the deliberations over the course of a shaping experience. Sometimes the small things can make a large difference; so attention to the details is critical. For example, stopping to review where a team is at in progressing through the method can lead to reflections about how to proceed.

Embed shaping in analysis projects

Shaping can then be embedded in a sequence of analysis projects. Individuals who have experienced shaping in one project can serve to transmit key learnings to another project. A team of individuals who have been involved in one or more shaping experiences can come together to assess whether specific organizational factors impede or facilitate shaping.

A final comment

Shaping aims to transform preliminary inferences into one or more tentative insights. The three cases discussed in this chapter demonstrate that the shaping method is always characterized by extensive analysis back and forth and interpersonal ebb and flow. Thus, the deliberative side of the insight discipline must be carefully managed. A commitment to building a shaping capability must be a goal for any organization that is serious about deploying the insight discipline.

Notes

157. The steps involved in moving from a tentative to an accepted insight serves as the focus of the next chapter.

158. Suggested insights have not yet been subjected to the vetting and refinement discussed later in this chapter.

159. This suggestion is strongly advocated in Steven Johnson, *Where Good Ideas Come From* (New York: Riverside Books, 2010).

160. The differences "burst into the open" because as the shaping analysis moves in the final steps (steps 8–10 in Table 5–1), individuals recognize that the window is closing on their ability to influence the final content of the tentative insight.

161. The role and importance of immersion in data as a means to enabling the mind, especially the non-conscious mind, to think about the data and its context has long been advocated by both theorists and empirical researchers. See, for example, John Seely Brown and Paul Duguid, *The Social Life of Information* (Boston: Harvard Business School Press, 2000).

162. This is a major theme in much of the recent output in neuroscience. It's a major focus in Steven Pinker's groundbreaking book, *How the Mind Works* (New York: W.W. Norton, 1997).

163. The tacit or unconscious side of reasoning is well established. It's the essence of Kahneman's System 1: thinking that happens automatically and quickly, with little or no effort and no sense of voluntary control. Daniel Kahneman, *Thinking Fast and Slow* (New York: Farrar, Straus and Giroux, 2011).

164. The work of Nicholas Rescher, a leading philosopher of science was especially helpful in extracting the principles. See, for example, Nicholas Rescher, *A System of Pragmatic Idealism, Volume 1: Human Knowledge in Idealistic Perspective* (Princeton,: Princeton University Press, 1992), and Nicholas Rescher, *Philosophical Reasoning, A Study in the Methodology of Philosophizing* (Malden, MA: Blackwell Publishers, 2001).

165. The pathway involved in reasoning, that is, getting from data to some form of conclusion or assertion, is of course the focus of many historic streams of philosophy and more recently neuroscience. See, for example,

Robert Nozick, *The Nature of Rationality* (Princeton: Princeton University Press, 1993), and Stephen Toulmin, *The Uses of Argument* (Cambridge: Cambridge University Press, 1958).

166. The emphasis upon deliberation and method as separate but related pillars of the insight discipline advocated throughout this book stems from the time it requires to get from "data" to something we refer to as a suggested or accepted insight. Deliberation can take many twists and turns, what we dub "analysis back and forth."

167. The tortured and convoluted path reflects both the analysis back and forth and the interpersonal ebb and flow that were briefly outlined in the introduction to this chapter.

168. The aha moment results from the cognitive unconscious processes at work in the brain. Eric Kandel discusses how these processes may determine the approach adopted by individuals to solve a problem or make sense of a situation. Eric R. Kandel, *The Age of Insight: The Quest to Understand the Unconscious in Art, Mind and Brain, from Vienna 1900 to the Present* (New York: Random House, 2012).

169. The role of our intuitions as the source of orchestrated reasoning is exemplified in the interconnections between System 1 and System 2 modes of thinking described by Kahneman. Daniel Kahneman, *Thinking Fast and Slow* (New York: Farrar, Straus and Giroux, 2011).

170. Intuition's role in the computations of the brain is especially well developed by Steven Pinker. See, Steven Pinking, *How the Mind Works* (New York: W.W. Norton & Company, 1997). For another perspective on the power of intuition to spark the mind, see, Daniel C. Dennett, *Intuition Pumps and Other Tools for Thinking* (New York: W.W. Norton & Company, 2013).

171. This point illustrates the role and importance of the "see" IF (insight factor).

172. The argument is most famously associated with Polanyi. Michael Polanyi, *The Tacit Dimension* (New York: Anchor Books, 1967). It's also consistent with a number of points made by Eric R. Kandel, *The Age of Insight: The Quest to Understand the Unconscious in Art, Mind and Brain, from Vienna 1900 to the Present* (New York: Random House, 2012), and Jonathan Haidt, *Why Good People are Divided by Politics and Religion* (New York: Pantheon Books, 2012).

173. See, for example, Jonathan Haidt, *Why Good People are Divided by Politics and Religion* (New York: Pantheon Books, 2012).

174. This is akin to the argument advocated as the purpose of structuring in Chapter 3; use the structuring analysis components to generate fresh indicators and thereby fresh inferences.

175. The role of cognitive biases as an influence on our intuitions and, more generally, how we think, is central to Kahneman's notions of thinking fast and slow. Daniel Kahneman, *Thinking Slow and Fast* (New York: Farrar, Straus and Giroux, 2011).

176. Karl Weick, *Sensemaking in Organizations* (Thousand Oaks, CA: Sage Publications, 1995).

177. See, for example, Dan Ariely, *Predictably Irrational: The Hidden Forces That Shape Our Decisions* (New York: HarperCollins, 2008).

178. The provisional nature of inferences and insights was noted in Chapter 3.

179. The discussion in Chapter 3 about the need to manage the choice of those involved in structuring is also relevant here.

180. This point reinforces congruency, that is, compatibility with the current and potential marketplace, as a desired insight attribute, as discussed in Chapter 1.

181. This observation reinforces the point made in the prior paragraph: the need to treat suggested integrated inferences and suggested insights as provisional, and thus requiring vetting.

182. This point has long been a staple of the output of philosophers of science. It's especially well developed in Nicholas Rescher, *A System of Pragmatic Idealism, Volume 1: Human Knowledge in Idealistic Perspective* (Princeton: Princeton University Press, 1992).

183. It's worth emphasizing here that in the absence of conceptual innovation, it would hardly be possible to craft insight manifesting significant new understanding of possible futures.

184. Invoking new points of view, or more broadly, the need to innovate conceptually, places a heavy onus on the 6IFs, especially the need to see differently and to thinking differently.

185. It's necessary to resort to drawing inferences based on their words, behaviors, and deeds as to what their tacit understanding is. Once we do

so, we can then test if they agree with our inferences or we would like to refine or reject them.

186. The refining of the tentative insight reflects the wordsmithing of an insight discussed as a key step in the vouching activity addressed in the next chapter.

187. This point has been emphasized and explained in each of the first three chapters.

188. The possible disjunction between the prevailing mental model and the current and potential change in the marketplace underpins the importance of congruence as a desired insight attribute as discussed in Chapter 1.

189. The competitor may not have crafted a similar or somewhat similar customer insight.

190. The emphasis here is worth noting: competitor insight, as noted earlier in this chapter, leads to CSI and GMI, both of which are critical to identifying and assessing business implications.

191. It was obvious that a few individuals had feelings of disquiet and discomfort and maybe even anger that their proposed suggested insights didn't get the consideration they expected.

192. This point is developed in detail in Chapter 9 when we address the influence of emotions.

193. We pick up this consideration in the final section of this chapter, building the organizational capability in shaping.

194. These are detailed in the right-hand column of Table 5-2.

Chapter 6

Stipulating: Vouching and Validating Change Insight

A health care company specializing in diagnostic technologies developed a tentative customer insight: both physicians and laboratories didn't appreciate the diagnostic superiority of a potential new technology the firm would take to the market within six months and hence physicians didn't understand how they could enhance the patient's health and laboratories didn't understand how they could enhance the quality and speed of the service they could provide to physicians and hospitals. This was significant new understanding for the analysis team: it contradicted the team's prior beliefs about physicians and laboratories. It led to the team developing two GMIs: the market opportunity was far larger than originally estimated in the early stages of development of the technology and assumptions about the speed of market penetration were greatly increased. The analysis team and the firm's marketing leaders were so excited and energized by the estimated sales projections, they dispensed with any further assessment of the customer insight. In short, they accepted the customer insight for decision-making purposes; they didn't conduct one final assessment of the customer insight, which we refer to as vouching.

The health care company also learned the need for what I call *validating,* assessing over time whether a change insight at any level—domain, CSI or GMI—holds up or needs to be revised. As the product was about to be launched, and especially in its first three months on the market, the analysis team monitored the reactions of physicians (for example, the extent to which they prescribed it) and laboratories (for example, the extent to which they preferred it to long-established alternatives). The results were disappointing. The two GMIs were sharply downgraded: the opportunity appeared to be far smaller than anticipated and initial market penetration assumptions were grossly optimistic. The result: the firm adjusted downward its resource commitment to the product and added the newly available resources to marketing another product line and to advancing early stage R&D.

The health care company case reminds us that shaping culminates in tentative change insights. Vetting challenges and refines the reasoning supporting each tentative insight. However, the analysis back and forth and the interpersonal ebb and flow typically combine to prolong the deliberations. The temptation to continue vetting and refining is difficult to resist. Yet, it can't go on forever! Thinking needs to conclude, decisions need to be made, action needs to be taken. In short, at some point, change insights need to be accepted, what I call "stipulated," for purposes of decision making.

This chapter details what is involved in stipulating change insights, why it's critical in crafting and leveraging insight, and what it means to validate a change insight over time.

Vouching for the insight

At some point, the analysis team becomes confident enough to stipulate the change insight as that which we will accept, that is, "take as stated for now" for the purposes of thinking, deciding and acting. Vouching involves the final review, assessment, and acceptance of a change insight. When the vouching steps are complete, the analysis team stipulates that the change insight has been fully tested to the best of its ability. The stipulated change insight constitutes the final output of the insighting process.[195]

The insight discipline's methods and deliberations leave their imprint on the transition from shaping to stipulating. The focus of deliberations in vouching shifts to whether you're willing to accept the tentative insight as final for the moment, as an input to extracting business implications. The accepted change insight, of course, isn't locked in stone; it remains open to alteration over time, subject to further data acquisition, analysis, and reflection.[196] Because it implies the imprimatur of those involved, the deliberation's interpersonal ebb and flow around final acceptance of the insight often become especially intense. It's the last opportunity for an individual or group to influence the insight's content.

Vouching entails a set of analysis steps (Table 6-1) that serve to orchestrate the deliberations. They frame the questions that must be asked and how they might be answered. The vouching process can be applied to all levels in the insight funnel (Figure 1-2) outlined in Chapter 1: domain insights, competitive space insights (CSIs), and generic marketplace insights (GMIs).

Table 6-1   Vouching: Key Steps

State the suggested insight

 Step 1: "Announce" the shift to vouching.

 Step 2: State the suggested insight.

 Step 3: Obtain agreement that the insight is worth vouching.

Review and assess the insight

 Step 4: Pose key questions.

 Step 5: Value test the insight.

 Step 6: Assess prior analysis conflicts.

 Step 7: Assess prior interpersonal conflicts.

 Step 8: Suggest amendments to the insight content.

 Step 9: Amend the insight.

Wordsmith the insight

 Step 10: Finalize the insight content.

 Step 11: Recognize the wordsmithing prescriptions.

Stipulate the accepted insight

 Step 12: Stipulate the insight as accepted for the moment.

 Step 13: Ensure that all recognize insights need to be validated over time.

When vouching doesn't occur

The importance of vouching as the lead up to stipulating an insight becomes evident in its absence. First, there's no recognized stopping point to the deliberations. The analysis back and forth may become protracted; without an agreed method to bring closure around an accepted insight, the participants can invoke every analysis and interpersonal means at their disposal to question and attack the opinions and assessment of others. Second, what passes for an accepted insight leaves a trail of discontented individuals: they frequently feel they didn't have an opportunity to have their voice heard. Third, not surprisingly, because individuals continue to question publicly either its content or the process by which it was crafted, the accepted insight may not be taken seriously by decision makers. Consequently, the decision value of the efforts to shape and disseminate change insights is substantially foregone.

When to apply vouching

Ideally, vouching takes place where the time invested in it generates organization (thinking, decision, and action) value. Nobody wants to waste time and energy in unnecessary activity. Here are three questions to ask to determine whether the full force of the vouching method (Table 6-1) should be applied to any tentative change insight:

- Does the change insight represent a dramatic shift in understanding?[197] The greater the change in understanding, the greater the need for vouching.

- Could the change insight give rise to a significant shift in the organization's thinking, decisions, and actions?[198] Answering this question requires a quick assessment of the change insight's potential business implications. It's often relatively straightforward to determine that a change insight might well have significant implications for key marketplace assumptions and beliefs, or how a major decision might be reframed or whether some new actions might be required.

- Did substantial analysis conflicts and interpersonal differences emerge in crafting the change insight? If the answer is yes, vouching provides an opportunity to revisit whether and how these differences impact an insight's content.

Vouching: Characteristics of insight render it necessary

Assuming affirmative answers to the criteria questions just noted, involvement in the final stages of critiquing and refining insights has convinced me of the importance of taking the time to go through the vouching process before finally stipulating an insight. This is so for a number reasons.

Insighting is a process: it's not a one-time event; it takes time.[199] Especially in the presence of analysis conflicts and interpersonal differences, getting to an acceptable stated insight proves difficult. One result is a protracted process and sometimes closure becomes impossible. Vouching as the pathway to stipulating a change insight aims to avoid these outcomes.

The opposite tendency is also prevalent: analysis teams often bring insight stipulation to a rapid conclusion. A suggested insight, the product of shaping, gets a quick review and is immediately accepted. Any value in terms of enhanced thinking, decisions, and actions inherent in vouching is lost.

Words make a difference to insight content. As you'll see later in this chapter, in any stipulated insight that emanates from the vouching activity, small changes can make a substantial difference. And, they may lead to considerably greater thinking, decision, and action value.

Sometimes the underlying intensity of the interpersonal ebb and flow only becomes evident in the vouching activity. Thus, vouching allows differences in opinions and their associated emotions to be put on the table one last time. One consequence is that the tentative insights (and underlying integrated inferences) get fully challenged and a genuine reconciliation of the differences becomes possible—they're no longer under the table. If that occurs, the likelihood of a superior insight is greatly enhanced.

Preparing the mind for vouching

It's necessary to devote attention to preparing the mind for vouching given some challenges specific to its method and deliberations. The most fundamental challenge, perhaps, requires individuals to step back from their involvement in structuring, sniffing, and shaping, to take a "fresh" look at the tentative change insights—the outputs of shaping. Given that it's the last opportunity to craft the change insight, an open mind becomes particularly important. But it especially tough to do: individuals are required to adopt an open mind in assessing what they've already produced!

Thus, to avoid vouching degenerating into merely rubber-stamping shaping's tentative change insights, many of the mind, data and reasoning principles need to be revisited and invoked. The non-referential mind principle (see Table 3-1) reminds an analysis team that it can't presume that a tentative insight accurately depicts or projects change—hence the need not only for an open mind but one that is enduringly curious. An open mind may be at least partially attained by disciplined diversity in perspectives: it suggests the need for new DNA—individuals new to the insighting process who can take a perspective that isn't hobbled by involvement in shaping. And, a reminder that the insight context profoundly matters (see Table 3-2) should help an analysis team commit to analyzing again whether change in the marketplace context supports the tentative insight.[200]

Reacquainting an analysis team with the reasoning principles noted in Table 5-2 underpins any effort to achieve an open mind. Recognizing the reasoning principle that no one individual's perspective should be privileged impels individuals to express their opinion and create the tension so critical to productive deliberations. But every individual's reasoning comes with cognitive biases (see Table 5-3): they make it difficult to disengage from the points of view and judgments advanced in shaping (and maybe even in structuring and sniffing). Hence, it may be especially necessary in stipulating to identity personal and organizational biases associated with the reasoning and choice of data supporting any critique of the tentative insight. Reaffirming that reasoning is the engine that powers conceptual innovation (new descriptions and explanations) may inspire one or more individuals to reconsider the "logics" or arguments enabling the tentative insight. One desirable outcome: insist on developing the strongest possible counter data and reasoning. The counter-reasoning likely revisits substantive elements of vetting the suggested and tentative insight in shaping.

The vouching method and deliberations

Vouching, as a method, involves four analysis steps that culminate in stipulating the insight as accepted for decision-making purposes (Table 6-1). They allow the analysis team and others who may be involved to have one final opportunity to contribute to crafting the change insight.

The deliberations stemming from these four questions require careful management. As you'll see, those leading vouching walk a tightrope: provide sufficient time to proceed through the method's steps but not to allow it to linger unnecessarily in nonproductive refinements of the tentative insight.

State the tentative insight

Step 1: Announce the shift to vouching

It is important to let all involved know that a transition of vouching is now occurring. The focus shifts to one final opportunity to amend the tentative insight.

Step 2: State the tentative insight

Stating the tentative insight, the output of shaping, for all to see, confirms that the analysis team is now moving into vouching. At first glance, it may seem superfluous and unnecessary. Indeed, I've heard it put rather bluntly: "All we're doing here is repeating what we have already agreed is the (tentative) insight." However, stating the tentative insight as a kickoff to vouching isn't an event, it's a process—a means for the analysis team and perhaps others to (re)focus their attention on the insight. Stating the CommodityCo case's customer insight, customers, recognizing that they need more than the base functional capabilities delivered by their providers, are seeking an offer rather than just a product, or the DipCo case customer insight, customers are falling into distinct needs-based segments (some want a full solution, others want a basic solution) requiring customized solutions and in the full solution segment customers will walk away fast from their longtime providers invites the analysis team and possibly others to consider whether they would like to amend it in any way. It reminds all involved that any tentative domain insight is really that—tentative until finally stipulated as that which we accept for decision-making purposes.

Step 3: Obtain agreement that this insight is worth vouching

Often stating a competitive space insight (CSI) or generic marketplace insight (GMI) reinforces its potential business implications and hence the importance of one last consideration of its attributes, including congruence and novelty. Take the suggested GMI from the DipCo case: a new marketplace opportunity (driven by an emerging customer need and the ability of at least one firm to serve that need) significantly larger than the current product solution would evolve over the next two years. Stating the tentative GMI allows all involved to recognize that if it stands the rigors of one last scrutiny test, its thinking, decision and action implications might be significant.

Review and assess the insight

The analysis team now understands it has one last opportunity for the moment to revisit and possibly refine the tentative insight. However, a word of caution is required here. The intent isn't to reopen shaping's deliberations or to fully execute again its complete method. It may be appropriate to do so if vital flaws are evident in the analysis back and forth or the interpersonal ebb and flow has skewed the deliberations in unacceptable ways. This decision tight rope results in a set of questions that determine whether and to what level of detail to engage in vouching.

Step 4: Pose key questions

The deliberations are driven by a set of questions that focus the assessment and refinement of the tentative insight(s). Answers to the questions quickly indicate whether vouching is likely to be protracted:

- Has preliminary value testing of the tentative insight indicated that it's worth expending the time to refine it?
- What's the rationale for each initial amendment to the tentative insight?
- What difference does each amendment make to the tentative insight? Is it more novel? Does it have wider applicability?[201]
- What's the rationale or argument of those opposed to the tentative insight?
- Are you comfortable vouching for the insight if you're questioned by your colleagues?

The questions, particularly the first two, indicate the analysis challenges faced in the vouching process. If they're not surfaced and considered, vouching can degenerate into an over-easy assessment that adds little value and may mean that the stipulated insights aren't fully vetted.

Step 5: Value test the insight

A quick value testing exercise confirms or denies the merit of proceeding with vouching. It revolves around two questions: Does the change insight shift what you see and your thinking in ways that make a difference to your beliefs, assumptions, and point of view? Partly because of the shift in thinking, could the change insight have a significant impact on the organization's intent, decisions, and actions?[202]

Another quick review of the DipCo GMI noted above quickly determined its potential thinking, decision, and action implications. It strongly suggested the possibility of significant opportunity, thought whether the firm had or could develop the capability to pursue the opportunity remained to be seen.

In the Gorilla Competitor case, one of the competitor insights—that the competitor was intent on reaching a new level of global market dominance through its R&D and marketing commitments that would make it exceptionally difficult for some current rivals to remain in the business—raised fears among the analysis team that if it proved congruent with how events unfolded, their own firm would find it difficult to realize the marketplace goals it current strategic plan aimed to achieve. Hence, they were extremely willing to invite others within the organization to engage in one final assessment of this competitor insight.

Step 6: Assess prior analysis conflicts

If analysis conflict has characterized the late stages in getting to the tentative insight, one immediate analysis pathway presents itself: is there any significant benefit to reviewing why these conflicts emerged and were sustained and whether and how they influenced the content of the tentative insight? This pathway gives rise to several questions. For example, what new eyes might be invoked to add a fresh perspective or to frame a new set of analysis questions? It might help to bring in relevant outsiders such as regulatory or technology experts who might ask questions that had been overlooked or downplayed. A second question: how different might the suggested insight be because of the new perspectives and questions? What if the new eyes provide fresh understanding of the forces that might influence the size and timing of the opportunity?

This analysis pathway is only warranted if there's a strong argument, that is, powerful reasoning that, in effect, extending shaping might result in significant, and perhaps radical amendment of the tentative insight.

Step 7: Asses prior interpersonal conflicts

If getting to the tentative insight has been marked by deep differences in the interpersonal ebb and flow, another pathway presents itself: is there any significant benefit to revisiting why these differences persisted and whether and how they influenced the content of the suggested insight? This pathway also gives rise to several questions worth considering. For example, what biases might have shaped the insight in one direction or another? If one or more individuals were biased toward advancing the need for a radical redirection of the firm's strategy, they would have been inclined to state the opportunity in very positive terms. What mix of positive and negative emotions were evident as the analysis team finalized the tentative insight? It might be worthwhile to ask what caused these emotions and how they played out in reaching some form of consensus around the tentative insight. Widespread negative emotions might indicate that a number of individuals felt uncomfortable and dismayed with the eventual suggested insight.

Again, this analysis pathway focusing on the interpersonal considerations influencing insight content is only warranted if there's significant evidence that interpersonal issues unduly influenced the tentative insight.

Step 8: Suggest amendments to the insight content

In most instances, because shaping's method and deliberations largely exhaust the analysis possibilities, vouching quickly zeros in on raising and assessing possible amendments to the tentative domain, CSI or GMI. If one or more of the possible amendments significantly alter the change insight, the deliberation assumes some of the aspects of the final stages of shaping (see steps 8–10 in Table 5-1).

Step 9: Amend the insight

If the amendments don't dramatically alter the change insight, the deliberation quickly moves to what I call *wordsmithing*.

Wordsmithing the insight

Wordsmithing an insight is the final opportunity to determine its specific and precise content. In some instances, even what initially appear to be relatively minor changes, can significantly alter the insight's content. Not surprisingly, wordsmithing typically reflects a continuation of the deliberations begun in step 2.

Case: DipCo

Consider the DipCo case customer insight: a new customer need (a particular operation's problem) with specific technology specifications was emerging, driven in part by evolving technology and by customers' discontent with existing solutions. As the team began to finalize the insight wording, a discussion ensued about whether the need was likely to be largely similar across customer groups. It led to the insight being restated: a new customer need is emerging that will vary greatly across customer groups. In effect, this is a distinctly different insight to the tentative insight that emerged in the shaping stage. It reflects deeper understanding of the customer change that could take place. The insight was then further reframed: a new customer need evolving out of a persistent customer operations problem with specific technology specifications will require distinctly different solutions across customer groups. The restated customer insight resulted in specific implications across the 6IFs, which I'll discuss later in this chapter.

Returning to the DipCo case GMI noted above: a new marketplace opportunity (driven by an emerging customer need and the ability of at least one firm to serve that need) will open a competitive space that will eventually obsolete the current product solution. A brief deliberation led to a wordsmithing change: a new marketplace opportunity, possibly doubling the size of the market for the current product (driven by an emerging customer need and the ability of at least one firm to serve that need) will open a competitive space that will eventually obsolete the current product solution within three years. The changes added clarity and specificity to the insight: the new market would be double the size of the existing one; obsolescence of the current product could occur within three years. Again, as noted later in the chapter, the 6IF implications were non-trivial.

Case: Gorilla Competitor

The tentative competitor insight, the Gorilla Competitor was intent on reaching a new level of global market dominance through its R&D and marketing commitments that would make it exceptionally difficult for some current rivals to remain in the business, did indeed give rise several suggested amendments. After some deliberation, the competitor insight was amended: the Gorilla Competitor's intent is to achieve global R&D and marketing dominance in the product domain, broadly defined, to the point that rivals without a strong R&D capability and the ability to develop global marketing and sales collaborations, will be forced out of the business within three years.

Some wordsmithing guidelines

The discussion above suggests several guidelines for wordsmithing the final content of a stipulated insight. First, don't overdo the wordsmithing, unless the answers to the questions noted above suggest it's necessary. Second, continually ask if the amendments to the insight content are adding clarity, that is, are they adding to the understanding inherent in the insight. To return to the Gorilla Competitor insight, the restated competitor insight now asserts that rivals without strong R&D and marketing capabilities won't be able to stay the course in this product arena. Third, where possible be specific. For example, adding a time dimension often frames an insight: The Gorilla Competitor insight now states that some rivals may not be in the marketplace in three years.

Stipulating the insight: The final act

The final step in vouching is to stop and declare this is the change insight you're willing to adopt for the moment as input to the next insight stages, deriving implication insights and business implications. Thus, the Gorilla Competitor analysis team might stipulate the competitor insight as stated above.

The stipulated insight brings closure to the insight process. It doesn't, however, end consideration of the insight: the need to validate the insight over time must be brought to the attention of all involved—those who have contributed to crafting the insight and those who will be involved in assessing its business implications.

Stipulating and the 6IFs

Change insights assume significance only to the extent that they make a difference in thinking, decisions, and actions. As noted in Chapter 1, the 6IFs can be used to enhance preparedness for the 4S cycle [203] and to assess the extent an insight makes a difference. I'll use the notion of making a difference to illustrate the distinct applicability of the 6IFs to the "input" and "output" sides of vouching.

Influencing the input side of vouching

Some analysis and interpersonal challenges specific to vouching require that application of the 6IFs in determining readiness for vouching must go beyond what was discussed in Chapter 3 in preparing individuals for structuring (see Table 3-4).[204] These challenges include the need to stringently review shaping's outputs to which individuals may have already contributed, to achieve closure on the insight process, to enable precision to be brought to bear on articulating insight content through wordsmithing, and, to facilitate the opportunity for individuals to express their judgments in the final interpersonal ebb and flow. Because people often fail to recognize the benefits of vouching, whether and to what vouching makes a difference must be directly addressed. In short, questions specific to each IF can be posed to assess readiness for and willingness to participate fully in vouching (Table 6-2).

Table 6-2   6IFs and Stipulating: Does It Make a Difference?

	Input side: Can stipulating make a difference?	Output side: How do stipulating outputs make a difference?	Output side: Sample key questions
See	Do we see how it might make a difference to final insight content?	What do we now see differently? What can we now imagine that we couldn't previously?	See new trends and patterns? See new discontinuities? See new opportunities and risks?
Think	Do we appreciate how we might need to change our modes of thinking as part of vouching?	What's different in what we think about and how we think? Are there specific nuances that are new in our thinking?	Thinking about new things? Focusing on new assumptions, beliefs, and projections? Using new modes of thinking?
Intend	Do we understand how the purpose of stipulating is different that shaping?	Does the new insight content suggest new goal possibilities or modifications to existing goals?	Establishing new goals? Establishing goals in new domains?

Decide	Are we willing to consider how and why stipulating might make a difference?	Is it possible the new insight makes a difference to the organization's intent and goals?	Making new decisions? Reframing existing decisions? Developing new decision options?
Act	Do we know which behaviors will help stipulating to make a difference?	What might be different about how we act?	Behaving in new ways? Adapting existing behaviors
Feel	What emotions might need to change to enable stipulating to be productive?	How might the stipulated insight lead to more positive emotions and overcome prior negative emotions?	Sensing new emotions?

The input-side questions noted in Table 6-2 provide a focus for deliberations aimed at enabling the team to learn about vouching and the difference it can make to the ultimate content of any change insight—domain, CSI, or GMI. Addressing each input-side question allows the team to see how vouching might alter insight content, how new modes of reasoning or challenging thinking might help to wordsmith any tentative insight—in short, how vouching could add significant value to the outputs of shaping (intent). If the team fails to see how vouching can enhance the quality of the insight content, they're unlikely to contribute earnestly to reviewing an accepted insight, much less to wordsmithing. If the team is unable to get beyond the thinking that led to the accepted insight, they're unlikely to advance new modes of reasoning to challenge the insight's content.

A prelude to these see, think, and intend inputs may be getting the team to consider how and why vouching might make a difference to their understanding of the change context, their judgments about change factors, and their willingness to amend tentative insights (the outputs of shaping). Consideration of the actions involved in stipulating's method (Table 6-1) encourages the team to understand what they need to do to enable vouching to achieve its goals. Not surprisingly, consideration of emotions may reveal substantial inhibitors to people being willing to undertake vouching. In the absence of attention to the 6IFs, the team is unlikely to advocate vouching (intent) or act in ways to identify vouching opportunities and suggestions that vouching be undertaken is only likely to lead to negative emotions (for example, feelings of discontent and loathing that they've been asked to do something they believe is unnecessary).

Analysis team leaders need to initiate deliberations that allow those involved in insight work to understand the role and intent of vouching—how it can make a real difference not only in the content of eventual stipulated insights but to the business implications to which it gives rise.

Assessing the output of vouching

As noted in Chapter 1, change insights possess value only to the extent they make a difference to the organization's thinking, decisions and actions. Developing a preliminary value testing of the proposed insight is integral to the vouching method (Table 6-1). A final value assessment of the tentative or accepted insight can never be conducted in vouching; that is the intent and focus of determining implication insights and business implications, as discussed in the following two chapters. But it's often useful to pose the output-side questions noted in Table 6-2 during vouching and when the insight is formally stipulated. These questions compel deliberations to assess, albeit in a preliminary way, whether the insight is likely to make a genuine difference along each of the 6IFs—in effect, whether it will contribute distinctive value to the organization's thinking, decisions, and actions.

Take as an example the customer insight from the DipCo case: a new customer need evolving out of a persistent customer operations problem with specific technology specifications will require distinctly different solutions across customer groups. The new understanding at the heart of the insight led the firm to see a significant new marketplace opportunity—the potential emergence of new customer need.[205] The opportunity would compel the management team to think about whether and how to exploit the opportunity: they would have to think about the scope and scale of the opportunity, what the customer need really was, and what new assets and capabilities would be required to pursue the opportunity. The insight could lead to a distinctly new intent and new decisions: the intent might be to develop a new strategy with the aim of reconfiguring a traditional market space. The associated decisions would also be new to the organization: it had never attempted to develop and market anything comparable to the projected solution. Of course, numerous new action streams would also have to be initiated and executed to go after the opportunity. The new product development and marketing context doubtlessly would ignite many emotion challenges; feelings of anxiety, discomfort, and insecurity would certainly be prevalent in the early stages of assessing the opportunity. It's important to note these are only preliminary assessments of the change insight's value; a complete assessment occurs in the deliberations around implication insights and business implications—the focus of the next two chapters.[206]

Vouching: Don't take it for granted

Teams sometimes view vouching as an afterthought to shaping. They don't relish taking the time out to do a final critical review of the tentative insight. However, involvement in the final stages of refining and delineating change insights at all marketplace levels has convinced me of the importance of taking the time to go through the vouching process before finally stipulating an insight. This is so for a few reasons. First, a natural tendency exists to bring insight stipulation to rapid closure; a "good enough" mentality often prevails that results in initially identified tentative insights receiving only minimal assessment.

A lot of the value of the insighting process thus is never realized. Second, as illustrated in the DipCo case, small changes can make a substantial difference in the stipulated insight that emanates from the vouching activity. And, they may lead to considerably greater thinking, decision, and action value. Third, sometimes the intensity of the interpersonal ebb and flow only becomes evident in the vouching activity. Thus, vouching allows differences in opinions and their associated emotions to be put on the table one last time.

One consequence is that the suggested insights (and underlying integrated inferences) get fully challenged and a genuine reconciliation of the differences becomes possible—they're no longer under the table. If that occurs, the likelihood of a superior insight is considerably higher.

Some stipulating errors

Stipulating's value resides in the refinement of any tentative insight—refinement that as illustrated in the DipCo case can sometimes fundamentally shift the insight content, and, thus, potentially its decision-making value. That additional value can be frittered away through the commission of the errors noted in Table 6-3. The largest error, of course, isn't entering the stipulating activity at all: once the insight is shaped (even as a first pass), immediately declaring it stipulated—we now accept it as an input to decision making. The impulse to get through stipulating as quickly as possible—which translates into an "over easy" pass—must also be resisted; experience teaches me that there's always a surprise or two lurking around the corner once stipulating is embarked upon.

Table 6-3   Fundamental Stipulating Errors

Overall stipulating process

- Ignoring stipulation entirely: "There's no need to test and refine the insight; our first definition of it is more than adequate."
- Moving through it rashly: "We've done the analysis, we've spent the time in shaping; there's no need to stop now and revisit it all in the form of vouching."
- Paying lip service to vouching: "We don't have much time to refine and test the suggested insight; can't we go with what we have?"

Stating the insight

- Not "announcing" that the transition from shaping to stipulating is now taking place: "We can wrap this up pretty quickly."
- Once it's announced, invitations to participate are restricted to a few: "A few of us can get this done without bothering others."

Review and assess the insight

- Not taking it seriously beyond one or two refinements of the tentative insight: "There's no need to refine further; these suggested refinements obviously don't add anything."
- Not encouraging individuals to wordsmith—to suggest amendments to the alleged insight: "Let's not waste time trying to be cute with our suggestions for how to improve the insight."
- Not allowing tension to emerge in the discussion around amendments to the alleged insight: "There's no need to eagerly contrast these two statements; these aren't really different descriptions of the insight."

Wordsmithing the insight

- Accepting the first rewording of the insight: "That's good enough for now."
- Not asking if the rewording is adding additional understanding: "we do not need to state the insight in the best possible language."

Stipulating the insight

- Not using the 6IFs to develop a preliminary assessment of its thinking, decision, and action consequences: "The insight obviously has significant implications; there's no need to refine them at this stage."

Another understandable error occurs when individuals shy away from anything resembling serious wordsmithing; they just don't believe it can make a difference. In short, a more refined understanding of change is missed.

A final error worth noting is failure to fully employ the 6IFs to assess the outcomes of a stipulated insight to determine if its business implications are likely to be trivial or significant. As noted previously, the 6IFs quickly reveal the potential import of a tentative or accepted change insight; they don't provide an assessment of the insight's business implications.

Validating change insights

Deep understanding of change encapsulated in a stipulated insight may become obsolete due to unanticipated change or by anticipated change that unfolds faster or slower than expected. In each case, the stipulated insight no longer holds and if adhered to likely results in inappropriate thinking, poor decisions and ineffective actions. Consider the following two examples I experienced in the last few years:[207]

- A competitor insight that a dominant rival would invest heavily to ramp up its market strategy to gain share at the expense of non-aggressive rivals suddenly lost its vintage when a year later the competitor was acquired by a large corporation which saw the business as a source of major positive cash flow and thus reverted to a steady state strategy.
- A customer insight developed by an electronics firm, consumers want a specific type of product functionality and will migrate quickly from rivals to obtain it, proved true for what might be described as "early innovators." However, the mass of the market rejected the new product functionality.[208]

These examples illustrate the importance of congruency as an insight attribute; insight content may become incongruent with marketplace developments. Thus, any change insight, no matter the depth of evidence and strength of reasoning buttressing it, must be continually validated. Validating involves assessing whether the stipulated change insight continues to hold. It addresses the question: in view of emerging and projected marketplace and organization change, do we need to amend the content of the insight? Validating an insight can occur only after it's been vouched for and stipulated.

To describe validating, I'll address four change insights in Box 6-1.

Box 6-1

Change Insights: Validating Examples

Case	Insight	Description
VP	Customer insight	Customers are falling into distinct needs-based segments (some want a full solution, others want a basic solution) requiring customized solutions and in the full solution segment customers *will* walk away fast from their longtime providers.
AbsoCo	Competitor insight	A currently insignificant player in one product area, could, through a single acquisition and a change in direction in its R&D investments generate within three years a new customer solution that would be a product generation or two ahead of all current rivals in that product space.
CommodityCo	Competitive space insight (CSI)	The undifferentiable commodity has now been differentiated.
VP	Generic marketplace insight (GMI)	Strategy vulnerability: Some rivals will find it impossible to make the transition.

The insight perspective

The insight discipline's interplay between deliberations and method emphasizes not only capturing, but also anticipating marketplace change as the critical input to validating a change insight. The deliberations involved in validating revolve around three questions:

- Is the content of the change insight holding up over time?
- If it isn't, how should the insight content be amended?
- If the insight is significantly changed, it leads to the value-testing question: What are the consequences of the amended insight for implication insights and business implications?

These three questions reflect and reinforce the characteristics of insights and insight work emphasized throughout this book. Change insights typically involve a view of the future. Change is never-ending; thus, all insights no matter how extensively vetted and vouched, have a definite shelf life. The judgments at the heart of an insight may be correct at the time an insight is stipulated but over time may become incongruent with marketplace and organization change. Thus, insighting as a process is never complete.

The future orientation of validating leads to an analysis method that focuses on identifying relevant marketplace indicators and monitoring and projecting change along them. The analysis steps drive deliberations that aim to amend insight content before it becomes obvious that it's necessary.

Preparing the mind for validating

Validating's central question is the content of the accepted change insight holding up, which requires systematic monitoring and projection of marketplace change. Thus, the mind principles (see Table 3-1) emphasizing the need to remember that all insights have a shelf life and to be perpetually inquisitive become especially important. Indeed, it may be necessary to hard-wire reminders of the shelf life of insights into the organization's procedures: for example, reviewing insight validity as a component at various stages of the annual strategic planning cycle or budget allocation across analysis projects.

Validating's central question can't be fully addressed without projecting the direction, speed and intensity of marketplace change. Customers' adoption of new products, competitors' shift in strategy, technology diffusion across geographies all necessitate projections of how broad and fast such change will occur. As you'll see shortly, projections of change provide early indicators of the need for insight review. Thus, the reasoning principles noted in Table 5-2, especially a willingness to invoke pictures (projections) of the future and that reasoning and its outcomes change over time become particularly relevant. Unfortunately, insight validating sometimes is severely circumscribed because an analysis leader and others feel uncomfortable crafting future projections and applying them to critique accepted change insights.[209]

Both monitoring and projecting change—without which validating's central question can't be addressed—obviously require data inputs. Many of the data principles noted in Table 3-2 assume added importance because of validating's future orientation: data is always in question (there's no guarantee that any projection reflects the "real" state of the world at some future time); data is likely contaminated in many ways (the biases of those crafting the competitor or customer change infuse the projections); understanding the data context is even more important (projections are always driven by change factors). Moreover, no type of data or data source can be privileged (indicators can come in many forms and different human data sources can provide distinct understanding of why projected trends, patterns or discontinuities will move in specific directions).

Analysis team leaders and others need to initiate and manage deliberations around the relevance of the mind, data, and reasoning principles to monitoring and specially to projecting change. Those involved in validating need to understand that it's never simply a matter of executing one means of projecting change. As noted in Chapter 1, the future is a cognitive construction. So it's appropriate to develop alternative methods to project change such as scenarios. The alternative competitive futures enable different indicators to be identified, thus enhancing the likelihood that relevant change will be detected sooner rather than later.

Validating: The method

Validating involves a set of steps designed to craft understanding of an inevitably changing marketplace (Table 6-4). Depending on the insight content, as discussed below, these steps may be executed at different speeds. However, the intent remains constant: amend the change insight content when it's deemed necessary; in other words, restipulate the change insight. The amended insight may reflect modest wordsmithing at one end or a drastically overhauled insight at the other end. In some instances, the marketplace change may so overwhelm the insight content that it's abandoned.

Table 6-4   Validating: Key Steps

Identify key indicators

    Step 1: Review the relevant context.

    Step 2: Identify insight-specific indicators.

    Step 3: Identify context-specific indicators.

Monitor and anticipate change

    Step 4: Monitor Indicators.

    Step 5: Derive Inferences.

Anticipate and project change

    Step 6: Identify potential change trajectories.

    Step 7: Project change.

Amend insight content

    Step 8: Develop preliminary amendments.

    Step 9: Amend insight content.

Identify key indicators

Validating addresses whether the stipulated insight remains congruent with the current and anticipated marketplace realities. It thus requires determining key change indicators and monitoring (and projecting) change along the indicators.

Step 1: Review the relevant context

The relevant marketplace context of any change insight doesn't remain constant. Change in and around customers, competitors, marketplace dynamics, and technology continues unabated. Thus, the intent of reviewing an insight's context is straightforward: identify change vectors that could not be detected simply by analyzing the change insight itself. For example, the emergence of an unexpected substitute product has caused many CSIs to be suddenly "off target" and if they continued to be "accepted" would lead to misleading business implications. Corporate customers' motivations may shift due to change in their internal situation; thus, insights into customers' purchasing patterns may quickly prove no longer congruent with how customers see the world. In short, the quality of a change insight may degrade or augment due to developments in its relevant context.

Two questions help determine the relevant context:

- What marketplace change would challenge the change insight's content?
- What is the evidence that the change is real? That is, is it already transpiring or might it emerge at some future time?

The competitor insight (Box 6-1) led to the identification of a set of potential change vectors that were expected to dominate change in the competitive context: developments in three specific technology domains, change in current rivals' R&D strategies, emergence of one or more rivals in related product domains, technology development within lead and follower customers, shifts in specific regulatory policies and rules. The evolution of change along any of these vectors could have dramatic impact on the competitor insight. For example, if the projected technology trajectories did occur, a rival product solution might make it to the marketplace within three to four years, thus challenging the core content of the competitor insight: the competitor's projected product might well be ahead of all current rivals but might be behind the substitute rival.

Step 2: Identify insight-specific indicators

It's advisable to identify insight-specific indicators before trying to determine context-specific indicators; the former helps the team recognize indicators that are truly context related. Every change insight, irrespective of its marketplace level, gives rise to indicators specific to its content. These indicators become a dominant focus in identifying and monitoring marketplace change over time relevant to the change insight.

Consider the customer insight noted in Box 6-1. Specific indicator categories include: customers' statements about need-related challenges, operations problems that need to be solved, and possible investment expenditures; variations in these statements across customers; technology advances by multiple technology development firms; discussion of specific technology advances in the trade literature, technology presentations at trade shows, and statement by particular technology experts; solution configurations being advanced by different potential vendors; early adoption by customers of some form of the solution.

Consider the competitor insight noted in Box 6-2. Specific indicator categories include: the competitor's statements about all facets of its business strategy; its actions specific to change in its operations; statements specific to its intent to do one or more acquisitions; resource commitments in its R&D program; interactions with customers; behaviors of the sales force; search for technology alliance partners.

Step 3: Identify context-specific indicators

Capturing relevant context change vectors, as discussed above, enables identification of context-specific indicators. Critical context change affecting the shelf life of a change insight often lies outside the range of insight-specific indicators.

With respect to the customer insight, context indicator categories include: competitors' statements and actions that might affect the possible operations solution; announcements of developments in new technologies, new technology launches, trials of specific technologies by customers; introduction of new regulatory rules or governmental hearings focused on industry developments or societal concerns. For example, the emergence of new technologies might drastically alter the underlying customer need; indeed, it might obso-lete the customer need before it's ever satisfied. Sometimes, regulatory change reshapes an insight's competitive space or enables or inhibits competitors' or customers' ability to realize their stated goals.

The CSI noted in Box 6-2 gave rise to a number of indicator categories: competitors' current customer offers; change in customers' offers; competi-tors' announcements of change in their marketing strategies; customers' product/solution inquiries and requests; analysis outputs and statements by industry observers (for example, consultants, technology experts).

The faster the need to amend insight content is detected, the earlier think-ing, decisions, and action can be adapted. As noted in Chapter 2, leading indicators provide early indications of emerging and potential marketplace change. Two questions guide determination of which indicators might be dubbed "leading" and thus receive critical attention: Which indicator catego-ries provide the earliest indications that amending insight content may be warranted? What change is already occurring along these indicators?

Consider the GMI noted in Box 6-1. Two early indicators might be rumors in the industry grapevine that a competitor is seeking to sell one or more manufacturing plants or has opened negotiations with vendors to lower its contract commitments for particular raw materials, components or sup-plies. Clearly, change along these and other indicators needs to be monitored to confirm or refute early inferences that they might give rise to.

Monitor and anticipate change

Tracking change along leading and other indicators provides the fodder for assessment of whether the change insight needs to be amended. If validating involved only monitoring change along context and insight specific indicators, it would be relatively straightforward. However, the real challenge and the source of the value of validating is in anticipating future change. Projections allow direct assessment of whether an accepted insight needs to be amended. As discussed in Chapters 2 and 3, change can be depicted and projected in terms of trends (change along single indicators), patterns (intersection of trends), and discontinuities (a change in direction in a trend or pattern).

Step 4: Monitor indicators

The CommodityCo firm (CSI in Box 6-1) asked itself two questions: How fast and widespread will differentiation take hold across rivals and customers?

And what might the dynamics of rivalry look like two years out? Answers to these two questions can only emerge by tracking context and insight specific indicators over time and hazarding projections based in large part on the detected change. For example, indicator categories associated with rivals' strategies including product configuration, service elements, promotion messages, sales force behaviors and pricing terms and conditions, allow inferences about the scope, speed and intensity of rivals' commitment to and execution of differentiation.

Consider the GMI noted in Box 6-1. Competitor specific indicators meriting tracking include: marketplace and financial performance, statements emanating from rivals about (for example) the future of the industry, what it takes to win in the industry, and, their ability to compete in the industry; investments in R&D, technology and marketing; change in customer offers (for example, change in products, services, terms and conditions).

Step 5: Derive inferences

Change along indicators enables the team to make judgments that eventually determine if the content of the change insight needs to be amended. The judgments involve two types of inferences: what is the current state of the change? What might be the future direction of the change? In effect, they conduct many of the elements of sniffing described in Chapter 4.

Consider the customer insight case (Box 6-1). Tracking the insight specific indicators noted above might give rise to an inference (based on their behaviors and statements) that some customers are currently moving quickly to obtain a possible customized solution. The analysis team might then judge (partly based on the intensity of customers' efforts) that further customers might migrate toward the customized solution segment.

Reverting to the GMI noted in Box 6-1, tracking key competitor-specific indicators noted above might allow inferences to be drawn that specific competitors were already struggling to stay in the business (lower performance along many indicators and executives' statements) and others were considering reducing their presence in the industry (for example, reductions in investments, executives' statements, comments from third parties).

Anticipate and project change

Step 6: Identify potential change projections

The critical output of the change inferences typically comes down to a projection of change (trends, patterns, and discontinuities) that provides the basis for determining whether and to what extent the change insight(s) needs to be adapted. In many respects, the assessment of these projections can be seen as an extension of the vetting and vouching that went into the insight's stipulation and acceptance.

Step 7: Project change

Consider the competitor insight noted in Box 6-1. The previously noted change vectors and their associated indicators provide a focus for the change projections. The projections address both the competitor context and the competitor. Competitor specific projections might include: how and when the competitor might consummate an acquisition, what entity might be an acquisition candidate, how its R&D initiatives might unfold, how an alliance with a technology house would provide a missing technology component. Context specific projections might include: emergence of new lookalike and substitute competitors, changes in rivals' strategies, shifts in customers' buying patterns and purchasing choice criteria.

The inferences noted above regarding the customer insight noted in Box 6-1 allowed the projection to be made that the pattern of a segment of customers moving toward a full solution was likely to strengthen and happen more quickly than previously thought.

The inferences noted above regarding the GMI case allowed the projection that the number of competitors who would remain in the market would be considerably smaller than initially projected.

Amend insight content

Step 8: Develop preliminary amendments

Eventually, an analysis team must determine whether the accepted insight content needs to be amended. The two guiding questions noted at the beginning of this section must again be brought to the fore: What marketplace change would challenge the change insight's content? What is the evidence the change is real, that is, already transpiring or might emerge at some future point in time?

The analysis steps in large measure mirror those in stipulating (Table 6-2): Suggest amendments to the insight content; finalize the insight content; wordsmith the final insight content; stipulate the insight as accepted for now; ensure that full recognition is given to the fact that the newly accepted insight will need to be continually monitored for its congruency with marketplace and organization change.

Step 9: Amend insight content

Not surprisingly, many of the characteristics of shaping and stipulating resurface: a tendency to protract the deliberations, especially if a strong or dominant argument supporting an amendment isn't present; analysis back and forth that reflects the ability to develop alternative statements of the desired insight content; and, interpersonal ebb and flow driven by the commitment of individuals or groups of individuals to their preferred insight content.

The competitor insight, a currently insignificant player in one product area, could, through a single acquisition and a change in direction in its R&D investments generate within three years a new customer solution was amended to the currently small competitor will launch a new product that will create a new product-market in which most current rivals won't have a presence.

Managing validating

Fast- and slow-cycle validating

In many circumstances, validating is best viewed as a sequence of rapid assessments of an increasingly more "accepted" insight. For example, a customer insight is continually tested against customer data that is collected through a sequence of customer-site visits and customer interviews. The customer insight may be amended several times until the analysis team judges that the insight can now be accepted for decision-making purposes. Such fast-cycle customer insight validating underpins the now popular lean-innovation approach to understanding customer change.[210]

Fast-cycle validating of a long-accepted competitor insight may be provoked by recognition of change along some relevant context or insight-specific indicators. A quick assessment of the potential business implications spurs the relevant data collection. In the competitor insight case cited at the beginning of the validating discussion, statements by the competitor's executive team supported by execution decisions including the withdrawal of a planned advertising blitz resulted in the amendment to the accepted insight—the competitor would treat the business as a cash cow.

Validating errors

At the level of the entire validating method (Table 6-4), some crucial errors that impede its execution stem from not preparing the mind appropriately. Not appreciating validating's role and importance as a prerequisite to superior thinking, decisions, and actions means that ongoing insight review and assessment receives minimal attention. Hence, there's little intent to execute validating. Second, deliberations sometimes are driven by a desire to amend the insight based upon judgments in the early stages of the validating method rather than proceeding through all the steps noted in Table 6-4, even if they're completed quickly. For example, in one customer insight case, an analysis team drew some quick inferences from the first indicator, a statement by a competitor that the institutional customer was fundamentally shifting its purchasing criteria and immediately suggested a significant change to the insight content, only to discover a short time later that they had badly misinterpreted the competitor's comments and had to withdraw the suggested insight modification.

Third, not asking emphatically enough whether the amended insight makes a difference and to whom. Consequently, falling into the trap of spending a lot of time amending and wordsmithing a change insight that may not be worth the effort.

Using the 6IFs

Many of the "making a difference" questions noted in the case of stipulating (Table 6-3) are also relevant to validating. The input side questions aim to prepare individuals or an analysis team for validating. The output side questions enable a preliminary assessment of the thinking, decision, and action value of the amended insight.

The making a difference mind-set can be further sharpened by focusing the 6IFs on validating's method and deliberations (Table 6-5).[211] The preparing the mind discussion above revealed how difficult it can be for an individual or analysis team to address seriously the central validating question: is the content of the accepted change insight holding up? On the input side, each IF can be used to identify key challenges likely to be confronted in any organization's efforts to introduce validating (Table 6-5) as a formal method. These method challenges can then be the focus of deliberations. Each IF also generates questions to guide deliberations as to why validating isn't appreciated or not routinely deployed. For example, one might ask: what is the state of each IF that inhibits understanding and acceptance of validating? Specifically, an analysis team might ask: why do individuals not "see" the value of validating or how it enables more incisive "thinking" or why individuals don't know how to "act" (what it takes to execute validating). Answering these types of questions helps pinpoint interventions required to develop preparedness for validating as one part of building a validating capability (see the next section).

Table 6-5   6IFs and Validating: Method and Deliberations

IFs	Method (key challenges)	Deliberations (key questions)
See	Getting individuals and leaders to see the need for and benefits of a validating method. Identifying key inhibitors to seeing the benefits of validating.	Why do individuals not see the uses and benefits of validating? What would the "ideal" in validating look like?
Think	Individuals resist the need to monitor change as an input to validating. Identifying why thinking about future change is so difficult.	Why do individuals not want to address indicators of future change? What would the ideal in thinking look like?
Intend	Individuals don't perceive a purpose to validating (even when its value and benefits are described).	How to get individuals to engage in deliberations around the purpose of validating? How to build a business case for validating?
Decide	Getting individuals and leaders to commit to validating and to manage the necessary deliberations.	How to get individuals to discuss what it would take to get them to decide that validating was worth the effort?

Act	Getting individuals and a team to adopt the steps in the validating method. and to engage in serious deliberations.	How to "teach" what it takes to execute the validating method? How to initiate discussions around a first execution of validating?
Feel	How to recognize the influence of emotions in various phases of deliberations? How to engage individuals in deliberations about emotions?	How to recognize the influence of emotions in various phases of deliberations? How to engage individuals in deliberations about emotions?

Each IF can be used to develop "the ideal" IF state with respect to validating. The ideal provides a guidepost to aim for in developing a validating capability. An individual or team can ask: what would we see, think, intend, decide, act and feel if we were ideally prepared for and fully engaged in validating? For example, what would individuals "see" if they were ideally prepared for validating? They might see how validating should be executed and they might see how an amended insight would be more congruent with emerging and potential marketplace change. Ideally also they would understand how individuals would act if they wished to maximize the value of validating.

On the output side, as illustrated in the case of stipulating (Table 6-3), you can use the 6IFs to identify and assess the consequences of successful validating. Again, the emphasis is on answering the question: what difference does validating, and specifically the amended insight, make to what and to whom? For example, do you see new marketplace opportunities? Are you thinking about new ways to augment your customer value propositions? Do you intend to pursue new goals?

Building validating capability

Validating results in accepted insights that hopefully reflect the insight attributes noted in Chapter 1. Validated insights ensure that the best understanding of change informs strategizing and decision making. Thus, the need to embed and sustain a validating capability: the ability to efficiently and effectively validate insights as part of the organization's ongoing analysis routines.

In keeping with the tenets of the insight discipline advanced in this book, it requires attention to both method and deliberations.

The prescribed method to build a validating capability (Table 6-6) incorporates execution of the validating steps (see steps 6–9 in Table 6-4) detailed above. However, embedding and sustaining a validating capability also needs to address the challenges noted in the discussion above of "preparing the mind," validating errors, and use of the 6IFs to enhance validating method and deliberations. Hence, the importance of the first five steps noted in Table 6-6; they aim to ready the organization to execute validating.

Given that a validating capability is likely to be poorly developed in most organizations, priority should be given to developing the business case for validating (step 1 in Table 6-6). The business case attracts attention when key change insights are identified (step 2) and screened to determine those especially meriting validating (step 3). Organizational impetus is created when one or more individuals assume the role of validating "overseer" (step 4): they push the need for validating and to monitor execution of individual validating projects. Validating gets accomplished only when a team is created to execute the work (step 5).

Table 6-6   Building Validating Capability

Build the business case for insight validating

- Show the consequences if one or more change insights don't hold.
- Show the potential benefits of amending the content of one or more insights.

Choose stipulated insights for validating attention

- Identify the set of potential validating candidates.
- Array in terms of time urgency.

Assess which should be the focus of validating

- Determine which change insights are most critical.
- Assess potential business implications of each change insight.

Appoint overseer of the validating process

- Nominate an individual or team to oversee validating process.
- If necessary, allocate insights to specific individuals.

Create an analysis team

- Team to determine appropriate analysis.
- Team to conduct analysis.

Identify context and insight specific indicators (for each insight)

- Identify relevant indictors.
- Determine potential leading indicators.

Arrange for data collection along indicators

- Identify how data is to be collected.
- Determine how data to be organized.

Conduct early analysis

- Draw inferences as data is collected.
- Assess preliminary need to amend individual insights.

Complete analysis

- Identify tentative insight amendments.
- Finalize accepted amendments.

Learn and apply across validating projects

- Identify key learnings for each validating project.
- Apply learnings to individual validating projects.

Once a validating infrastructure is in place, validating projects can be executed (steps 6-9). It's helpful to ensure that at least one individual in each project team has prior experience in validating: it becomes a means to transfer learning from one Validating project to another.

Each validating step involves deliberations; especially dialogue around the role and importance of each step, how best to execute it, how to leverage learnings from prior validating projects, and, perhaps most contentious of all, how to move expeditiously through the steps without compromising analysis quality. A few points merit emphasis. Initial deliberations need to center on what a validating capability consists of: "how will we know it if we see it" is a question that is often raised.

Building the business case presumes a clear description of the purpose: Here's what we mean by validating capability, here's what it entails, and here's how it benefits the organization. Then as progress through the method steps (Table 6-6) occurs, deliberations need to be sharply focused on building validating capability: for example, how to enhance execution of each step, how to anticipate and avoid errors associated with each step, how to improve the overall validating infrastructure.[212]

It's also helpful to celebrate a validating win, that is, where an amended insight led to thinking, decisions, and action that made a difference.

A final comment

It's all too easy to overlook the role and importance of stipulating. However, it provides a critical opportunity to review the content of a change insight—especially critical to do so if the insight is likely to lead to significant thinking, decision, and action implications. Validating an insight assumes special importance in the presence or projection of turbulent marketplace change. It reminds all concerned that change insights have a shelf life.

Notes

195. Again, the insight process refers to the 4S cycle, structuring, sniffing, shaping, and stipulating.

196. This is the rationale, as discussed later in this chapter, for validating.

197. The importance of a shift in understanding as a core attribute of an insight was elaborated in Chapter 1.

198. This is an obvious reference to the 6IFs: thinking, decision making, and action as they key criteria to assess the impact of change insight.

199. Insighting here is shorthand for the 4S cycle: structuring, sniffing, shaping, and stipulating.

200. Presumably, they've already done so as part of shaping the tentative insight.

201. One could ask questions specific to each of the desired attributes of change insights noted in Chapter 1.

202. It's evident here that the assessment criteria reflect the 6IFs, initially introduced in Chapter 1 and applied in each chapter in this book.

203. Assessing readiness or an individual or team to engaging in vouching involves the 'input side" of doing insight work.

204. However, all the considerations noted in Table 3-4 are relevant to vouching.

205. This a classic example of a GMI, a generic marketplace insight; an opportunity that would be available to any rival should they seek to pursue.

206. Consideration of implication insights and business implications represent phases 3 and 4 in insight work (see Figure 1-1 in Chapter 1).

207. These examples remind us that an accepted insight may turn out to be true for a period and then turns out not to be true, hence the need for validating. These examples remind us also of the importance of "enduring" as a desirable attribute of any insight.

208. These examples remind us again that marketplace change insights deal with the future and therefore are the outcome of judgments (inferences) made about the future, hence, the need for validating.

209. This is an example of how emotions can negatively influence validating.

210. See, for example, Steve Bland, "Why the Lean Start-Up Changes Everything," *Harvard Business Review*, May 2013, 4–9.

211. Linkages between the 6IFs to the insight discipline's method and deliberations were initially introduced in Chapters 1 and 2.

212. Validating infrastructure refers to (among other things): having one or more individuals who possess expertise in validating, the transfer of validating learning from one analysis team to others, and maybe even a portal where individuals or teams can deposit their experience and learning.

Chapter 7

Implication Insights: The Segue to Business Implications

How often have you found yourself in the following situation? You and your colleagues are sitting around a table reviewing the detailed outputs of an extensive piece of analysis work. It could be the analysis of the shifting forces in an industry, the next generation of disruptive technologies, the projected strategies of diverse rivals, or changing customer behaviors across market or geographic segments. You're looking at myriad tables, charts, diagrams, and spreadsheets. You may have shaped and stipulated some domain insights, or possibly competitive space insights (CSIs) or maybe even generic marketplace insights (GMIs). The task at hand is clear: determine the business implications.

But a common outcome in this situation results in the deliberations going around in circles. Possible implications are noted, then discussed, another implication is suggested, further discussion ensues, and the pattern continues. Different perspectives stemming from participants' position in the hierarchy or functional department fuel distinctive preferences for what should be decided; various potential action plans attract groups of adherents. There seems to be no reasonable way to get to a set of business implications. In short, a distinct and accepted method to anchor and focus the deliberations isn't present.

The insight discipline advocated throughout this book suggests one way out of this circular deliberation trail: identify key implication insights before moving to specifying the final business implication details. This chapter expands on the notion of implication insight introduced in earlier chapters and shows in detail its contribution to intelligence insight. I'll illustrate how change insights provide the grist for the development of implication insights and how implication insights, in turn, facilitate and drive the determination of business implications. We begin by describing the role and importance of implication insight and why it's necessary to distinguish between implication insights and business implications—a distinction that is rarely made in organizations today. The bulk of the chapter details how to identify, assess, and leverage implication insights.

Understanding implication insight

The insight discipline emphasizes intelligence insight, that is, change insights and their implications for the business. Implication insights serve as the critical lynchpin between change insights and business implications (Figure 7-1). They provide critical high-level guidance for the organization's thinking, decisions, and actions. As noted in Chapter 1, an implication insight constitutes a fundamental "so-what" or "given" about consequences for the business that is derived from consideration of change insights but it doesn't indicate specific business implications. It requires you to identify and vet key implication insights, which is the focus of this chapter.

FIGURE 7-1

The Pathway to Implication Insights

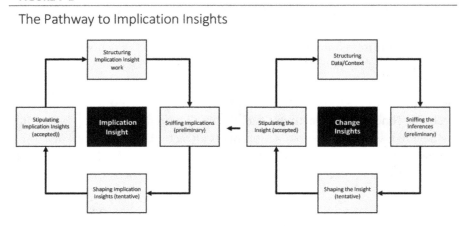

Implication insight always involves a change in understanding

Fundamental to understanding implication insight is that it involves a shift in understanding about the business that is crucial to future success.[213] The CommodityCo case illustrated how a small set of key domain change insights led to an implication insight that the firm's longstanding strategy had to change or it would rapidly lose market position and share—an example of an implication insight that fundamentally shifted the analysis ground on which the business implications were crafted (see Figure 1-1). The VP case also generated two core implication insights: how the organization thinks about winning and retaining customers' needs to shift, and the organization needs to massively reconfigure how it is managed.

Following are some examples of implication insights from specific industry settings (some of which are discussed later in this chapter). Each illustrates a critical shift in understanding that most likely leads to new business implications such as the need to change strategy direction, adopt distinctly new assumptions, or execution in a different way.[214]

Medical instruments: Without economies of scope, we can't compete in this industry against our current rivals (historically we thought we could compete and win by focusing on a few products).

R&D intensive technology: We can no longer depend on our own resources (capital, knowledge, skills, and so on) as the platform for new product breakthroughs if we wish to retain our historic goal of first mover advantage (previously our dominant assumption was that we "could go it alone" in R&D).

Manufacturing intensive: We will need to develop distinctly different solutions across customer groups if you're to go after a new opportunity evolving out of a persistent customer operations problem (we tend to offer the same core product to many customer groups).

Here's a further example of implication insights that make clear that any implication insight doesn't axiomatically suggest what the business implications should be, even though they involve a distinct shift in understanding.

The experience of a pharmaceutical company succinctly illustrates the connections between change insights and implication insight and business implications. An industry analysis led to a short list of CSIs and GMIs. Extensive deliberations about the potential business implications led to one core implication insight, political strategy, the management of external stakeholders, is fundamental to marketplace success (Figure 7-2). The accepted implication insight reflected new understanding in multiple ways. It was the first time that political strategy[215] was taken seriously as a form of strategy. Indeed, some managers had suggested previously that there really wasn't any such thing as a political strategy. It was the first time that extensive agreement was reached on the fact that some stakeholders were changing their political strategy and thwarting the organization's marketplace goals in new and somewhat unanticipated ways. It was the first time that some senior executives accepted that political strategy success was a prerequisite to winning in the product marketplace. The core business strategy implication: develop a political or stakeholder strategy.

FIGURE 7-2

Implication Insight: Pharmaceutical Case

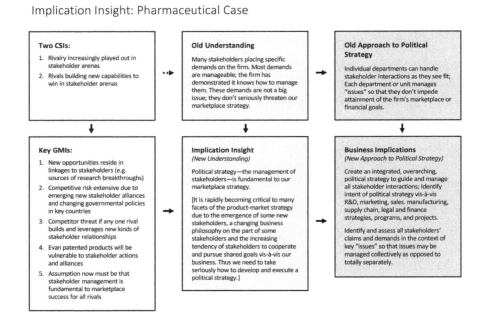

Ignore implication insights at your peril

Not identifying implication insights on the pathway to business implications can not only slow down deliberations[216] around business implications, but also lead to lower quality business implications. Consider these examples:

Biosciences case: A cross-functional team, guided by senior members of the intelligence function, conducted an extensive analysis of the industry and macro-environmental forces shaping the future of specific therapeutic areas. Specific findings were catalogued and agreed, some of which might be described as competitive space insights (CSIs) and generic marketplace insights (GMIs). Yet, when it came to determining key business implications, the extended analysis team found it almost impossible to come to agreement. Key individuals appeared to have distinct interpretations of what the findings implied for thinking, decisions, and actions.

Business services case: A six-month study of the "drivers of the emerging market" for a professional services business in a narrow "solution" area generated a clear and agreed set of factors, many of which might be considered CSIs and GMIs. Yet, in the appraisal of the core business implications, in the words of chief strategy officer, "all hell broke loose." The executive team simply could not agree on the key implications for the firm's strategy and operations.

Consumer case: At a recent market research conference, a VP of consumer insight told the story of how his team had produced an "incisive and comprehensive" set of consumer insights, with particular emphasis on understanding the motivations influencing consumers' purchasing behaviors. However, the marketing management team became highly exasperated[217] when it became evident that they could not reach agreement on key business implications. He noted in strong terms that individual marketing managers seemed to draw their own conclusions as to the marketing implications and they were highly reluctant to relinquish them.

The role and importance of implication insights

The importance of paying attention to implication insights before moving to determining "final" business implications—what the organization should do—is exemplified by the difficulties encountered in each of the three cases. First, it compels an analysis team to identify the base implications—the big so-whats—from change insights specific to the organization before the team members embark on fully specifying and assessing business implications. What the change insights mean for the business get encapsulated in one or a small number of short and compelling implication insights. In the case of the pharmaceutical firm noted above, the implication insight, political strategy—the management of external stakeholders—is fundamental to our marketplace strategy, transformed all the change insight deliberations into one sentence that shaped a set of significant business implications. Not doing so, as we saw in the case of the business services and consumer goods firm gives rise to a protracted and non-productive business implications' deliberations resulting in wasted energy, attention, and emotion.

Frequently, identifying and assessing possible implications takes time: the understanding embedded in implication insights often isn't self-evident in the content of change insights. The pharma firm, as illustrated later in this chapter, engaged in extensive deliberations to shape the political implication insight just noted. In the CommodityCo case described in Chapter 1, the analysis team in conjunction with members of the management team literally took several months to identify and accept the key implication insight—the firm's strategy could not win if it didn't undergo extensive change (see Figure 1-3).

A fundamental premise underpinning the insight discipline throughout this book is that implication insights help focus the deliberations inherent in getting into the details and nuances of business implications. If the pharmaceutical firm hadn't identified and accepted the political strategy implication insight, the analysis back and forth in the deliberations about how to create and execute a political strategy would inevitably keep circling back to whether a political strategy was required. In the CommodityCo case, once the core implication insight was accepted—the firm's strategy must change—the analysis team and members of management then dedicated themselves to developing and putting in place the new strategy. In effect, in both the pharmaceutical and CommodityCo organizations, most of the misgivings and doubts about the strategy direction were laid to rest in the deliberations aimed at determining the key implication insights.

A separate point implicit in the above observations is worth making here: implication insights become a powerful means to convey the need for change in and around the organization. The importance of the change insights only gets crystallized when an implication insight emerges. It's the pivotal first step in answering the so-what questions raised in Chapter 3.[218] Executives, when presented with one or more implication insights, glean why they need to (for example) review the viability of the current strategy, develop new strategy alternatives, or reframe how they think about strategy execution. In the pharmaceutical case, a small number of executives, for the first time, appreciated the importance of political strategy and the critical need for the firm to institute a process to develop a comprehensive approach to dealing with its myriad stakeholders. Note that their appreciation for the role and importance of political strategy preceded the determination of what the political strategy should be and how it might be executed.

Implication insight: Insight into what

The examples noted above and throughout this chapter indicate that implication insights address almost any facet of the business. However, they're likely to concern, directly or indirectly, the four core implication domains: strategy, operations, organization, and leadership (Table 7-1). It's easy to imagine a range of topics in each core implication area that might serve as the focus of an implication insight. Each example in Table 7-1 illustrates the old and new understanding at the heart of any implication insight, as emphasized above. Again, each example doesn't indicate what the firm should do; that becomes the focus of determining the relevant business implications.

Table 7-1   Implication Insights: Differences between Old and New Understandings

Implication domain	Old understanding	New understanding
Strategy	Our strategy will take us through the next two to four years. Our large market share rivals continue to be our dominant adversary.	Our strategy will be made obsolete in the next two years by the actions of rivals. Increasingly, our focus needs to shift to the upstart innovators and substitute product rivals.
Operations	Our global supply chain is fast reaching equivalence with our key rival. Our manufacturing facilities enable us to outperform rivals' product functionality.	Our major rival is rejuvenating its regional supply chains; we're fast falling behind. Due to one rival's adoption of new process technologies, we're now lagging behind.

Organization	Our R&D pipeline will provide a sequence of winning product solutions because our R&D capabilities far outdistance rivals. Our long-established culture drives our customer-facing employees to deliver unparalleled service quality.	Our R&D pipeline won't be the source of winning products—customers are already migrating to substitute products. Many of our culture driven behavior norms are getting in the way of rapid customer response.
Leadership	Our leaders have shifted our culture so that we're now far more agile than previously. Our leadership team understands what it takes to deliver value to key customer segments.	Due to the actions of rivals and customers in the pursuit of customized solutions, we need to redefine what we mean by agility. Our leaders need to embed themselves in the context of customers; their sense of customer needs must be updated.

Preparing the mind for implication insight work

Nothing short of a fundamental mind-set shift is required in moving from change insight to implication insight. The focus, content, and details of implication insight work are fundamentally different than in the case of change insights. The focus shifts from marketplace change to internal implications; the analysis switches from understanding marketplace change to highlighting its high-level thinking, decision and action implications for the organization. Consequently, critical challenges and issues must be confronted in the transition from change insights to implication insights (Table 7-2). Not surprisingly, therefore, even in the presence of carefully crafted and "vouched for" change insights, the deliberations inherent in the transition to implication insights, as you'll see later in this chapter, are anything but linear, straightforward, and easy to execute. Moreover, implication insights (and business implications) often are anything but obvious, and some tentative and accepted implication insights may run counter to strongly held historic perspectives and viewpoints. Thus, preparing the mind for implication insight work can't be avoided.

Table 7-2   Some Challenges and Issues in Transitioning from Change Insight to Implication Insight

Key questions	Sample issues and questions
What are the big organizational challenges we face in getting to implication insights and business implications?	Many people, including some senior and seasoned managers, find it more interesting and challenging to grapple with and make sense of external change than to transform it into implication insights and business implications. Getting the team to break from their deeply entrenched historic routines in business implications analysis to take seriously the need to develop and assess implications insight.
Do we have the right mind-set in place?	Are we willing to adopt the fundamental mind-set shift required in move from change insight to implication insight because the focus, scope, content, and details of implication insight work are fundamentally different than in the case of change insights?
Do we bring sufficient imagination to the task?	Are we willing to see and think differently? Are we willing to adopt new modes of analysis?
Do we have the right knowledge and skills in place?	Do we have the deep knowledge of the firm's context, strategies, issues, and decisions required to (quickly) identify relevant implication insights? Do we have the skills to manage the interpersonal ebb and flow in deliberations?

Do we imbue our deliberations with sufficient vigor and intensity?	The transition often results in the analysis team having to grapple with the organization's sacred cows, "non-discussables" and other implicit facets of the culture. Does the organization culture support the time required for penetrating deliberations? Do analysis teams develop methods that embrace different analysis frames, foci and perspectives?
What inhibitors are getting in the way and how do we deal with them?	Many staff professionals recognize the personal and professional risks associated with putting forth business implications that run against the tide of current "thinking" within the organization. Executives and others react negatively to learning that their long-held customer, competitor, or industry assumptions are incongruent with the emerging realities of marketplace change.
What significant errors are we making and how do we avoid committing them?	Acquiescing to the stated desired outcomes of senior members of the organization's hierarchy: thus, sabotaging the process and the spirit of insight work. Not taking the time to sniff possible implications: thus, moving far too quickly to a lower quality implication. Accepting the first implication that seems plausible and convincing: thus, missing out on the dialogue that likely would lead to a superior implication. Viewing the proposed (recommended) implications as having a longer than probable shelf life: thus, failing to monitor the proposed action against the undoubted marketplace change.

The mind and data principles (see Tables 3-1 and 3-2) as well as the reasoning principles (see Table 5-2) are equally applicable to addressing the challenges and issues (Table 7-2) that are unavoidable in developing and leveraging implication insights. Some mind and reasoning principles are especially pertinent.

An open mind exempts nothing about the organization from questioning; all facets of "how we've always done business around here" are challenged. In the pharma case, executives' minds had to be opened over the course of extensive deliberations to recognize the potential power and value of political strategy as an enabler of product-market strategy. The challenges inherent in reflecting on prevailing mental models such as assumptions and beliefs about what it takes to win in the marketplace are unlikely to be addressed if curiosity about possible implications is shut off. Of course, the dominant cognitive and organizational biases may dramatically shape deliberations in many ways that inhibit or suppress consideration of implications. In the DipCo case, organizational biases including an affinity for "facts" as opposed to judgments about the future inhibited many individuals from seriously considering whether and how the firm could pursue the identified marketplace opportunity.

Vigor and intensity can only be brought to bear in the deliberations when members of the analysis team recognize that multiple modes of reasoning are not only appropriate, but required, and no one individual's preferred reasoning mode should be privileged. Variation in the reasoning serves as an antidote to accepting the first statement of an implication insight that seems possible. In the Gorilla Competitor case, a suggested implication insight proposed by a well-respected leader of the strategy department that the firm would need to rationalize its product line to survive rivalry with the Gorilla Competitor immediately attracted strong support from others but was eventually rejected when alternative assumptions about the firm's capabilities were considered.

The data principles (see Table 3-2) also inform the mind-set required to develop implication insights. It's imperative to recognize that the organization's own "data" is always time dependent: for example, in the DipCo case, the firm's beliefs about the merits of its core value proposition were fast proving incongruent with its experience in the marketplace. Moreover, recognizing that data about our own organization is always contaminated by biases requires a willingness to involve multiple functions and deploy methods that build tension through diverse and even conflicting reasoning modes.

And, it may be especially important to recognize that specific types of data are never privileged, particularly in the early stages of transforming change insights into implication insights. In the pharma case, sales and market share data were initially privileged at the expense of data addressing stakeholder positions and relationships; hence, a strong but undetected bias toward product-market strategy inhibited serious deliberations focused on the relevance and need for political strategy. It's also worth noting that a focus on domains with plentiful data may mislead the search for implication insights. In the Gorilla Competitor case, an abundance of R&D and technology data led to deep deliberations about R&D/technology implications at the expense of considerations of marketing and partnering implications—areas in which the firm had limited experience.

Finding a pathway to intelligence insight

The transition to implication insights, and thus, intelligence insight, involves a pathway similar to the structuring, sniffing, shaping, and stipulating activities described in the previous four chapters. As with change insights, there's no single pathway to implication insights that analysis teams can follow in every situation. However, key elements of the 4Ss will be evident in every pathway. For purposes of illustrating the 4S cycle, I'll use the BSC case (the biosciences company described in Box 7-1) and draw on the pharma case (Figure 7-1), and the VP, DipCo, and Gorilla Competitor cases discussed in earlier chapters.

Box 7-1

Case: BSC—R&D

A product development team within a basic science intensive global corporation began to prepare its presentation to the executive team for an investment decision. The product under review was in the middle stages of R&D development; the product and management teams agreed that it was considerably behind the competition.

The team conducted an intensive competitive landscape analysis to determine: the key forces shaping the potential dynamics of rivalry in the new product space (no products were on the market as yet; when rivals might enter the market; and the comparative strengths and weaknesses of rival's products.

A series of meetings over a four-month period culminated in a meeting chaired by the product vice president. Intensive discussion around the findings to date resulted in requests for further data and analysis. After another round of both formal and informal meetings, a consensus evolved around the following key change insights:

- The product space wouldn't incur intense competitive rivalry until two years later than expected (previously the company believed a sequence of rapid entries would ignite head-to-head competition within the next three years)
- Competitors had their own unique way of behaving, driven by their capabilities and senior managers' strategic intent (previously the product team had presumed that competitors would behave as they would)
- Although most competitors' development research programs in the focal product area were advancing considerably more slowly than previously projected (the company had thought that some of the rivals would be ready to launch a product before it had completed its own product development work), one competitor had identified a process to accelerate their respective program

A number of rounds of discussions were involved in accepting and buying in to the content and direction of the change insights. As the dialogue shifted to what it all meant for the company, a series of implication insights began to take hold:

- The company could take advantage of the precedents set by the lead competitor and accelerate its own product, shaving considerable time from its R&D program
- Getting to the market before all rivals except one could be made to happen (previously the firm believed that was emphatically not a possibility)
- The firm would need to accelerate its own product development or it would come to market just after multiple competitors, ensuring no differentiation of its product versus several others.

Once the product development team and the executives involved accepted the implication insights, a few amendments were made to the investment proposal. The most critical included:

- A segmented approach to the focal product area, in the past the company had brought products to market that appealed to all comers, however plans were developed to demonstrate how the target audience could be expanded with later R&D investments
- An accelerated development plan, which was a step change in how the company had previously brought products to market
- A significantly higher product forecast, based on the faster time to market and the decreased number of competitors at launch

As a result, the company's product development cycle was shortened by two years or so. It now looks like the company will be second to the market. Some executives in the company have estimated that the shortened development cycle and the faster market entry will result in at least $3 billion additional revenues beyond the originally projected financial returns.

Structuring implication insights

Structuring prepares the organization for the tasks inherent in getting to intelligence insights. Structuring's three elements detailed in the case of change insights—identifying key opportunities, applying analysis context components, and managing personnel—are also relevant to implication insights. Structuring is especially important if implication insight has not previously been a focus in the organization's development of business implications. Preparing for implication insight work requires consideration of a set of unavoidable questions, each of which is addressed in this chapter (Table 7-3). Structuring's intent is to ensure that all involved in key analysis projects as well as decision makers understand the role and importance of implication insight and its interplay with business implications.

Rather than regurgitate the nuances of structuring detailed in Chapter 3, this section highlights how specific aspects of structuring enable a wider range of possible implications, and thus, superior implication insights.

Table 7-3   Structuring: Preparing for Implication Insight Work

Key questions	Common errors	Sample recommendations
Do we understand the iterative nature of implications work?	Presuming it involves a set of sequential steps with no backward loops.	Develop a visual that illustrates the inherently iterative flow of the steps involved in determining implication insights and business implications.
Is (sufficient) attention paid to implication insight?	Implication insight isn't a focus of analysis. Business implications not tested against implication insights.	Make the determination of implication insights a required component of the development of business implications.
Is deriving implication insight accorded sufficient importance?	Accorded verbal importance but not seriously assessed. Reviewed as part of larger assessment of decision making but not isolated as a separate topic.	Separate as a focal point for assessment in the case of whatever analysis tools and techniques are employed. Perhaps establish a team to conduct the analysis and make recommendations.
What is the relevant implication insight focus?	Defining the focus too narrowly. Employing only one definition of the business focus.	Start with a broad definition and work back to a narrower definition.
What should be the scope of the questions asked?	Work largely from a predetermined set of questions. Use analysis frames to determine the relevant questions.	Adopt a largely open-ended approach to asking questions. Encourage individuals to ask novel implication questions.

Who should be involved?	Insisting largely on the same set of individuals and/or single department or unit. Not involving different individuals/units at different times.	Use individuals from multiple functions and departments. Involve pockets of expertise where appropriate.
What vantage point should be adopted?	Not adopting the vantage point of customers, channels, suppliers, competitors, government agencies, and others.	Ask someone to take the vantage point of customers and others. Compare and contrast the vantage points of various stakeholders.
Is imagination and creativity nurtured and appreciated?	Efforts to stretch the boundaries of thinking about implications are quickly squelched.	Ask the team to identify possible implications that others have not yet noted.

Determine opportunities for identifying implication insights

Any analysis project in which change insights have been crafted warrants the determination of implication insights. However, it may be especially critical to determine implication insights if an analysis project has one or more of the following attributes:

- It addresses or uncovers significant change patterns or discontinuities in the marketplace: the business implications may not be obvious.
- Significant disagreement emerges in the final stages of stipulating one or more change insights: identifying implication insights may provide a pathway to resolving the disagreement.
- If a consensus quickly emerges once change insights are crafted around significant change in business implications, for example, a radical shift in assumptions or a change in strategy direction: attention to

implication insights will likely clarify the thinking behind the proposed change in business implications.

Applying analysis context components

Change insights are more likely to transform into valuable business implications when the analysis context components described in Chapter 3 are applied to broaden the range of possible implication insights. Here we emphasize the analysis context components that have proven most critical as an antidote to the tendency of analysis teams to fall back on "how we've always done it around here" routines.

Frame and focus: Asking different questions

How to frame implication analysis rarely receives attention yet it constitutes a critical rationale for structuring. The question, how should you frame the analysis to get from change insights to implication insights to business implications, should never be considered one with a settled answer. A variety of initial frames generate different questions. Here are some examples of different frames:

Implication domains

Asking the question, what might be possible implications in each of the core implication domains (strategy, operations, organization and leadership) enable organization-specific vantage points, as described in the next section, sniffing. Each domain affords questions that spark different deliberations about possible implications—the raw ingredients out of which implication insights and later, business implications, will be crafted.

6IFs

Each IF also frames very different issues and questions to be addressed. The seeing IF challenges the analysis team to look beyond the obvious and the historically accepted purviews. For example, a team member might ask: how do these change insights enable us to see strategy alternatives or marketplace opportunities or technology challenges that we previously missed? In the CommodityCo case, the team challenged itself to imagine how the firm might create services to significantly differentiate its offering from key rivals.

The intend IF could lead an individual to ask how change insights might enable the organization to pursue new marketplace goals such as establishing a new customer value solution. The act IF might provoke an individual to ask what the analysis team should do to ensure that maximum DNA variety is brought to bear on the deliberations. The feel IF should cause all those involved to review how emotions might be inhibiting some individuals from contributing their best thinking and analysis.

I'll demonstrate in sniffing how GMIs serve as a powerful segue to surfacing possible implication insights. To cite merely one example, if all or most competitors are deemed to be vulnerable to an emerging or disruptive technology, an array of questions then presents itself that might lead to preliminary implications: What might be the effects on our current products? What breakthrough products might be possible to conceive and create? How might we have to redirect our R&D investment programs? One outcome eventually might be a significant implication insight, for example, we need to access new technologies to be competitive in a specific product category.

Stretch

In the VP case, the analysis team might ask, what if we were to develop a distinctive new customer value proposition? Stretching the group's thinking in this way might lead the team to generate a suggested implication insight: we need to move fast to build an alliance development capability.[219]

Scope: The business context

One factor implicit in the framing analysis discussion if not recognized can severely affect the derivation of implication insights (and business implications). The scope of the business context taken to the analysis of any change insight, and especially GMIs, critically influences the range and specificity of the implications generated. Here's one example:

An industrial product firm amid significant technology change crafted the following customer insight: many corporate customers' negative emotions about the firm's products are overwhelming their assessment that the products represent good value for the price. If the analysis focus is integrated marketing communications, the customer insight is assessed only for its implications for communication concerns: What messages should be communicated to overcome the negative emotions? What language should be used? What media should be used to communicate to customers? On the other hand, if the analysis focus is marketing strategy, or even more broadly, business unit strategy, then fundamentally different questions are asked and distinctly different implication insights emerge. For example, if the analysis focus is supply chain management, a question might be posed about the implications for purchasing strategy about components and supplies. Were the customer change insight interpreted to mean that product sales might decline and perhaps precipitously, then implications for product development would need to be considered.

Perspective: Assume varied vantage points

Structuring also recognizes that the desired DNA variety is enabled by adopting different vantage points.[220] The intent is to extend the range of preliminary and suggested implications.

Internal functions and positions

Functional areas such as R&D, marketing, sales, finance and legal identify outcomes and consequences that could affect any of the four core implication domains. In the pharmaceutical case, the legal department might identify the need to develop new types of contractual relations with specific external entities. The marketing group might generate potential alliances with specific external entities as a prelude to developing new customer value propositions.

External entities

External vantage points almost certainly surface preliminary implications beyond those identified by internal stakeholders. Competitors often see what a firm should do long before executives in the firm figure it out.[221] Customers are often only too happy to tell a supplier how they can improve their offer, the irritants they need to eradicate, or the marketplace opportunities that might be emerging. NGOs increasingly affect how a strategy plays out as many firms in the health care, oil, chemical, consumer packaged goods, and industrial product sectors have discovered.

The future

One vantage point can't be forgotten: start in the future and work backwards. In many respects, we can only know the present by taking a lens at some point in the future.[222] As many firms can attest, strategy and operations implications that are strongly preferred now given current marketplace conditions are rejected when they're tested against projected market conditions a few years out.[223]

Theory

In many ways, implicit theories[224] about what causes business success or failure has the most impact on how the team approaches the challenge of identifying possible and potential implication insights. Consider the following three examples:

- A team that only considers product and functional attributes in its development of marketing strategy options may not generate options that might emanate from analysis of emotional needs.
- A team that believes all R&D must be done in-house will have difficulty seriously entertaining alternative R&D strategies that include any form of collaboration with other entities.
- A team that is locked into incremental changes to strategy isn't likely to consider "inventive" strategy possibilities.[225]

Getting the right people involved

Structuring directly addresses the question of who should be involved in developing and accessing implication insights (and business implications). The frequent and appropriate initial response is to suggest some combination of individuals with varying backgrounds:[226] different levels in the organization, involvement in different functions, different education and professional backgrounds, and, different external work and life experiences. However, as with change insight, we can't leave the DNA variety goal to chance. The challenges inherent in shifting from change to implication insights (Table 7-2) add to the importance of using the 6IFs to assess whether individuals are willing to "live" the "frame of mind" noted above.[227] Echoing the discussion in Chapter 1, individuals need to prepare and test themselves against the 6IFs:

- See: Do we push the boundaries of what we see in and around the business?
- Think: Do we challenge what the organization should think about and how it thinks?

- Intend: Do we want to stretch the organization in all it does?
- Decide: Are we willing to reconsider decisions already made or put new decisions on the table?
- Act: Are we committed to doing what is necessary to craft possible and potential implications?
- Feel: Are we willing to surface and confront the emotions behind specific contributions in any phase of the deliberations?[228]

Each of the 6IFs provides a yardstick against which to assess the readiness and potential contribution to the 4S cycle—structuring, sniffing, shaping, and stipulating—involved in generating implication insights.

Open-ended analysis

It may also be appropriate to encourage open-ended analysis: no bounds are placed on how individuals or a team interacts, they can adopt any vantage point, and use any method to generate possible implication insights.[229] Imagination and creativity become drivers of how a team sees and thinks.[230]

Case: BSC

The role and importance of structuring is evident in what the BSC development team did and didn't do (Box 7-1). Initially, structuring was largely non-existent: the team leadership didn't ensure that all team members understood the role and importance of implication insight; the team didn't reflect on the mind-set challenges; nor did the team raise any issues about the need for DNA variety. It's no surprise then that the team executed a conventional competitive landscape analysis, with the assistance of a third-party vendor as a data collection provider. After the initial research, the team framed the required analysis as largely a "check the box" exercise: there was little expectation that the analysis would generate new change insights or lead to new implications

One senior manager, however, was concerned that the team hadn't pushed themselves sufficiently to "see" what could happen in the competitive context or to assess what key competitors were really doing in this product R&D space. He initiated what in effect was a structuring process.[231] He asked an internal marketplace intelligence specialist to manage the analysis process. She was specifically requested to challenge the team's and the organization's point of view and working assumptions with respect to the product space. She immediately met with the team members and others in the organization to understand how they saw the issues pertaining to the R&D investment proposal.

The role and importance of framing to inaugurate a pathway to implication insight for the BSC team can be readily illustrated. For example, if the team challenged itself to be in the market with a viable product within months of the first entrant to this product segment,[232] possible implications would quickly have become evident: we need significant increments of new resources (personnel, capital, knowledge); the firm must make this R&D stream a top investment priority; one or more senior leaders would need to make this investment stream their personal key performance goal.

The implication insight eventually derived, getting to the market before all rivals except one could be made to happen (previously the firm believed that was emphatically not a possibility) most likely would have been crafted considerably earlier.

Sniffing preliminary implications

Structuring and sniffing are closely intertwined. Devastating errors on the road to implication insights include not structuring vantage points widely enough and moving far too quickly to accepting and vouching for an implication insight or specific business implications. Thus, curtailing the generation of possible implication insights. The pharma company had it not taken the time to identify myriad potential business implications almost certainly would have missed the importance of crafting an integrated political strategy. Consider also the many examples of firms that quickly but incorrectly determined if they refined their current strategy they could fend off the attack of potential rivals' offerings driven either by disruptive technologies or substitute products. They precluded the generation and adoption of implication possibilities to address the threat of the new type of rivals.

The intent of sniffing: Possible implications

The intent in sniffing is to identify preliminary or possible implications without immediate reference to their relevance or importance. The inhibitors to sniffing (Table 7-4) suggest the importance of sniffing a wide range of possible implications (as a prelude to shaping implication insight) without immediately judging their relevance or value. Sniffing, as described in this section, aims to avoid a common occurrence: a single team is responsible for most or all implications work; it generates a narrow set of reasonably self-evident implications; it does so quickly without attempting to stretch the band of possible implications.

Table 7-4   Inhibitors to Implication Insight Work: The 6IFs Framework

6IFs	Common inhibitors to doing quality implication insight work	Statements associated with the inhibitors	Recommended actions
See	Mental models don't allow alternative "views." No expectation that individuals should "imagine" what the future might be. Commitment to current strategy and action plans. Culture frowns on stepping outside prevailing norms.	"We're so focused on ensuring the current strategy wins, we don't allow ourselves to look beyond it." "We don't want to be seen as crafting futures that aren't self-evident today."	Ask individuals to imagine what the most positive and negative (preliminary) implications might be. Ask individuals if there are key implication takeaways that they might have missed.
Think	Leaders don't challenge assumptions and beliefs. Reluctance to discuss different viewpoints. Unwillingness to question established analysis modes.	"Our analysis methods always seem to generate strategies that win." "Our assumptions don't need to be reviewed, not much has changed."	Ask the analysis team to apply each of the analysis context components to help identify preliminary implications.

Intend	Leaders and others unwilling to consider major change to current business intent and goals. Don't see the need to conduct a full-scale implications analysis.	"Our intent and goals stretch us as far as can go." "Our strategy is set." "We know what it is we want to achieve." "The implications are obvious."	Ask what goals now seem possible. Ask individuals to identify one or more goals that have been overlooked. Ask which goals need to be tweaked.
Decide	Key decision makers often fail to seek inputs from support functions and others. Consider that current decisions don't need to be challenged. High faith in prevailing approaches to decision making.	"Our strategy is pretty much set; our challenge is to execute well." "We have covered all the bases with respect to that decision."	Ask individuals how the emerging implications might reframe current or even past decisions. Ask the analysis team to identity how the timing around specific decisions might be affected.
Act	Don't believe there's a need to review and reassess current action programs. Assert that implications assessment is too difficult and not worth it.	"We don't need to spend much time identifying key takeaways from our change insight work." "We don't have a leader to do that work."	Ask individuals to identify how and why current action programs might need to be adapted in view of emerging implications.
Feel	Individuals feel comfortable with the status quo. Some feel that others won't be able to handle the inevitable tension in identifying implication insights.	"I feel it takes too much mental energy to do the work properly." "I feel extremely hesitant to take on this assignment."	Ask individuals how they feel about executing specific steps in the method to identify implication insights. Then discuss why they have these feelings.

Sniffing possible implications is driven by questions specific to each of the frames noted above in the discussion of structuring:

- What might be possible implications in each core implication domain (strategy, operations, organization and leadership)?
- What might be possible implications if you're sitting in a specific functional unit or department such as finance, marketing, sales, R&D, and human resources?
- What might be possible implications if you were to take the vantage point of external entities such as channels, customers, suppliers, or government agencies?
- What possible implications are suggested by each IF?[233]
- What questions might be asked if you start at a point in the future and worked backwards?

The purpose here is to create a laundry list of preliminary implications that can be integrated later into a set of suggested implication insights. I'll emphasize again: there's no intent to assess the relevance, importance, or value of preliminary or possible implications.

Sniffing: The role of inferences

The transition from change insight to implication insight requires you to draw inferences. Otherwise, it's impossible to generate preliminary and suggested implication insights.[234] Inferences lie at the heart of preliminary implications whether derived from domain insights, CSIs or GMIs, or any open-ended process.

Domain insights

Any domain insight, for example a competitor insight or customer insight, can be the source of multiple preliminary or possible implications.[235] To revert to the pharmaceutical case (Figure 7-2), a regulatory domain insight, because of badly managed review procedures in one high-profile drug case, the approval process for all cases will be significantly more stringent and slower, could lead to the following inferences of preliminary implications: the firm will need to invest new resources in preparation of all submissions for the approval process; senior leaders will need to invest more oversight time in all preparations for the approval process; the projected launch time of one specific new product may have to be delayed for at least 18 months; cash flow targets two to three years out may be off by at least 15 percent.

Competitive space insights (CSIs) to implications

Each CSI should be assessed individually for its possible implications. Two or more CSIs will likely generate both common and different implications, thus, reducing the likelihood that preliminary implications will be overlooked or missed. As described in Chapter 2, the pathway from a single CSI to business implications passes through generic marketplace implications (GMIs).

CSIs to GMIs

The analysis facilitates inferences from the CSIs to the five GMI components described in Chapter 2. Each GMI involves a different focus and distinct questions. An inference about possible opportunities compels different considerations than inferences about competitor threats or assumptions. Team members working individually or as a group need to consider what is happening or could happen in each GMI area before they move to deriving possible implications—either implication insights or business implications. The importance of this point can't be overstated for two reasons. First, it enables individuals and the analysis team to develop a more refined sense of the competitive context before seriously deriving business implications. The result: it sharpens the implications they derive.

If an individual thinks through the consequences of the CSIs for the opportunity array that could emerge, she is better positioned to draw possible implication insights for the business. Second, the possible implications derived are likely to be broader in scope. By being immersed in the vulnerabilities that might arise or the competitor threats that could materialize, individuals are likely to "see" possible implication insights that they might otherwise not detect.

CSIs to GMIs to Implication insight

It's worth noting again that each GMI that emanates from an insight project provides a powerful focus for deriving preliminary implication insights. Many times, they're anything but self-evident; the possible implication insights result from immersion in the context and deep reflection on the part of individuals and the team conducting the analysis.

Take as an example the following GMI assumption: average market growth will be 12 to 15 percent over the next five years. The company had previously presumed a 5 to 7 percent average growth rate. Some possible leadership implications surprised the team: leaders need to "recalibrate" their point of view and base assumptions about the business; and key leaders will have to reconfigure significant commitments expected from our business partners—some relationships may be severely tested; a few marketing leaders will need to work hard to build the relationship with our sales force; the leadership team will need to act decisively if major market opportunities aren't to be foregone. None of these possible implications for the Leadership domain would have been expected or projected a mere two months earlier before the industry analysis project was completed.

Managing the range of possible implications

An analysis team leader needs to take a firm role in sniffing. She needs to guide the team through an initial meeting, typically no longer that three or four hours, dedicated to surfacing possible implication insights. She also needs to emphasize that the deliberations won't succumb to any temptations to stray into consideration of business implications. A stern focus on the task at hand concentrates the attention of all involved to refine and reword preliminary and suggested implication insights as they're proposed.

Here's one example that was noted earlier: the real marketplace opportunity involves this set of customers' needs. Earlier renditions of the implication insight included: customer needs defined in this way…represent an emerging opportunity; our products can be transformed to satisfy this particular customer need; if we accept this customer's articulation of its needs, here's what the marketplace opportunity will be. The extensive deliberation eventually led to an agreement that the real opportunity resided only in the needs of one set of customers.

In sniffing we place no limits on the range of preliminary or possible implication insights. In the words of one manager, "There's no such thing as a dumb possible implication." In a three or four-hour session, it's amazing to observe the breadth of possible implications and even possible implication insights that a team of five or six individuals can generate from a set of domain insights, CSIs and GMIs.

The 6IFs as enablers of sniffing implications

When appropriately used, the 6IFs serve to stimulate inferences of preliminary implication insights. They help ensure that the object of inferences isn't
dominated by what's top of mind for the team. Each IF, as noted earlier, serves
as a source of possible implications by suggesting a set of questions that individuals might ask as they seek to identify and extend the range of possible
implications beyond those that prevailing mental models might indicate.
Consider two IFs, thinking and seeing.

The IF, thinking, as noted in earlier chapters, provokes two broad questions: what to think about and how to think. Thus, given any change insight,
individuals ask the question: what should the organization or elements of it
think about? If we revert to the GMI assumption insight and the Leadership
domain possible implications noted above, the IF, thinking, should cause
several questions to be asked: How might the assumption insight affect the
leadership team's historic assumption set about the marketplace, competitors
and customers? Which leaders might find that their resource commitments
may inadvertently concede market share to rivals? Why might leaders in specific functional areas need to rebuild their relationship with other parts of the
organization if the current plans are geared for a market size considerably
below what it might turn out to be?

The IF, seeing, illustrates how the range of issues and questions that
should be asked in identifying possible implication insights runs far wider
than typically addressed. Asking the related questions, what do you see differently and to what "does the difference make a difference," stimulates the
opportunity to delve deeply into possible implications within individual topic
areas. Staying with the GMI assumption example, you may "see" differently
the range and scope of the marketplace opportunity, what competitors are
doing or are likely to do, why customers are responding to various rivals at
unexpected rates, and, how rivalry might play out over the next three years.
In short, you see the marketplace context in a new light.

What you "see" then leads to the difference question: what difference does
it make for implications in any of the four implication domains. If you see,
that is, judge that a variety of distinct opportunities are emerging faster than
you expected, you then ask: what are the possible implications for strategy,
operations, organization, and leadership? One suggested implication insight
might be: the scope and scale of the marketplace opportunity across our
product lines is far more extensive than previously thought.[236]

The need for imagination

Imagination serves as the fuel that generates inferences about possible implication insights. There's no substitute for it. All too often what I observe is the following: individuals can't commit to raising implication insight possibilities that aren't essentially self-evident. One team, for example, was completely comfortable addressing short-term technology implication issues but found it nearly impossible to think about marketing and customer issues.

The output

Sniffing results in a laundry list of preliminary implications, and maybe even some suggested implication insights. This outcome is by design; there's no intent to organize the list into related or imaginative groups. There's no way to know what the list may include. Depending upon the business focus, there might be a list of possible implications addressing several facets of the four core implication domains. For example, new strategy alternatives, the current customer value proposition, execution of the strategy, the need to create new alliances along the value chain, or new issues for leadership to address.

Case: BSC

Once the key change insights were developed and accepted, the product development team in a series of meetings began to focus on, articulate, and list possible implications. Several possible implications had been noted but not collated in the deliberations leading to the change insights. The list of preliminary implications included:

- We can't win if we're the fourth or fifth entrant to this product space; rivals will be too far ahead.
- We need to act differently than our rivals wherever the opportunity presents itself.
- Science alone isn't enough to get to market before the current leading candidate to be first to the market.
- If we invest appropriately, we can speed up our R&D development cycle, faster than we had previously believed.

- Adding key personnel with the right knowledge will be essential to speeding up our R&D development cycle.
- Market entry strategy can't simply replicate any rival that is the first entrant.
- Senior leaders in the company need to be behind the R&D commitment.

Shaping suggested and tentative implication insights

A list of possible implications (and, perhaps some preliminary implication insights) gives rise to an obvious analysis challenge: how to integrate them into a short set of implication insights that enhances the likelihood of generating value-generating business implications. Shaping aims to achieve that goal: to craft suggested implication insights that merit serious vetting and vouching to move down the pathway to accepted implication and, later, recommended business implications.

The guiding questions are:

- How can the preliminary implications list be integrated to capture the core or underlying implication insights?
- How can we then vet and vouch for the proposed (tentative) implication insights?

Thus, in shaping, the deliberation shifts to determining and vetting a small set of tentative implication insights, often no more than three or four. This is often a tougher task than expected. Again, a large part of the challenge revolves around "getting the wording right." Changes in the wording can make a substantial difference to the content of individual implication insights. Consider this example: our vulnerability to technology change implies a need to redirect our R&D investments and program was reworded to our vulnerability to technology change implies a need to quickly adapt our product development investments and programs. The latter statement represents a fundamentally different implication insight that would likely lead to different business implications than the former statement.

Some systemic shaping errors and difficulties

Unfortunately, a simple algorithm to guide the shaping of possible implication insights doesn't exist. It's not a deductive exercise—far from it! Many judgments need to be made by the team as they project and assess how events might unfold in any industry or competitive space and whether and how the organization can muster the resources and the will to respond to anticipated marketplace change. The absence of a guiding algorithm-like analysis structure partly accounts for several common errors I've observed in getting to a small set of crucial implication insights (and business implications):

- Not developing an a priori structure or hierarchy of implication levels.
- Letting a single perspective or functional area dominate the analysis.
- Not making any effort to get outside the organization's mental models.
- Premature closure of the analysis due to executive imprimatur or planning deadlines.
- Significant analysis paralysis due to the inability to move beyond functional biases and the absence of a hierarchy of implication levels.
- Not recognizing the influence of emotions on the contributions of each individual.

Involvement in several transitions to implication insights has highlighted for me the difficulties analysis teams encounter in overcoming the systemic errors just noted. They include:

- Not being able to agree on a starting point (see the next section) for the determination of implication insights (as well as business implications).
- Getting bogged down in the transition from a laundry list of possible implications (the output of sniffing) to a short set of integrated or core implication insights.
- Not knowing how to simultaneously address several implication categories, such as strategy, operations, organization, and leadership.
- Inability to reconcile (intense) differences in judgments among team members.

The discussion that follows addresses these common errors and the difficulties in overcoming them.

Getting to a set of suggested implication insights

In many respects, transitioning to a set of suggested implication insights from a laundry list of possible implications follows the sequence discussed in Chapter 5 in the case of shaping change insights.

Form a list of categories

One starting point is agreement that the analysis needs to categorize the (often long) laundry list of preliminary or possible implications. Though this may seem obvious, how to get to implication insight categories has sometimes led to intense discussion because individuals immediately suggest different ways of getting there. An important lesson learned over many years is that superior implication insights, and thus superior business implications, are created when more than one approach is adopted. In short, two or more starting points prove useful to generate a diverse set of categories that in turn are more likely to produce higher-quality implication insights. Here are three possible starting points:

- Use a predetermined set of categories. Categories might include key implication domains such as strategy, operations, organization and leadership or various sub-categories of each domain.
- Ask individuals to quickly review the laundry list and then suggest plausible categories.
- Let the categories emerge from the analysis.

Analysis back and forth

The transition to implication insight categories necessarily involves an analysis back and forth and interpersonal ebb and flow[237] irrespective of which of the three pathways are adopted. Team members combine possible implications in different ways, reflecting their perspectives and local knowledge.

In one case, an individual considered two preliminary implications: our current price levels will be difficult to sustain, and customers will more and more demand that we provide a solution tailored to their needs. From this, an integrated implication was drawn: we need to assume that our current product line will have little marketplace appeal three years from now.

Another individual connected these two preliminary insight implications with another—we're likely to lose some key accounts due to the efforts of competitor X to deliver superior value though at higher prices than ours—and developed the following more integrated implication insight: our current product line has already lost a lot of its attractiveness in some key customer accounts. A back and forth then ensued among several the team members to derive a higher-level implication insight in the strategy domain: we urgently need to configure our offer in some market segments.

The analysis challenge is to craft one or more key implication insights related to one or more of the core implication domains[238] and/or other domains identified by the analysis team. It's critical to distinguish between implication insights and general business implications.

Interpersonal ebb and flow

Some of the errors and difficulties noted above have their genesis in or are reinforced by the dynamics evident in the ebb and flow of the interpersonal interactions that accompany the deliberation's analysis back and forth. Emotions, biases, and politics, interweave to drive the dynamics, sometimes productively, sometimes in ways that degrade and protract the analysis. The extraction of higher-level or integrated implication insights is most assuredly not simply a function of so-called rational thinking: clear rules and criteria that lead to a single outcome that all can immediately agree is the best or optimal choice.[239]

Emotions enter the fray in many ways.[240] If a few individuals feel energized, excited and secure that we urgently need to configure our offer in some market segments, then they'll likely support and advance that inference. If, on the other hand, one or more individuals feel insecure, uncomfortable, and hesitant about that inference, they'll likely question it, seek more data and evidence to assess it, and ask that others reconsider how they see it. Emotions thus may speed up or slow down the analysis process.

Personal biases, as noted in Chapter 5, are always present. I'll note two specific biases here. Confirmation bias, the tendency to seek data that confirms our prior judgments and beliefs, serves to reinforce prevailing mental models. If an individual genuinely believes that we urgently need to configure our offer in some market segments, he will seek data to confirm that belief and may ignore or downplay data that calls that belief into question. Recency bias, the tendency to give priority to recently encountered data, may account for some of the ebb and flow in the deliberations: individuals who have just seen an analysis report or have just heard the observations of a supporter or protagonist may change their opinion or viewpoint and thus give voice to a stance opposite of what they had previously advocated.

Politics here means how relationships influence the ebb and flow of deliberations. Individuals who want to ingratiate themselves with senior members of the team often concur with their opinions or choose not to voice their objections or counterviews. Alliances among individuals, though nothing is agreed formally, may result in larger numbers supporting or refuting a judgment made by an individual team member.

Vetting suggested implication insights

A question inevitably arises as a team moves towards finalizing a set of implication insights, that is, moving from a list of suggested to a small set of tentative implication insights: how do we know we got it right?[241] The question really being asked is: what is the evidence that supports or refutes each suggested implication insight? Vetting aims to provide an answer to these questions. As with change insights, implication insights can also be vetted for quality and novelty.

Implication insight quality

Suggested implication insights implicitly address the future more than the past or the present. Critical judgments thus underpin each insight. Often, they're not made explicit and therefore aren't tested. Three quality tests must be performed: scrutiny, explanation, and scope.[242]

Scrutiny test

The scrutiny test aims to assess whether a suggested or even a tentative implication insight holds up in the face of a rigorous critique. It involves posing the following questions:

- What reasoning supports the suggested implication insight?
- What would have to happen in the future for it to be accurate?

- What counter data and reasoning can be assembled to provide a challenge to it?
- What judgments (if any) are required to reconcile the suggested and counter arguments?

In the pharma case cited throughout this chapter, the analysis team found itself attracted to a suggested[243] political strategy implication insight: our political strategy is poorly executed. The analysis team identified a small set of judgments that underpinned the evolving political strategy implication insight: change reflecting in the GMIs indicate the need for a coherent political strategy; it's possible to execute political strategy as a coherent set of related actions; political strategy has the potential to dramatically influence product market success. Each of these judgments can then be "scrutinized' through the application of the four questions just noted. Not surprisingly, such scrutiny typically leads to modification of individual suggested implication insights. In the pharma case, the analysis back and forth led eventually led to the accepted political strategy implication insight noted in Figure 7-2: political strategy—the management of stakeholders—is fundamental to our product-market strategy success.

The scrutiny rigor is typically enhanced if a separate set of individuals is asked to challenge and refine each suggested implication insight. They provide a degree of protection from the biases associated with the team that develops the initial or preliminary insight statements. The analysis back and forth that then ensues when the two teams come together sharpens everyone's understanding of the implication insights and their business context.

Explanation test

A suggested or tentative implication insight provides new understanding for the organization. If you accept that it has a high degree of congruence,[244] the question that follows is: what does the implication insight help to explain? Stated differently, what is it the implication insight helps you to better understand? The importance of these questions resides in the fact that if they're not answered, the value of an implication insight, that is, its ability to help generate value-generating business implications, is less likely to be fully exploited. For example, in the pharma case, if members of the analysis team or individual managers or executives didn't understand that the political strategy insight explains why the firm needs to respond to evident change in the competitive context or what might happen to its marketplace performance if it didn't respond, they're less likely to treat seriously the implication insight and its business implications. In the CommodityCo case discussed in Chapter 1, the CSI, the undifferentiated product has now been differentiated, enabled a few managers in the firm to understand what was taking place in the marketplace, but it took them several months to accept the CSI and its marketplace and organization implications.

Scope test

A suggested implication insight may have broad or narrow business implications. The pharma implication insight had consequences for each implication domain: it affected decisions in the strategy, operations, organization, and leadership domains. The wider the range of potential business implications, the more stringent should be the application of the scrutiny and explanation tests.

Implication insight novelty

An implication insight more likely contributes to value generating business implications such as new marketplace opportunity or change in strategy direction or modifications in strategy execution when it meets the novelty tests noted in Chapter 1.

New to the firm

Without question, radically new as opposed to incremental understanding, assuming it meets the quality tests just discussed, is likely to cause major questions about potential change in each core implication domain: strategy, operations, organization, leadership. Radical new understanding may involve accepting premises that are the opposite of those historically accepted, as happened in the pharma and CommodityCo cases.

Application of the 6IFs helps assess the degree of newness of any suggested or tentative implication insight. If the implication insight doesn't enable you to see differently and to think differently, its newness is slim. The pharma firm personnel began to see the relevance and importance of the stakeholder environment for strategy determination and execution. As they pondered the need to address stakeholders in new ways, it became clear that they had little choice but to accept the fact that an integrated political strategy—the opposite of the firm's prior behaviors—had to be seriously considered: a new intent and decisions were now "on the table". And if the political strategy insight was accepted, a whole new action stream was required. Newness may also be reflected in emotions: executives in the Pharma firm clearly felt more comfortable and content that they now had a deeper understanding of the broader marketplace and less hesitant to initiate political strategy actions. Thus, the 6IFs clearly indicated it was not merely an incremental insight.

New to the world

An implication insight that has not been derived by direct or indirect rivals opens the possibility of significant value generating business implications. To test the extent of newness to the world, an analysis team asks the following questions:

- What is the evidence in the form of words or actions that one or more rivals have already developed the same implication insight?
- What is the evidence that one or more rivals are moving toward deriving the implication insight?

Thus, the pharmaceutical firm reviewed statements and actions of rivals with respect to political intentions and actions. The intent was to determine if any rival had reached the conclusion that it must develop a coherent, broadly focused political strategy or is already well down the road to doing so. The judgment was that rivals were not yet indicating or behaving as if they reached a similar implication insight.

Case: BSC

The transition from the list of possible implications to the set of implication insights noted in Box 7-1 involved a series of meetings. The deliberations centered on the potential order of entry of the known R&D participants and where BSC might fall in that entry order given alternative levels of investment and organization commitment. Assessments of rivals' likely entry times and their market entry strategy evidenced intense analysis back and forth. As individual implications in the list of preliminary implications noted above were discussed, the team developed and tested some judgments about the firm's R&D capabilities, its capacity to speed up R&D, senior leaders' commitment to the product area, and the importance of getting to the market as soon as possible after the first market entrant.

The intensity of the analysis deliberations was reflected in and drove some significant interpersonal ebb and flow. Emotions became evident as individuals supported and refuted others' judgments and suggestions. One team member described the ebb and flow as the product of respectful disagreements. The intelligence specialist and the VP kept the deliberation moving forward, not allowing any one individual to dominate.

The team vetted each implication insight noted in Box 7-1 as it began to crystalize. If any of the three implication insights proved off the mark, the business consequences would be severe. For example, if the firm could not shave considerable time off its originally planned R&D timeline, the likelihood of reaching the market before three or four of its key rivals was essentially zero. Thus, the scrutiny test was stringently applied to each emerging implication insight.

The novelty test also proved to be crucial. The team admitted how shocked they were that the lead rival was not as far ahead in its product development as it had initially believed and even more shocked that its own R&D timeline could be significantly advanced. Each realization caused the team to reassess the evidence. Team members also made a judgment that the thrust of the implication insights might well be new to the world: there appeared to be little evidence that rivals suspected the firm could come to the market with a product as quickly as it was now projecting. If this were the case, rivals would likely not commit resources to getting to the market earlier than their current plans intended.

Stipulating: Accepting the implication insight

At some point, the set of implication insights must be vouched for: you're willing to offer it as the output of our analysis and present it as a stepping-stone to determining business implications. The analysis steps involved in stipulating an implication insight mirror those discussed in Chapter 6 in the case of change insights. Stipulating's output may be only one fundamental implication insight, as was the case of the pharma firm (see Figure 7-2). It was two implication insights in the CommodityCo case and three in the BSC case.

Case: BSC

When the analysis team seemed to be close to finalizing the three implication insights, the intelligence leader moved the team into stipulating. It was then that the importance of wordsmithing became apparent. For example, getting to the market before all rivals except one could be made to happen, (previously the firm believed that was emphatically not a possibility), evolved from a prior stating of the implication insight as we can beat all rivals to the market, perhaps even the market leader.

Validating

Determining and detailing business implications creates the need to revisit and possibly refine each implication insight.[245] The validating method outlined in Chapter 6 in the case of change insights is equally relevant to monitoring the need to amend implication insights.

Every implication insight has indicators associated with it that can be tracked to assess whether it needs to be amended or even scrapped entirely. Because implication insights refer to the organization rather than the external marketplace, sometimes change along one or more indicators may occur quickly to cause change in how it's viewed or stated. The implication insight, our traditional core technology competencies are becoming less relevant to some customers due to the evolution of their technology platforms, crafted by a professional services company had a number of relevant indicators including customers' purchases of technology, customers' statement about their technology and operations intentions, and customers' responses to the salesforce's offers. New data along any of these indicators might shift the suggested implication insight from less relevant to customers to not relevant to customers, with significant consequences for business implications.

Institutionalizing insight implications: Key action steps

Making implication insights an integral element in the organization's analysis processes and deliberation protocols requires both a method and careful management of deliberations along each step in the method (Table 7-5).

Table 7-5   Institutionalizing Implication Insight Work

Identify extent of current implication insight work

- Are implication insights identified in current analysis projects?
- Are implication insights included in strategy planning documents?
- To what extent is there an established method to identify implication insights?
- Who is typically involved in implication insight deliberations?

Prepare for implication insight work

- Identify and address the key questions associated with implication insight work (Table 7-2).
- Be aware of the typical errors in Implication insight work and know how to avoid them (Table 7-3).
- Identify key inhibitors to insight implication work and how to manage them (Table 7-4).

Create an infrastructure for Implication Insight work

- Appoint an individual to "teach" what implication insight work is all about.
- Ask that individual to oversee the capturing and sharing of learnings from individual analysis projects.

Choose one or two initial projects

- Identify an initial project.
- Apply the implication insight method.
- Assess relevance of the implication insights for other analysis projects.
- Document the learning from the project.

Integrate into all analysis projects

- Establish the generic need for implication insights.
- Execute the implication insight method.

The first step requires carefully documenting whether and to what extent the organization currently identifies implication insights. It involves thorough due diligence: assertions that "we determine key implications of our analysis work" often mistake business implications for implication insights. Working under this false impression relieves an analysis team of the commitment to review past and ongoing projects to determine if implication insights are a genuine focus.

It's also important to document the analysis method employed to determine (the alleged) implication insights. Doing so becomes a test of whether the (alleged) method is real or imaginary. In one firm, the purported method turned out to be nothing more than a brief deliberation as to what "big takeaways" might be drawn from a lengthy industry analysis; the first assertions were not subjected to any scrutiny.

Any analysis team must prepare for implication insight work if the concept is new to it. In short, it needs to develop an understanding of what implication insight entails: what it is, what the analysis method involves, what errors typically characterize initial efforts to transform change insights into implication insights, and, the role of the 4Ss (structuring, sniffing, shaping and stipulating) in determining and assessing implication insights. This learning can be made a part of any team's initial effort to develop a set of implication insights.

A core element in the preparation involves "preparing the mind" for implication work: fully understanding the challenges and issues involved in transitioning from change insight work to implication insight work (Table 7-2).

A modest organization infrastructure helps to get insight implication work off the ground and share learning across analysis teams and functional units. Something as simple as appointing one individual to "teach" the concept, show what the method is, and illustrate the types of deliberations required in going through the 4Ss, takes much of the mystery out of what it requires to get to implication insights.

Ultimately, implication insight needs to be incorporated into analysis projects. Choose a project, an industry, competitor, or technology analysis or a scenario or competitive gaming exercise, or a big data engagement. Then ensure that implication insights are developed before the determination of business implications. Deploy the 4S method detailed above to generate preliminary implications and transform them into tentative and accepted implication insights.

Identify the key execution learnings during the first project application. Note specific analysis difficulties, for example, the steps in the method that caused the most difficulties, perhaps analysis back and forth that resulted in impasses or bottlenecks. In the same vein, note specific issues and challenges with respect to the interpersonal ebb and flow; for example, what seemed to cause individuals or sets of individuals to push or react to specific suggested or tentative implication insights. Pay attention to emotions, especially in early efforts to incorporate considerations of implication insights in analysis projects: individuals' emotions supporting or resisting the time and energy required to identify implication insights go a long to explaining why the work meets with success or failure.

These learnings then inform the next efforts to integrate implication insights into specific projects. Leaders of analysis projects should use these learnings to ensure that prior errors aren't repeated.

A final comment

The insight discipline advocates the role and importance of implication insights in getting from marketplace understanding (change insights) to business implications. Attention to implication insights enables any analysis team to identify the critical few "pivotal so-whats" that guide the determination of business implications. Although crafting implication insights will be new to most organizations, doing so enhances the likelihood of superior business implications—the focus of the next chapter.

Notes

213. The importance of a shift in understanding to the concept of any level of marketplace insight was outlined in Chapters 1 and 2.

214. Few strategy and marketing textbooks come close to identifying implication insights. They jump straight into determining and specific business implications, once they've gone through the "environmental analysis" considerations. The closest they come to implication insights is when they identify key assumptions, but the focus of the assumptions is predominantly external.

215. Political strategy refers to the collection of "influence" initiatives that an organization creates and executes to influence its many stakeholders in the external competitive space. Stakeholders include any entity that can place a "demand" on the organization. They include all the market players in an industry as well as entities in the socio-political domains such as local, state, and federal agencies, unions, community groups, and NGOs. See, for example, Ian C. MacMillan and Patricia E. Jones, *Strategy Formulation: Power and Politics* (St. Paul: West Publishing Company, 1986).

216. The circuitous movement from one business implication to another noted at the beginning of this chapter provide a good illustration of how the deliberations get slowed down.

217. This is example of the influence of emotions in the transition from change insights to business implications. Feelings of exasperation may drive the marketing management team to short-circuit the analysis process and simply assert what the implications are or it might drive the team to adopt a new analysis approach to the transition.

218. The pivotal so-what questions include: what are the implications for our thinking, decision making and action. Think, decide and act are three key factors in the 6IFs (insight factors).

219. Note this is still only a possible implication insight. It needs to be analyzed in the context of other possible implication insights.

220. The notion of DNA variety was introduced in Chapter 3. It implies the need to have individuals with different perspectives, experience and background involved in analysis so that a greater variety of issues and questions are raised.

221. It's for this reason that competitive gaming (often referred to as war gaming) almost always identifies actions the focal firm should take that come as a surprise to the firm's executive team.

222. Starting from a vantage point in the future is of course a fundamental principle in scenario work. It's an argument found in many books detailing novel approaches to competitive strategy. See, for example, Gary Hamel and C.K. Prahalad, *Competing for the Future: Breakthrough Strategies for Seizing Control of Your Industry and Creating the Markets of Tomorrow* (Boston: Harvard Business School Press, 1994).

223. Scenarios provide the methodology to view the present from the vantage point of the future. Scenarios emphasize the importance of dealing with uncertainty. See, Paul De Ruijter, *Scenario Based Strategy: Navigate the Future* (Surrey, U.K.: Gower Publishing, 2014).

224. Implicit theories reflect mental models that shape what we look for and how we see the world around us. Peter Drucker, among many others, has described how a theory of the business can be so powerful and yet remain largely implicit. Peter Drucker, "The Theory of the Business," *Harvard Business Review*, September/October 1994, 95–104.

225. Inventive strategy involves creating a new white space in the market, that is, a customer offer that is fundamentally new. It has many of the elements of a "blue ocean" strategy. See, W. Chan Kim and Renee Mauborgne, *Blue Ocean Strategy: How to Crete Uncontested Market Space and Make the Competition Irrelevant* (Boston: Harvard Business School Press, 2005).

226. See the discussion in Chapter 3 of the role and importance of getting the right personnel involved in structuring.

227. We are referring here to the need to adopt the frame of mind advocated earlier in this chapter.

228. The influence of emotions is treated in detail in Chapter 9.

229. Open-ended analysis here is largely similar to that discussed in Chapter 5 with respect to inferencing. The difference is that the focus is on the organization rather than the external marketplace.

230. The need for and role of imagination is discussed later in this chapter.

231. He was not aware of the structuring activity as we discuss it in this chapter; yet many of the items he initiated clearly fall within structuring.

232. This is an example of the "stretch" frame noted earlier.

233. The 6IFs as enablers of preliminary inferences are addressed later in this section.

234. Suggested inferences emerge from the amalgamation of two or more preliminary inferences.

235. It's important to note that while marketplace domain insights can and do lead to individuals or an analysis team to derive preliminary implications, they're just that: preliminary implications.

236. The discussion here illustrates again the iterative nature of identifying implication insight and business implications.

237. Analysis back and forth and interpersonal ebb and flow were described and discussed in the previous chapter.

238. Implication insights needn't apply to all four core implication domains—strategy, operations, organization, and leadership—though they frequently do.

239. The reasoning behind this argument is discussed in Chapter 8.

240. The influence of emotions on the crafting of both change insight and implication insight will be the focus of Chapter 9.

241. The real question is: how do we know we got it reasonably right? We can't ever be certain that an implication insight will turn out to be completely congruent with how events evolve over time.

242. These are the three criteria used to assess *change* insight quality. See Chapter 5.

243. Again, It's important to note that *suggested* here means the implication insight has not been subjected to the scrutiny tests advocated in this section.

244. As described in Chapter 1, by congruence we mean that it's largely accurate in what it describes or projects about the external marketplace.

245. This point is developed in detail in the next chapter.

Chapter 8

Business Implications: Thinking, Decisions, Action

At the beginning of Chapter 1, the executive asked two questions of the analysis team: what are your key insights into this competitive space, and what's their relevance and importance for our current and future strategy and operations? Implication insights, as described in the previous chapter, constitute the first element of a response to his second question. We now address the final element of his second question, what are the business implications? We have emphasized four interrelated implication domains—strategy, operations, organization, and leadership—throughout this book.[246] Because so many others have done so, it's not our purpose here to document and detail what is entailed in determining a preferred strategy and its associated initiatives, action programs, and plans.[247] Rather, this chapter illustrates how the insight discipline augments many facets of the analysis necessarily involved in the determination of business implications.

Determining business implications: Value of the insight discipline

Most organizations have established analysis processes and organizational routines to turn analysis of the change domains indicated in the insight funnel (see Figure 1-2) into a set of business implications, especially in the strategy and operations domains. These processes and routines address two questions: What are the major business implications in terms of thinking, decisions, and actions across the key implication domains?[248] And, will the thinking, decision, and action choices enable the firm to generate superior marketplace performance and financial returns? The insight discipline enhances the quality of the analysis method and deliberations inherent in these processes and routines in three related ways, what we refer to as the three business implication principles:

- Emphasize new understanding.
- Revisit and refine change and implication insights.
- Articulate insights specific to the implication domains.

I'll use the cases discussed in earlier chapters as well as the case briefly described in Box 8-1 to illustrate how the three principles impact determination of business implications.

Box 8-1

A Small Technology Development Company

A cross-functional team in a small technology development (STD) company conducted an extensive industry analysis using multiple industry frameworks. The team identified a number of key change drivers and developed a set of simple scenarios around the interactions of the change drivers. The team then involved a number of other members of management to identify and detail specific decision and action implications. Unfortunately, all those involved could not come to agreement as to what the key business implications should be. Eventually, a few key staff reporting into the executive team decided on the key implications and action plans.

In retrospect, here's a set of three implication insights that should have been the output of the initial assessment of the change drivers and the set of industry scenarios:

- Our traditional core technology competencies are becoming less relevant to some customers due to the evolution of their technology platforms.
- Small players (like us) will need to enter into technology alliances due to a few competitors making major investments in technologies to get to next generation products.
- Our marketing needs to focus on creating customer niches for our current and about to be introduced new products.

Emphasize new understanding

The insight discipline pushes for new understanding—without which insight isn't possible—as the crucial means to putting in place the thinking, decisions, and actions required to drive marketplace and financial value for the organization. An emphasis on insight reminds everyone involved in business implications deliberations that they should be obsessive in their attention to shifts in their understanding of both the external marketplace and the organization (Table 8-1). Thus, two questions should be top of mind for those involved in identifying and assessing proposed business implications:

- What is our current understanding of change in both the marketplace and our organization? For example, our current understanding of customer needs across distinct segments or competitors' likely strategic moves or the potential evolution of key emerging technologies?
- How has the understanding changed? Is the shift in understanding significant?

These two understanding questions[249] ensure that the deliberations oscillate back and forth between the development and choice of business implications and the knowledge base[250] underpinning the analysis process, including all previously accepted change and implication insights.

The emphasis on shifts in understanding reminds the team to focus on why issues and questions[251] and not just the "what and how" sides of decisions and action streams that typically drive the development of business implications. For example, developing a set of strategy alternatives around the customer offers we want to take to market and how we want to compete against rivals requires consideration of the customer, competitor, and broader marketplace factors influencing the choice of alternatives. Critical questions include: What do we believe are the underlying customer needs? What are we assuming about competitors' responses to our moves? What will influence customers' adoption of our offer? What projected technology or regulatory change is shaping how we see the marketplace evolving in the next few years? Consideration of these questions compels attention to why we wish to adopt one strategy alternative rather than others. It may surface a shift in understanding of customers' needs or rivals' likely strategy moves or customers' product adoption propensities.

Table 8-1   Business Implications: Difference between Old and New Understandings

Implication domains	Old understanding: Old thinking, decisions, action	New understanding: New thinking, decisions, actions
Strategy	We win by delivering product functionality that is largely similar to rivals across all product lines but at significantly lower prices to customers in all geographic segments. Our strategy has succeeded in creating winning products without resorting to alliances along our value chain.	Rivals' commitment to enhancing product functionality means that we need to focus on outperforming them in functionality in one or two product groups and delivering superior services with prices somewhat higher than rivals. Be selectively developing alliances along the value chain, we can generate a wider range of high-quality products than any rival.
Operations	Our sales organization has always identified the next generation of marketplace opportunities. Manufacturing and outbound logistics were the primary cost rivers we addressed.	Because of rampant technology change, we've committed to building cross-functional teams to identify emerging and potential opportunities. We now address in detail the cost implications of every key business activity.
Organization	We've always allowed marketing and sales to operate as individual fiefdoms. We decided that our culture was a major source of our customer-facing capabilities and thus should be left alone.	We now manage the interdependencies with great care; they now report to the same person. We've initiated action programs to make our culture more customer focused, partly to reinvigorate all customer-facing capabilities.

| Leadership | There was no need for members of the executive committee to visit customers regularly. The monthly executive committee meeting didn't review key strategy assumptions. | Regular customer meetings are now scheduled with every member of the executive committee. How key assumptions are holding up is now an agenda item in each month's executive committee meeting. |

Revisit (and, if necessary, refine) change and implication insights

The insight discipline's emphasis upon change in understanding inevitably implies that business implications method and deliberations can't be self-contained; it inevitably needs to revert to consideration of change and implication insights. And, sometimes reconsidering change and implication insights leads to amending them, as they're never set in stone.[252]

VP case: The analysis team struggled to agree on specific strategy and operations implications. The difficulties at the heart of the struggle arose in large part from the unwillingness to revisit the core implication insights and even the GMIs that helped shape the implication insights. For example, some of the heated discussions about refocusing and retraining the salesforce stemmed from some individuals not fully internalizing one of the key implication insights, the need to shift to intangibles as a critical component of the firm's customer value proposition.[253] Once more time was devoted to assessing why the shift to intangibles was "one platform" for the required customer proposition differentiation, the decisions and actions being recommended by the analysis team were far more acceptable.

Articulate insights specific to implication domains

The emphasis on the *what* and the *how* in determining business implications results in an absence of attention to crafting insights specific to each core business implication domain. An emphasis upon change in understanding generates issues and questions specific to each domain (Table 8-2). A change in strategy direction or a shift in resource commitments in operations raises issues and questions about understanding specific to each core business implication domain. If the change in understanding is sufficiently significant, it may constitute a strategy or operations insight, that is, new understanding about strategy or operations that is substantially different than our prior understanding.[254] In short, as demonstrated later in this chapter, the deliberations get redirected to identifying and vetting insights specific to each implication domain.

Table 8-2   Business Implications: Foci and Domains

Domains/Foci	Thinking	Decisions	Action
Strategy	What's our new understanding about strategy alternatives? *The assumptions underlying our historic strategy are now outdated; the new set of assumptions are the following...*	What's the new understanding about how we should approach one or more decisions? *Our key strategy decisions now need to focus on substitute rivals as our biggest threat; previously we only considered lookalike product rivals.*	Has our understanding of key actions streams shifted? *We need to launch our new product in a number of geographies simultaneously not sequentially as we have previously done.*
Operations	What's our new understanding about key facets of operations? *We need locally focused supply chains; an integrated global supply chain carries too many vulnerabilities.*	What's our new understanding about key decisions in and around operations? *Our manufacturing decisions should be driven by margins and profitability, not by "asset load."*	Has our understanding of key actions streams in and around operations shifted? *Treat all of our alliance partners as genuine partners, not as entities with whom we have a financial relationship.*

Organization	What's our new understanding of the need for organization change? *We need customer-centric teams, not functions dealing separately with customers.*	What is the significant new understanding of what detracts from our decision making? *We need to examine the culture inhibitors behind our decision failures and not just structural issues.*	What's the new understanding of how we become customer-centric? *We need to "live with" customers as opposed to using third parties and surveys to gain customer understanding.*
Leadership	What's the big new shift in our understanding about the role of our senior leaders? *Leaders need to openly challenge long-held beliefs and assumptions.*	What's new in our understanding of how leaders can augment decision making? *Line leaders need to visibly exude what it takes to be an insight advocate.*	What's the new understanding about the behaviors of the leadership team? *Leaders need to create and sustain extensive tension in key strategy deliberations.*

Avoiding business implication errors

When the three business implication principles noted above are adopted, as I'll illustrate in this chapter, they ameliorate a number of common analysis tendencies in the determination and assessment of business implications:

- Not recognizing the iterative nature of business implications deliberations; thus, unintentionally suppressing the ability of the analysis team to address the inherent ambiguity of the competitive context.[255]
- Moving too quickly to the final analysis outputs: thus, not allowing time to critically reflect on the potential implications of marketplace change;[256]

- Concentrating analysis efforts in a narrow set of implication domains: thus, for example, issues and questions with respect to leadership often receive cursory, if any, attention;

- Not challenging the organization's prevailing mental models; thus, accepting historic points of view and assumptions and beliefs that may be incongruent with implication and change insights;[257]

- Accepting too easily the dominant analysis orthodoxies; thus, not adopting new or alternative analysis frameworks that would cause new questions to be asked;[258]

- Constricting the analysis to a small set of individuals; thus, not engaging a variety of disciplines that probably already exist within the organization;[259]

- Neglecting to focus on developing superior understanding of the organization (its assets, capabilities, performance attributes, vulnerabilities, and so on). Thus, failing to leverage existing organization attributes.[260]

Applying the insight discipline

The 4S activities described in the case of change and implication insights—structuring, sniffing, shaping, and stipulating—can also be deployed to enhance the analysis method and deliberations throughout the development and assessment of business implications (Figure 8-1). Each activity plays a distinct role in ensuring that the business implications eventually derived enhance the chances of the organization to win in the external marketplace.

FIGURE 8-1

The Pathway to Business Implications

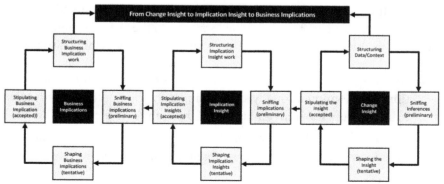

Structuring

Unfortunately, the business implications errors noted above are often hard-wired into the organization. Structuring lays the organizational groundwork to address each error. It's especially important to do so because business implications critical to future marketplace and financial performance often don't jump off the page; indeed, they're rarely identified in the first or even the second work session.[261] Structuring serves as the initial means to put the three business implication principles into practice.

Structuring analysis

In part because of the iterative nature of implications work, many of the points noted in the discussion of structuring implication insights are relevant to business implications: developing an appropriate framing mind-set, adopting distinct perspectives as a focal point for asking question, the role of the 6IFs in preparing and testing individuals' readiness, as well as taking a future-backward stance. However, because all organizations already have established approaches to determining business implications, structuring needs to address some specific analysis and personnel issues.

The following five structuring recommendations bring the three business implication principles to bear on the analysis methods and deliberations inherent in determining business implications. The intent is to enable sniffing to generate a more extensive listing of preliminary or possible business implications[262] and in doing so to allow analysis and organization leaders to keep a persistent focus on the two core understanding questions noted above.

Connect the insight discipline to key analysis tasks

Multiple analysis tasks are involved in any effort to determine key business implications in the core implication domains: strategy, operations, organization, and leadership. Organizations typically follow a set of analysis processes and routines in choosing a strategy, developing a set of operations initiatives and plans to execute a strategy, determining how to reconfigure a supply chain or realigning leaders and resources across a set of business units or functional departments.[263] Frequently, the deliberations involved in determining the contours of a strategy change or the details of an execution plan take place over several weeks or even months. Analysis leaders and others face extensive analysis back and forth and interpersonal ebb and flow in the deliberations. Thus, one or more leaders need to assume the charge of keeping the insight discipline at the forefront of successive tasks at the heart of the deliberations. A question they should continually ask: how can the insight discipline enhance the execution of each task?

STD case: Assessment of the organization's assets and capabilities constitutes a critical analysis task in strategy development. In the STD case, the analysis team and others recognized the limited marketing assets and capabilities possessed by the firm compared to key rivals. The organization insight, the marketing deficiency in assets and capabilities compared to rivals was the major limitation on the firm's ability to achieve its strategic objectives, was new to many members of the management team. Initially, only one or two individuals could see[264] that this was possibly the case. They structured a sequence of meetings to enable others to think about why it was so and what actions might be required to rectify the marketing deficiency. It was only much later in the deliberations that the intent emerged to address the marketing challenge as an organization-wide commitment.

Emphasize thinking

As an analysis team proceeds through the stages and tasks in developing business implications, a general question should be continually asked: how do the deliberations affect our thinking, for example, our assumptions, beliefs and point of view? Here is one recent example:

In assessing the most appropriate go-to-market strategy for a new product, the analysis team determined some of its previously accepted assumptions needed to be radically changed. Two organization resource insights emerged: the organization was no longer willing to invest the resources that were now evidently required for a launch of the desired scale and its channel partners were no longer willing to engage in co-marketing activities at the level previously projected. Both resource insights led to a new assumptions set that some key managers were initially unwilling to accept. In effect, a new mental model emerged about what the organization could achieve in the marketplace.

Broaden the range of implication domains

Structuring also alerts analysis leaders and others to monitor carefully the range of the implication domains or sub-domains considered. It's here that the insight discipline can exert some of its strongest influence. The question that should be continually asked: how can insight discipline extend the focus of deliberations to include previously neglected implication domain components? Below are some examples:

STD case: The deliberations intended to specify key business implications spent an inordinate time detailing key actions to acquire, incorporate and leverage various technologies but little time considering the marketing strategy required to identify and serve individual market niches. STD executives later developed the marketing insight that the absence of marketing capability constituted the principle constraints on the firm's ability to break into new customer segments and to retain some key customer accounts.

Professional services firm: In PowerPoint template-driven organizations, the range of implication domains considered in determining strategy is, in many respects, largely predetermined.[265] In one professional services firm, the templates guiding analysis outputs asked for details on each market opportunity that was the focus of the proposed strategy but didn't ask for potential competitor threats. The emphasis was on opportunities, not the associated risks. Pushing hard to identify emerging and potential rivals would likely have generated possible competitor insights that might have placed particular opportunities in a less positive light.

Extend the depth in implications deliberations

All too frequently, the deliberations around specific business implication contexts exhibit a surprising level of superficiality.[266] Deliberations around a proposed strategy or its alleged winning value proposition don't go beyond a top-level or first-cut analysis of the scope, scale and nature of the marketplace opportunity. For example, the underlying customer need gets a "once-over" discussion but the real issues, pain points, and problems confronted by different customers receive surprisingly little detailed attention. Sometimes the lack of a deep-dive in the deliberations stems from a presumption that those involved know the relevant context—a dangerous presumption. The question that should be continually asked is how the insight discipline might help generate deeper understanding in specific implication domain topics.

Consider these two examples:

Pharma case: In working toward a set of political strategy decisions and actions, the analysis team had to dig deeply beyond the first few questions to fully understand many of the key stakeholders who were to be the object of its political action programs. Initially, there was little inclination to inquire about individual stakeholders' market position in their respective competitive contexts, the nature of the rivalry with their competitors, or what their interests and needs were with respect to the pharmaceutical firm. The recommended influence action program directed at individual stakeholders changed as the team developed more in-depth understanding of the context of key stakeholders.

DipCo case: As the DipCo analysis team began to develop an action plan to address the competitor's value proposition shift, it recognized that the absence of a shared understanding of key competitors around how they might be affected by the projected change in the competitive space. The team decided to conduct a "deeper dive" to assess which specific competitors might not be able to stay in the market and what others would have to do to remain in the market. The vulnerability faced by some current rivals encouraged the team to develop a more aggressive strategy in the unavoidable battle with the rival to whom its valued customer had migrated.

Stretch the scope of deliberations

The temptation not to go beyond the traditional scope of deliberations in business implications frequently isn't resisted. Yet sometimes it's necessary to do so. For example, extending the consideration of strategy possibilities way beyond incremental strategy change to include renovative[267] and even inventive strategies challenges the prevailing understanding of the marketplace opportunity, identifies hidden vulnerabilities of the current strategy and limitations in the organization's capabilities. The question that should be continually asked is how the scope of the deliberations should be stretched to develop new understanding.

BSC case: The analysis leaders had to push to ensure that the market strategy implications went beyond the firm's historic one-size-fits-all approach to market segmentation: the opportunity to deliver customized offers to specific customer segments was a real possibility but one many members of the analysis team didn't immediately appreciate. It led to the development of a new understanding of customers' needs.

Professional services firm: Senior members of the executive team intervened in a number of strategy development meetings to prevent discussion of a fundamental new customer offer that had been generated by a middle management task force. They didn't believe that key customers were ready for the potential new offer and that consideration of the alleged new marketplace opportunity was outside the remit of the first quarter strategy review process. Adherence to the organization's procedures and protocols overruled attention to a key customer insight that was in fact diametrically the opposite of the senior management mind-set asserting that customers were not ready for the customer solution. Consideration of the new strategy possibility was postponed for six months.

Structuring personnel

Structuring emphasizes getting the right individuals, with the appropriate mind-set, organized in productive teams, and fully understanding the need to deploy the insight discipline in the determination of business implications. The case examples discussed above in the application of the five structuring recommendations suggest how the 6IFs provide one set of ideal standards to help achieve that goal.

See: Individuals are committed to imagining and reflecting on strategy, operations and organization possibilities that might be outside anything previously considered.[268]

Think: Breaking out of traditional ways of thinking about strategy, operations and organization requires leaving behind what are often long accepted, and indeed, largely tacit points of view, assumptions, beliefs and projections.

Intend: Teams driven by the intent to push all organizational, cognitive and analytical boundaries in sniffing and shaping business implications that lead to winning strategies are likely to invest the time, energy and resources to achieve that goal.

Decide: The intent just described ultimately gets tested in whether the team is willing to shape and make decisions that previously might have been avoided or postponed. Relatedly, individuals decide they want to enter and commit to the necessary deliberations.

Act: Leaders and analysis team members push each other to adopt the insight discipline, to move beyond early assertions of appropriate thinking, decisions, and actions, to develop novel ways to vet suggested implications, and validate over time proposed goals and actions.

Feel: Deliberations around business implications reflect careful attention to emotions, especially how feelings of support or opposition drive forward or side tract efforts to apply the implication principles noted earlier.

Each of these structuring ideals aims to enable sniffing to generate possible business implications that might otherwise be missed.

Sniffing

Sniffing involves drawing inferences about preliminary or possible business implications in predetermined or emergent business domains. Each of the three business implication principles noted above influence sniffing. *Emphasize new understanding* encourages drawing inferences about new topics or new aspects of existing topics. Revisiting and refining change and implication insights encourages inferences even though they may suggest issues or questions challenging previously accepted change and implication insights— a reminder once again that both change and implication insights have a shelf life. *Articulate insights specific to implication domains* reminds all involved that inferences should be drawn with respect to any implication domain without reference to whether they'll withstand scrutiny.

BSC case: Considerable uncertainty marked the analysis addressing how best to proceed given the three implication insights (Box 7-1). What actions should be taken to advance the R&D program? How fast could the program be advanced? What go-to-market strategy would be most appropriate given the anticipated market position of the presumed market leader? Again, multiple inferences about these and related topics provide the fodder for the requisite business implication deliberations.

Each level of marketplace change insight noted in the insight funnel (see Figure 1-2) serves as a source of preliminary business implications.

Implication insights as the source of inferences

Implication insights provide the most immediate source of inferences of possible business implications. An obvious question drives sniffing: What possible business implications can we infer from each implication insight with respect to each core implication domain?[269] As a team delves into identifying and noting possible implications, the five structuring analysis recommendations give rise to sequences of questions that push sniffing in many directions simultaneously (Table 8-3). The generic questions noted in Table 8-3 (second

Table 8-3   Structuring Analysis Recommendations: Linkages to Sniffing (BCS Case)

Structuring analysis recommendations	Key structuring questions	Sample sniffing questions	BSC case sniffing example questions
Connect to key analysis tasks	How can the insight discipline enhance the execution of each task?	What are the possible implications for: New market opportunities? Potential new products? Change to our current value propositions? New execution initiatives?	Do we have the capabilities to pursue the alleged marketplace opportunity? When will the key competitor actually launch its product? What might be the market dynamics when we enter the market?
Emphasize thinking	How do the deliberations affect our thinking, for example, our assumptions, beliefs, and point of view?	What are the possible implications for: Our point of view, assumptions, beliefs, and projections? Past and current decisions? Future decisions we might need to make? Current action streams? New action streams we might need to take?	What assumptions do we want to accept about the key competitor's strategic intent in this product segment? When do we make the decision to speed up R&D investment? When do we refute our past R&D investment decisions? What stream of actions must we execute in order to speed up the R&D trajectory?

Broaden the range of implication (sub) domains	How can the insight discipline extend the focus of deliberations to include previously neglected implication domain components?	What might be possible implications for: New products or product line extensions? New customer needs and segments we might serve? New technologies and how they might acquire or leverage them? How we might reduce cash flow vulnerability rather than focusing only on cash flow variability?	Can we segment our customers around needs and determine how those needs can be met? Can we determine the go-to-market strategy of individual rivals who may enter after us?
Extend the depth in implications deliberations	How might the insight discipline help generate deeper understanding in specific implication domain topics?	What are the possible implications if we: Ask different kinds of questions about why our strategy is winning or losing? Ask how we might change the focus of future value propositions beyond what we have previously considered? Ask how we might augment our current value propositions?	What might be a radically different way to develop an R&D plan? How might we leverage external resources to design a novel go-to-market strategy? How might we add new increments of value to specific customer segments? How might we finance an R&D program in a way that would be novel to the industry?

Stretch the scope of deliberations	How should the scope of the deliberations be stretched to develop new understanding?	What might be the possible business implications if we: Considered a truly inventive strategy instead of an incremental strategy? Choose a goal of doubling revenue in the next five years instead of an annual increase of 5 percent?	What if we chose to shorten the R&D timeline not by 25 percent but by 50 percent? What if we collaborated with a rival in distributing our new product?

column from the right) are merely suggestive of the questions that can be asked so that an analysis team pushes itself beyond the first or second obvious inference that might be generated. Each of the five structuring recommendations compels individuals to ask questions that broaden and deepen the analysis and thus help avoid the business implications analysis errors noted earlier.

BSC case: The power and importance of the questions stemming from the structuring analysis recommendations are evident in the BSC case (Table 8-3). Each set of questions drove the BSC analysis team to draw inferences (The right hand column in Table 8-3) and thus consider implications that went way beyond where the team started. For example, the structuring analysis recommendation, connect to key analysis tasks, caused the team to derive inferences that led it to review carefully when the key competitor might actually launch its product, what its market entry strategy might be, and what might be the competitive dynamics once the competitor and our firm were in the market.

Pursuit of the types of questions noted in Table 8-3 led the BSC analysis team to identify specific preliminary implications in each of the core implication domains (Figure 8-2). A number of these implications were not anticipated by members of the analysis team.

FIGURE 8-2

From Implication Insights to Possible Business Implications: the BSC Case

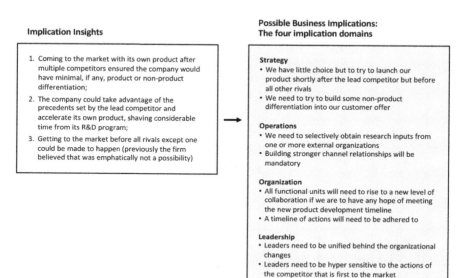

VP case: It's important to note that each implication insight may give rise to somewhat unique possible business implications. Thus, it's critical to subject each implication insight to extensive application of structuring's five analysis recommendations. In the VP case, the implication insight, how we think about winning and retaining customers' needs to shift, gave rise to a series of preliminary implications about marketing options, the opportunities associated with each alternative, the competitive risks that might have to be addressed, customer value propositions, rivals potential actions, assumptions about marketplace change, what the marketplace execution challenges might be, and what marketplace success might look like. The second VP case implication insight which says we need to massively reconfigure how we manage the organization, led the team to develop a long series of preliminary business implications addressing the assets and capabilities that would be required to win, the issues leadership would need to focus on, how the organization's values and mind-set might have to change, behaviors required of the salesforce, and how marketing would need to be managed.

Implication Insights as a driver of business implications

The BSC and VP cases demonstrate how implication insights not only focus and inspire the derivation of possible business implications but implications likely to result in thinking, decisions, and actions that lead to superior marketplace performance and financial returns. This is so for at least three reasons. First, implication insights represent a synthesis of key implications derived from change insights, that is, what is truly important for the organization. Thus, the presumption is that the business implications they give rise to will be most relevant to the organization's future. For example, in both the BSC and VP cases, a number of the possible business implications were a surprise to those involved; consequently, it's safe to suggest that the business implications eventually determined wouldn't have been expected.[270]

Second, implication insights, if taken seriously, grant the analysis team and others permission to dig deeply into possible business implications across the core business implication domains and indeed other domains that may arise in the course of the analysis. In the VP case, the two implication insights led the analysis team to conduct a full-scale assessment of what it would take to win in the marketplace and how and why the firm's mind-set and assumptions had to dramatically change. Without question, the extent and intensity of the analysis wouldn't have occurred in the absence of the accepted implication insights.[271]

Third, the deliberations always circle back to the organization's realities, as noted earlier. Issues got to do with the organization's assets, capabilities, mind-set, culture, and other attributes arise as an off-shoot of addressing marketplace strategy and operations thinking, decisions, and actions. Thus, organization insights, distinct from change and implication insights, become a focus and output of the analysis.[272]

Also, the interplay between implication insights and business implications, including the forays into crafting implication domain insights, such as strategy and organization insights, is a reminder of the iterative nature of the back-end stages of insight work, that is, generating intelligence insight. Implication insights are determined at one point in time. As business implications are suggested and tested, it causes reflections about individual implication insights and they may need to be amended.[273]

Extending the range of possible business implications

Each level of change insight along the insight funnel (Figure 1-2) leading to implication insights can also serve as a source of potential preliminary implications.

Generic marketplace insights

The deliberations inherent in generic marketplace insights (GMIs), as noted in Chapter 7, give rise to implication considerations that often quickly morph into preliminary business implications: items that one or more individuals suggest the organization should consider in terms of its thinking, decisions, and actions. Deliberations around the foci of GMIs—marketplace opportunities, competitive risks, competitor threats, strategy vulnerabilities, and marketplace assumptions—spark possible implications rather quickly that can be used to augment the list of possible implications derived from implication insights.

VP case: Possible business implications stimulated by the implication insight, how we think about winning and retaining customers' needs to shift, could be extended and sharpened in view of the GMI, an opportunity is rapidly emerging for a new customer offer. Preliminary business implications might address: how extensive the opportunity might be, the features of what the customer offer might be, the types of customers most likely to adopt the customer offer, and why customers might be attracted to the offer. Again, the iterative nature of insight work is evident in this analysis back and forth.

Competitive space insights

Competitive space insights (CSIs), as described in Chapters 1 and 2, go further back in the insight funnel than GMIs (see Figure 1-2). Along with domain insights, they provide the raw material to generate GMIs. CSIs also often give rise to possible business implications: individuals and analysis teams quickly identify what the preliminary thinking, decision, or action implications might be.

VP case: The CSI, strategy will need to be based on multiple dimensions of value. It will transform which rivals win and which lose; some won't be able to make the transition, could be the source of possible implications about many facets of thinking (for example, assumptions about customer value, rivals' actions, and, customer needs), decisions (for example, the need to reconfigure the base customer offer, whether to pursue specific rivals' customers before they exit the market), and actions (for example, how to pursue rival's customers, development of new marketing and sales programs).

Domain insights

Many of the examples throughout this book illustrate how significant domain insights such as customer, competitor, technology, economic or governmental insights enable individuals to derive possible business implications in one or more of the implication domains. Again, the emphasis here is on preliminary or possible business implications: when considered in the context of CSIs or GMIs, it's likely the possible implications may change.

Customer Insight: A technology company discovered that for a variety of technological, cost and application reasons, Chinese corporate customers in a small number of related industries wouldn't accept what it had believed was the key technical differentiator of its dominant product line. The eventual customer insight: a set of changes in how the product line was presented and sold to Chinese customers in conjunction with modest changes in the product could overcome many of the initial purchase inhibitors. A long stream of preliminary design, manufacturing, marketing, sales, and service implications were then quickly derived as input to determination of the China market entry strategy.

Competitor insight: A firm in a traditional industrial product area crafted an insight about a rival's interactions with customers from a pattern of behaviors and words, the competitor was signing "agreements" with major and mid-sized customers faster than any rival as a way to "tie-up" the customers for many months and, in some cases, a few years. The result; many customers simply wouldn't engage with the firm's sales force or even executives from the firm. A stream of preliminary implication inferences was derived with respect to marketing, sales, PR, value propositions, and organization change required to combat the rival's behaviors.

Comparison to the status quo

One way to sharpen the focus in deriving preliminary or possible implications from change and implications insights is to place an emphasis upon differences with the status quo in the framing questions that are asked. Doing so helps to give a voice to the two core understanding questions noted at the beginning of this chapter: what is the current understanding, and how has that understanding changed? Thinking, decisions, and actions, in keeping with the three implication principles noted earlier, provide one point of departure to frame relevant questions.

- What difference do the change and implication insights imply for our mind-set? For example, what we think about customers or rivals and how we think about them? How is our thinking about customers shifting?

- What difference do they make for how we approach decisions—past, current and future decisions—or how we should view a specific decision? For example, is there a set of strategy and/or operations decisions that we will be facing for the first time? How is our understanding of the major drivers of key decisions shifting?

- What difference do they make for how we go about developing our action plans or whether and how we need to alter a previously accepted plan? For example, do we need to develop new initiatives and associated action streams, given specific change in strategy direction? How is our understanding of what it takes to execute particular initiatives and action streams shifted?

STD case: The implication insight, small players (like us) will need to enter into technology alliances due to a few competitors making major investments in technologies to get to next generation products, could have brought immediate clarity to the connections among a set of possible business implications that unfortunately remained hidden and disconnected in the protracted deliberations. The thinking, decision, and action inferences noted in Figure 8-3 suggest that a new point of view about competing in the future was necessary: old assumptions about the relevance of alliances to the firm's strategy would have to be immediately discarded; new alliance related decisions needed to be addressed in the next few months; action would have to be taken quickly to discern who might be potential alliance partners.

Forthrightly pursuing thinking, decision, and action questions pushes individuals not to settle for trivial differences.[274] An analysis team leader who challenges team members to identify other inferences that might have been

FIGURE 8-3

From Implication Insight to Thinking, Decisions and Action; the STD Case

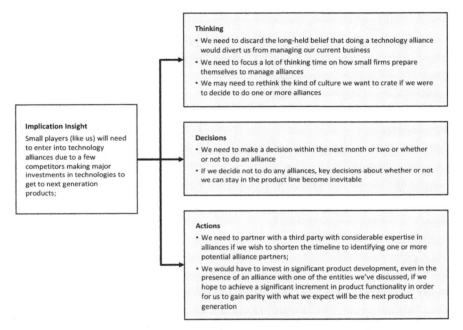

Thinking
- We need to discard the long-held belief that doing a technology alliance would divert us from managing our current business
- We need to focus a lot of thinking time on how small firms prepare themselves to manage alliances
- We may need to rethink the kind of culture we want to crate if we were to decide to do one or more alliances

Implication Insight

Small players (like us) will need to enter into technology alliances due to a few competitors making major investments in technologies to get to next generation products;

Decisions
- We need to make a decision within the next month or two or whether or not to do an alliance
- If we decide not to do any alliances, key decisions about whether or not we can stay in the product line become inevitable

Actions
- We need to partner with a third party with considerable expertise in alliances if we wish to shorten the timeline to identifying one or more potential alliance partners;
- We would have to invest in significant product development, even in the presence of an alliance with one of the entities we've discussed, if we hope to achieve a significant increment in product functionality in order for us to gain parity with what we expect will be the next product generation

missed in the first go-around or team meeting gives everyone involved the opportunity to identify more significant implications.

Predetermined questions

In keeping with the three business implication principles, it's possible to develop a predetermined set of questions with respect to each core implication domain to foster and stretch the generation of preliminary business implication inferences. These questions are likely to be largely distinct from explicit thinking, decision, and action questions.[275] For example, with respect to the strategy domain, the following questions might be asked:

- Given our current strategy, what would it take to go after one or more of the identified marketplace opportunities?
- How fast could we adapt our strategy if we choose to go after a specific opportunity?

- How might the new strategy direction affect our brand?
- Do we have the resources to pursue the strategy?
- Do we have the will to adapt our strategy?

The intent of predetermined questions is to ensure that questions pertaining to each implication domain are asked and to encourage individuals to ask follow-up questions that are often the source of possible implications that otherwise would likely be missed.

The output
Sniffing leads to a list of preliminary business implications across the predetermined and emergent implication domains. The sets of possible business implications noted in Figures 8-2 and 8-3 and Table 8-3 stemming from one or a few CSIs and/or GMIs indicates how extensive lists of preliminary or possible business implications can be.

Shaping

The intent of shaping is to generate an agreed set of suggested, and later, tentative "thinking" outputs (assumptions, beliefs and points of view), decisions and action programs in the strategy, operations, organization and leadership domains that can then be fully vetted and vouched for. Anyone who has been involved in the deliberations around strategy determination and its associated action plans has experienced extensive analysis back and forth and considerable interpersonal ebb and flow.[276] Again, our purpose here isn't to deconstruct and detail the analysis method involved but to illustrate how the insight discipline can augment the quality of the deliberations around it.

Four shaping recommendations
Here are four shaping recommendations to enhance the content of the deliberations involved in getting to a tentative set of business implications. They enable application of the three general business implication principles noted at the beginning of this chapter. Each shaping recommendation encourages analysis team members to keep the insight discipline, and, in particular, the emphasis upon new understanding, at the forefront of the analysis back and forth as they move down the pathway from a laundry list of preliminary

business implications to a short set of key implications in each core implication domain.

As deliberations proceed, opportunities emerge to revisit and possibly refine prior change and implication insights and to generate implication domain insights. Because it has not been addressed in prior chapters, I'll again pay special attention to crafting implication domain insights (strategy, operations, organization and leadership).

Emphasize change in understanding

As the analysis team moves toward consensus on implications in each implication domain, questions should be asked about how the deliberations may reflect or have caused shifts in marketplace understanding. For example, how might our understanding of stakeholders such as customers, channels, or rivals have changed? Unfortunately, such understanding shifts may be implicit; thus, extensive insight learning is missed and the opportunity to enhance business implications may also be foregone.

BSC case: As the BSC team moved toward refining and accepting an accelerated development plan, a genuine step change in how the firm develops products for market introduction, it was compelled to analyze how it had previously done so, the constraints that had inhibited it from moving more quickly through product development, and how it actually executed product launches.

Consideration of these questions afforded an opportunity to review the previously determined change and implication insights as well to refine understanding of the BSC organization. The analysis team was now in a position to develop implication domain insights—insights that would reframe the firm's understanding of itself. For example, a clearer understanding of what the company could actually do to ramp up its product development might suggest the following organization insight: by developing tight linkages among all the functional areas involved in R&D, the company could eliminate a series of prior constraints and bottlenecks that would enable it to match any rival's R&D timeline. This organization insight also led to a leadership insight: Leaders by being involved in both oversight of and execution of the R&D plan could shift the R&D culture from one that was largely product focused to one that was heavily marketplace focused.

STD case: As the team's deliberations moved toward determining the need for a revitalization of the product line—a major strategy implication—a new understanding of customers was emerging but not explicitly stated and agreed: some key customer needs, though not yet fully articulated, would be fulfilled by one or more rivals' projected product introductions. Had the new customer understanding been captured, new customer insight could have been crafted and tested.

The STD analysis team and others also asked why they didn't "see" and appreciate these customer needs before they were made visible by the projected launch of rivals' products. Deliberations around this and related questions eventually led to an organization insight with significant decision and action implications: *we're poorly structured to understand marketplace change—we don't "see" and "think" in ways that allow us to anticipate customer and market change.* This organization insight, once it was accepted, led to intense deliberations around how to structure and sniff for detection of marketplace change.

Focus on thinking

As progress is made toward agreement on potential decisions: for example, which strategy alternative to pursue or how to amend the current customer value proposition, it's imperative to address the thinking that lies behind the preferred choices.[277] For example, what trade-offs might have been made that warrant more careful attention? What if the decision is go after market share rather than cash contribution, what tacit marketplace and organization assumptions might we have made that we now need to scrutinize? Might we have assumed that market share will lead to lower unit costs that in turn will give rise to enhanced margins and cash flow? These questions lead to the opportunity to explicate and test assumptions and beliefs that the analysis team can choose to accept or reject for the purposes of strategizing and decision making.

CommodityCo case: The CommodityCo case (Figure 1-2) provides a powerful example why focusing on the underlying thinking, that is, assumptions and beliefs, informs the context for decisions and action. Once the assumption and belief shift became accepted, that is, differentiation, customer value, and competitors' moves now had to be the focus (and not the product, price and commoditization), the management team was able to reverse years of strategy and investment commitments associated with thinking of rivalry in terms of a commodity business. For the first time, they addressed how they could "add value" for customers, build relationships with customers, and use the sales force as a means to sell and deliver value for customers.

Revisit decision rationales

Choices among decision alternatives sometimes garner momentum that overpowers reflection on the underpinning rationales. Thus, revisiting decision choices as a degree of consensus begins to emerge around a set of business implications causes the why questions to be posed.

Pharmaceutical case: As decisions are on the verge of being taken to develop action plans specific to individual stakeholders, questions arose as to why we need to take action now, why we need to develop actions specific to individual stakeholders and why we believe that stakeholders will respond to our initiatives in particular ways. The deliberations due to these questions led to a new tentative execution or operations insight: the political strategy needs to be executed more broadly and faster than anyone had initially believed.

Consider action consequences

Actions have consequences; sometimes they're not anticipated because nobody assumes the task of projecting what they might be. Consideration of action consequences, of course, leads to revisiting thinking and decision rationales.

STD case: Committing to an action program to identify, develop and finalize an alliance agreement with one or more technology sources brought into stark relief the fact that the firm had little if any alliance-related capability. The STD firm backed into an organization (capability) insight, alliance related capability may be the source of our ability to stay in this product space. It became a capability the firm had little choice but to develop.

Professional services firm: Accepting a set of action initiatives intended to reach new customer segments caused the management team to address whether and how it could educate and train its marketing, sales and service teams to develop value propositions specific to each chosen customer segment. As the firm embarked on detailing these key elements in its action plan, one outcome became clear that it transformed into an organization insight: the firm is poorly positioned in terms of its marketing, sales and service integration compared to its key rivals to deliver even modestly customized solutions to key customer segments. This insight came as a surprise and shock to many managers in the firm; they thought they had achieved significant alignment across these functions. An action program was immediately initiated to fill what was now an obvious void.

Vetting proposed recommendations

The four shaping recommendations influence every phase of the deliberations on the pathway to accepted[278] business implications. However, as agreement begins to harden around a set of tentative recommendations, some of the business implication errors noted above may begin to kick in: there's little interest in challenging the prevailing mind-set, analysis orthodoxies get reinforced, and, the need to get done with the action plan overwhelms any desire to conduct a critical review of why you're moving in the proposed direction. In part because of these errors, comprehensive vetting and vouching, as outlined in Chapters 5 and 6, especially need to take place. Although many different frameworks exist to assess or vet a proposed strategy, initiatives, and action plans, the insight principles and recommendations noted in this chapter receive little attention. However, vetting offers an ideal opportunity to focus on the two core understanding questions noted at the beginning of this chapter: What is our current understanding of change in both the marketplace and our organization? And how has the understanding changed? Is the shift in understanding significant?

Scrutiny: Reality congruence

Proposed strategy and related recommendations succeed if they're appropriate for the emerging competitive space they must play out in.[279] Of course, only time can tell if they are. However, vetting enforces an assessment of marketplace congruence.[280] The insight discipline suggests posing the following set of questions as one way to stress-test proposed recommendations:

- Do the thinking, decision and action components of the proposed game plan support and reinforce each other?
- Are the recommendations supported by the previously derived change and implication insights?

- If yes, is there sufficient "stretch" in the proposals? Do they need to be "pushed" further?
- If no, do the change and implication insights need to be amended? Or, do the proposed decisions and actions need to be changed?
- Do the implication domain insights hold and support the proposed decision and action direction?

Tackling these questions compels any analysis team to first critically assess connections between the thinking underpinning the recommendations on the one hand and the decision and action elements[281] on the other hand.

BSC case: The commitment to segment customers through the development of product variations was predicated on specific assumptions: R&D could develop product variations that would attract distinct groupings of customers; the customer segments would be sufficiently large to warrant marketing and sales programs to reach them; the firm had the in-house capabilities to develop the necessary product variations. However, it was only in the development of the details of the product strategy and the operational changes it required that careful consideration of customers' potential behaviors were carefully examined. A new understanding of customers emerged: even if customers responded to the proposed product variations, the marketing and sales costs to reach these "hidden customer segments" was likely to far higher than initially projected. This new customer insight led to deliberations around marketing and sales resource allocation.

VP case: The vetting task was clear: do the assumptions about the marketplace and the organization support or conflict with the proposed strategy and associated action plans? If the team judged they don't support the proposed strategy direction and action stream, then attention quickly moves to reassessing whether the assumption set is truly indicative of the emerging and potential competitive environment. If their best judgment concludes the answer is yes, then attention shifts to how the proposed strategy direction may have to be adjusted.

If the analysis team in the VP case determines that the strategy recommendations are understated, for example, the proposed value proposition can be augmented in new ways that hadn't previously received much attention, the implication insight, *we need to massively reconfigure how we manage the organization,* might be modified to we need to reconfigure the organization to focus on significantly augmenting customer value. The restated implication insight focuses senior leaders' attention on many aspects of marketing which hadn't been the strong suit of the firm. Thus, a leadership insight: leaders need to learn the "what and how" of marketing, otherwise the new customer value propositions are unlikely to be realized.

Novelty: Action distinctiveness

Even if a set of proposed recommendations generally meet the scrutiny test, without a substantial novelty element they're not likely to generate exciting marketplace outcomes and financial results. The entrepreneurship content[282] test firmly poses the novelty question: what is fundamentally different about the proposed strategy and action game plan compared with rivals that will lead to advantage in the marketplace?

CommodityCo case: There was little doubt that the firm's customer offers would be distinct but whether the offer distinctiveness would translate into customer advantage was still an open question. Some doubt began to emerge among the team members that customers might not respond in the projected numbers. Thus, the analysis team was compelled to revisit its understanding of customers: what did we really understand about customers' needs? The team was also compelled to revisit its understanding of competitors: what offers might different competitors take to the market and why would customers see them as superior or inferior to our offers? The analysis team eventually reframed its key customer insight, Customers, recognizing that they need more than the base functional capabilities delivered by their providers, are seeking an offer rather than just a product to Customers recognizing they need more than base functional capabilities delivered by their providers, are seeking lasting relationships with providers that will enable co-creation of the customer offer. The restated customer insight led to an organization domain insight, collaborating to co-create customer offers requires us to develop a new set of customer-interfacing skills.[283]

Novelty: Insight distinctiveness

Even if proposed business implications largely pass the marketplace congruence and action novelty tests, the insight discipline still raises the fundamental insight novelty question at two levels: the marketplace change levels depicted in the insight funnel (Figure 1-2) and implication domains. Marketplace change categories take us back to the central insight challenge outlined in Chapter 1: what is novel about the firm's change and implication insights and do they meet the full set the tests outlined toward the end of Chapter 1? The same questions can be asked of implication domain insights that emerge during the determination and assessment of business implications. The insight novelty question, at least in my experience, is rarely if ever, raised and seriously treated in the development and testing of business implications.

Validating change and implication insights continues during development of business implications. If it proves necessary to amend specific change or implication insights,[284] novelty of the amended insights can be assessed as outlined in Chapter 6.

Because they emerge during development of business implications, implication domain insights won't have previously been vetted. Subjecting them to the tests inherent in the desired insight attributes always generates new understanding of the insight context and may greatly impact the unfolding business implications.[285] Take the organization (capability) insight noted above in the STD case: alliance related capability may be the source of our ability to stay in this product space. The insight did involve distinctive new understanding for the firm; alliance related capability previously was not recognized as necessary. Its novelty could be tested against rivals' use of alliances as the building blocks of critical capabilities. Rivals did have alliance-based capabilities but no firm had crafted unique capabilities. Its obviousness was rather low; it was not counter-intuitive and it could easily be detected by any firm in the business. Its congruence was high; alliance partners possessed skills and knowledge the firm didn't and could not easily develop. It explained why the firm could not win by depending on its own resources. Its endurance depended on the firm's ability to develop and enhance the capability over time. In summary, the desired attribute criteria can be deployed to sharpen understanding of the implication domain insight's context and assess its potential marketplace and organization value.

Rivalry: Winning execution

Consideration of execution issues and challenges during development of business implications provides another opportunity to exploit the three business implication principles. Any strategy that passes the scrutiny and novelty tests may still run into significant, and in the worst case, insurmountable execution difficulties. Execution in the marketplace may be hobbled by the actions of rivals and other stakeholders. Execution may also fall prey to the organization's inability to adjust its infrastructure, policies, culture, or leadership. Marketplace difficulties offer the opportunity to revisit and perhaps refine prior change and implication insights. Organization difficulties present the opportunity to revisit and perhaps refine prior and emerging implication organization insights.

BCS case: Consideration of execution issues and challenges led the analysis team to critically assess the firm's ability to make happen the proposed marketplace strategy and R&D action plan. The speed-to-market requirement required the firm to develop an R&D capability considerable beyond its current state. The organization insight around its deficient R&D capability (which was initially strongly denied by some individuals) resulted in the company, as previously noted, committing to building the requisite R&D capability and arguably becoming the best in its competitor set.

Pharmaceutical case: Strategies become sitting ducks for rivals when they don't change over time. Thus, a constant need exists to develop strategy specific insight. The aforementioned implication insight, political strategy, the management of external stakeholders is fundamental to marketplace success, led to extensive deliberations focused on determining the appropriate political strategy content and how to execute it. New understanding about political strategy slowly emerged. One political strategy execution insight can be simply stated: build alliance networks specific to each key business issue rather than presuming that one large network of relationships could be tailored to each key issue.

Value testing

Assessing the value generation potential of strategies and action plans provides a critical opportunity for deployment of the insight discipline.[286] This is especially so because value assessment so often devolves into the manipulation of financial spreadsheets; developing and analyzing alternative configurations of the revenue, cost and cash flow numbers. The presumption is that vetting, to the extent it occurs, has exhausted all avenues to fully understand the merits and deficiencies of a set of recommendations. The insight discipline's notion of value testing emphasizes pursuit of new understanding[287] as value assessment is executed.

Projected marketplace outcomes and financial results can only be validated over time.[288] But, they can be value tested in terms of their acceptability, and perhaps, even their likelihood, before they're executed.

Projections

The insight discipline suggests using projected outcomes and results as a learning framework to review, challenge, and, if necessary, amend change and implication insights as well as implication domain insights. Projected marketplace, technology, and financial outcomes play out in the future; thus, judgments necessarily involved in projecting outcomes become one critical focus.

Pharmaceutical case: Projected marketplace results included: stakeholder responses to influence action programs (for example, supporting the firm in public forums such as industry association meetings, legislative bodies, and regulatory agencies) and stakeholder behaviors in collaborative initiatives (for example, aligning with the firm to push for shared goals such as preferred tax policies and control of drug importation). The Pharma firm judged that a number of specific stakeholders would align with it in support of a particular regulatory issue. If some of them didn't fully commit to and help resource the planned initiatives to influence the regulatory and legislative bodies, they were less likely to succeed. This concern caused a review of the assumptions underpinning the proposed political strategy. As a consequence, the base implication insight was amended, political strategy—the management of stakeholders—is fundamental to our marketplace strategy, but significant marketplace results would take more than two years to be realized. The result: the initially projected cash inflows had to be reduced.

Thinking, decisions, actions

Thinking, decisions and actions provide a related way to initiate value testing proposed business implications. Any set of recommendations necessarily includes a stream of specific decisions and related action initiatives and plans. The emphasis upon understanding suggests a set of questions:

What would have to happen in and around the marketplace for a set of decisions to generate the stated marketplace results? For example, the decisions involved in moving a strategy in a new direction might be predicated on rivals not reacting aggressively for six to twelve months and a specific number of customers migrating to the firm's new value proposition within six months or so. Sensitivity analysis might suggest that the projected marketplace results are highly dependent on the competitor not reacting aggressively for twelve months. This sensitivity result suggests the need to analyze whether, when and how the competitor might initiate a major marketplace response. If the analysis indicated new understanding that the competitor didn't possess the marketing, sales and manufacturing capabilities to launch an aggressive response within twelve months, a significant competitor insight may have been created—this is especially so if the new competitor understanding is opposite to what was previously believed and it caused the firm to advance its resource commitment to executing the new strategy direction.

What would have to happen within the organization for an action stream to be executed as planned—would it adhere to the intended timeline, meet all milestones, and facilitate realization of the desired marketplace results? For example, an execution plan might require specific capabilities such as a global supply chain process be further developed and specific assets such as customer relationships and knowledge be further augmented. In the CommodityCo case discussed in Chapter 1, if recruitment, development and training of the sales force were to fall behind schedule, the sales projections would come up short.

The decision and action streams of questions illustrate the unavoidability of thinking issues and questions arising once the future is the focus of consideration.

Current results and outcomes

Of course, real-time marketplace and financial results provide the inputs to value test past strategy choices, decisions and action plan. They tell us in definitive terms how well or badly past projections have turned out. While the value assessment may be relatively straightforward—past projections have turned out well or badly—the connections to understanding shifts are often not so evident. The insight discipline cautions us to be careful and thorough in addressing two contexts.

First, positive results may cause an analysis team not to reflect on accepted change insights or implication insights. Yet we know that change insights have a definite shelf life. Indeed, the change insights becoming incongruent with the environment may prove to be a harbinger of required change in a strategy delivering highly positive results.

Second, negative results may cause an analysis team to cast aside or disparage the underlying change and implication insights. However, the strategy may take longer to bear fruit than expected or the fault may lie in poor execution.

Stipulating

Eventually, those involved in the analysis reach a point where they must offer the business implications. That is, assert that they've fully vetted and can vouch for the recommendations when they forward them to an executive team or others. They do so recognizing the fact that the recommended thinking, decision and action outputs are subject to change, and especially so, if the underlying change and implications insights need to be amended in view of the never-ending change in the external world.

Validating

Finally, as with change and implication insights, the insight discipline advocates validating business implication recommendations. Reflecting the three business implication principles, it emphasizes three foci. First, validating the underlying change and implication insights as precursors of the need for change in thinking, decisions and actions at the heart of the recommendations associated with one or more of the implication domains. Second, validating thinking, decisions, and actions through the results and outcomes they generate over time. Third, validating execution. Indicators can be monitored to assess whether execution is meeting operating targets, timelines, milestones, avoiding bottlenecks and other limiting factors.

A final comment

The insight discipline ensures that determining and assessing business implications doesn't get isolated from the learning necessarily involved in shaping change insights and implication insights. It also provides an opportunity to craft core implication domain insights—strategy, operations, organization, and leadership. It's a reminder that it is humans who make the judgments about what thinking, decision, and action implications are accepted.

Notes

246. Strategy encapsulates the offers the organization makes to customers, how it competes to attract, win and retain customers, and the goals it seeks to attain. Operations entails the activities the organization engages in to create, produce, market, deliver, sell and service the customer offers. Organization refers to how the entity configures and manages itself including its structure, systems, processes, procedures and culture. Leadership addresses what leaders do and how they do it.

247. See, for example, George S. Day, *Strategic Market Planning: The Pursuit of Competitive Advantage* (St. Paul: West Publishing, 1984). For a more recent example, see, A.G. Lafley and Roger L. Martin, *Playing to Win: How Strategy Really Works* (Boston: Harvard Business School Press, 2013).

248. Again, it's worth emphasizing that thinking, decisions and action constitute the three core Fs (factors) in the 6IFs. In this chapter, we are of course addressing the output side of the 6IFs.

249. These two understanding questions represent more than a trivial change in focus in the determination of business implications. Many of the analysis routines at the core of developing business implications such as detailing individual strategy alternatives, assessing the threats and risks associated with a potential strategy, translating a proposed strategy into action programs and projects, and developing projected cash flows, become projects in which frequently the dominant motivation is to get them completed.

250. By underlying knowledge base we mean all the analysis outputs that have been accumulated and crafted as inputs to determination of business implications.

251. An emphasis on the why questions and issues, by definition, involves a focus on thinking.

252. In other words, validating change and implication insights continues through the course of developing and assessing business implications. This should not be surprising given that the marketplace and the organization continue to change.

253. The struggle involving heated discussions illustrates how the analysis back and forth is often not linear or simply analytical; it stems in part

from the interpersonal ebb and flow—individuals advocating their point of view, often feeling that their point of view is correct.

254. Each domain insight should demonstrate the desired attributes noted in Chapter 1.

255. Although it isn't uncommon for the deliberations around business implications to go on for months, often three to six months in the final phases of the annual strategic planning cycle, the deliberations don't intentionally and explicitly address the ambiguities and complexities that are inherent in marketplace change. For a good discussion of the consequences of not deal forthrightly with complexity and ambiguity, see Michael E. Raynor, *The Strategy Paradox: Why Committing to Success Leads to Failure (and What to Do About It)* (New York: Currency-Doubleday, 2007).

256. This common error provides justification for the 6IFs, the need to take time to apply each IF to get on the table issues and questions that otherwise wouldn't be surfaced, much less addressed.

257. Many others have noted this error. This is a persistent theme in Richard P. Rumelt, *Good Strategy, Bad Strategy: The Difference and Why it Matters* (New York: Crown Business, 2011).

258. The error has also been noted by many. See, for example, Gary Hamel and C. K. Prahalad, *Competing for the Future: Breakthrough Strategies for Seizing Control of Your Industry and Creating the Markets of Tomorrow* (Boston: Harvard Business School Press, 1994).

259. This error has also been noted by many others. It's also a direct cause of the restricted mentality error just noted. See, for example, Willie Pietersen, *Reinventing Strategy: Using Strategic Learning to Create and Sustain Breakthrough Performance* (New York: John Wiley & Sons, 2002).

260. This error has been forcefully noted by many others. It's consistent with the resource-based theory of the firm. See, for example, Rajendra K. Srivastava, Liam Fahey, and H. Kurt Christensen, "The Resource-Based View and Marketing: The Role of Market-Based Assets in Gaining Competitive Advantage, *Journal of Management* 27 (2001): 777–802.

261. This accounts in part for the intensity of the deliberations that so frequently characterize determination of business implications, for example, the disagreements that arise with respect to whether a specific

strategy alternative merits full development or whether a particular customer value proposition would attract customers away from rivals.

262. A more extensive set of preliminary business implications helps to
address the errors in business implications analysis noted earlier.

263. The four examples just noted refer to the four implication domains,
strategy, operations, organization, and leadership.

264. This example illustrates the importance of seeing differently as the
impetus for consideration of the remaining 6IFs (think, intend, decide,
act, feel).

265. This is because the templates to be completed indicate the implication
domains to be addressed.

266. A particularly egregious example is the amount of time spent refining
financial projections of revenues, costs, and cash flows without critically
examining the marketplace assumptions underpinning the estimates of
product sales across the relevant market segments.

267. Renovative strategy refers to situations in which a firm takes its current
strategy as a base but then extensively renovates it. For example, a firm
moving from selling products to delivering solutions or when a firm
moves from price driven strategy to a services driven strategy.

268. The earlier discussion of both the BSC and STD cases recognizing key
capability deficiencies illustrates the importance of "seeing" in identifying and addressing our own organization's realities.

269. Others will emerge as sniffing proceeds.

270. In my experience, identifying unexpected business implications occurs
quite frequently as a result of a strong commitment to surfacing preliminary implications.

271. This is a good example of how application of the insight perspective
sometimes takes deliberations in unanticipated directions.

272. Hence, the importance of the third of the three business implication
principles advocated at the beginning of this chapter: identify insights
specific to the business implication domains.

273. In short, implication insights should always be a focus of attention. Validating serves the role of constantly monitoring and adapting implication insights.

274. The importance of project or team leaders (indeed leaders at any level of the organization) asking questions as a driver of an insight culture is addressed in more detail in Chapter 10.

275. See, for example, the thinking, decision and action questions raised in Chapter 7 in the development of implication insights.

276. The notions of analysis back and forth and interpersonal ebb and flow were extensively treated in the prior chapter.

277. This admonition had been made by many others across a range of disciplines from cognitive science to political science to many functional literatures in management.

278. "Accepted" means the final stipulated set of recommendations.

279. This observation is a reminder that strategy is always *conditional*: It's designed to fit the competitive context in which it will play out. In other words, a one-size-fits-all strategy can't win across market segments with distinct market conditions.

280. Congruence with current or emerging marketplace change was identified in Chapter 1 as one of the critical insight attributes.

281. Again, remember that thinking, deciding, and acting are the three core components of the 6IFs.

282. The strategic management literature emphasizes entrepreneurial content as a critical element in any business strategy.

283. Previously the firm thought it had the necessary skills to develop customer offers.

284. This exhortation is of course the execution of the second of the three business implication principles identified early in this chapter: revisit and refine change and implication insights.

285. Because implication domain insights are specific to the firm (rather than the external environment), the desired insight attributes noted in Chapter 1 are applied primarily from the perspective of the firm though considerations of external marketplace often have relevance.

286. Value testing, as noted in Chapter 2, explicitly addresses what the projected marketplace performance and financial results might be and whether they might be acceptable.

287. Again, this is one on the three business implication principles noted earlier.

288. This point was emphasized in Chapter 3.

Chapter 9

Insight Work: The Influence of Emotions

Earlier chapters emphasized that the brain draws inferences and organizes them to craft integrated inferences and insights. It can do so at stunning speed. And, even more critically, the mind can invoke views of the future that aren't contained in the present: it can think in terms not just of "what does happen" but "what would happen if." Thus, inferences and insight can be about the future. However, neuroscience, in the last few decades, has demonstrated that a (more) complete picture of how the mind works in the context of the present and the future requires that we address the role and influence of emotions. This chapter begins with a brief discussion of what we mean by emotions. We then illustrate how emotions can influence, positively and negatively, each of the 4I components and each of the 4S activities. The final section of the chapter suggests some approaches to diagnosing and managing the influence of emotions in insight work.

Emotions are integral to how we think and what we do

Many renowned neuroscientists, including Stephen Pinker, Antonio Damasio, Eric Kandel, and Joshua Greene argue convincingly with the support of extensive research that our minds' computations don't occur in isolation from emotions. Eric Kandel asserts, "The longstanding idea that thinking and emotion are in opposition to each other is no longer credible."[289] Joshua Green argues, "Like the automatic settings on a camera, emotions produce behavior that is generally adaptive, and without the need for conscious thought about what to do."[290] Stephen Pinker concludes, "no sharp line divides thinking from feeling, nor does thinking inevitably precede feeling or vice-versa."[291] Antonio Damasio has argued persuasively that "emotions, thinking and behavior are never far from each other—they're inextricably intertwined."[292] In short, there's little dispute that emotions are an integral part of being human—in fact, we simply wouldn't be human without emotions.[293]

Despite the critical influence of emotions on our thinking, analysis, and behavior, there's surprisingly little agreement as to what emotions are. To explore the influence of emotions on insight work, I'll take a somewhat simple view: emotions can be thought of as our feelings—how we feel about something or other.[294] You're biologically hard-wired to have emotions: to feel (for example) excited, uncomfortable, serene, proud, dismayed, rejected, joyful, sorrowful, and hesitant. Emotions are always present (Box 9-1). We simply can't switch on and off our capacity to have emotions. Once we accept that "the mind is as the brain does," an old maxim so often quoted by leading neuroscientists and others, we must accept that emotions always influence what is happening within our minds.

Box 9-1

Emotions at Work in a Meeting

If you sit in a meeting in which executives and others analyze and debate any topic or issue (for example, a consulting team's study findings and their business implications), you can't but quickly conclude that something other than so-called analytic rationality is at work. You note that comments are made with varying degrees of exuberance; individuals react in ways that don't seem to be congruent with the facts or the data; past events and experiences are recalled with vigor and conviction; and, the dialogue seems to be driven by more than simply recourse to the analysis outputs. That elephant in the room is called emotion—how individuals feel about themselves, others, topics being discussed, specific bits of data, conclusions being advocated, and many other items.

Here are some examples of emotions or feelings in the context of the type of executive meeting noted above: "I feel insecure about my job"; he feels hesitant to confront a colleague about something she said; I feel attracted to an analysis approach to solving a specific point of contention among us; she feels energized by way her boss responded to her presentation. A moment's reflection will demonstrate how each of these emotions possesses the capacity to influence individuals' behaviors:

- I'm insecure about my job; I'm reluctant to question some obvious misstatements of others.
- I'm hesitant to confront a colleague about something she said; I'll discuss it with her in a sidebar to avoid embarrassing her.
- I'm attracted to an analysis approach to solving a specific point of contention among the team; I'll push my preferred analysis approach even though it's obvious others are reluctant to accept my preference.
- I'm energized by the way my boss responded to my presentation; I'll augment my point of view with details I omitted in the presentation.

Emotions influence all facets of insight work

Every experience we have within or outside an organization takes place within the context of our emotions (both conscious and non-conscious) prevailing at that point in time.[295] Each experience provokes new emotions, reinforces or suppresses existing emotions or even causes new or deepens existing emotion conflicts (Figure 9-1). Past experiences embedded in our memory, and, mostly in our subconscious memory, are laden with emotions.[296] For example, our observations of customers' responses to competitors' announcements or hearing about a new technology being developed by a competitor could provoke new emotions: we suddenly feel exasperated that our market research or marketplace intelligence groups hadn't already developed and disseminated an understanding of what customers and competitors were doing and feel nervous and angry that our firm was likely to fall further behind in the race to launch the next generation of new products. A prior insight engagement that led to deep interpersonal tensions resulting in an "analysis breakdown" may be cloaked in feelings of hurt, unease, angst, and regret. These feelings may be resurrected when someone suggests conducting another insight project.

FIGURE 9-1

Emotions Influence All Facets of the Insight Context

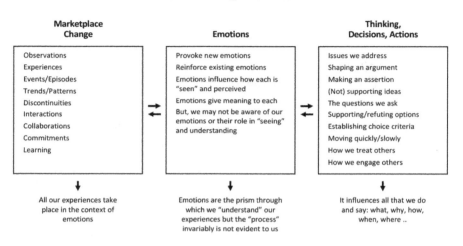

Marketplace Change	Emotions	Thinking, Decisions, Actions
Observations	Provoke new emotions	Issues we address
Experiences	Reinforce existing emotions	Shaping an argument
Events/Episodes	Emotions influence how each is	Making an assertion
Trends/Patterns	"seen" and perceived	(Not) supporting ideas
Discontinuities	Emotions give meaning to each	The questions we ask
Interactions	But, we may not be aware of our	Supporting/refuting options
Collaborations	emotions or their role in "seeing"	Establishing choice criteria
Commitments	and understanding	Moving quickly/slowly
Learning		How we treat others
		How we engage others

All our experiences take place in the context of emotions	Emotions are the prism through which we "understand" our experiences but the "process" invariably is not evident to us	It influences all that we do and say: what, why, how, when, where ..

Emotions also influence our experience. Our emotions at any point in time influence what we look for in the environment, where we look, and how we look. If we feel exultant and joyous because we believe you're on the verge of a quality insight, we may search for additional supporting indicators, especially domain indicators we hadn't previously sought, to add further credence to the emerging insight.[297] If we feel jubilant and secure because our market performance is better than projected, then we may be less inclined to actively seek indicators that might suggest competitive turbulence ahead.

Humans have a mix of conscious and unconscious emotions

Emotions are either pleasant (positive) or unpleasant (negative).[298] In relation to any issue or topic or challenge, you're likely to possess a mixture of positive and negative emotions. You may have positive feelings about some team members involved in an insight project and negative feelings about others. Indeed, you're highly likely to have both pleasant and unpleasant feelings about a single individual. For example, an inference strongly advocated by one person may provoke mixed emotions: "I'm excited and relieved that the inference has been well articulated and evidences compelling reasoning, but I'm annoyed and dismayed that the person chose to reveal the inference in front of the management team before we had a chance to vet it and support its presentation."[299]

However, you may or may not be conscious of these emotions. In many instances, people can articulate their emotions; they can express how they feel about something or other. A variety of emotions relevant to some facets of insight work are noted in Table 9-1. It's possible to imagine yourself making any of the statements shown in the "Emotions" column.

Table 9-1   Initiating an Insight Project: The Influence of Emotions

Insight project issues	Emotions	Implications
We need to embark on an insight project.	I'm eager and pleased that we have the opportunity to demonstrate our insight capabilities. I'm frustrated and annoyed that we have to devote scarce time to another insight project.	May impact who gets involved in the insight project. May affect the speed with which the insight project gets off the ground.
Let's review what we learned from previous insight work.	I'm determined and inspired to capture and promote what we've learned. I feel foolish and unsettled that we've been asked to review work we completed long ago.	Team members may embark on the insight project with varying degrees of enthusiasm.
We need to sell this insight project to the executive team.	I'm exasperated and fatigued that we have to sell another insight project. I'm comfortable and secure in meeting with the executive team to discuss the project.	The tone and body language observed by the management team may reveal different levels of commitment to the project.

We need to be clear about the purpose of this insight project.	I'm content and confident that a discussion of the project goals will inspire commitment to the project. I'm confused and flustered that we don't yet know what the project goals are.	Emotions can lead to a contentious or aligned discussion of the project goals. Conflicting emotions may lead to clarity and agreement on the goals.
We need to quickly generate results from this insight project.	I feel overwhelmed and depressed that the rush to get an output may supersede our willingness to do the necessary analysis work. Others are expressing dismay that "timing" will drive us to prematurely advance one or more insights.	Negative emotions may propel team members to express their concerns and thus cause a reassessment of the proposed project timing (maybe leading to the allocation of more time to properly do the analysis).
How do we get started in this insight project?	I'm distraught that no one on our team has prior experience in doing this kind of work. Some team members seem overconfident and casual about how to kick off this project.	The conflicting emotions may cause team members to engage in a nonproductive way about how to initiate the project.
Can we get some people with knowledge of insight work involved?	I'm hesitant to commit to this project in the absence of any experienced people. I feel exhilarated that we have a chance to design the project without interference from the so-called experts.	The project may go down several dead-ends due to lack of guidance from experienced hands.

However, one of the truly critical outputs of neuroscience is the realization that a lot of our emotions reside at the unaware level: you're not able to express them but we can appreciate them once we become aware of them. One consequence is that what we say may not be how we feel. The brain's biology enables emotions to operate as an unperceived process that is an inherent part of how the mind works. The existence of non-conscious emotions isn't trivial with respect to their implications for how the brain/mind works. It's now commonly argued that these tacit emotions can serve as the dominant influence on what we "see" and how we think and behave.[300] They can be viewed as a built-in prism through which all formal and informal computational work of the brain must pass. More broadly, these tacit emotions influence our preferences in almost every sphere of life including all facets of analytics.

Human interaction never occurs in an emotion-free zone

People's emotions influence, and sometimes, dictate their choices. Alternatives that are economically equivalent may be distinctly emotionally unequal: people feel more inclined toward one rather than others.[301] More generally, emotions aren't just something humans possess; many have noted that they often have specific action tendencies.[302] Customers who feel anger due to the appalling service they've received are likely not to buy from that firm again. Emotions, thus, often provide the motivations for our choices and behaviors—the why behind what we decide and do.[303]

Emotions influence every facet of how we engage with each other, what we engage about, and whether the engagement contributes positively or negatively to accomplishment of the relevant tasks. If the quotations from leading neuroscientists noted above are correct, then any line of argument or reasoning we construct in engaging with others is influenced directly or indirectly by our emotions. In short, even though we may not be able to articulate our feelings, they nonetheless shape how we react to others' suggestions, commands, and inquiries.[304]

The insight context as an opportunity for emotions

Insight work represented in the transition through the 4I stages, indicators, inferences, insights and implications, and especially the 4S activities: structuring, sniffing, shaping, and stipulating, that enable the transition, presents innumerable opportunities for the positive and negative influence of emotions. Stated more strongly, the influence of emotions isn't incidental to the behaviors and choices of those involved in insight work; it often proves pivotal in shaping the inputs, processes, and outputs of each 4I stage and each 4S activity (Figure 9-2).[305]

FIGURE 9-2

Connecting Emotions and the 4S Cycle

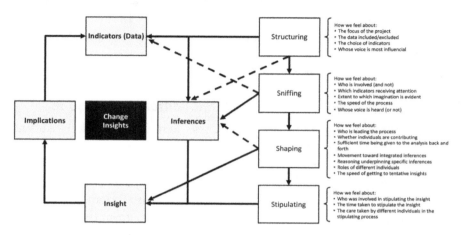

Structuring: Indicators/data

Structuring aims to generate change indicators that will eventually lead to high quality insights. At the heart of structuring lie the choices involved in the determination, range, source, and use of indicators. Each of these choices provides a context for the influence of emotions. And, how these emotions play out at both the individual and group levels directly affect the inferences and insights that eventually emerge. Even well-established data and indicator procedures are often embedded in emotion conflicts that determine the choices made and how they're "presented," that is, justified to others. Emotions influence the three structuring elements addressed in Chapter 3: identifying structuring opportunities, applying the analysis context components, and determining the appropriate personnel.

Identifying structuring opportunities

The steps involved in identifying structuring opportunities identified in Chapter 3 give rise to insight project issues and associated emotions (Table

9-2). All the phases involved in identifying, proposing, advancing, accepting, and managing insight projects are influenced, and in some instances, determined by the emotions at play. For example, whether an insight project once identified is deemed worthy of execution may be a function of individuals' positive or negative emotions associated with prior insight projects and with the need to "sell" the project to senior managers. Determining the purpose of an insight project may give rise to a flurry of emotions that cause contentious deliberations pertaining to the project's specific goals. The emotions may be lurking behind but driving the "lines of reasoning" at the core of the conflicting points of view. Some may feel exasperated and even despondent that another insight project is being proposed; others may feel comfortable and secure that the project is needed and will lead to positive results.

Analysis context components

Execution of the analysis context components described in Chapter 3 occurs in a whirlpool of emotions. Emotions affect the data practice prerequisites to successful execution of structuring (Table 3-2). Specifically, emotions influence deliberations addressing data/indicator sources, preferences, sufficiency, range, and type—considerations at the core of each analysis context component.

Data/indicator sources

Few topics provoke contentious emotions as choices about relevant data sources and appropriate modes of data collection. Deeply entrenched feelings that come to the fore frequently dictate the choices made. Consider these comments:[306]

- "Every time we use our sales force as the source of information on emerging customers' needs, I'm extremely frustrated that you're limiting our potential understanding of customers."
- "I'm increasingly embarrassed that we continue to depend on third-party sources to develop depictions of our competitors' likely moves."
- "I'm totally exasperated and bewildered that we don't ask customers who have walked away from us what they think of us. Go do it and quickly."

Emotions such as those expressed in these statements are likely to drive people to do or say things that affects structuring:[307] to ask questions in meetings why these circumstances persist; to identify and express their concerns to relevant decision makers; to try to cause others to take specific actions (for example, to use sources other than the sales force as providers of data on emerging customers).

Data/indicator preferences

Emotions sometimes spill out into the open when individuals express their preferences for specific data or indicator types. Consider these comments:

- "I get so angry when I see the team using numbers with minimal reference to their context."
- "We use the same indicators repeatedly to monitor competitors' and customers' behaviors. No wonder the executive team exhibits so little confidence in our explanations of surprising shifts in their behavior."
- "I feel so relieved, and indeed, excited, that for the first time you're using non-technology indicators to track and project rivals' potential shifts in manufacturing technologies."

Few will argue against the assertion that these types of emotions are likely to shape what these individuals say about how numbers are used or what indicators should be deployed.

Data/indicator sufficiency

The tone of comments uttered about data (in)sufficiency often conveys the presence of intensely felt emotions that may drive the direction and tone of analysis back and forth due to how they affect the interpersonal ebb and flow evident in deliberations:

- "Why do we persist in getting more accuracy in the numbers beyond their obvious decision value? It energizes some people, but it thoroughly depresses me."
- "I get so exasperated and depressed when analysts tell me that we can never have enough data!"

Range of indicators

Structuring addresses the relevant range of change domains.[308] It's always a difficult challenge. And, the breadth of focus within domains is a neverending challenge; for example, how many different types of competitors should we track and monitor? The deliberations around these decisions sometimes give rise to and reflect emotions—feelings that can determine the decision outcomes.

- "I'm more comfortable and secure in the judgments of the research team since they expanded the domains that they now routinely monitor for change indicators."
- "I'm honored and gratified that I've been asked to assess whether and how we can do a better job of identifying relevant indicators in specific domains."
- "I'm dismayed and distraught that we only use financial indicators to assess our marketplace performance."

Type of indicators

Organizations sometimes are unaware they've fallen into the trap of preferring and using specific types of indicators and ignoring others. Efforts to remedy this error may be energized by emotions provoked by its recognition.

- "I'm beginning to feel proud and relieved that we're at least having a discussion that we need to develop some non-quantitative indicators as inputs to tracking and projecting customers' needs."
- "I'm sad and embarrassed to have to point this out again, but why do we insist on emphasizing lagging rather than anticipatory indicators[309] with respect to rivals' strategic moves and overall performance?"

Influence on analysis context components

Each analysis context component[310] is greatly affected by the influence of emotions on the deliberations around data and indicator issues just discussed. Here are some examples:

If specific sources of data such as lost customers, smaller competitors, NGOs, and government agencies are deemed unnecessary or inappropriate, the *scope* of an insight project may be restricted because relevant and critical data isn't sought.

Emotions about data (in)sufficiency may limit or extend the *analysis frame*. If an analysis team shares emotions of distrust and discomfort regarding customers' emotions as an influence on purchasing decisions, it's unlikely to ask for an analysis of customers' emotions as one means to explain purchasing choices.

Emotions influencing preferences for data and/or indicator types significantly impact *focus shift*, the types of questions asked. Individuals who feel secure, comfortable and contented dealing with facts are typically ill-disposed to grappling with the uncertainties inherent in analyzing what the marketplace might look like five years out or in assessing rivals' potential strategy shifts. Such questions tend to get shunted aside.

Emotions influencing data/indicator sources and data preferences may extend or restrict the range of *perspectives* employed to draw preliminary inferences. An analysis team that becomes increasingly loath and disconcerted that analysis is always dependent on the same sources and the same data types is more likely to seek new perspectives, that is, new data sources that will bring a fresh point of view. I recently encountered a set of managers who had become distraught and dismayed that the firm's customer solution processes were dominated by the point of view of teams within the firm. In the words of one manager, "they reached an emotional fever pitch," which led them to seek multiple external perspectives—current, past and prospective customers, competitors, relevant third parties and industry experts.

Emotions influencing each of the data/indicators considerations affect how individuals or an analysis team view the relevant context. For example, an individual who feels satisfied and secure that the current range of customer indicators is sufficient to explain key customer change isn't likely to seek indicators external to customers (such as competitors' changing customer offers) that might elaborate the *context* within which customers make their choices.

Though typically unrecognized, emotions drive or constrict *imagination*. Feelings of excitement, inquisitiveness and exploration incite the enthusiasm to broaden the types of acceptable data and indicators that underpins imaginative structuring such as inventing competitors' strategies or crafting scenarios that paint competitive future distinctly different than today.

In summary, even the early stages in the insight process are subject to the influence—both positive and negative—of individuals' emotions. Choices and uses of indicators may be cloaked in "rational" language[311] but be determined by emotions that may not be articulated nor fully understood.

Sniffing: Inferences

Perhaps nowhere along the 41 Diamond Framework do emotions so strongly impact the outcomes yet be so well concealed as in sniffing—drawing inferences. Individuals experience analysis back and forth and interpersonal ebb and flow in every step along the pathway in inference derivation, as described in Chapter 4. That experience is both a reflection of prevailing emotions and the cause of shifting emotions.

Individuals drawing inferences

Consider the following examples derived from conversing with individuals while drawing inferences:

- Reluctance to draw an inference: I don't know enough about the context to feel comfortable drawing a strong inference now. The person is unwilling to draw preliminary inferences.
- Acceptance of the data sources: I'm elated that these established external data sources (industry experts) provided the base data for the inferences. The feelings of trust and acceptance about the industry experts lead the person to not seek other data and viewpoints and thus not to question the proposed inference.
- Questioning the reasoning: I'm loath to accept the logic connecting the data and the asserted inference. The person is unwilling to consider "what-if" the inference is largely on target.
- Who derived the inference: I have great faith in the person who derived and advanced the inference. The person is likely to accept a false inference.
- Conflicting inferences: I'm uncomfortable and insecure because I can draw conflicting inferences from this set of indicators. This person isn't likely to fully develop the conflicting inferences and then try to reconcile them.
- If the inference is incorrect: If my inference proves false, I'll feel like a fool in front of my peers. This is a common impulse that obviously inhibits inference drawing and development.

We've all heard comments like those noted here. They illustrate the centrality of emotions to the choices made by individuals that affect what inferences are drawn, how fast or slow they're drawn, the extent and intensity of the interactions among those involved, and whether and how inferences are vetted.

Groups drawing inferences

As illustrated in many examples throughout this book, deriving, vetting and accepting preliminary, tentative, and accepted inferences typically involves groups of individuals. The back and forth of the analysis process and its outputs reflect the ebb and flow of the interpersonal dynamics of the group. And, the dynamics so often reflect the emotions in play. Consider the three central steps in inference derivation described in Chapter 4, perception, derivation, and articulation.

Perception: Detecting sniffing opportunities

Sniffing possibilities aren't detected and executed by minds that might be described as "blank slates" ready to scan, monitor and project change. Emotions shared by a team or a unit at a point in time ensure that each team member's mind isn't a blank slate. These emotions may be provoked by an event or a prolonged experience; in either case, they support or suppress perception of sniffing opportunities. For example, a team that has just been told in no uncertain terms by a senior executive that technology isn't the source of the business unit's poor market performance won't be inclined to scan for technology indicators—feelings of hesitancy and fear inhibit its search for technology explanations of the unit's inferior performance.

Derivation: Sniffing a potential inference

Even if sniffing opportunities are perceived, emotions driving group dynamics may help or hinder inference derivation. Here are two examples:

The head of a marketing group was feeling pangs of angst and dismay that progress toward insight development was too slow. He issued a dictate that the team should cease seeking new indicators; the time had come to draw some solid preliminary inferences and move quickly to shape a few core insights. Members of the team disagreed strongly; as a result, team members felt highly discontented and had feelings of dread and hesitancy engaging with the marketing leader. One consequence was that the team emotionally disengaged from the insight work; they simply agreed to go through the motions on the theory that "this insight initiative too will pass."

On the other hand, shared positive emotions may serve to motivate and speed up preliminary inference derivation. A series of insight experiences resulting in significant intelligence insight is likely to generate feelings of self-esteem, accomplishment, and delight. Team members, thus, are likely to draw preliminary inferences by adopting the role and perspective of competitors or customers.

Articulation: Stating a preliminary inference

It's worth repeating that preliminary inferences don't exist in a vacuum. Individuals sometimes engage in language outbursts revealing deep emotional reactions to the articulation of a simple, preliminary inference. Here's one case:

A team member merely states that she infers from a corporate customer's comments that key individuals within the customer organization seem increasingly willing to talk openly about "our firm's unwillingness to address persistent complaints about the product line's functionality compared to rivals." Others on the team immediately challenged the inference, not by addressing the underlying indicators and logic, but by calling into question her customer knowledge and understanding, as well as her analytical competence. Some team members felt energized by collectively "attacking" the purveyor of the preliminary inference. The result: they became even less inclined to analyze whether evidence existed to support or refute the preliminary inference. The woman who advanced the preliminary inference and who considered it merely a preliminary inference needing further development and vetting, not surprisingly, experienced feelings of disgust and disrespect for her colleagues. The outcome: she disengaged from articulating preliminary inferences in front of her peers.

Shaping: Insight

Emotions influence each of the steps in the shaping method (Table 5-1). Progression through the shaping steps always brings into the open differences in judgments about insight content and, partly, therefore, tensions evident among and between individuals and groups. These differences and tensions constitute a breeding ground for evoking or reinforcing emotions. No wonder interpersonal ebb and flow typifies shaping. Emotions, therefore, are never far from the surface as an insight is shaped and stipulated. And, new emotions may kick in once the "aha" insight moment arrives.

Refining preliminary inferences

Refining preliminary inferences and moving forward toward integrated inferences and suggested insights is a pathway paved with emotional involvement and expression which can dramatically influence how it evolves. The need to refine a preliminary inference arises for several reasons: the architect of the inference or others are concerned about its accuracy; it conflicts with other preliminary inferences; or, questions may be raised about the indicator quality or the reasoning connecting the indicator to the inference.[312] Whatever the reason, emotions may be playing a significant, and possibly even a dominant role. Consider the following case:

The preliminary inference, a substitute technology may be developed by a firm not considered to be in our industry within the next two years, provoked intense discussion. Individuals from different functional backgrounds offered varying opinions on the inference. Two individuals with strong R&D experience expressed feelings of dismay and disbelief that the inference could possibly be accurate. A sales manager, on the other hand, felt extremely uncomfortable that the inference might turn out to be accurate. Feelings about the potential consequences of the inference led to a major refinement of the preliminary inference: a (particular) technology could be developed by a (specific) firm within a two to three-year period if a certain level of R&D investment was sustained over that time.[313]

Accepting a preliminary inference

Unlike the technology inference just discussed, most preliminary inferences, thankfully, are accepted for what they are—inferences drawn as preliminary statements that serve as fodder for the development of integrated inferences. Yet, sometimes a dynamic unfolds among individuals around the precise wording of the preliminary inference. Consider the following example. The initial statement read: The technology announcement will lead to a dominant new product feature being on the market within one year. This statement directly contradicted an assumption explicitly stated in the annual plan document that no new major product change would occur for at least two years (based on extensive technology analysis and projections). Some members of the strategy team immediately became rather irate that their projection was being indirectly challenged. They objected to the one-year timeline without asking for the data and reasoning that led to it. The immediate upshot was that a question mark was placed after the statement!

Integrating inferences

As hinted in the above discussion, the transition from preliminary to more refined and integrated inferences often leads directly to emotional turbulence and its expression.

Early stage movement to integrated inferences

It requires a series of analysis efforts to combine preliminary inferences into a broader inference; opinions are likely to be different even as to which preliminary inferences should be combined and related to each other. Each time a broader inference is suggested, others jump in with their observations and suggestions; the back and forth can test even the most patient of individuals. Ultimately, the shift to a more integrated or refined inference depends upon individuals' judgments.

The analysis dynamics just described causes and is reflected in a parallel dynamic of emotions. Individuals can easily feel disrespected, tired, aggravated, and hesitant as their inference offerings are scrutinized and reconfigured by colleagues. On the other hand, some individuals may feel invigorated, energized, and even joyful at the prospect of making an inference and insight breakthrough, or at least, of getting to a higher level of understanding about the topics being investigated.

In the DipCo case, the apparently simple task of grouping preliminary inferences spawned emotions that prolonged the development of inference categories. Some individuals' feelings of self-worth and trust in others were shattered when their initial groupings were essentially ridiculed as "overly-simplistic" and not reflecting serious analysis. In response, they challenged the reasoning behind the initial suggestions of their critics. One result: although it led to a more protracted categorization process, it produced more diversity of thinking in the deliberations—everyone had to provide support for their first suggested categories.[314]

Later stage movement to integrated inferences

By later stages here we mean that drafts of integrated inferences are the focus of the deliberations. Many preliminary inferences have been consolidated into an integrated inference, which may be close to a suggested or tentative insight.[315] Here, as noted in Chapter 5, the interpersonal ebb and flow, fueled by differences in judgments, often becomes sharply evident.

In the Gorilla Competitor case, it took several iterations through the suggested integrated inferences to reach a working consensus on a few clearly articulated integrated inferences. As individuals developed rationales to support their contributions, they began to develop feelings of contentment and comfort with their judgments, and thus, often argued more vehemently for their point of view. Sometimes it led to others admitting the "wisdom" of their argument; other times, it led to a spirited discussion of how best to aggregate sets of preliminary inferences into a more refined integrated inference. One result: the initially suggested integrated inferences were subjected to levels of scrutiny that clearly otherwise wouldn't have occurred.

Vetting suggested and tentative insights

The reasoning and judgments required in the tests of insight scrutiny and quality can't be separated from emotional influences.[316] Individuals' emotional reactions to the judgments of others are colored by multiple biases, for example, preferences for specific types and source of data as well as assessments of individuals' knowledge and analysis capabilities. Thus, the reasoning supporting an assertion of high insight quality, that is, it's highly congruent with the emerging marketplace, may be accepted or challenged depending on the emotions provoked by the argument's proponents.

In the VP case, vetting the suggested insights gave rise to intense interpersonal ebb and flow, in large measure caused by emotions—though efforts were frequently made to keep them from public view. What was taken as compelling and convincing evidence by the advocates of a tentative insight provoked feelings of disbelief, regret, and disquiet on the part of others that saw the alleged evidence as contradictory, or insufficient or poorly presented. These emotions could result in positive or negative consequences for the subsequence deliberations. The positive result: questioning of the evidence (reasoning and data) leads to a more thorough critique of evolving insight. The negative result: the emotions cause individuals not to "hear," that is, not to take seriously the reasoning of others. In the VP case, the analysis leader had to intervene: he asked each side to articulate why they supported or rejected each "set of evidence" which often caused the underlying emotions to be surfaced. For example, feelings of uneasiness and skepticism were sometimes more associated with the person(s) advocating a line of reasoning than with the reasoning itself.[317]

Aha hits or insight moments

When that aha moment arrives—when the insight "hits"—it's not simply a cognitive experience. Far from it—it's emphatically also an emotional event, and more broadly, an emotional experience. We have emotions about the insight; indeed, it may affect how we feel about many things! It's crucial to note that the emotions evoked may be positive or negative or both. For example, we may feel proud and contented and worthy that we have crafted an insight that provides a new explanation of events or isolates a market opportunity that others seem to have missed or specifies a solution to a long-standing problem. These positive emotions are likely to propel us to disseminate and propagate the insight with vigor and conviction; we will become a vocal participant in the arena of ideas and possibilities within our organization.

This is what occurred in the CommodityCo case discussed in Chapter 1. Once the analysis team crafted the competitive space insight, the undifferentiable commodity has now been differentiated, feelings of exuberance, excitement, and delight penetrated the team members: they realized that the insight explained what they sensed was happening in the marketplace and that it possessed significant potential business implications. These emotions energized their commitment and efforts to engage the management team in deliberations about the insight's business implications.

On the other hand, recognizing an insight may evoke feelings of despair, dismay, and rejection when we consider what it will take to "push" the insight in deliberations with colleagues and others who may be disbelievers. Sometimes, we may be overcome with feelings of disappointment, shock, and sadness that it took us so long to apprehend the insight!

This is what occurred in the Gorilla Competitor case discussed in Chapter 5. Some members of the analysis team were overcome with feelings of angst, foreboding, and despondency when they assessed the deliberation challenges they would encounter in engaging with certain members of the management team who had expressed the opposite of one key competitor insight:[318] the competitor would find it impossible to extend its global reach, given its resource pool and the intensity of competition in all regions of the global marketplace. They had to steel themselves to engage in the first presentation of the insights.

Stipulating the insight

Stipulating an insight as "accepted for now" as input to thinking, decisions, and actions requires the agreement of those involved. As in the earlier steps in shaping an insight, the pathway to concurrence involving analysis back and forth opens opportunities for emotions to influence both the process and the outcome. Here are three reasons why this is so.

Those who don't subscribe to the stipulated insight (or early drafts of it) often feel antagonized and distressed that their viewpoint isn't being accorded due consideration. If they choose to promote their viewpoint, it slows down the pathway to an agreed statement of the insight. It they win or partially win the analysis battle, the stipulated insight will have changed. Wordsmithing a tentative insight proves to be fertile ground for emotion-driven clashes around deeply held perspectives on insight content. Wordsmithing the DipCo case customer insight discussed in Chapter 6 initially led some members of the team to feel disturbed and alienated that their suggestion to significantly reword the tentative insight was being ignored. They expressed their alienation. In response, more serious attention was paid to rewording the tentative insight. The resultant customer insight reflected their belief that distinct customer segments was critical to the insight: a new customer need evolving out of a persistent customer operations problem with specific technology specifications will require distinctly different solutions across customer group.

Those who do (largely) subscribe to the stipulated insight but believe that their voice has not been sufficiently headed may feel that they're not respected. They may be less willing to promote and support the insight and its implications in later discussions. In the Gorilla Competitor case, a few individuals felt disrespected and aggrieved that their suggestion of a minor rewording of one insight was essentially ignored by the team leader. They supported the accepted insight but believed it would benefit from a modest rewording.

Some may judge that the insight has been stipulated too quickly or it has taken too long to do so. They may feel troubled and uncomfortable about the process. They may ask for further reflection on and refinement of the stipulated insight or they may deem it necessary to ask for an assessment of the insight stipulation process.

Developing business implications

The shift in focus from understanding change to identifying and assessing its business implications[319]—what it means for thinking, decisions, and action—gives rise to a new emotional context. For those involved in shaping and detailing the change insight, assessment of potential implications means that the judgments of others who may have had little or no role in the change insight process must now be considered. These judgments aren't emotion free! Executives, managers, staff units, and others who were not involved, or involved only peripherally, to this point bring their own perspective, history, and hopes to the dialogue—and, hence, their own emotions. Anyone who has been involved in this transition will recognize the powerful role emotions play and their consequences for the generation, discussion, and acceptance of implications.

Transitioning to implications: An introduction

The emotions evoked within the team by the need to ferret out the business implications of a set of change insights may slow and even stultify the transition or energize and propel it. Unfortunately, in many instances, the need to bring forward not just change insights but their business implications, even if it's only thinking, decision and action options or possibilities (and not recommendations) stirs feelings of dread, hesitancy, and discomfort in many individuals. The personal risks of having suggested implication insights and business implications questioned, challenged and perhaps even rejected by executives and others send feelings of angst and trepidation up the spine. One result is that caution overrules imagination; only implications deemed "safe" are brought forward.[320] Open-ended identification and assessment of potential implications dies on the vine of distaste of another rebuke by executives or others. Great change insights are shortchanged in terms of their potential business implications; the value generating capacity of the insights is severely limited.

Yet, emotions can work in favor of a productive transition. Indeed, they may be essential to it. The challenges identified earlier with respect to the transition[321] that lurk behind and often directly cause the negative emotions just discussed need to be explicitly addressed. The mind-set shift in transitioning from the subtleties of change insight to the high-level view inherent in implication insights[322] and the specific details of business implications must be supported by creating and harnessing positive emotions. The analysis team needs to feel committed and confident that they can tease out implications that will warrant executive attention. They need to feel secure and even joyful that they have the capacity to identify implications that may be new to executives and others.

Implication insight

The analysis back and forth characteristic of getting to suggested and tentative implication insights inevitably gives rise to emotional challenges both for individuals and the analysis team. For example, to the extent that a suggested implication insight repudiates long-held understanding of why the firm was successful, or indicates that the firm's historic technologies no longer contain the seeds of future success or that the firm's key alliances don't provide the channel access required by the new products likely to dominate the marketplace, emotions very quickly come to the fore. These emotions may be positive or negative; without question, they drive the interpersonal ebb and flow.

In the CommodityCo case, as the team moved toward an implication insight that we need to change how we manage the organization, individuals began to experience disturbing negative emotions and energizing positive emotions. I feel distraught that we have so much work to do to reconfigure the organization and hesitant to undertake that work were probably two common negative emotions (based on statements they made). One consequence of these emotions: some individuals asked that all phases of the analysis be reviewed; shaping and stipulating the implication insight clearly underwent additional analysis back and forth. Not surprisingly, a sharper edge on the interpersonal ebb and flow emerged: vetting the emerging insight was characterized by questions asking for refinement of the data and evidence supporting and refuting evolving statements of the implication insight. On the other hand, positive emotions were also evident: I feel excited and joyous that we will finally get the organization that is a prerequisite to marketplace success and I feel comfortable and secure in my judgment that we develop the necessary organization represent pleasant emotions (again based on individuals' statements). These emotions led some individuals to be more inclined to accept the emerging implication insight and to push to get more quickly to a tentative and accepted form of the insight. The tension in the interpersonal ebb and flow reflected the clash of underlying emotions.

Presenting implications

Intelligence insights come alive and are fully tested only when they're presented to an audience. Regrettably, on far too many occasions the change insights and their associated implications for thinking, decisions, and actions fall flat, that is, don't give rise to invigorating deliberations, in large measure due to the prevailing emotions on one or both sides of the presentation fence.

The emotions involving fear, dread, and sorrow are to be expected if the business implications constitute "bad news." Feelings of discomfort, hesitancy and insecurity are likely to be prevalent if the change insight involve GMI (generic marketplace insights) that suggest (for instance) a heretofore presumed opportunity is considerably smaller than expected or that a competitor threat is "real" or that the business unit is dramatically more vulnerable to marketplace discontinuities than indicated in the strategic plan. Even if the implications reflect "good news," similar negative emotions may lead to a rather timid, dry, and "sheepish" presentation; the full force of the implications may be drowned out by the presenter's understated tone and tenor.

Thinking implications

The transition to business implications and deliberations addressing their relevance, importance, and urgency necessarily provoke and challenge what the organization should be thinking about and how it should think. It's difficult to believe that asking anyone to consider changing what they think about and how they should think doesn't provoke some form of (intense) emotional response. How the emotions play out heavily influences thinking implications; they can reinforce old thinking habits and ways of thinking or they can provoke commitment to reviewing, challenging, and adopting new thinking foci and approaches. Consider the following case I recently observed:

An assessment of key competitors led to a specific GMI: the competitors' collective new plant capacity coming on stream over the next three years drastically reduced the presumed and asserted opportunity for all rivals in one product area. Consequently, the projected cash flows from this product that were intended to fund other product areas would be substantially less; hence, projected revenues in the next five years were almost certainly significantly overstated. The CEO's feelings of disappointment, fear and even shame (he indicated that it was shameful that the analysis teams hadn't previously "picked up" the size of the emerging plant capacity extension) led him to immediately express in harsh language the need for a "full and thorough" review of the competitor's planned strategies and their implications for "our firm's strategies, investments and commitments." The thinking behind the strategic plan needed to be and would be reassessed.

In most circumstances, if you're asking the executive team to reconsider some long-held assumptions and beliefs, feelings of anxiety and suspicion as to why it's necessary to do so emerge. The battle to identify, assess, and refine assumptions may be just as much about the encompassing emotions as about the analysis schemes and protocols. In the CommodityCo case discussed in Chapter 1, the executive team when first presented with the analysis team's findings (including the insights) and tentative implications gave vent to feelings not just of discomfort and doubtfulness but of anger and consternation: they simply didn't accept the proposed implications and wondered aloud why they would even be presented. These emotions had to be overturned through a series of meetings, often involving direct challenging of each other's judgments, before key members of the executive team felt sufficiently comfortable and secure to take seriously the suggested implications.

Decisions

Everything addressed so far in this chapter confirms that developing, assessing, and choosing among decision options is never an emotion-free zone! And, it's true for both big and small decisions. Developing strategy options that break away from the current strategy always brings forth supporting and opposing emotions. Pricing decisions always seem to unearth and make visible emotions that appear to support a price move as obviously appropriate or equally obviously without merit. Even small decisions in the broader scheme of things can provoke emotional firestorms. I've seen a suggestion to conduct one more quick review of a decision allocating workloads between two sales persons ignite feelings of disgust and annoyance ("why do we have to do this one more time?") and feelings of relief and hope ("maybe there's a possibility that we can adjust the allocation").

Deliberations and action

Getting to specific business implications, especially actions, necessarily entails extensive dialogue. Typically, it involves the team advancing different judgments, assessments and recommendations. However, the espoused rationales often conceal strong emotions at work.[323]

In the VP case, some executive team members initially could not accept the action stream suggested by the analysis team. The proposed actions awoke feelings of comfort, delight, and contentment with the historic strategy and feelings of resentment and dismay that a distinctly new course of action was being proposed. On the other hand, the feelings of elation and excitement that the proposed actions were the only pathway to competitive success propelled the analysis team to adopt multiple different analysis approaches to show the executive team why the old strategy could only loose in the fast-changing external marketplace. Without these positive emotions, it's doubtful the analysis team would have committed themselves to "winning over" the executive team to their point of view.[324]

Accepting the challenge to influence emotions in insight work

The potential influence of emotions in all four stages of the 4I Diamond Framework and the 4S cycle detailed above suggests the inappropriateness of leaving to chance whether and how emotions affect the quality of intelligence insights. Yet, as noted earlier, widely accepted protocols to detect and manage emotions don't exist.[325] However, if you accept the challenge to influence emotions in insight work, here's a set of recommendations.

Recognize the importance of emotions

Everybody needs to recognize and understand some basic facts of life in any organizational setting: emotions always influence thinking, decisions, and action. As long as humans draw inferences and craft change and implication insights and develop business implications, emotions won't sit idly by. But as many of the examples above illustrate, emotions on the one hand and thinking, decisions, and actions on the other constitute a two-way street: they influence each other, the causal relationship runs in both directions.[326]

It's absurd to assert that people "keep emotions out of it" or expect that reasoning should only be the preserve of "objective" analysis.[327] Thus, it's critical to recognize that emotions are always involved in structuring, sniffing, shaping, and stipulating both change and implication insights. In short, sensitivity to the potential influence of emotions in insight work is the vital first step to leveraging the positive effects and mitigating the negative effects of emotions in all phases of insight work.

Be attentive to emotions

But recognition of the influence of emotions isn't sufficient; the team involved in insight crafting and leveraging insight needs to be attentive to the presence, role, and impact of emotions. In every phase of insight work, it's important to ask three questions:

- How are my emotions being influenced by and influencing the insight process?
- Whose emotions are impacting the insight context and how are they doing so?
- What actions do I need to take (or influence others to take) to leverage positive emotions and ameliorate negative emotions so that insight work achieves its desired goals?

Because emotions don't announce themselves and the truly influential emotions often reside at the tacit or implicit level, addressing these three questions is far from easy. Yet, failure to endeavor to discern key emotions—your own or those of others—as the many examples in this chapter attest means you won't understand the whys behind the behaviors and actions you observe in insight work—including your own.

Conduct emotion self-diagnosis

Despite wide recognition of the importance of emotions as an influence on behaviors and the efforts of many specialist research and consulting organizations, there are no widely accepted algorithms available to detect and categorize emotions.[328] The presence of non-conscious emotions renders the task extremely difficult and is a reminder of the great care required in asserting which emotions are dominant at any one time in respect to any specific context.

Yet, with these caveats in mind, it can still be extraordinarily useful to conduct some careful self-diagnosis of the prevalence and influence of our own emotions in specific insight contexts. Consider the hypothetical analysis depicted in Table 9-2. It shows a sequence of emotion-relevant questions that might be addressed in any phase of insight work. The intent of the questions isn't just to understand our own emotions but to try to diagnose how they might be influencing your thinking, decisions, and actions (or non-decisions and non-actions). It's highly likely that unless you go through some set of such questions, you don't understand the whys behind your words, your behaviors toward others, or the motivations behind your words and deeds.

Table 9-2   Emotion Self-Diagnosis: Guiding Questions

What is the specific insight context?

- We've just generated an intelligence insight: the product evolution likely to be driven by these emerging technologies and the investments of entities outside the historic competitive space implies that our current asset and capability base will be significantly less leveragable than our strategic plans envisaged.

How do you feel about this specific insight context?

- I'm dismayed and angry that we didn't craft this insight before now.
- I'm elated that we may have the chance to avoid investments stipulated in the strategic plan that might not pay off.
- I feel a strong interest in wanting to vet this insight in case it's a product of faulty reasoning.

How do you feel about your own behaviors or actions?

- I'm embarrassed that I didn't push harder to test the transition from raw inferences to the core or integrated inferences.
- I'm confident that I asked a number of the right questions to assess the acceptability of the insight.

How do you feel about other team members who are involved in this insight context?

- I'm angry and worried that some team members didn't fully commit themselves to the process.
- I admire those few individuals who really drove the insight process.

Why are these emotions present?

- I'm uncomfortable with the way parts of the analysis were conducted.
- I don't think I was fully involved and committed in parts of the analysis process.
- I resent how a few individuals tried to dominate the entire process.

How are these emotions influencing how you see this context?

- We were slow to get to this insight. We didn't spend enough time teasing through the steps from some key (integrated) inferences to the purported insight. I could have done more to enhance the insight process.

How have these emotions influenced your behaviors, actions, and words?

- I think I'm going to ask that the insight be subjected to a full vetting exercise.

How are these emotions enabling or hindering you in contributing to this insight work?

- Because I'm angry and worried that some team members didn't commit themselves fully to the analysis process, I'm reluctant to engage with them and thus I may be inhibiting their contribution to the overall process.

Ascertaining linkages between our emotions and thinking and (non) actions serves as a prelude to action. Because of the two-way influence between emotions and thinking, decisions, and actions, it's important to note here that managing our own emotions can't be separated from managing our own behaviors and actions. Thus, in the case highlighted in Table 9-2, the individual feels uncomfortable with the way the analysis process unfolded and thus wants to have the insight subjected to a full vetting process.[329]

Diagnose context emotions

It's never enough to conduct only emotion self-diagnosis; others are always involved in every insight context. We need to try to detect the emotions most likely driving what others do as well as how and why they do what they do in various phases of the 4S cycle. The sequence of questions outlined in Table 9-3 provides one road map to detecting and analyzing others' dominant emotions as well as determining what the appropriate actions might be.

Table 9-3   Diagnose Context Emotions

What is the insight context?

- What is the focus of the insight work (where is it in the 4S activities)?

What are the issues and tasks?

- What specific tasks need to be accomplished?
- What are the key analysis issues?

Who is involved?

- Which individuals are involved?

What roles are they playing?

- What analysis are they conducting?
- What influence roles are they playing?
- What actions have they taken?

What emotions do they manifest?

- What "cues" (words, behaviors, actions, expressions, and so on) suggest what emotions?
- Which emotions are positive? Which emotions are negative?

What is the source or cause of these emotions?

- What is giving rise to or causing the emotion?
- Is there a pattern in the sources or causes of a set of emotions?

What is the influence of these emotions on the work?

- How does each emotion or set of emotions affect individuals' words and actions?
- What emotion dynamics might be at play across individuals or groups?

What interventions might be required and why?

- What actions might be required to address the source of emotions (especially negative emotions)?
- Should these actions be executed "behind the scenes" (privately) on in quasi or full public view (for example, in meetings or small groups)?
- What is the intent of each intervention or action?

Who executes those interventions?

- Who should execute each intervention?

How should the results/outcomes be monitored over time?

Individuals' or teams' emotions may be reinforcing or conflicting or some combination at any point in time at any phase of insight work. For example, in shaping an insight, one or more individuals might be revealing positive emotions supporting the transition from a small set of integrated inferences to forming an accepted insight.[330] Their words and body language suggest they feel comfortable, confident and fulfilled, and even euphoric that the analysis process is moving to determining an acceptable insight. Others, on the other hand, may feel troubled, frustrated and vulnerable, and even diminished and overwhelmed that the process is moving toward what they view as premature closure. The obvious challenge (and it's not an easy task) is to ascertain what is the source or cause of each dominant emotion. For example, what is giving rise to the positive emotion, fulfilled? It might be that the person considers she and her colleagues have put forth a best possible effort to get to a rich insight or might simply be that she is happy that she has completed the task and can now get on to more urgent tasks.

Negative emotions more often reveal deep-seated issues that must be addressed. For example, if he feels vulnerable with respect to the transition to an insight specification, it may be that he considers his reputation and integrity within the larger work group could be jeopardized by moving too quickly and not generating a valuable insight. Or, he may feel vulnerable because others didn't see his contribution to the analysis and discussion as worthwhile and thus that he had no standing to seek a continuation of the process.

Actions

Actions can be organized into three groups: discerning the source or cause of specific emotions; acting to leverage or ameliorate emotions; and monitor the consequences of the interventions.

Discerning the source of emotions

Although there clearly is no foolproof way to discern another person's emotions specific to any task or phase in insight work, two approaches are helpful. First, once you identify a possible emotion, try to identify what might be causing it. So, if this individual seems to be feeling proud and joyful, ask what might be giving rise to it? Merely asking the question may alert us to some underlying issues or challenges that we had previously overlooked. Second, if may be helpful to ask the individuals how they're feeling about the relevant insight process task or phase. However, bearing in mind that "what we say is often not how we feel", it may be best to ask open-ended general questions and work backwards to the specific feelings that may be in play. Thus, ask: what is your assessment of progress in completing this task? Are you satisfied with the outcomes? Did everyone contribute to the process? Responses to these types of questions likely will suggest the presence of specific emotions.

Emotion guided actions

The actions one takes to "manage" emotions depend upon the why behind the specific emotion (why this person feels this way in this specific context) and the context objectives at that time. For example, if the individual feeling vulnerable noted above is due to concerns about his reputation and integrity, the work project leader may need to reassure him that others don't share his concern and that a time constraint is due to the need for a (tentative) deliverable to the senior executive team. The specific actions taken depend upon whether the specific emotion is due to, for example, misinformation or a false understanding of the context or a faulty assessment of the intent or motivations of others.

Monitoring action results

Tracking emotion change and the outcomes of interventions to influence specific individuals' emotions across insight stages never ceases. If the emotion interventions are successful, individuals will exhibit greater inclination to contribute in a positive manner; their deeds and words will constitute the evidence. The individual feeling vulnerable can be observed to determine if the words of the project leader had the desired effects.

A final comment

The analysis back and forth and the ebb and flow of the interpersonal dynamics inherent in drawing inferences and crafting insight reflect the interplay of emotions. A failure to attend to emotions—your own and others'—means that a full understanding of both the how and the why of insight work will be elusive.

Notes

289. Eric R. Kandel, *The Age of Insight: The Quest to Understand the Unconscious in Art, Mind and Brain, from Vienna 1900 to the Present* (New York: Random House, 2012), 371.

290. Joshua Greene, *Moral Tribes: Emotion, Reason and The Gap Between Us and Them* (New York: The Penguin Press, 2003), 134.

291. Steven Pinker, *How the Mind Works* (New York: W.W. Norton & Company, 1997), 373.

292. See, for example, Antonio Damasio, *Descartes' Error: Emotion, Reason and the Human Brain* (London: Penguin Books, 1994).

293. I am grateful to Tom Snyder for many useful discussions about the nature of emotions and the interconnections between emotions and behaviors.

294. For one view of the distinction between feelings and emotions, see, Antonio Damasio, *Descartes' Error: Emotion, Reason and the Human Brain* (London: Penguin Books, 1994), 143-155.

295. For a comprehensive review of the role and influence of emotions in interpersonal and organizational settings, see, Hillary Anger Elfenbein, "Emotion in Organizations, A Review and Theoretical Integration," *The Academy of Management Annals* 1, no. 1 (2007): 315-386.

296. This point is strongly emphasized in Jeff Hawkins, *On Intelligence: How a New Understanding of the Brain Will Lead to the Creation of Truly Intelligent Machines* (New York: St Martin's Griffin, 2004).

297. This is an example of confirmation bias discussed in Chapter 4.

298. This is the most fundamental categorization of emotions. Steven Pinker provides one illustration of this basic categorization: "We not only register events but register them as pleasurable or painful." Steven Pinker, *How the Mind Works* (New York: W.W. Norton & Company, 1997), 143.

299. Some emotion issues with respect to presentations are discussed later in this chapter.

300. This is another reason why "feel" is necessary as one of the 6IFs discussed throughout this book.

301. This point is nicely articulated by Daniel Kahneman, *Thinking Fast and Slow* (New York: Farrar, Straus and Giroux, 2011), 364.

302. Joshua Greene, *Moral Tribes: Emotion, Reason and The Gap Between Us and Them* (New York: The Penguin Press, 2003), 135. (italics in the original).

303. This assertion is consistent with the emphasis on addressing the "why" questions throughout this book.

304. This illustrates how emotions often drive the dynamics of the interpersonal ebb and flow that is always associated with every analysis back and forth.

305. Again, this observation illustrates why we have included "feel" as one of the 6IFs.

306. The "comments" noted in this chapter reflect observations I've heard in analysis projects. I've rephrased many of them to fit the structure: show an emotion and its implications.

307. This is an example of the tendency noted earlier of emotions having action implications.

308. The analysis context component, Scope, specifically addresses the breadth of focus in insight work.

309. Leading and lagging indicators were described in Chapter 3.

310. Eight analysis context components were detailed in Chapter 3.

311. Rational refers to business or company specific factors. For example, it costs too much to generate new data; we don't have the time to search for new indicators.

312. The sources of analysis back and forth involved in the transition from preliminary inferences to a tentative insight were detailed in Chapter 5.

313. It's not uncommon for preliminary inferences that are considered important to be the subject of extensive attention leading to their refinement. It's one step in the analysis method involved in shaping (Table 5–1).

314. This is a classic example of emotion conflicts leading to positive impact on deliberations. Again, it illustrates the importance of including "feel" in the 6IFs.

315. See Chapter 5, summarized in Table 5–1, for a discussion of the steps involved in the transition from preliminary inferences to an accepted insight.

316. This point was also emphasized in the discussion of vetting suggested insights in Chapter 5.

317. For example, individuals from marketing might not respect the R&D function; hence, negative emotions such as feelings of disbelief and disquiet might be associated with any judgment or line of reason presented by R&D personnel.

318. The Gorilla Competitor insight: *The Gorilla Competitor was intent on reaching a new level of global market dominance through its R&D and marketing commitments that would make it exceptionally difficult for some current rivals to remain in the business;*

319. The challenges involved in this transition were addressed in some detail in Chapter 7, especially Table 7–2.

320. Safe here means highly likely to be accepted by the management team.

321. These challenges (Table 7-1) should not be understated. They ask individuals to undertake analysis and interpersonal tasks that present extensive difficulties.

322. The mind-set shift required to enable the transition from change insights to implications insights was detailed in Chapter 7.

323. This reflects the earlier observation that what people say often doesn't reflect how they feel.

324. The role and influence of emotions in the VP case's deliberations around actions were also addressed in Chapter 2.

325. A sharp distinction must be drawn between detecting and managing emotions. Many different technologies are now employed to capture emotions. See, for example, www.emotionmining.com.

326. Again, this observation is supported by the comments of Kandel, Greene, Pinker, and Damasio, noted earlier in this chapter.

327. Philosophy makes clear that objectivity can never be an attribute of a single individual.

328. See, for example, www.emotionmining.com.

329. The details of a full vetting process were described in Chapter 5.

330. See the VP case in Chapter 2 for an illustration of this transition.

Chapter 10

An Insight Culture: The Role of Leaders

In Chapter 1, the CommodityCo executive asked his analysis team two questions after they had presented a comprehensive analysis of change in a specific industry context: What are your key insights into this competitive space? And what are their relevance and import for our current and future strategy and operations? Asking these two questions exemplifies a leader's role in bringing the insight discipline to the fore in any organizational setting.

In this chapter I'll address the role of leaders in establishing an insight culture. By insight culture, I am referring broadly to an organization that exhibits insight-related values, norms and practices. The presumption is that leaders make the difference: what they do and say shapes and drives whether and how an insight culture evolves and survives. In keeping with prior chapters, the focus will be on enhancing insight method and deliberations, with emphasis on the questions that leaders should ask.[331]

This chapter lays out a set of action prescriptions for leaders who desire to establish an insight culture. The prescriptions are based on my observations and analysis of the efforts of firms to adopt an intelligence insight approach to analysis. No firm that I'm aware of has established and institutionalized the action program detailed in this chapter. However, for any organization that seriously wishes to move toward an insight culture, each of the elements detailed below enables that intent.

One view of organization culture

Organization culture is ephemeral, intangible, and illusive. Nonetheless, it's real; it constitutes the organizational world in which individuals live and work gets done. It may be difficult to define and describe but its implications are tangible and evident. Definitions and descriptions of it abound but most authors agree that an organization's culture directly influences and is manifest in "how and why we get things done around here."[332] But what are the elements of the culture that shape how work gets done?

An organization's values, norms, and practices provide one established means to capture culture and trace its impact on how and why work gets accomplished (or not).[333] Values constitute the embedded, widely dispersed, tacit preferences about what the organization considers to be important: what it should strive to attain, and to be, and how to do so. Values are often difficult to articulate; they're especially difficult to change. Values, ultimately, are manifest in words (what leaders and others say, where they say it, and how they say), behaviors (what leaders and others do in specific contexts and circumstances), and deeds[334] (decisions and actions leaders and others take or commit to). Thus, whether an organization is driven by or is striving to create insight-related values is evidenced in its leaders' words, behaviors, and deeds.

Behavior norms are associated with every facet of insight work. These include how wide to scope the search for relevant data and indicators, how to draw preliminary inferences, who should be involved in shaping inferences, how openly to question suggested implication insights, and how detailed intelligence insights should be. It's not an overstatement to assert that unless leaders focus on aiding desired and correcting inhibiting behavior norms, their efforts to shape an insight culture are destined to have limited effect.

Practices involve the details of repetitive or recurring behaviors. They constitute the processes and procedures that can be observed in "how we get things done around here." Practices range from the relatively mundane and highly repetitive such as how the telephone gets answered or how report forms get completed to more intricate and involved activities such as how meetings get structured and managed and how presentations are conducted. All functions and disciplines have practices associated with them—it's how they accomplish work. In general terms, insight-related practices include conducting all the tasks previously noted in the 4S cycle: structuring, sniffing, shaping, and stipulating.

The leader's role: Set the stage for insight work

Leaders at every level of the organization face three challenges with respect to insight work: how to set the stage for insight work; how to influence others in the execution of insight work; and how to leverage the outputs of insight work in thinking, decisions, and actions. Each leader challenge can be transformed into a question that helps to focus and shape the leader's role in sparking and sustaining an insight culture's values, norms, and practices:

- How can the leader enable a more receptive culture for insight work?
- What can the leader do to enhance the conduct of insight work?
- How can the leader guide and leverage insight work so that the organization performs better along each of the 6IFs (that is, in terms of how it sees, thinks, intends, decides, acts and feels) because of the change and implication insights generated and, thereby, enhance marketplace performance and economic returns?

The three leader challenges connect directly to the four phases of insight work identified in Chapter 1.[335] The leader guidelines advocated in the remainder of this chapter aim to answer these three questions.

Setting the stage for insight work

A leader at any level of an organization faces a crucial insight culture challenge: how to set the stage for the inculcation of insight values, norms and practices into the organization's everyday analysis methods and deliberations. Ideally, a leader becomes a role model: she lives the values, engages in the behaviors and drives the practices that others can aspire to and emulate.[336] By doing so, both overtly and subtly, she initiates movement toward adoption and execution of the insight discipline's analysis methods and modes of deliberation outlined in earlier chapters.

Not surprisingly, setting the stage involves three elements that relate explicitly to values, norms, and practices. We briefly introduce each element here and the remainder of the chapter details how leaders execute the three elements.

Set expectations (values)

A leader demonstrates over time that the insight perspective is a way of life when it comes to the conduct of analysis. In other words, it constitutes the values (the preferences) that drive organization members' work in all forms of analysis and engagement; it's not something that is allowed to fall into that well-known organizational wastebasket—this too shall pass! The two questions posed by the executive in Chapter 1 and restated earlier in this chapter represent a strong statement of values—a preference articulated in the presence of many colleagues that an outcome of analysis deliberations must be a set of core change insights and their business implications.

Set the behaviors (norms)

The leader's words, behaviors, and deeds help put in place and reinforce desired insight behavioral norms. For example, if the leader challenges the linkages between a proposed insight project and key business goals, then social (behavior) norms are likely to evolve that it's both appropriate and acceptable to ask for and substantiate how and why a potential insight project would advance what the business wants to achieve in the marketplace. If the leader demands that implication insights be clearly and succinctly stated as a transition from change insights to business implications, social norms will quickly emerge that significant efforts must be expended to generate implication insights.

Set the standard (practices)

Expectations and norms need to be transformed into standards to be achieved in and around business practices. Often the leader's focus revolves around inculcating insight-specific practices into ad hoc or established organization practices. For example, with respect to deliberation, a leader could ask if multiple different perspectives or vantage points were adopted in sniffing or if counterarguments were developed as part of vetting and vouching for an insight. A leader could also insist that any team conducting a specific domain analysis generate and present one or two core insights, instead of the typical stream of PowerPoint slides. A leader might also suggest the types of questions that should be addressed at various stages in analysis.

In summary, setting the stage contributes to individual leaders becoming a role model for the role and influence of insight in how the organization thinks, decides and acts.

Analysis project leaders

Leaders of analysis projects reside at the coalface of any organization's efforts to drive an insight culture into day-to-day expectations, behaviors and practices with the intent of enhancing the methods and deliberations that constitute the 4S cycle.[337] Team members look to them for cues as to what is important (values), what behaviors are appropriate (norms), and how to execute routines and protocols (practices). A team leader can raise issues and ask questions that stem from the topic areas noted in Table 10-1 to develop a preliminary assessment of the presence (or absence) of insight values, norms and practices. I'll highlight some key areas that analysis leaders must be attentive to in the case of both change insight and intelligence insight.

Table 10-1   Evidence of the Presence (or Absence) of an Insight Culture in and around an Analysis Team

	Values: What we consider important	Behavioral norms: Desired modes of deliberation	Practices: How we execute methods
Change insight	Key business issues and challenges drive our insight work. We address the most critical insight issues or topics. Analysis is driven by the goal of developing a small set of insights? Insights must meet desired insight attributes. We have established methods to execute structuring, sniffing, shaping, and stipulating. We pay explicit attention to institutionalizing each of the 4Ss.	Continually ask what's the new understanding (insight). Questioning each other's modes of thinking/reasoning is acceptable. Individuals support their point of view with the strongest possible reasons and best data. Individuals/teams rebuke others if they don't try to "see" from different vantage points. Individuals willingly challenge suggested inferences and insights.	We have a protocol to assess if a proposed insight meets desired insight attributes. We invest the time to identify indicators (as distinct from treating all data similarly)? We sniff as quickly as we should (rather than waiting until all the data is collected)? We develop different ways of shaping an insight (rather than sticking with one tried and trusted approach)?

Impli-cation insight	Implication insights are a prominent component in all insight projects. Analysis teams obsess on generating implication insights before detailing business implications. An established method to generate and assess implication insights exists. Deliberations involve multiple perspectives. Analysis back and forth is managed to create productive tension. Co-creation of implication insights between analysis team and managers.	Individuals discuss why they need to generate implication insights. Analysis teams address how to move quickly to address implication insights. Individuals ask what are the key inhibitors and how to remedy them. Individuals push each other to identify multiple preliminary and integrated inferences. Questioning the reasoning supporting tentative implication insights is mandatory.	Analysis teams develop an execution plan and timetable to generate accepted implication insights. We sniff multiple preliminary implication inferences from each change insight as well as from GMIs, CMIs, and domain insights).

Change insight

Analysis project leaders keep their eyes firmly focused on the prize—creating change insights that can be evaluated against the desired insight attributes noted in Chapter 1. Here are several pointers for project leaders that help ensure the prize is realized:

Insight potential

Analysis processes have a habit of degenerating into routines; we analyze the same things, in the same way, developing the same types of outputs, and generating the same deliverables. The potential for insights is thus greatly lessened—to say the least. Analysis team leaders, on the other hand, imbued with the insight discipline, reinforce insight values, norms and practices, by always asking two questions:

- Are we addressing the most critical change topics or issues, that is, those with potentially the highest business impact? Stated more colloquially, are we looking in the right places?[338]
- Are we asking the kinds of questions that enhance the probability of crafting value generating insights?[339]

Project leaders will find many of the questions noted in later tables in this chapter relevant to these two questions.[340]

Insight focus

Analysis leaders insist on crafting a small set of insights.[341] Analysis teams take as their primary charge to drive beyond traditional outputs including findings that remain largely descriptive of change. They recognize that a few key insights enable executives, managers and others to "see" more clearly than a ream of descriptive statistics, detailed historical narratives and Power Point slides that demonstrate the team's capacity to create and "present" data. They push for the explanations of change that can never emerge from a focus upon description. They continually ask: what's the potential insight here? Is this analysis moving towards an insight? In the VP case, discussed in Chapter 2, the team leader intervened on several occasions to refocus the team away from further detailing the competitor's value proposition and the customer's response to developing new understanding of why the value proposition was winning.

Insight relevance

The "relevance test" implied in earlier chapters is never far from the mind of analysis leaders: as analysis proceeds, questions about potential business relevance enter the fray.[342] In the pharma case, discussed in several chapters, the team leaders had to insist on members seriously considering the relevance of the emerging political strategy insight; they just didn't see that it would be relevant to the firm's competitive market strategy. Reinforcing the expectation (value) that change and implication insights would be fully assessed established the behavioral norm that it was acceptable to tease out implications even though there might be early opposition to doing so.

Here are two functional department examples:

- A team in the finance group projecting cash flows for the next three years tests the sensitivities of cash inflows and outflows to key assumptions about rivals' strategies, governmental policies and general economic conditions. It then asks what new assumption understanding is emerging and whether it reaches the level of a change insight, and might it then have relevance to current or potential business issues and decisions.

- An R&D team assessing how other firms develop external networks as sources of potentially valuable knowledge crafts a new insight (for the R&D function) that small investments in a few start-up firms could shorten the R&D development cycle in two specific product/solution areas and enable superior product attributes to what might be expected by depending on the firm's historic approach to R&D project management. This import of this new understanding for the firm's R&D strategy was initially downplayed by the analysis team and others to whom it was presented. But a team leader posed the question: how might it have implications for the firms R&D future? Some unexpected preliminary implications eventually led to a redesign of how the firm conducted R&D.

Insight scrutiny

Perhaps nowhere do the values, norms and practices that should epitomize an insight culture come more into play than in the vetting and vouching of suggested or tentative insights. The analysis back and forth reflects values that emphasize the importance of stress-testing emergent insights. The norms and practices that support behaviors designed to challenge others' contributions enable change insights that can be vouched for. As noted in the VP case in Chapter 5, behavior norms and practices that encourage intensive and detailed analysis back and forth just don't happen; they need to be encouraged and supported. It's critical to ask for the strongest supporting and counter evidence for suggested and tentative change insights.

Insight novelty

The insight discipline sets a high bar—the clear expectation (values) that insights should be novel, not just to the organization but also to rivals. Thus, questions are persistently posed by the analysis team leader (behavioral norms) to assess whether the tentative or stipulated insights pass the novelty tests outlined in earlier chapters.[343] Not surprisingly, when purported insights fail the novelty test, the analysis team turns its attention elsewhere in the pursuit of change insight and avoids the embarrassment of bringing forward purported insights with little value-generating potential. Vetting insight novelty, illustrated in the DipCo and VP cases in Chapters 5 and 6 requires the project leader to remind team members of the role and relevance of the mind, data, and reasoning principles (see Tables 3-1, 3-2, and 5-1 respectively) to buttress specific insight values, such as the importance of an open and deeply inquisitive mind; behavioral norms, such as using multiple modes of reasoning; and desired practices, such as testing insight novelty before it's advanced as an output of analysis.

Insight evolution

Interpersonal interactions always heavily influence the pathway through analysis. Emotions reflected in the interpersonal dynamics, as described in Chapter 9, frequently account for the "back and forth" in the analysis pathway. Thus, project leaders attend to the interpersonal side of analysis work (values); they intervene in many of the ways described in Chapter 9 to affect behavioral norms and practices that make it acceptable to address emotions as a driver of the interpersonal ebb and flow.

Intelligence insight: Implication insight and business implications

Analysis leaders make a difference and earn their spurs not through the quality of change insights but through value generating intelligence insights: business implications that make a substantial contribution to winning in the external marketplace constitute the ultimate value test, as outlined in Chapter 1. Beyond being the spearhead of the 4S activities—structuring, sniffing, shaping, and stipulating—described in Chapters 7 and 8, analysis leaders drive the insight culture in the context of intelligence insight in several ways:

Intelligence insight obsessiveness

Analysis leaders obsess about what change insight means for the business; they enforce the expectation (value) that the work isn't completed until implication insights and business implications are generated. The obsessiveness is conveyed through persistent questions and questioning—both behavior norms are important. Questions about the topic areas noted in Table 10-1 drive home the need to focus upon business implications. Infusing questioning, as a process, into the dialogue along the pathway from suggested through tentative to accepted implications, as outlined in Chapters 7 and 8, establishes key norms and practice elements: it's not just acceptable to question the relevance, importance and merit of implications, it's mandatory to do so.

Intelligence insight inhibitors

Analysis project leaders identify and manage inhibitors to developing and leveraging intelligence insight. Some inhibitors may be within the project team: for example, how emotions influence the analysis pathway, a reluctance to put up one's hand by suggesting potential or proposed implications, or even a lack of relevant organizational knowledge. Other inhibitors, such as many of those noted in Chapter 7 (Table 7-4) may be associated with the broader organizational context. A willingness to identify and discuss individual inhibitors, and take corrective action, is a powerful expression of insight values and a powerful illustration of integrating insight practices into the broader project practice. Consider the following example:

A senior executive made clear in a strategy review meeting that he didn't see the merits of developing a set of implication insights. The analysis team leader insisted on including the implication insights and presenting them before a discussion unfolded on business implications. She encouraged questions and discussion around the implication insights. The executive recognized the value of determining implication insights and asked that they be made a regular component of all strategy analysis projects. A new insight value, norm, and practice took root.

Intelligence insight engagement

Analysis leaders know that violating the "mind" principles noted in Chapter 4 impedes the pursuit of higher quality intelligence insights. They make explicit several values (for example, they don't privilege the judgment or perspective of one individual or function above others); behavioral norms (for example, they recognize that the back and forth in analysis must be infused with multiple modes of reasoning); and practices (for example, they insist that the team's assessments need to be tested against the judgments of others external to the team or group). Leaders, therefore, manage the dilemma caused by the need to complete analysis (though often faced with largely arbitrary deadlines) and the need to fully engage the minds of all team members to get more vital and vibrant business implications.

Intelligence insight collaboration

Analysis leaders also recognize that engagement isn't sufficient: generating and vetting intelligence insights require collaboration among team members and with decision makers. How well analysis project leaders collaborate with executives, managers, and functional leaders in reviewing and assessing their outputs (such as potential and proposed business implications) determines what intelligence insights eventually get developed and executed. In many organizations, such collaboration necessarily involves creating new insight values (for example, the importance of co-creating implication insights with executives and managers), behavioral norms (for example, asking individuals from different functional areas to evaluate tentative implication insights), and practices (for example, establishing one or more meetings involving managers and project team members to identify possible and potential business implications). In the BSC case, discussed in Chapters 7 and 8, the intelligence professional serving as the project leader intervened to "bring all parties to the table" to develop the implication insights and business implications rather than doing so in series of hand-offs.

Intelligence dynamics

Just as in creating change insight, analysis leaders pay close attention to the interpersonal ebb and flow in and around the 4S activities. Often, interpersonal issues[344] undergird the analysis bottlenecks, regression, and failures to create productive tension.[344] The attentive analysis leader notes how emotions may be influencing behavior norms that negatively impinge upon any of the 4S activities and takes appropriate corrective action.[346]

In one example, a manager of competitive analysis noticed that some team members were reluctant to originate possible or preliminary implications given a set of study findings, including a small set of change insights, which were the output of a "deep dive" into the changes driving a specific product sector. When she asked why, one of the team quickly responded that they felt unhappy and insecure searching for possible implications that would be outside what some executives and managers might consider acceptable. She then assured the entire team that it was their obligation to challenge the organization's long-help routines and ways of doing things and she would take responsibility to bring forward to the executive group what the analysis team considered its best professional judgments. In short, she established a new insight value for the team (our professional opinion is what counts), a new behavior norm (we pursue possible implications wherever they take us), and a new practice (we develop new routines to help us identify possible business implications).

Role of mid-level leaders

We take a broad view of mid-level leaders: directors, managers, and VPs. They're in the best position to drive "local" knowledge and insight work. They often oversee major business initiatives, provide day-to-day guidance of action programs and projects, are central to most work processes, and influence significant numbers of people through their leadership roles. By virtue of where they sit, they possess many specific opportunities to lead, shape and reinforce insight values, norms and practices—which if well executed go a long way to achieving and sustaining an organization-wide and deep insight culture.

If the insight discipline is to truly influence how an organization executes insight methods and deliberations, it's not enough for mid-level leaders to express their buy-in; they must live it.[347] If they manifest insight-related values, norms and practices in their sphere of influence,[348] then the organization has a reasonable chance of adopting and exuding an insight culture. So how might mid-level leaders live an insight culture? Here's a set of prescriptions based on observations of several leaders at different levels across many types of organizations.

Getting to change insights

VPs or functional heads of, for example, marketing, sales, operations, manufacturing, engineering, human resources, and finance need to know the trajectory of change in the relevant marketplace domains. Change insight at all levels of the insight funnel (domain, CSIs, and GMIs) ought to be a stable element of their understanding of current and potential marketplace change. Thus, their own decision-making needs should serve as the motivator for involvement in change insight work—they need to be attentive to what they need to do to enable the organization to enhance the quality of change insights.

Structuring

The early stages of change insight work present several opportunities for any mid-level leader to pose questions that advance an insight culture's values, norms, and practices (Table 10-2).

Table 10-2   Structuring and Sniffing: Insight-Related Questions Mid-Level Leaders Should Ask

Insight value questions

- What marketplace change are the insight projects intended to address?
- What business issues, challenges or needs are the insights intended to inform?
- How can I leverage these insights in the work I do?
- How do the insights affect decisions confronting us now?
- How do the insights help shape emerging and future decisions and actions?

Insight work scope

- What major analysis projects are now underway?
- How is the insight discipline influencing these projects?
- What major analysis projects will we be initiating?
- Given our key business issues and objectives, what insight work (analysis projects) should we be undertaking?

Proposed insight work

- How does each proposed insight project connect to specific business issues and goals?
- If it were successful, how would it influence how the organization thinks, makes decisions and acts?
- How might the project be better focused to enhance thinking, decisions, and actions?

Insight work participants

- Who is involved in the insight work?
- Who isn't now involved, but could contribute to the work?
- Who should I influence to become involved in a project?
- Who external to the organization should be involved?

Insight work perspective

- Is there excessive dependence on specific data types or data sources?
- Does one individual, functional area, or organizational level dominate deliberations?
- Does one mode of reasoning dominate analysis and deliberations?

Influence the insight work scope

Mid-level leaders bear the responsibility for ensuring that key business issues and challenges drive insight work. Developing interesting change insights that have minimal implications for the organization's thinking, decisions and action clearly serve no purpose. Here's one example of a mid-level leader influencing the scope of insight work: a chief marketing officer asked that insight projects address (among other things) customers' and potential competitors' likely responses as part of the firm's preparations for a new go-to-market strategy in launching a product intended to create a new market space.

Influence proposed insight work

Mid-level leaders review and approve proposed work initiatives. Here's where a leader can help determine the content and direction of immediate insight work. The types of questions noted in Table 10-2 compel consideration of the crucial linkage between the firm's core business issues, challenges and decisions and the thrust of insight work. Simply asking the question—how a proposed analysis project will aid and abet the organization's thinking, decisions and action—reinforces the value (expectation) that analysis by itself serves no purpose. Here's one example:

A chief strategy officer challenged an analysis team that was about to engage a small consulting firm to conduct an analysis of the buying behaviors of a segment of the firm's key accounts to identify what they expected to learn that would be different than what they already knew based on extensive prior research. The analysis team found it difficult to identify what the difference might be and found it largely impossible when pushed by the chief strategy officer to explain how the possible difference would have a major impact on the organization's thinking, decisions and action. The proposed project was dropped.

Influence insight work participants

As illustrated in many examples in earlier chapters, who is involved in all stages of insight work greatly influences the nature and quality of the insights derived. Mid-level leaders exert tremendous influence on shaping an insight culture's norms and practices by asking who is involved in an emerging insight project, suggesting the value of a role for different individuals or units, or even on occasion dictating the need for contributions from specific individuals internal or external to the organization. Leaders in marketing, sales and operations functions sometimes can pinpoint individuals in their external networks that could be the sources of critical information. It's here of course that the 6IFs can be used to structure the composition of any analysis team.

Influence the work perspective

As outlined in Chapter 3, and illustrated in many examples throughout this book, structuring strives to obtain data from many distinct sources, address multiple distinct entities as potential sources of insight, build different perspectives into insight work, and scrutinize data conflicts, dilemmas, and anomalies for their potential valuable inferences. Thus, a critical leader role is to ensure that, as detailed in Chapter 3, dependence upon a small set of data sources or a single mode of analysis or a dominant mode of reasoning doesn't arise. Again, the questions noted in Table 10-2 send clear signals that a manager wants to see evidence of specific desired values, norms and practices.

Sniffing

Anticipating and understanding marketplace change constitutes a fundamental responsibility of any leader. Thus, sniffing, as an activity, becomes a responsibility of every leader; it's not preserved for those formally involved in insight projects. In fact, the ultimate dream of anyone imagining what an insight culture might be would surely entail everyone in the organization sniffing as the opportunity arises in pursuit of the next breakthrough intelligence insights.[349] Mid-level leaders play a few critical roles in the pursuit of the dream:

Perform sniffing

An undeniable fact of organizational life is that as managers climb the organizational hierarchy, they encounter opportunities for sniffing that aren't available to those beneath them. VPs and managers meeting with their peers in supplier or customer organizations may capture indicators of potential change in many domains. One marketing manager attending an industry trade show drew an inference from conversations with multiple customers that sales of the industry's dominant product could fall precipitously if the application-in-use problems experienced by a respected customer were to make it into trade press. This inference was new to the firm's market intelligence team.

Conveying the inference to the intelligence team reinforced the expectation (value) that sniffing should be conducted where possible and the practice that the outputs of sniffing should be made available to those who are able leverage it.

Ask others about sniffing

Questions always embody signals. Leaders convey their concern, interest and desire by asking questions of others about whether and when, how, where and why they engage in sniffing. Even a broad question such as "what customer behaviors provide you the opportunity for interesting inferences" signals not only the leader's knowledge of the need for and possibilities of sniffing but the intent to make sniffing part of the organization's values, norms and practices.

Collaborate in sniffing

The leader's collaboration in sniffing serves as an even more powerful signal of the role and importance of sniffing and its potential contribution to insight. For example, if a leader, at any level in the organization attends an external meeting, he or she can sniff inferences about a range of topics and then convey those inferences to a team involved in a specific analysis project. Conveying these inferences to others may initiate pathways to insight that might not otherwise occur. The application-in-use inference just noted led the analysis team to review multiple inferences it had drawn about the future of that specific product-market space.

Shaping

Mid-level leaders' presence in shaping is typically more visible than in sniffing. It drives home to all involved that they value insight work and are willing to develop and reinforce behavior norms and practices that make it central to the organization's thinking, decisions and action. Mid-level leaders can ask many questions (Table 10-3) and play many roles in shaping, sometimes as a central figure, sometimes as a peripheral figure.

Table 10-3   Shaping and Stipulating: Insight-Related Questions Mid-Level Leaders Should Ask

When tentative change insights (before they're finally stipulated as accepted) begin to emerge, mid-level leaders should ask

- What's surprising about this tentative insight?
- Is it possible to do further analysis (vetting) to strengthen or refute the insight?
- Should we get others involved to challenge the insight? Who might be most suitable for this task?
- How might this change insight lead to high-value intelligence insight?
- How might this insight affect our thinking on this or related topics or issues?

When insights have been stipulated, managers and executives should ask these questions, which relate to the desired insight attributes discussed in Chapter 1:

- What's new in each insight? Is it new to the world?
- What was the old understanding? Was it explicit or implicit?
- How significant is the difference? Who might view the difference as significant?
- What does the insight help to explain?
- What are the preliminary judgments on how each change insight could influence our thinking, decision, and action streams?
- What reasoning or argument connects the data to the insight?

As insights are incorporated into analysis, mid-level leaders (as well as executives) should ask:

- How can we (more quickly) move to identifying implication insights?
- Are we prepared to address business implications?
- Are we continuing to validate each insight?
- Do we need to amend specific insights?
- If we do, what is the new insight content?
- How might the new insight content affect implication insights and business implications?

Review insight focus

As insight work progresses through shaping, the leader can never presume the work will be decision value generating. Thus, the questions noted in Table 10-2 can be asked again; they reinforce insight values and behavior norms. Asking these focus questions, serves two purposes in the early stages of shaping. First, it enables the leader to get (re)acquainted with the focus and scope of individual insight projects as well as the overall insight program (the collection of projects). The leader then can question the potential value and returns of individual projects—thus, influencing the allocation of resources to insight work. Second, it again sends a strong signal to all involved that the leader isn't just thinking "big-picture" when it comes to insight work but is also willing to invest the time and energy to learn what is necessary to enable the big-picture thinking.

Address the insight funnel

A leader at any organizational level can buttress insight values and norms by insisting that GMIs (generic marketplace insights) be a focus and output of shaping. All too often in traditional modes of industry and market analysis, key GMI components (opportunities, competitive risks, competitor threats, vulnerabilities and assumptions) aren't isolated as separate inputs to strategy development. Here are some examples of questions I've seen managers pose:[350]

- How does the analysis affect the array of opportunities confronting us? And, what's the opportunity we had previously missed?
- What forces are propelling the competitive risks you've identified? And, how might the trajectory of these risks change over time?
- What competitor-specific factors might cause competitors to alter the strategy projections you have presented?
- Why do some of the vulnerabilities you identify seem to be relevant to most firms and some seem to be relevant to only one or two firms?
- What if one of your key assumptions proves incorrect—what are its implications for the set of insights you present?

Ask insight content questions

Asking insight content questions captures others' attention and alerts them to be prepared for leaders' questions.[351] Questions such as the insight funnel questions just noted, as well as those in Table 10-3, force a dialogue around the evidence and rationales for progress from preliminary inferences through integrated inferences to tentative and accepted change insights. The manager's questions augment and may direct the vetting of insights—sometimes in full public view of the leader's colleagues. Sometimes, one simple question can force a shift in the "back and forth" characteristic of vetting. The VP in the BSC case, discussed in Chapters 7 and 8, guided the analysis process by persistently asking questions about how the change insights were evolving and later what their business implications might be.

Consider also the following example: A VP asks how the competitive space insight (CSI) proposed by the team changes the understanding of what will happen in the marketplace. The analysis team and others in the room immediately discussed what was new in the suggested insight. It was quickly agreed that the difference between the old and new understanding had to be clarified and that the rationales underpinning the new understanding (the suggested insight) had to be revisited.

Attend to emotions

Leaders attentive to detecting, assessing and managing the emotional context, often revealed in the ebb and flow of interpersonal interactions during shaping, are likely to observe both the emotional impediments to and facilitators of productive dialogue. Thus, leaders addressing the emotional context in ways suggested in Chapter 9, reinforce their strong preferences (values) for the importance of insight work and behavior norms and practices that should be evident in its execution. Consider the following example:

Two junior individuals in a meeting designed to elicit possible implications of a set of CSIs and GMI were obviously unhappy with the responses they got to some of their suggestions (facial reactions sometimes betray more than we wish!). A VP later asked each one why they seemed to be disturbed and spoke less as the meeting progressed. They indicated the source of their discomfort and dismay: more senior members in the room frequently didn't acknowledge their contributions and sometimes didn't write down key words from their comments, as they did for others. The VP in his opening comments at the next meeting talked about the importance of listening to each person (values), taking note of each contribution (norms) and making sure that all comments were included as they moved toward potential and proposed implications (practices).

Manage responses

Although it may appear at first glance as relatively inconsequential, how leaders manage their responses to others' questions and inquiries reinforces or impedes desired insight values, norms, and practices. Uttering the tart response, "that's the dumbed question I've heard today" hardly empowers those present to fully vet emerging insights or to challenge each other's reasoning. On the other hand, asking probing questions to extend team members' observations may authorize others to put that behavior norm into practice.

Stipulating

Mid-level leaders can intervene in several ways to drive home insight values, norms, and practices when it comes to stipulating insights.

Force stipulation

While sufficient time needs to be devoted to the final stipulation of an insight, it's probably more common to find analysis procrastination and delaying tactics stalling the determination of change insights that can be taken as inputs for implications analysis. A leader may need to intervene to push the process along to avoid postponing serious analysis of business implications. In the words of one middle-level manager, "A change insight that is 80 percent correct is infinitely better than a persistent muddle as to what the insight might be."

Ask content questions

As with vetting, when leaders ask questions about the content and process of vouching for an insight, everyone involved gets a clear message that vouching isn't something to be done quickly and lightly. Therefore, norms and practices associated with vouching are more likely to be developed and assessed. For example, individuals are more likely to challenge each other's reasoning and evidence supporting and refuting a suggested and stipulated insight if they know that they may be required to describe and defend the analysis process and its outcomes.

Post-stipulation

Although it may seem obvious, mid-level leaders (and executives) need to ask a set of critical questions once a change insight has been stipulated (Table 10-3). To revert to the CommodityCo case in Chapter 1, once the change insight, the undifferentiable commodity has now been differentiated, was stipulated, the executive team could then ask a series of questions both to better understand the change insight and to develop a sense of its potential business implications. Each of the questions noted in Table 10-3 possesses the capacity to shape deliberations around the stipulated change insight and how it might influence thinking, decisions, and actions. For example, leaders can again ask the question, how significant is the difference between the old and new understanding inherent in the change insight; again, it leads to a discussion of what the difference is, the evidence for the difference, why the difference was not previously detected, and, of course, what its possible business implications might be.

Getting to intelligence insights

Leaders at every level of the organization quickly learn that change insights may be interesting but it's intelligence insight that leads to marketplace results and economic value. Thus, whether and how an organization generates intelligence insights constitutes the critical test of any organization's insight culture. Leaders' interventions at all levels in the organizational hierarchy[352] are necessary to drive and sustain a concern with and focus on business implications.

Rather than focus on the steps involved in the 4S activities described in Chapters 7 and 8, I'll briefly note key inhibitors[353] (Table 10-4) and then address the key business implication elements—thinking, decisions, and actions.[354]

Table 10-4   Sample Intelligence Insight Inhibitors and Their Cultural Underpinnings

Sample intelligence insight inhibitors	Sample culture issues	Sample potential leader actions
Not clear what our strategy is.	Importance of clear sense of the strategy not valued by leaders.	Summarize and publicize direction and content of the strategy.
Deep commitment to past decisions.	Behavior norms don't allow discussion and re-appraisal of past commitments.	Establish required norms and practices in documents and appropriate meetings.
Deeply entrenched mental models.	Diagnosing and assessing elements of shared mental models not valued.	Develop diagnostic practices as part of strategy and decision analysis.
Move quickly to implications and then "lock-in" on them.	Norms and practices don't support review of implications once tentatively agreed.	Initiate a review process as a norm within decision and strategy processes.

Reluctance to engage around signifi- cant differences in opinions.	Values and norms around the need to identify and reconcile differences in view- points and opinions missing from day-to-day practices.	Use one or more meet- ings as a venue to illustrate the requisite norms and practices to move beyond viewpoint differences.
Lockstep, time- sequenced protocols and routines for getting to business implications.	Value of adhering to schedules and protocol deemed more important than allowing flexibility in the analysis processes to generate implications.	Work with selected others to test different approaches to identify- ing and assessing busi- ness implications.
Don't see the value of devoting time to identifying possible implications.	Practices to gener- ate and review pos- sible implications not developed.	Appoint individuals to develop and institute relevant practices.
Reluctance to iden- tify and deal with underpinning emo- tion issues.	Absence of behavior norms to ask individuals what is motivating spe- cific behaviors and then discuss the answers.	Establish venues (such as "safe harbors") to diag- nose motivations behind behaviors and to address actions required.

Address inhibitors

Understanding the range of potential intelligence insight inhibitors, espe- cially those noted in Chapters 7, 8 and 9, constitutes one crucial starting point for mid-level leaders committed to infusing the insight discipline into their part of the organization. It's not enough to be aware of key inhibitors to tran- sitioning to implication insights and business implications; mid-level leaders need to know how to manage them (see right-hand column in Table 10-4). I'll merely address one common inhibitor noted in Table 10-4, the prevalence of lock-step, time-sequenced protocols and routines deployed to generate business implications. Mid-level leaders need to take the initiative to estab- lish specific routines to provide an analysis team and others the "space" to develop implication insights and to challenge each other in the deliberations during development of business implications. One commonality across the cases described in this book was the deliberate attempt on the part of many mid-level (and project team leaders) to isolate time for undisturbed focus on developing implication insights. Unless they did so, the tendency to glide by implication insights on a fast pathway to determining business implications proved irresistible.

Focus on thinking

If, as suggested in earlier chapters, insights shift thinking in distinct and fundamental ways, then it can't be left to chance that leaders' actions (words, behaviors and deeds) challenge their own or the organization's thinking.

The leader's own thinking

Unfortunately, an organization's mental model, its shared point of view, assumptions, and beliefs, proves stunningly difficult to change. However, culture is always lived and changed at your own doorstep. If you don't reflect on and endeavor to change your own values, norms, and practices, you become the obstacle to culture change.[355] Thus, leaders must devote some time to considering and extracting the consequences of each key change and implication insight or set of insights for their own thinking. It requires the commitment to ask challenging questions (Table 10-5); otherwise the necessary reflection isn't likely to occur.

Table 10-5   Questions to Provoke Reflection on Your Own Thinking

What I should think about:

- How do change insights affect what facets of marketplace change I should think about? For example: change in and around competitors, customers, marketplace dynamics, governmental shifts? What specific questions should I be asking?
- What elements of each business implication domain (strategy, operations, organization and leadership) should I be thinking about? What specific questions should I be asking?
- Given the change insights, what new decisions should we be addressing? What's new about these decisions?

- How might the focus of individual current decisions need to change? Why?
- What action streams do we need to reassess? Why?
- What new actions may be on the immediate horizon?
- What longer-term actions might we need to consider?
- How are these attention foci different than what was previously the object of my attention?
- How might these attention differences lead to change in my mental model? For example, my "point of view," assumptions and beliefs about how the marketplace may evolve?
- What might be the implications of that difference for our goals, what we decide, and the actions we take?

How I should think:

- How can I manage deliberations so that I'm exposed to diverse perspectives?
- How can I engage with others in ways that allow me to be more imaginative?
- Can I use scenario-like methods to think backwards from the future?
- Do I need to stress test my assumptions and beliefs—perhaps through sensitivity analysis?
- What supporting and refuting data and reasoning should I seek to assess my point-of-view about the evolving marketplace?
- How can I use others to challenge my reasoning?
- Is my reasoning overly dependent on specific data types and data sources?

Leaders who are willing to reveal that change or implication insights have caused a shift in the focus of their thinking buttress and reinforce the insight value that elements of our mental models should always be open to adaptation and sometimes to complete change. Consider this example:

A VP stated in strong terms in a strategy review session how a few CSI (competitive space insights) had compelled him to adopt a new assumption set about the future of the industry: he now accepted that dramatic product change would occur in the next two years as opposed to what had happened in the prior five years. Articulating his assumption change helped establish the behavior norm that it was acceptable for individuals to make visible to their peers how and why their "view of the future" had changed.

Unit or organization-wide thinking

Change insights always present a leader with the opportunity to consider and assess the state of the organization's thinking from the perspective of both the content (what the organization thinks about) and process (how the organization thinks). This is an underappreciated leverage point to instill some facets of insight values, norms and practices.[356]

Each case discussed in this book offers myriad examples of the downside of not doing so early, rather than later, in an insight project. In the Gorilla Competitor example, discussed in Chapter 5, it was only after the implication insights were determined and key business implications developed, that it dawned on key leaders that "thinking issues" regarding their own firm needed to be addressed. Had issues about the firm's assumptions and beliefs received some serious attention during the development of the implication insights (and maybe even earlier), the insight analysis project would have been accorded greater urgency and, most likely, action taken sooner.

Here's another example from recent experience: In one professional services company, two CSIs, customers are rapidly moving away from the historic pricing model and rivals are testing different pricing models with large individual customers. These tests are made with the intent of reshaping their entire pricing structure and ended up providing an opportunity for a few members of the executive team to revisit and fundamentally shift the firm's historic marketplace assumption set. One outcome was that the insight practice, always review and stress-test key assumptions, became an accepted tenet of the firm's strategy and marketing analysis.

Focus on decisions and decision making

Mid-level leaders shape the context for the transition from change insights to implication insights and, finally, to thinking, decision, and action implications. Insight values, norms, and practices facilitate or inhibit the transition.

Determining the decision focus

Change insights afford leaders a golden opportunity to ask a powerful question: what is the real focus of the decision you're exploring? In some instances, it may fundamentally shift the focus and attention of those involved in a specific decision context. GMIs (generic marketplace insights) sometimes provide the vehicle to do so. Referring to the DipCo case, the customer insight that the customer need centered on a solution and not a product, moved the focus of the marketing decision from "how do we enhance the design and performance of our product" to "how do we develop the knowledge and competencies to create a genuine solution for the customer." Openly shifting the decision focus reinforced the insight value (expectation) that it was appropriate to initiate deliberations that might result in a new decision focus.

Reframing existing decisions

Even more expansive than determining the decision focus is the possibility of reframing an existing set of decisions. In the words of one executive "we now see what we thought was the decision set in a totally different light."

The CommodityCo case described in Chapter 1 provides a classic example: instead of being consumed with a set of decisions that stemmed from viewing the product as a commodity, they now had to deal with a set of decisions that addressed how to compete with a competitor that had somewhat de-commoditized the customer experience. In short, it had to reframe its marketing, sales and operations decisions to fulfill a distinctly different customer value proposition.

Managing (structuring) the decision context

Decision focus and framing typically evolve when leaders influence and shape the decision context: who is involved, what roles they play, whose perspective they adopt, and, the expectations (value) articulated for the type of outputs and outcomes desired (norms and practices). Here are two examples, one relatively formal, one less so:

In the professional services firm mentioned earlier, the customer and competitor insights led members of the executive team to establish a set of analysis teams to determine what the firm's strategy should be, to question what offers should be taken to which customer segments, and how the firm should compete against specific rivals in different geographic markets.

They intentionally established some overlaps in the remit of the teams; a new behavioral norm and practice. The intent was to obtain the perspective and judgment of each team with respect to a set of fundamental issues confronting the business.

Although it's often overlooked, one simple but powerful means to structure a decision context involves influencing "who should be in the room" when the intent may be to generate potential implications or to move all the way to specific decision and action implications. I frequently witness how the content and direction of the deliberations switches dramatically when marketing personnel are added to a predominantly R&D and engineering function driven meeting. Suddenly, a different perspective on customers is evident in the room. Again, the behavioral norms involving multiple and sometimes conflicting perspectives are endorsed.

Managing the decision process (shaping analysis)

All too often, decision processes solidify, if not ossify, over time in many organizations.[357] The back and forth in the deliberations becomes staid, non-inquisitive, and predictable: the dominance of the accepted mental models suppresses inclinations to try new modes of analysis or to raise business implication questions that might "rattle someone's cage." Leaders exercising the insight discipline inherently challenge the modes and content of deliberations along each stage of the decision process. In doing so, issues relating to values, norms and practices inevitably arise. Consider these widely applicable examples:

- When a leader declares she wants to see the key change and implication insights, or the assumptions that stem from key insights, that serve as input to identifying strategy alternatives, she shapes the decision's analysis context. Values associated with the importance of exposing and assessing insights get reinforced.

- Leaders can influence the decision process by insisting that the strongest possible arguments, pro and con, be created and tested, as part of the evaluation of the strategy alternatives. Norms around analysis behaviors get exposed and reinforced.

- Asking specific questions about the sensitivity of change in change insights to the implications that were derived and advocated often leads to shifting the dynamics in the back and forth of vetting potential and proposed implications. Practices involved in vetting get integrated into the organization's strategy development and choice protocols.

Shaping the decision process (interpersonal)

As described in Chapter 8, observation of the ebb and flow of interpersonal interactions in the dialogue about business implications enables leaders to detect the role and influence of emotions in shaping deliberations. Leaders can then choose where and how to intervene, sometimes to leverage positive emotions, sometimes to mitigate negative emotions. Here's one recent example of a leader's actions to address emotions influencing the ebb and flow of deliberations:

A visible emotional attachment to what a segment of the organization believes underpins its historic marketplace success even though strong evidence suggests it's no longer relevant to winning in the rapidly changing marketplace. A VP asked for a set of individuals who held this belief to make the business case that the factors it espoused were critical to winning customers in the emerging marketplace. During the analysis, the team concluded that other factors were far more crucial to marketplace success. The manager avoided haranguing them or belittling their analysis in public and they became supporters of the firm's new strategy initiatives. The value of asking individuals to substantiate a belief was established; the behavioral norms around challenging individuals to support their viewpoint were supported; the practice of following through on the request to buttress an argument was clearly initiated.

Focus on action

The insight discipline doesn't stop at thinking and deciding—it traces all the way to action and beyond. Mid-level leaders know that the organization's actions (not just what it thinks or decides) determine whether it wins in the external marketplace, how fast it does so, and, if success can be sustained. Choosing a strategy direction gives rise to myriad action choices. Thus, extensive deliberations are also required to address the action choices. The focus should be on how change insights inform the following set of questions:

- How might we need to change specific actions we're now taking?
- What new actions might we need to take?

- How might we need to alter the execution of actions?

Answering these questions of course connects directly to what is determined in the focus on thinking and decisions discussed above. They also afford further opportunity to identify how and why the prevailing insight culture supports or inhibits desired action streams.

Insight work

Executing the 4S cycle also involves action; thus, insight work should also be subjected to the three questions just noted. This is especially so given that insights, as noted many times previously, have a shelf life due to neverending marketplace and organizational change. In parallel with action streams (see next item), leaders continue to ask many of the questions already noted about ongoing insight projects and whether new insight projects are warranted.

Initiatives and projects

Strategies and decisions get translated into initiatives and projects, in short, action streams. One focus requires the identification of new action streams and changes to ongoing action. Consider one example:

A set of decisions culminate in the commitment to changing the firm's customer value proposition. A new action stream focuses on developing a new solution for the chosen customer segments. However, the absence of insight norms supporting the development of intimate customer relationships greatly hampers the early stages of one initiative—co-developing with customers the intended customer solutions. Insight values exhorting the importance of customer learning, including the need to learn from inside customer organizations, were glaringly absent. The management team had to initiate an insight project to illustrate how to develop customer intimate relationships with special emphasis on the behavior norms and practices around customer data collection and analysis.

Action execution

As a focus on execution replaces strategy development concerns, it's especially important for mid-level leaders to ask two questions: what insight values, norms and practices are hindering or facilitating execution? What values, norms and practices are needed to support and drive higher quality execution? Indeed, as just illustrated in the case of the customer value proposition case, every initiative and project can be viewed as a test case of the organization's prevailing insight culture. It's important to note that these two questions can be applied to initiatives that are largely internal or external.

Learning and adapting

Executing any action stream affords learning linkages back to thinking and decisions—linkages that also test the organization's prevailing insight culture. Consider the following example:

The leader of a new product launch initiative called a meeting to challenge the proposed action plan. In effect, he asked that the plan be reassessed against a set of GMI (generic marketplace insights). He was concerned that key vulnerabilities that had been identified as part of the marketplace analysis hadn't been given sufficient consideration. In short, he believed the proposed action plan could fall prey to these vulnerabilities. One outcome was that the plan's timetable was altered extensively—a far slower launch was agreed upon. As part of the action plan reassessment process, the product launch leader made it clear that individuals should voice their concerns about the feasibility of plans, and, at a minimum, find a "safe harbor" to do so—which for this organization at the middle levels would be nothing short of a radically new behavioral norm.

Senior leaders as drivers of insight culture

Senior (C-suite) leaders play a limited but pivotal role in shaping and sustaining an insight culture. However, because of their authority position, executives can "set the stage"[358] for the infusion of insight values, norms, and practices in ways that others simply can't.

Provide "air cover"

A senior market intelligence professional put it this way: "if the executive VP and his colleagues hadn't protected our big competitor and customer insight projects from the ravages of the finance department and the persistent inquiries of other senior executives as to when the projects would be completed, they would have died on the vine in their very early stages." Without appropriate air cover,[359] many insight project teams find that the analysis method is short-circuited and deliberations are short-changed in the interests of meeting deadlines or simply constrained so that projects can be deemed to have been completed. A commitment to air cover expresses in the strongest possible terms the value associated with insight work.

Ask for change insights

Executives can single-handedly in one moment shift insight values, norms and practices by asking that the relevant change insights with respect to a specific business issue and its context be highlighted in any meeting, presentation or document. When the executive asks this question for the first time, it becomes a show-stopper! Consider this example:

A CMO asked his strategy development team what key change insights they had generated about the Chinese market as an input to developing the proposed market entry strategy. He proclaimed loudly that he didn't want to see any more "data dumps" on what was happening in the China market. The team got the message as to what outputs they needed to create as well as what was no longer acceptable.

Asking that the change insights be succinctly stated also conveys a desired behavioral norm and announces a new desired practice.

Ask for implications

In the same vein, asking for implication insights (and business implications) in many instances transforms the nature of deliberations; it slows down the rush to agree on the actions that should be taken. It enforces the expectation (value) of implication insight as an analysis output and input to thinking and reflection.

Perhaps the ultimate manifestation of an insight culture is when executives not only ask for change and implication insights and business implications but use them to reflect on their own thinking, decision, and action commitments.

Challenge thinking

Executives can use insight outputs to test and refine their own "points of view," assumptions, and beliefs. The explanation component[360] of change insights frequently causes executives (and others) to reflect on long-held assumptions and beliefs that may turn out to be tenuous or questionable. For example, GMIs that provide the rationales for emerging opportunities or competitive risks or strategy vulnerabilities provide an opportunity for executives to challenge what are often tacit assumptions about where marketplace opportunities reside or the key competitive risks or vulnerabilities that should be addressed. In the VP case discussed in Chapter 2, the senior executives belatedly reflected on the incompatibility of the marketplace assumptions generated by the insight study and the firm's historic strategy. Had they done so in the early stages of the deliberations around the study's business implications, the time lag between the study's completion and the decision and action implications would have been shortened considerably. And, significant economic costs to the business would have been avoided.

Shape deliberations in decision making

Another pivotal role available to executives involves building and sustaining a spirit of deliberation in decision making: asking the questions noted in Table 10-5; seeking the judgments critical to both change and intelligence insights; ensuring that differences in perspective, opinion and rationales are exposed and discussed; insisting that time be made available for the necessary deliberations. Insight values, norms and practices get embedded in the organization without drawing attention to them. In both the VP and CommodityCo cases, senior executives initially didn't orchestrate deliberations to ensure that many of the questions noted in Table 10-5 would be the focus of serious dialogue. Therefore, the decisions eventually made took far longer than they should.

Reassess action commitments

Executives can also continue to review ongoing initiatives and action plans. Asking if initiatives and action streams are supported by validated change and implication insights enables executives to (re)assess whether their support for specific initiatives should be amended. The question reinforces the expectation (value) that change and implication insights should be at the forefront of analysis.

Meetings: An ideal intervention point for leaders

Because they consume an inordinate amount of time, meetings afford leaders at all levels in the organization a convenient and critical opportunity to embed and reinforce an insight culture. Deliberations take place in meetings, mostly in formal, but also in informal settings. Meeting thus present executives and others an ideal location to "set the stage" for motivating others to adopt insight values, norms and practices

The organization's culture comes alive and is fully experienced in meetings—for better and for worse. Meetings reveal and reflect all facets of the organization's culture: the values that underpin, for example, what topics are addressed, how they're discussed, what's considered important (and not); the norms that undergird how a meeting's agenda is established and followed, behavior expectations, and the tone and tenor of interactions tolerated; and, the practices including how the meeting is organized and chaired, who speaks, in what way and in what order, the dynamics of interactions, and the nature of responses.

Here are some ways that leaders can use meetings to make an insight culture a living and breathing driving force in the organization:

- Executives and others use meetings judiciously as platforms to evangelize about the importance of insights as a way of thinking, a mode of analysis, a frame for dialogue—in short, a means to enhance the quality of the organization's deliberations;
- Executives and others raise questions about the relevance of insights to the issues and topics at hand;
- Meetings are used as appropriate to address insight content issues and questions;
- Leaders use regularly scheduled meetings to bring an insight focus to specific topics or issues;
- Leaders use meetings to introduce insight related topics where they hadn't previously been present;
- Insight is set as part of the agenda for the next "regular" meeting;
- In some case, it may be appropriate to establish an insight specific meeting.

Meeting presentations

Leaders can make a dramatic insertion into the prevailing culture by influencing presentations of analysis outputs. How often have you sat through a presentation that offers a parade of data-dense decks that may last for thirty minutes or more but never get to insights? The presentation never addresses the two questions posed by the executive at the beginning of Chapter 1 and restated at the introduction to this chapter. Any effort to develop and sustain an insight culture must address a critical issue: how best to use "presentations" as a driver of attention to insight not just within meetings but as a focal point in analysis deliberations.

Here's one set of insight-oriented guidelines leaders can enforce for those making presentations where the intent is to convey the outputs of analysis:

- Highlight the insights, as the summary outputs of the analysis, early in the presentation;
- Emphasize the competitive space insights (CSIs) and the generic marketplace insights (GMIs) as the segue to the business implications;
- Highlight the business implications and how they connect to the key insights;
- Provide the rationales for the core insights (without getting lost in the data details or the analysis nuances);
- Leave sufficient time for discussion.

Simple as these "guidelines" may seem, an analysis of presentations in your organization will likely find that they're mostly violated.

Meeting participants

Leaders can also drive an insight perspective through their influence on any meeting's participants. Meeting participants aren't idle observers in an insight culture; insight values, norms, and practices should be manifest in how they contribute. Leaders, by dent of their own example, can exhort others to adopt the following norms and associated practices. The intent is to ensure that insights are surfaced, critiqued, and leveraged:

- If insights aren't presented, they ask that the analysis be revisited to identify relevant insights;
- When insights are presented, they orient the discussion toward the rationales supporting and refuting the insights rather than requesting a complete walk-through of all the background data and indicators;
- They focus on intelligence insights. They orient the dialogue toward implications for the organization's thinking, decisions, and actions.

These suggestions may seem obvious and perhaps insignificant. Yet, their absence goes a long way to explaining why so many meetings that involve consideration of analysis outputs fail to manifest any serious deliberation.

A final comment

The thrust of the argument throughout this book is that deliberation plays a pivotal role in insight generation. The deliberative prescriptions outlined in earlier chapters aim to enhance analysis, and especially, the dialogue around it, in the pursuit of insight. Generating change insight, and particularly, intelligence insight, requires collaboration among individuals and across functional units, as well as up and down the organizational hierarchy. Leaders play many crucial roles in instigating, nurturing, sustaining, and leveraging the necessary collaboration.

Leaders influence and drive insight work by focusing on the underlying insight culture. They need to "live" the values, serve as the role model of the desired behavioral norms, and drive the necessary insight practices into the day-to-day life of the organization. They can't be observers on the sidelines of deliberations; by being engaged, they enable the co-creation of intelligence insight—understanding of change that affords superior thinking, enables better and faster decision making and drives action that wins in the marketplace.

Notes

331. The role and importance of asking questions is a theme in many descriptions of what it takes to be a leader. See, for example, Ronald A. Heifetz, *Leadership Without Easy Answers* (Cambridge, MA: Belknap Press, 1994).

332. Edgar Schein has heavily influenced the understanding and study of organization culture. He defined it as: a pattern of shared basic assumptions that the group learned as it solved its problems of external adaptation and internal integration that has worked well enough to be considered valid and, therefore, to be taught to new members as the correct way to perceive, think and feel in relation to those problems. See Edgar H. Schein, *The Corporate Culture Survival Guide* (San Francisco: Jossey-Bass Publishers, 1999).

333. See David W. De Long and Liam Fahey, "Diagnosing Cultural Barriers to Knowledge Management," *Academy of Management Executive* 14, no. 4 (2000): 113–27, for a discussion of the importance of these three

culture components in shaping whether and how organizations succeed in creating the productive management of knowledge.

334. Individuals' behaviors (their interactions with others) and deeds (decisions, commitments and actions) may indicate different values. Deeds, as a category, involve organizational activities.

335. In Chapter 1, we noted that the disciplined approach to insight work required individuals to address how to prepare themselves for insight work, how to enhance the conduct of insight work, and how to leverage change insight by transforming it into intelligence insight, that is, business implications.

336. This is in large part what was meant earlier by the need for a leader to "live" or "exude" an insight culture.

337. Although Moorman and Day don't directly address the role and influence of an insight culture, shaping and sustaining an insight culture can be seen as an integral and underpinning component of their Organizing for Marketing Excellence framework. Christine Moorman and George S. Day, "Organizing for Marketing Excellence," *Journal of Marketing* 80, no. 6 (2016): 6–35.

338. The questions link directly to the first element in structuring addressed in Chapter 3: are we focused on the most critical opportunities for insight work, that is, those that will make the greatest contribution to the organization's marketplace and economic performance.

339. The exhortation here reflects the distinction between change insight and intelligence insight (i.e. change insight and its business implications).

340. See Tables 10-2, 10-3, and 10-4.

341. Persistently emphasizing the need to generate a small set of change insights reinforces doing so as a dominant insight value.

342. The relevance test is implied in the vetting activity detailed in Chapters 5 and 6. It's made explicit in the development and assessment of implication insights.

343. The novelty test is detailed in Chapter 5 and is also addressed in Chapters 6 and 7.

344. See Chapter 9 for many examples of how and why emotions reflected in interpersonal issues cause analysis difficulties.

345. The intent isn't just to create tension but productive tension that leads to reflection and hence superior dialogue. See Lee Nichol, ed., *On Dialogue* (New York: Routledge, 1996).

346. Chapter 9 provides many suggestions as to what appropriate corrective actions might be.

347. I "buy-in" is frequently what executives and other say; it may or may not be evidenced in their behaviors and deeds. In other words, they don't live what they say.

348. The notion of living the insight culture in effect sets the stage for insight work, as discussed earlier in this chapter.

349. This observation is consistent with the argument that those throughout the organization with access to external entities and events should be focused on gathering data relevant to the organization's current and potential strategy and decision needs.

350. These questions are extensions of the insight funnel questions noted earlier (see Chapters 1 and 2).

351. The notion of insight content was introduced in Chapter 1. It addresses what the insight actually says.

352. Again, to be clear, the emphasis here is mid-level leaders; senior leaders are addressed in the next section.

353. Mid-level managers need to recognize inhibitors to insight work before they can begin to address them. Of course, it's even more productive if they anticipate inhibitors before they surface and negatively affect the flow of the work.

354. Again, we need to remind ourselves that thinking, deciding, and action, constitute the three core Fs (factors) in the 6IFs. The discussion here addresses the 6IFs at the output side.

355. This argument is consistent with the point of view that self-assessment is a critical input to developing strategies to influence others. See, for example, Allan R. Cohen and David L. Bradford, *Influencing Up* (New York: John Wiley & Sons, 2013).

356. Any effort to instill insight values focused on the need to enhance the organization's capacity to think about different things and employ different modes of thinking could deploy the Six Hat and Six Action Shoe modes of thinking and acting developed by Edward de Bono. See,

Edward de Bono, *Six Thinking Hats: An Essential Approach to Business Management* (New York: Little Brown, 1985), and, Edward de Bono, *Six Action Shoes* (New York: HarperBusiness, 1991).

357. Many of the inhibitors to intelligence insight work are noted in Table 7-4. It's easy to see how they could contribute to the ossification of decision routines and processes.

358. The earlier discussion in this chapter pertaining to setting the stage is equally applicable to C-suite executives.

359. Air cover is a commonly used phrase to signify that a senior person is providing protection from organizational interference for a more junior person to accomplish a specific task.

360. Chapter 1 notes that insights should provide an explanation (or lead quickly to an explanation) of the phenomenon they address.

Acknowledgments

This book wouldn't have been possible without the corporate organizations—large and small—that allowed me to develop and test insight-related ideas in projects, workshops, and consulting engagements over the last twenty-plus years.

I owe an enormous debt of gratitude to those who gave me detailed and constructive comments on one or more chapters, including Gaurab Bhardwaj, Kurt Christensen, Martha Culver, David De Long, Phil Dover, Stew Early, Francois Gau, John Grant, Kelsey Hare, David Harkleroad, Linda Hayes, Adrienne Jonsson, Rand Mendez, Ralph Oliva, V. K. Narayanan, Robert Randall, Clay Philips, Larry Prusak, Bill Sammon, Patricia Seeman, Dan Simpson, Elizabeth Swann, Hubert St Onge, Martin Wall, Wanda Wallace, and Fred Wiersema. They gave freely of their time to discuss nuances of the text, and pushed me to clarify concepts, explore particular facets of insight work, and explain the rationales for specific recommendations.

I'm also immensely grateful to the Intelligence Leadership Forum, who have allowed me to use the group as my personal learning laboratory. What an indescribable pleasure it is to meet three times a year with people who are genuinely interested in ideas, who render a constructive critique of any material, suggestion, or practice that comes before them, and who are always eager to test new ideas, new ways of thinking, and new practices.

I want to acknowledge the Leadership Forum, Inc. (LFI) team, who have made my professional life such a pleasure: Wanda Wallace, Peter Wright, Mary Lou Donovan, Kelly Nipp, Mandy Peele, and Candis Tate. Wanda, my LFI partner, has constantly encouraged me to "get that book done." I can't thank her enough for being my unrelenting source of inspiration to challenge how things get done in the corporate world.

Finally, I want to thank my wife, Patricia, for tolerating my incessant disappearances into my home office. A lifelong partner makes both the journey and destination worthwhile.

Index

About the Author

Dr. Liam Fahey is co-founder and executive director of Leadership Forum, Inc. (Liam.Fahey@leadershipforuminc.com) and the creator and leader of its Intelligence Leadership Forum.   He has been a faculty member at Northwestern University's Kellogg School of Management and Boston University, and he now serves as Professor of Management Practice at Babson College.

His consulting, teaching, research and writing focus is on enabling organizations to win in the marketplace through enhanced marketplace intelligence and insight. He advises leaders, conducts workshops, consults to analysis specialists and engages with work teams in all facets of generating and leveraging marketplace intelligence and insight.

The author or editor of eight books and over fifty articles or book chapters, he has won all three major awards from the Journal of Marketing (the Maynard, Alpha Kappa Psi, and Jagdish Seth Award) as well as the Marketing Science Institute's best paper award.